MW01234921

THE OTHER HOLLYWOOD RENAISSANCE

Traditions in American Cinema
Series Editors Linda Badley and R. Barton Palmer

Titles in the series include:

www.edinburghuniversitypress.com/series/tiac

THE OTHER HOLLYWOOD RENAISSANCE

Edited by Dominic Lennard, R. Barton Palmer, and Murray Pomerance

EDINBURGH
University Press

Edinburgh University Press is one of the leading university presses in the UK. We publish academic books and journals in our selected subject areas across the humanities and social sciences, combining cutting-edge scholarship with high editorial and production values to produce academic works of lasting importance. For more information visit our website: edinburghuniversitypress.com

Edinburgh University Press Ltd
The Tun – Holyrood Road
12(2f) Jackson's Entry
Edinburgh EH8 8PJ

Typeset in 10/12.5pt Sabon by
Servis Filmsetting Ltd, Stockport, Cheshire

A CIP record for this book is available from the British Library

ISBN 978 1 4744 4264 0 (hardback)
ISBN 978 1 4744 4265 7 (webready PDF)
ISBN 978 1 4744 4267 1 (epub)

CONTENTS

FIGURES

NOTES ON THE CONTRIBUTORS

Brenda Austin-Smith is Professor and Head of the Department of English, Theatre, Film, and Media at the University of Manitoba in Winnipeg, Canada. She teaches and publishes on cinephilia, screen performance, melodrama, film and emotion, cult film, adaptation, and film and the city.

Linda Badley is Professor Emerita in English at Middle Tennessee State University. She has published widely on American independent film, gothic and horror studies, gender and media, Nordic cinema, and Lars von Trier. With R. Barton Palmer, she co-edits *Traditions in World Cinema* and *Traditions in American Cinema*, companion series at Edinburgh University Press.

Rebecca Bell-Metereau teaches Film and English and directs the Media Studies Minor at Texas State University. She is the author of *Transgender Cinema*, *Hollywood Androgyny* and *Simone Weil*, and co-editor of *Star Bodies and the Erotics of Suffering*. She has also contributed chapters to edited books including *Acting for America*; *A Little Solitaire*; *Cinema and Modernity*; *American Cinema of the 1950s*; and *Authorship in Film Adaptation*. Her work has appeared in such journals as *College English*, *Quarterly Review of Film & Video*, *Journal of Popular Film & Television*, and *Cinema Journal*.

Dennis Bingham is Professor of English and Director of Film Studies at Indiana University-Purdue University, Indianapolis (IUPUI). He has published widely on film biography, and on stardom, gender, and acting in Hollywood and international cinemas. His books include *Whose Lives Are They Anyway?: The Biopic As Contemporary Film Genre* and *Acting Male: Masculinities in the Films of James Stewart, Clint Eastwood, and Jack Nicholson*. He is the editor of the *American Cinema of the 2010s* (forthcoming) and is currently writing a book about Bob Fosse.

David Desser is Emeritus Professor of Cinema Studies and Comparative and World Literatures and East Asian Languages and Cultures at the University of Illinois. He is the author and editor of numerous works, including most recently *Tough Ain't Enough: New Perspectives on the Films of Clint Eastwood*, and *Killers, Clients and Kindred Spirits: The Taboo Cinema of Shohei Imamura*. He is a former editor of *Cinema Journal* and the founding editor of the *Journal of Japanese and Korean Cinema*.

Lester D. Friedman is Emeritus Professor and former chair of the Media and Society Program at Hobart and William Smith Colleges. He is the author, co-author, and editor of over twenty books and numerous articles, his areas of academic specialties include: film genres, sports and media, American cinema of the 1970s, American Jewish cinema, British film of the 1980s, and Health and Humanities. Additionally, he has written books about Steven Spielberg, Arthur Penn, *Peter Pan*, *Frankenstein*, and Clint Eastwood.

Ina Rae Hark is Distinguished Professor Emerita of English and Film/Media at the University of South Carolina. Her eclectic scholarship emphasizes masculinity studies, science fiction, and Hitchcock, but she has ranged widely. She has written or edited books on *Star Trek*, *Deadwood*, films of the 1930s, film exhibition, road movie, and representations of masculinity in cinema.

Jonathan Kirshner is Professor of Political Science and International Studies at Boston College. He is the author of *Hollywood's Last Golden Age: Politics, Society and the Seventies Film in America* and co-editor (with Jon Lewis) of *When the Movies Mattered: The New Hollywood Revisited*.

Dominic Lennard is a Teaching Fellow in the University College at the University of Tasmania. He is the author of the books *Bad Seeds and Holy Terrors: The Child Villains of Horror Film* and *Brute Force: Animal Horror Movies*, as well as numerous book chapters and articles on cinema.

Vincent Longo is a Doctoral Candidate in Film, Television, and Media at the University of Michigan. His published and forthcoming work in *The Moving Image*, *Screen*, *JCMS Teaching Dossier*, and several anthologies focuses on multimedia theater, New Hollywood authorship, archival studies, and audiovisual essay pedagogy. He is also co-authoring a book about the anti-fascist and racial politics of Orson Welles's unmade adaptation of *Heart of Darkness*. The online edition of the book will also supply digital access to pertinent archival materials at the University of Michigan Special Collections Research Center.

Douglas McFarland is a retired Professor of English and Classical Studies at Flagler College, Saint Augustine, Florida where he taught Renaissance literature, Latin, and Greek. He has published on sixteenth-century English and French literature, as well as numerous articles and chapters on film. He is the co-editor of *John Huston as Adaptor* and *Patricia Highsmith on Screen*.

Terence McSweeney is a senior lecturer in Film and Television Studies at Solent University. He is the author of *Avengers Assemble! Critical Perspectives on the Marvel Cinematic Universe*, *The 'War on Terror' and American Film: 9/11 Frames per Second*, and numerous other books connected to film, popular culture, and history.

R. Barton Palmer is Calhoun Lemon Professor of Literature Emeritus at Clemson University, where he founded the World Cinema program. He is the author or editor of more than fifty books on various literary and cinematic subjects. Currently he is the editor of the *South Atlantic Review* and the *Tennessee Williams Annual Review*, and serves as one of the general, and often founding, editors of six academic book series at university presses.

Murray Pomerance is an independent scholar living in Toronto. He is the author of *Cinema, If You Please: The Memory of Taste, the Taste of Memory*, *A Dream of Hitchcock*, and *Virtuoso: Film Performance and the Actor's Magic*, as well as many other books including the BFI Film Classics monographs on *Marnie* and *The Man Who Knew Too Much*. His book *The Film Cheat: Screen Artifice and Viewing Pleasure* is forthcoming from Bloomsbury. He edits the "Horizons of Cinema" series at SUNY Press and the "Techniques of the Moving Image" series at Rutgers.

Nancy M. Roche is a lecturer in the English Department at Vanderbilt University. Her specialties are women in film, cinemas of the 1960s, and American Independent Film, with an emphasis on culture studies, race and gender, and identity performance. Her book *Cinema in Revolt: Censorship Reform in 1960s British and American Film* is forthcoming from Edinburgh University Press.

Steven Rybin is associate professor of film studies at Minnesota State University, Mankato, where he is also co-director of the Film and Media Studies Program.

He is the author of *Geraldine Chaplin: The Gift of Film Performance*, *Gestures of Love: Romancing Performance in Classical Hollywood Cinema*, and *Michael Mann: Crime Auteur*. He is also editor of *The Cinema of Hal Hartley: Flirting with Formalism*, co-editor (with Murray Pomerance) of *Hamlet Lives in Hollywood: John Barrymore and the Acting Tradition Onscreen*, and co-editor (with Will Scheibel) of *Lonely Places, Dangerous Ground: Nicholas Ray in American Cinema*.

Daniel Sacco teaches Film, Aesthetics, and Culture at Yorkville University. His research explores intersections between genre cinema, spectatorship theory, film censorship, and the sociology of film reception. He has published on the cinemas of Lucio Fulci, Vincent Gallo, and the film and television documentary work of Andrew Jarecki. His writing has appeared in *Cinephile*, *The New Review of Film and Television Studies*, and *Studies in the Fantastic*.

Maya Montañez Smukler heads the UCLA Film and Television Archive Research and Study Center. She is the author of *Liberating Hollywood: Women Directors & the Feminist Reform of 1970s American Cinema*, among other works on film.

Kyle Stevens is the author of *Mike Nichols: Sex, Language, and the Reinvention of Psychological Realism*, co-editor of the two-volume collection *Close-Up: Great Screen Performances*, and editor of the forthcoming *The Oxford Handbook of Film Theory*. His work has appeared in *Cinema Journal*, *Adaptation*, *Critical Quarterly*, *New Review of Film and Television Studies*, *World Picture*, as well as several edited collections.

I-Lien Tsay is working on a cultural history of the animal actor in film and television. Her research interests include animal studies, visual rhetoric, feminist film theory, theories of affect, and American melodrama.

Daniel Varndell is a senior lecturer in the English Literature department at the University of Winchester, UK. He is the author of *Hollywood Remakes, Deleuze and the Grandfather Paradox*, and has published on the work of Hal Hartley, John Barrymore, and Peter Sellers, as well as on the films *The White Ribbon*, *Jaws*, and *Shane*. His forthcoming monograph (2021) examines etiquette and torture in film performance.

Constantine Verevis is Associate Professor in Film and Screen Studies at Monash University, Melbourne. His publications include: *Film Remakes, Second Takes: Critical Approaches to the Film Sequel*, *Film Trilogies: New Critical Approaches*, *Australian Film Theory and Criticism, Vol. I: Critical*

Positions, US Independent Film After 1989: Possible Films, Transnational Television Remakes, Transnational Film Remakes, Flaming Creatures, and *Film Reboots*. With Claire Perkins he is founding co-editor of *Screen Serialities* (Edinburgh University Press).

Rick Warner is an Associate Professor and Director of Film Studies at the University of North Carolina, Chapel Hill. He is the author of *Godard and the Essay Film: A Form That Thinks* and coeditor, with Colin McCabe and Kathleen Murray, of *True to the Spirit: Film Adaptation and the Question of Fidelity*. His essays have appeared in several edited collections, as well as in such journals as *New Review of Film and Television Studies*, *Quarterly Review of Film and Video*, and *Adaptation*. His current book project examines contemplative styles in global art cinema from 1945 to the present.

THE NEW PICTURE SHOW:
AN INTRODUCTION

Dominic Lennard, R. Barton Palmer, and Murray Pomerance

Figure I.1a *The Last Picture Show*. (1970, Peter Bogadanovich). Digital frame
enlargement. Courtesy of BBS/Columbia Pictures.

Auteurism and Seventies American Cinema

With a focus on directors rather than on wider industry and cultural developments, this present volume complements rather than challenges the received
critical understanding of the early 1970s "Hollywood Renaissance" as the
modernist cinema of a few exceptionally talented auteurs. The critical consensus, with minor exceptions, identifies these mainstream industry directors
as Francis Ford Coppola, Stanley Kubrick, Robert Altman, Arthur Penn, and
Martin Scorsese (see Kolker, Jacobs, and Cook 1998, as well as Kirshner/
Lewis). In the eighties, after his career had taken a late turn toward art cinema
with *The Color Purple* (1985) and *Empire of the Sun* (1987), Steven Spielberg
was added to the canon of exceptional auteurs by Robert Kolker, who dropped
Coppola from the group for what he deemed a decline in aesthetic quality and

I

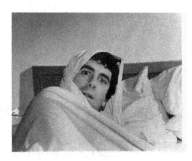

Figure I.1b   *I Love My Wife* (Mel Stuart, 1970) featured Elliott Gould's memorable performance as a disaffected husband who cannot save his failing marriage. Digital frame enlargement. Courtesy of Universal Pictures.

achievement. George Lucas, the other major figure of the era whose initial successes, like those of Spielberg, were based on genre filmmaking intended for a mass audience, has never been understood as an auteur.

The chapters collected in this book are devoted to figures chosen by the contributors. They examine in an auteurist vein the oeuvres of other noteworthy Renaissance filmmakers whose contributions to this loosely connected movement have been minimized or forgotten. Herein discussed are: newcomers to Hollywood (Jerry Schatzberg, Bob Rafelson, William Friedkin, Peter Bogdanovich, Joan Micklin Silver, Brian De Palma, Terrence Malick, Paul Schrader, Alan Rudolph, and Michael Cimino); those working in filmmaking who graduated in the era to the director's chair (Alan Pakula, Hal Ashby, Elaine May, Paul Mazursky, and Bob Fosse); émigré directors from the British industry (John Schlesinger, John Boorman, and Peter Yates); and established US directors whose participation in the auteur cinema constitutes a special period in their careers (Sidney Lumet, Mike Nichols, John Cassavetes, Sam Peckinpah, and John Frankenheimer).

The era's richness in emerging or renovating directorial talent is evident in the unfortunate circumstance that, for reasons of space, it was not possible to include essays on all who were responsible for some of the Renaissance's most interesting films, including those still more-or-less known today (Michael Ritchie, Frank Perry, Robert Mulligan, Irvin Kershner, John G. Avildsen, Martin Ritt, Jack Smight, and Claudia Weil) but also others who have slipped from collective memory, along with their films (Larry Peerce, Lawrence Turman, Frank D. Gilroy, Paul Sylbert, Henry Jaglom, and Mel Stuart, among others).

One notable absence here is Roman Polanski, responsible for two of the era's most important releases, *Rosemary's Baby* (1968) and *Chinatown* (1974). Polanski's career in the period, much of which was spent in France, will be covered in full in the companion to this present volume: *The Other*

French New Wave, edited by Charlie Michael, Frédéric Gimello, and R. Barton Palmer (forthcoming from Edinburgh University Press). A further important issue that could not be accommodated in the present volume is the connection, important for aesthetic and industrial reasons, between Renaissance filmmaking and one of the most important production trends of seventies Hollywood: Blaxploitation. Despite important historical work by, among others, Ed Guerrero, Blaxploitation still awaits the independent, book-length account it richly merits (see Guerrero 2012). It would be an understatement to say that there is much in seventies American cinema that needs rescuing from a memory hole.

Fifty years on, the aims of *The Other Hollywood Renaissance* are the memorialization, but also the celebration of a period in American filmmaking of wide-ranging accomplishments that are the perhaps surprising reflexes of political conflict, cultural transformation, and increasing uncertainty about national purpose. This volume builds on discussions of filmmaking in the era that have emphasized its aesthetic achievements and continuing political relevance, such as the essays collected in Lester D. Friedman's *American Cinema of the Seventies: Themes and Variations*. The editors and contributors to this present volume plead guilty to the charge of an enthusiasm for the subject. As far as the cinema was concerned, the seventies was a deeply paradoxical time, with the Hollywood system unraveling, having become irrelevant to the lives of many, even as enthusiasm for film as an art, and as the bearer of important messages, rose steadily among the cultural elite and, more generally, among the college-educated twenty-year-olds who were the first to study films and film history in the classroom.

The formation of the Renaissance canon reflected a growing cinephilia in important areas of the viewing public at the time, one shared by the critics whose work shaped the wide understanding of directors who were playing an increasingly central role. Of course, that Hollywood was undergoing a profound transformation would not have been apparent to every paying customer, but this was in fact what was happening. The emergence and flourishing of these auteurs marked the beginning of the post-studio (or post-classical) era that has become generally known as "The New Hollywood," in which, as Barry Langford puts it, there was a "changing of the guard." A loosely connected group he calls "new sheriffs" were now in charge of an industry "town" whose founders had passed or retired from the scene, even as their family-run studios had become assets in emerging conglomerate corporate structures (see Langford 107–56; Monaco 29–48; for an early assessment of the New Hollywood see Madsen). That there was a so-called "Renaissance" in Hollywood would have been news to cinemagoers, whose main interest was entertainment rather than the nature and cultural status of this prominent industry.

Figure I.2   Robert Redford stars in *The Candidate* (Michael Ritchie, 1973) as an idealistic politician caught up in the dirty business of electoral politics. Digital frame enlargement. Courtesy of Redford-Ritchie/Wildwood.

In its attempt to organize and promote a slice of cultural history, auteurism depends on the application to seventies American cinema of the evaluative protocols of the *politique des auteurs* that had been developed nearly two decades earlier and in France by the *Cahiers du cinéma* critics. This *politique* can be easily explained. Because of their signal qualities as artists, only some directors can truly be spoken of as authors, as the creative forces responsible for the films that bear their "signatures." However successful by industry standards, other directors are at most scene-stagers (*metteurs-en scène*), responsible for principal photography and some other aspects of production, but not creative forces who can be thought of as authors driven to mark every project with their personality.

The auteur "policy" deeply reflects neoromantic notions of individual energy, expressiveness, and, above all, resistance to conformity – qualities that emerge and are sustained only with difficulty in the practice of an industrial, profit-driven art form. Journalist Andrew Sarris set himself the task of explaining this intellectual development to American film enthusiasts who did not stay *au courant* with French developments, arguing for its application in his influential evaluative survey of studio-era production in *The American Cinema*, a bestseller first published in 1968. In faux Linnaean fashion, Sarris assigned Hollywood directors to a series of categories he confected with a waspish wit (e.g. "expressive esoterica" and "fringe benefits"). Most regrettably, he conferred a deceptive objectivity on French critical practice by mistranslating *politique* as "theory."

Cineliterate viewers in the seventies accepted that not every movie was worthy of being taken seriously, of course, but, especially after Sarris, they were inclined to believe that some Hollywood filmmakers proved more able than others in probing and extending the capacities of the medium. Well aware that film production was a collective, industrialized activity, enthusiasts had no trouble understanding that many, perhaps most, commercial releases were not art in the sense that some forms of European practice arguably were. Properly appreciating what Hollywood had done right, while ignoring its shortcomings, required a properly tuned critical sense. Informed by a field knowledge of Hollywood production, taste was needed to distinguish precious metal from dross through deploying the vague terms of distinction-making developed in Sarris's account. In any case, that talented directors in Hollywood could be understood as authors, a notion that, first developed in postwar French film culture, became a widely accepted touchstone in the US for would-be astute filmgoers.

In their collection of interviews with Peter Bogdanovich, Arthur Penn, Samuel Fuller, and others, *The Director's Event*, published in 1969 for a popular audience, journalists Eric Sherman and Martin Rubin evidence the percolation of auteurism into fan discourse. Sherman and Rubin argue that an interest in directors flows naturally from viewer experience: "We like or dislike a film according to the feelings it gives us." Inevitably understanding a film as a message of sorts, we "believe that the feelings in a film come from its director." Other films by the same director excite similar feelings, and we realize that he is "expressing the same personal ideas" (5). This is the essential of Sarris's auteurism, albeit naturalized with a bit of Aristotelian theory about the centrality of emotional affect. During the next two decades, auteurism offered a powerfully engaged approach to the contemporary scene for a newly constituting discipline of film studies. Director study proved more productive and enduring than the "great works" approach to film history whose literary affiliations for a while made it popular among the many *converso* English and language professors, the "first settlers" who took up the task of creating university film programs. Authorship, just to make the obvious point, was itself a time-honored approach to the creation of textual bodies thought to constitute the various national literatures. Thus it seemed natural to deploy it as an organizing principle in the chronicling and evaluation of another form of largely narrative art, one that could also be periodized and assigned a nationality as need arose, with a cadre of honored practitioners ready to hand to fill out a tradition.

Among filmmaking traditions, the Hollywood Renaissance seems unique in giving shape to the very method that simultaneously emerged for its mapping and evaluation. Auteurism took shape in part as a response to an evolving industrial practice, when the industry for its own reasons accorded directors more control over the projects they helmed. Enthusiasm for the director as a new kind of star permeates the perdurably influential contemporary accounts of Diane Jacobs, James Monaco, and especially Robert Kolker. All three of these writers were under forty in the early seventies, and they fairly represent an increasingly cineliterate, and youthful, culture that was hungry for film art on the European model. Reflecting the increasing awareness amongst the educated of how the political in its various forms pervaded collective experience, these youthful enthusiasts wished for a national cinema that eschewed mindless entertainment. They advocated for filmmaking of true artistic quality that would meaningfully engage with an American culture then experiencing, in the wake of (what some at the time thought of as) the disruptive sixties, a kind of freefall that was both terrifying and exhilarating.

From the vantage point of nearly a half century later, this auteurism 1.0 has proven mostly to be insight enabled by a certain blindness, in the sense promoted by literary critic Paul de Man (see de Man). For de Man, all critical approaches produce understandings by refusing to see and read from other perspectives. Though there has been some slippage in the members of the charmed circle (reflecting minor initial differences in assessment), the reputations of the major directors lionized by Jacobs et al. have only grown, even as the New Hollywood they helped found has taken some different turns in the twenty-first century. Auteurism has stimulated important understandings of the period's promotion of a rather narrow canon of favored directors, a grouping that, closely tracking Sarris's persnickety taxonomizing, depended on a blindness to more general developments. In France, the *Cahiers* group, reflecting the neoromantic humanism of its doyen, André Bazin, had also emphasized individual expression in their less comprehensive evaluations of Hollywood history. It bears remembering that many of the Hollywood directors lionized by *Cahiers*, such as John Ford, Howard Hawks and, of course, Alfred Hitchcock, found similar places of honor in Sarris's several panthea.

Finding "authors" in a collective industrial practice made sense only if one didn't struggle to account for how the many figures involved in making a film contributed to the final product; screenwriters, cinematographers, art designers, and performers, after all, could also be thought of as authors of a kind. For French cinephiles, the critical position opposing auteurism was an emphasis on the film as produced by artistic influences and cultural trends, a form of vaguely Marxist appreciation that also developed in postwar France. Associated with the left-wing journal *Positif*, this approach dominated in the way the French came to grips with the most significant artistic trend of Hollywood's postwar era: film noir. *Cahiers* writers were enthusiastic about some of the directors who worked in noir (Hitchcock, Nicholas Ray, Fuller, Robert Siodmak, Otto Preminger, Billy Wilder, and Joseph Losey chief among them), but never developed a group auteur approach to the series. Noir has never been theorized as yet another moment of auteur cinema in Hollywood history by Anglophone critics. Instead, the production trend has been chronicled by the *Positif* approach to film history. Raymond Borde and Étienne Chaumeton in their *Panorama du film noir américain* formulated the thematic/cultural understanding of noir that, with much further work done by Anglophone critics, has since become the conventional view, especially in its classic phase (see Borde and Chaumeton). In noir studies, scholars became preoccupied with how to think the impressive noir textual body in terms of genre theory; this discussion about taxonomy proved unproductive and has thankfully petered out in recent years. Scholars have not promoted an agreed-upon canon of favored noir directors to take its place.

Interestingly, for most film enthusiasts in the US, French notions of film noir would have to await the work of festivals and yet another popularizer, Paul Schrader. He did not write, as did Sarris, a book on the subject, but his 1971 essay "Notes on Film Noir" was widely read by academics and serious enthusiasts (see Palmer for early French work on noir and Schrader's essay). Borrowing an analytical page from Sarris, but changing the object of analysis, British scholar Raymond Durgnat proposed a series of taxonomic categories of films; his "family tree" diagram of the production trend famously recalls similar uses of the tree metaphor in genealogy and, perhaps most notably, in research on the connections between and among the various Indo-European languages (see Durgnat in Palmer). Something along the same analytical lines could be produced for the early seventies "break" from accepted Hollywood practice. However, no scholar, French or American, has thus far been moved to sketch out either a "panorama" or a family tree that outlines the production trend on which we are focusing here.

Instead, auteurist approaches in the course of the seventies claimed the field for themselves. It quickly became apparent that the agreed-upon major players would be Robert Altman, Francis Ford Coppola, Arthur Penn, Stanley Kubrick, and Martin Scorsese, who were misunderstood as in themselves constituting what was unmistakably a sea change in the national cinema, involving a broader range of directorial talent. Critics like Diane Jacobs, writing in 1977, properly saw the Renaissance as a "sudden harvest of grace" that was "gestating within the frenetic activity of the previous decade" and most spectacularly expressed itself in the "conglomeration of talent" that "descended" on Hollywood and insisted on "having a say in the future of movies" (Jacobs 1,4). For the first time, says Jacobs, channeling Paul Mazursky, one of the exciting new faces, "American directors were making personal films built on or, more soberly, seen as the cinematic reflex of the emergence, in the wake of the demise of the classic studio system, of a 'New Hollywood'" (4).

As a historical observation, this is plainly wrong; the country's directors had been at times making personal films since the 1910s. Jacobs and Mazursky are correct, however, about a surge in such approaches and projects. And it's surely easy enough for anyone wanting to tout a new product or production method to give it the spangling label, "New." In any case, individuality and institutional change as framing notions tend to be more distinctive

Figure I.3   A number of auteurist films discovered forgotten corners of American life, such as the southern coastal island in Martin Ritt's *Conrack* (1974), starring Jon Voight. Digital frame enlargement. Courtesy of 20th Century Fox.

than complementary. The emphasis of Jacobs's account quickly emerges as author-centered after some gesturing at larger, more diverse contexts. The difference between historical analysis and critical enthusiasm quickly becomes decisive. In this way, it differs importantly from that of Sarris, who creates the illusion that his categorizations are in the screen history he recounts and not in the subjectivity of his judgments.

Kolker points toward an interesting critical way forward by lauding the interest of Renaissance directors in "the films that preceded them" even as, with a series of self-reflexive gestures, they "confront and examine the form of what they do" (viii – from the preface to the study's first edition). Such self-consciousness marks these films as constituting a renaissance, a form of re-imagining and appropriating a tradition that is honored explicitly in its renewal. No doubt. More useful, however, is his observation that such inter-textuality (as we would now say) is also obtrusive, constituting cinematic objects as pre-eminently re-constructions and homages. He could have gone further. The filmmaking of the classic studio period is more complex and, at times, self-deconstructing than is suggested by the monologic notion of the "classic Hollywood text" then beginning to dominate film criticism after the appearance of important work on Hollywood by neoformalist critics, especially David Bordwell (see Bordwell et al.). The production history of the classic studio era is more irregular than Jacobs and company, in a manner ratified by Bordwell, tended to imagine it.

AMERICAN FILM CULTURE COMES OF AGE

Nevertheless, an ever-more sophisticated American cinema was emerging at the very moment when an efflorescence in stylistic and thematic complexity was there to be seen and appreciated on the nation's screens. That films could be art rather than just entertainment was, by the beginning of the seventies, an attitude widely shared among both the intelligentsia and the younger filmgoers who now constituted the most influential sector of the paying public. As screen historian David Cook observes, this was a generation that had "grown up with the medium of television, learning to process the audiovisual language of film on a daily basis" (*Lost Illusions*, 69). Without really trying, younger viewers had become well acquainted with the previous two decades or so of studio-era production, due to the decision of the networks and independent television stations to fill up many hours of the day with broadcasts of older Hollywood and foreign films (69). Many of this cadre were well-educated and some were more than a little cinephilic, having been exposed since adolescence to the international art cinema, then enjoying its greatest period of popularity, especially amongst young people and the better educated.

Television and the local art house informally offered an unprecedented and largely free exposure to the seventh art for the youth audience, who effortlessly acquired a vast knowledge of film history in ways that have not since been so readily available. The educational establishment did not lag far behind in catering to a widely shared enthusiasm, as some academics argued that the nation's filmmaking institutions, and their history, constituted legitimate objects of scholarly inquiry. "The rise of film study in American colleges and universities," Cook reminds us, "insured that this generation would know more about what it saw on the screen in academic terms than any generation before it" (*Lost Illusions*, 69). An enthusiasm for film was no longer seen as a misplaced endorsement of a necessarily debased popular culture that merited, so Frankfurt School thinkers like Theodor Adorno and Max Horkheimer opined, dismissal by those who knew artless manipulation when they encountered it. Though Hollywood had flourished for more than half a century, by 1970 US commercial filmmakers were threatened by the ever-increasing indifference of the national audience to the films they were turning out, offering support for the Frankfurt School's dismissal of this area of the so-called "culture industry." Most Hollywood releases of the era were time-honored formula projects, and these now held diminishing appeal in a society riven by rapid cultural change. However, the fact that many, especially in the youthful niche market, saw little but staleness in sixties production – not that the most perceptive of viewers would dismiss sixties filmmaking as uniformly stale (consider Frankenheimer's *The Manchurian Candidate* [1962], Kubrick's *Dr. Strangelove* [1964], or Nichols's *Who's Afraid of Virginia Woolf?* [1966]) –

interestingly contrasted with the same enthusiasm they showed for seventies films deemed artistically worthy and intellectually sophisticated.

For the industry, an obvious solution was to try something different in order to woo back patrons, especially the twenty- and thirty-year-olds who showed themselves more enthusiastic than their parents about moviegoing (see Cook *Lost Illusions*; Monaco; Langford 107–53). This audience segment enthusiastically supported the art house cinema, whose "sure seater" venues were consistently profitable precisely because they exhibited an ever-changing mix of foreign releases whose signal distinction, as Barbara Wilinsky observes, was to be found in their "differences from Hollywood films." The international art cinema offered, as she goes on to state, a kind of "counterprogramming" (15) whose appeal to the more sophisticated and intellectually-minded viewer prompted another and earlier kind of renaissance in American exhibition (chronicled by Tino Balio). Foreign films, not widely distributed since the early 1930s, once again became profitable, sometimes amazingly so, as they were screened in an increasing number of specialized "art houses" in metropolitan areas and college towns (see Balio). One of the editors here was able to watch Antonioni's *Red Desert* (1964) at such a venue in Colorado Springs in the earliest years of the decade.

The seventies and youth renaissances are closely related. Each is a reflex of changing values and tastes as the aesthetic compact between the US cinema and its public altered. After the unexpected success of several youth-oriented releases at the end of the sixties, most notably *Easy Rider* (1969), which was helmed by newcomers to directing Peter Fonda and Dennis Hopper, producers found themselves willing to finance projects with themes and styles that defied conventional wisdom, making for a different, often more challenging, kind of viewing experience. Significantly, many films in the era, writes Todd Berliner, manifested "an unusual manner of storytelling," indicating that they aimed for "moments of incoherence" that, even as they promoted the modernist principle of difficulty, violated the central principle of studio filmmaking that the story be always clearly and simply presented (5, 25). If only for a decade or so, an American art cinema emerged that aimed to locate that sweet spot of anti-commercial commerciality then achieved by many European releases. American producers, Wilinsky reports, had simply "commercialized art cinema" in the hopes of making films that would appeal to a mass audience (4).

Though far from uncontroversial, and often not particularly popular with the public at large, many films in what was welcomed by the intelligentsia as a renaissance for the national cinema were lauded for their artistry, but perhaps even more for their idiosyncratic engagement with the then fracturing national culture. Antiestablishmentarianism ran deep in these releases, and not just in their rejection of received industry wisdom. The films in this cycle are also often counter-cultural in terms of the era's politics, reflecting the leftward tilt of the majority of young people now constituting a vital niche audience. If grudgingly at first, the critical establishment expressed approval, with a key moment provided by the journalistic controversy over Arthur Penn's gangster biopic *Bonnie and Clyde* (1967). Though it ended with a bloody shoot-out that restored (if with shocking brutality) the power of law and order, this piece of genre revisionism unabashedly glorified the rebellion of a bank-robbing couple against the law and social convention, providing a historical precedent of sorts for contemporary street politics of protest and rebellion against authority. Within a year of this film's theatrical release, there were riots in the streets of major American cities – racism, poverty, and disenfranchisement all gathering force together.

Aided by new technology, *Bonnie and Clyde* pushed the representation of violence to new and shocking levels, while its frank exploration of sexual themes underlined how old-fashioned the Production Code, codified by 1934 and soon to be abandoned, now seemed to many. The nation's leading film critic, Bosley Crowther of the *New York Times*, was appalled by what Penn had produced, labeling it a "cheap piece of bald-faced slapstick comedy" (Crowther). The film's unanticipated sensational success, however, suggested to his editors that Crowther was now completely out of touch with the US film scene. They were correct. He was a victim, it seems, of the so-called generation gap then dividing young people from their elders, or so his publisher concluded. Crowther was summarily replaced by Pauline Kael, who felt compelled to offer her own take on the politics, both cultural and journalistic, that had led to *l'affaire Penn*. She sparked a debate about the cultural value of films that managed to remain national news for some weeks (see Kael). The urban, college-educated younger generation had now embraced edgy films that in one way or another said something meaningful about their world----of this there was no longer any doubt. In the next several years, US filmmakers addressed the now unmistakably rich "youth market" with other innovative releases that challenged long-held assumptions about the form of Hollywood films and the role these fictional stories could play in the national imaginary. Unsurprisingly, there was much directorial chaff along with the grain, as in any era. Many films reflecting the enthusiasms of this cinematic moment slipped into oblivion, sadly, perhaps, since those enthusiasms are another part of national and cinematic history that can fruitfully be explored.

Nonetheless, the auteur cinema featured challenging narratives that, as Todd Berliner describes, sometimes verged on, but ultimately refused, incoherence, unlike more relentlessly enigmatic art cinema releases such as Alain Resnais's *Last Year at Marienbad* (1961). Instead, in Berliner's apt metaphor, a "faint cacophony of incongruous ideas and narrational devices" makes itself heard in projects that were at least minimally conventional (Berliner 9). As he points out, this cacophony is also somewhat audible in releases of the era that were more acceptable to mainstream audiences, including *Patton* (Franklin J. Schaffner, 1970), *The Godfather* (Francis Ford Coppola, 1972), and *One Flew Over the Cuckoo's Nest* (Miloš Forman, 1975). Experimentation with various split-screen effects in the otherwise conventional genre exercises *The Thomas Crown Affair* (Norman Jewison) and *The Boston Strangler* (Richard Fleischer), both 1968, presaged more disorienting forms of modernist fragmentation in Renaissance productions such as Robert Altman's diptych, *Images* (1972) and *Three Women* (1977).

In the auteur cinema, challenges to conventional methods and themes were often voiced more stridently (if backed by less money and fewer resources) than in those films anticipating a broader viewership. By turns provoked and confused, viewers were pressured into a deeper intellectual engagement than was their custom with the entertainment cinema. In particular, a number of auteurist releases did short circuit the expectation that narratives, led by sympathetic protagonists, would make sense and climax in meaningful "points," thus resolving (or at least appearing to resolve) the problems or questions with which they began. In the auteurist films, conventional values were regularly not reaffirmed, while a justice that was at least somewhat poetic was often not much in evidence. The (Code-based) formula that had served Hollywood well for decades depended on sympathetic characters, incarnated by stars in the main roles who were capable of presiding convincingly over happy endings. Renaissance filmmakers could now bend those conventions, dispensing with stars altogether or using them against type. The auteurs were in effect redefining the industry approach to feature filmmaking that had delivered decades of success. A cycle of Hollywood films was emerging that bore striking similarities to the rather highbrow offerings of the international art cinema. What was emerging was an oppositional aesthetic, the "not-Hollywood."

The Art Cinema Renaissance

This was no accident, but a telling example of how the industry principle of investing in success was making its power felt. Since the end of World War II, foreign films rejecting the established entertainment model had been experiencing such a surge of popularity on US screens that Tino Balio also uses the term "Renaissance" to describe it (see Balio; Wilinsky). Inside the exhibition world, these venues became known as "sure seaters" because the films they screened had become predictably popular with a niche clientele that craved offbeat offerings. Art houses grew rapidly in number after the end of the war, serving an ever-increasing clientele until decline set in during the seventies and their numbers began to dwindle even after they developed the alternative strategy of the revival screening of Hollywood classics alongside foreign releases. The art cinema of the period, as David Bordwell has carefully anatomized, collectively produced a set of conventions that constituted an appealing alternative to the easy viewing that filmgoers had come to love (Bordwell).

If not in a wholesale fashion, American auteurs were now adapting this model, and exhibitors could hardly have ignored the promise of such a development since they had seen the emergence of a niche alternative audience even before the war (see Bordwell and Cook). As film distributor Joseph Burstyn wrote in 1939, "The audience for foreign films is still comprised of movie-goers seeking an escape from Hollywood escapism, people interested in unusual stories, mature treatment, and realistic performances" (qtd. in Wilinsky 24). If by 1970, the popularity of art cinema had begun to contract somewhat, it was still a significant presence on the American scene during the brief flourishing of Renaissance filmmaking and thus a worthy object of imitation, especially for limited-budget or small-scale projects.

Director-centered production, already a feature of pre-war filmmaking on the continent, garnered more notice with the advent of both Italian Neorealism and the French New Wave. As Renaissance filmmaking from Hollywood gained critical acceptance, new releases were often marketed as "signed" by their directors, following that well-established European practice of which art-cinema patrons were very much aware. Moreover, Renaissance projects were mostly small-scale, following the limited-budget/limited-profits model then proving successful enough to sustain a niche area of production for many of the foreign filmmakers who were eager to do business in the US market. However, it is important to remember that, as James Monaco reports,

> Every interesting movement in European film since the end of World War II . . . had been at least partly the result of temporary economic conditions that allowed filmmakers to do their work cheaply and expect a return sufficient to cover expenses and provide money to go on. (23)

The key word here is "temporary." The auteurist cinema was a movement that rejected the time-tested entertainment business formula. It was founded on an economic model of unproven, indeed unlikely viability.

This Hollywood Renaissance cycle raised a difficult aesthetic issue as well. If, as Wilinsky writes, art-cinema filmmakers imagined themselves as "working against the mainstream Hollywood system," then their approach would by its oppositional nature be "difficult to maintain in the face of success," at least on a regular basis, and there was, as ever, a need for a certain, self-sustaining level of profitability (35). This is to say than an arty auteurism was at best a highly unstable, liminal phenomenon, even if some compromises could be made to increase a difficult film's popularity. Unless arty films performed the role of reputation-enhancing loss leaders for production companies (as came to be true for much of the independent productions of the eighties), limited profits and sustainability were not likely to appeal to an industry founded on substantial bottom-line success. This was especially the case once the US film industry, entering the New Hollywood era, depended more on entrepreneurial/corporate investment and less on the bank (essentially the Bank of America) financing managed through the family-owned studios of the previous generation.

False hopes about the sustaining profitability of arty youth-oriented films had been aroused at the end of the sixties by the spectacular box office earned by *Bonnie and Clyde*, *The Graduate* (Mike Nichols, 1967), and *Easy Rider*, not to say the provocative promise of Michelangelo Antonioni's first English-language film, *Blow-Up*, a stunning vision and riddling narrative exhibited not in art houses but in mainstream cinemas through an arm of MGM. *Easy Rider* provided an especially appealing model in itself. It offered an intriguing mix of art-cinema stylings and a B-movie road narrative with two "outlaw" cineastes shooting many of their sequences guerilla style, in a fashion that recalled Godard's legendary making of *Breathless* (1960). *Rider* was produced on a budget of only about $400,000 by two erstwhile actors just barely into their thirties, yet it earned more than $41 million in several domestic exhibition runs, giving the lie to the general rule that you needed to put money on the screen in order to recoup it at the ticket counter. Theaters in major venues, such as Manhattan, were jammed full for *Rider*, as they had been for *Blow-Up*. The box-office success of *Bonnie and Clyde, Easy Rider,* and *The Graduate* fueled a production trend in which directors, often youthful or new to the task, came to play prominent roles in the conception, development, execution, and even marketing of projects that were marked as personal (see Cook, *Lost Illusions* 67–157).

The abandonment of the Production Code Administration and its replacement in 1968 by a more permissive ratings system (CARA) allowed filmmakers something of a greater freedom in representing sexual themes already enjoyed by art-cinema cineastes. The frank and sometimes calculatingly naughty treatment of the erotic life in many foreign films was a considerable source of their appeal for American audiences, and domestic producers followed suit. Nudity, what the industry termed "sexual situations," and even simulated intercourse became increasingly common in American films during the seventies, toward the end of the decade giving rise to a new genre, the so-called erotic thriller, in which simulated intercourse was a main attraction (see Martin). This was yet another US trend that borrowed from the international art cinema of the era. Few "art" films were more successful than Roger Vadim's *And God Created Woman* (1956), starring sex kitten Brigitte Bardot, which earned perhaps as much as $4 million in US exhibition. In the sixties, the (for the time) striking female nudity and sexual simulations in *Blow-Up* convinced American producers that audience tolerance of, not to mention desire for, less restrained representations of sex and the female body had increased in the past decade or so. More tolerance for explicit violence (not an art-cinema feature) was a unique feature of US seventies filmmaking in general, including in the auteurist cycle where it became a major and resonant theme in a society waging war at home and abroad.

The New Hollywood and Other Revolutions

As a production trend, and because of its promotion of a cinema of auteurs, the Hollywood Renaissance of the early 1970s holds considerable importance for the writing of US film history, since it is the first stage of what film historians have labeled as the New Hollywood. This institutional moment of considerable transformation extends from the demise of studio filmmaking during the sixties down to the present day (see Lewis for detailed discussion). In a film culture and industry where directors still have more importance than they regularly did during the studio period, the auteurism that emerged in the early seventies continues to be a central aspect of film culture and practice. To be sure, as historians such as David Cook and James Monaco point out, the auteurist model of small films appealed primarily to a niche audience of cinema enthusiasts. However, as a business plan auteurism was never going to displace a well-established model of an entirely different scale, successful for decades, and intended to appeal to a mass public, not film enthusiasts. The auteurist cinema deployed a niche-marketing model that had succeeded for the international art cinema, whose releases rarely generated huge box office since they played on a relatively small number of the nation's screens. With its "handmade" approach to project development and realization, the auteur-centered model simply could not be scaled up for the enormous US industry and the more diverse public it served.

Since the 1920s, investment-financed productions had always catered to established tastes in order to minimize risk. The crisis of steadily declining ticket receipts shook confidence in this model, as the studio system declined. Although the auteur cinema, promoting personality and idiosyncrasy, briefly dominated the American cinema's presentation of self to a national audience, auteur films could not offer sufficient uniformity and predictability based on formulaic repetition and the carefully calculated and always luminous presence of star performers. Still, by the end of the seventies, directors had achieved a prominence never to be surrendered even when the industry regained its financial health in the course of the next decade.

In the late sixties, by way of contrast, the national audience had become increasingly indifferent to big-budget genre projects (especially disaster films and musicals) that were designed and promoted to be the substantial hits they only sometimes were. The pressures of the marketplace thus made it possible for more wannabe cineastes outside the mainstream, supposed to be sources of something new and appealing, to gain access to a director's chair. Some signal successes at the end of the sixties with untraditional material endorsed this view. Marginal players within the industry (Robert Altman and Hal Ashby are prominent examples) were greenlit to make productions featuring a more personal approach that challenged or defied the long-established model of the well-made film. More important, appeal for directorial volunteers reached the arts scene generally, and university film schools in particular. There would be more tolerance of arty idiosyncrasy among those hopeful of connecting with what seemed to be rapidly evolving tastes in cinematic entertainment, as the slew of unconventional releases that hit US screens from 1970–73 proves (see Cook, *Lost Illusions* 171–2 for a listing of relevant films and filmmakers).

A focus on exceptional directors did much for the reputation of the American cinema, providing a cultural argument that strengthened Hollywood's hold on the entertainment sector, which was slipping away year by year as Americans, especially those over forty, gave up on regular moviegoing. Interestingly, this was happening at the very moment that American films (*not* movies) were taken up by the intelligentsia as, at least in part, more artistically significant than had been previously thought. With new recruits, directing talent was certainly not in short supply. It ceased being shameful for serious writers to work for the film industry at times (as Sam Shepard's career indicates), or for the graduates of film-schools' academic programs to migrate into directing. The industry also showed itself more receptive to the entrance of other promising outsiders, a change that did not always prove successful.

In terms of their serious themes, if not their innovative style and form (a *geist* adopted from the art cinema), many Renaissance films owed much to the celluloid past, constituting less a break from the studio era and more a respectful re-engagement with that industry's better angels. Films like *Taxi Driver* (1976) anticipated and soon became an element of the developing "independent" sector, a sector that would come to appeal in unpredicted ways. A later, telling example would be Scorsese's *Silence* (2016), a grim narrative about the campaign to extirpate an expanding Christianity in seventeenth-century Japan that checked none of the boxes that since the 1980s have ensured widespread audience appeal. While praising that film's artistry, Peter Debruge, writing in *Variety*, lamented that it was "too abstruse for the great many moviegoers who such an expensive undertaking hopes to attract" (Debruge). As one of its most famous practitioners, Martin Scorsese continues even at the end of his career to uphold the Renaissance commitment to an American art cinema despite the commercial challenges that have not changed significantly since the late seventies. The distinctive modernism of the Renaissance endures as an important strain within the alternative to the traditional entertainment film that has gained a continuing prominence since the eighties.

The economic and political upheavals of the 1930s, and the entrance of a number of engaged artists into filmmaking, had led to the emergence of, as Saverio Giovacchini reports, "a politicized modernism" in which a number of key directors were involved, such as Frank Capra and Fritz Lang. With regard to their engagement with modernism, they felt it important "to open up its message to the masses insofar as it was increasingly aware that the work of the previous generation of modernists had been hampered by the narrowness, elitism, and overall fragmentation of its audience" (5). A number of Renaissance productions can be seen as continuing this vein of engaged filmmaking, most notably Hal Ashby's reverential biopic of thirties activist Woody Guthrie, *Bound for Glory* (1976) and Sidney Lumet's indictment of New York City police corruption, *Serpico* (1973). Like others of the period, these films were not "challenging" or "incoherent" in the sense that many releases of the auteur period were (see Berliner).

If the Hollywood Renaissance was truly a cinema of mostly desperate loners, in part this was because its major figures drew for creative inspiration on themes explored in the noirs and small adult films of the previous decade (compare Martin Ritt's *Hud* [1963] with Peter Bogdanovich's *Last Picture Show* [1971], both of which drew on Larry McMurtry's demythologizing fiction about the American West and Texas in particular). Renaissance filmmaking revised interest in film noir, spawning a revival that with its updating merited a different label (neo-noir). The continuity across different trends of opposition to industry formulas was also a matter of personnel. Some of the

Figure I.4   Second-rate boxers who live on the margins, sometimes in success but mostly in failure, are the subject of John Huston's poignantly realist *Fat City* (1972). Digital frame enlargement. Courtesy of Columbia Pictures.

directors prominent in the small adult and noir series became important contributors to Renaissance filmmaking (John Frankenheimer, Stanley Kubrick, and Sidney Lumet most prominently).

The noirs and small adult films limned a very different portrait of America than that presented in another production trend from the fifties and sixties, whose influence would still be evident a decade later: what Chris Cagle identifies as "prestige" sociological productions (see Cagle). These films assume that some present social conditions constitute problems self-evidently in need of solutions, be they collective or individual. The remit of this production trend seems to be the transferring to the screen of the notion of the therapeutic, then becoming a dominant element in American culture, a notion whose value the small adult films tend to interrogate. These prestige productions were, in Cagle's view, a kind of "sociology on film" and often received industry awards and journalistic praise. They were an element of "middlebrow culture," consonant with and often derived from the problem fiction of the period, even as they provided a "self-critical commentary on middle-class life." This demand for an unaccustomed intellectual complexity meant that Hollywood filmmakers who undertook these projects were "challenged to search for new aesthetic formulas and new ways to deal with thematic directness in the context of entertainment cinema" (Cagle 15, 17–18).

Earlier prestige social problem films (such as Elia Kazan's *Gentleman's Agreement* [1947]) imagined the brighter, problem-cleansed future expected by many in postwar American culture. The Cold War torpor evoked in much of the era's philosophical/religious commentary (think Reinhold Niebuhr) found dramatic shape in such small adult fantasies of social breakdown as Kazan's *A Face in the Crowd* and Martin Ritt's *No Down Payment* (both 1957). Renaissance productions like *All the President's Men* (Alan J. Pakula, 1976), with its endorsement of an independent free-press investigation of government corruption, forcefully continue this tradition. In the same director's noirish *The Parallax View* (1974), however, an enterprising journalist discovers but then, before he can warn his fellow citizens, is destroyed by a powerful conspiracy that decapitates the government. Other seventies films in the "prestige sociology" series would include *Norma Rae* (Martin Ritt, 1979), *Kramer vs. Kramer* (Robert Benton, 1979), *Alice Doesn't Live Here Anymore* (Martin Scorsese, 1974), and *The China Syndrome* (James Bridges, 1979).

The emergence and flourishing of a production series in the early seventies, that offered a serious alternative to the industry's entertainment model and that depended on independent-minded directors and producers, was hardly unprecedented. In fact, it is easy to make the case that oppositional filmmaking of different kinds is a continuing feature of the classic studio era, a period otherwise supposed, with good reason, to be one of steady, limits-respecting production. A sense of shared oppositionality across the work of a number of directors suggests that the Renaissance films constitute a cycle or series that might be discussed in a way quite different from the auteurism adopted here. In such an account, similar aspects of production history might be emphasized (including the key role played by screenwriters), and so might narrative patterns and stylistic peculiarities (for a different, and provocative analysis of this issue, see Godfrey; see Kirshner for a useful "thematic" approach). If the Renaissance cinema were considered more of a group tradition, then the expressive idiosyncrasies of their individual films, what auteurism conceives as "signatures," would receive less focus. Moreover, projects that are not part of an oeuvre in any substantial sense but are otherwise significant in terms of structure or theme might draw more attention. A group approach to the phenomenon would emphasize its continuity with the way Hollywood was "renewed" and dedicated to distinct forms of seriousness/artistry several times in the course of its history.

From the point of view of the writing of the history of this period, the cost of canonizing based on a selective neoromanticism has been high. For one thing, other directors and releases worthy of respectful remembrance have been unjustly neglected. If they are not to be lost to history, these artists and their work should be given their due as the age of post-studio Hollywood revival recedes from memory, the surviving filmmakers approach their career

Figure I.5 Renaissance films often touched on contemporary politics, as in the chronicling of campus revolt in *The Strawberry Statement* (Stuart Hagmann,1970). Digital frame enlargement. Courtesy of MGM.

ends, and those scholars for whom these films were a lived cinematic experience (two of your humble narrators included) are joined on the scene by enthusiastic "young voices." However, there is a larger problem illuminated by the expanded survey of directorial accomplishment offered in this book. Because it is inherently resistant to the devising of informative generalities, even the more inclusive kind of auteurism proves inadequate as a driver of historical explanation. Viewed only through the lens of directorial accomplishment, what preceded the Renaissance, that is, classic Hollywood, forfeits its status as a site of cultural production with its own complex history. It becomes instead a usable past, less a shaping context and more a source of textual effects, mostly trace elements incorporated into individual films, such as gender bendings and other reworkings of classical conventions. Authorship establishes its independence through transtextualizing homages to studio era greats. Just to make the obvious point, there is more to history than records of exceptional accomplishment.

Kolker's description of the Renaissance movement as a *cinema of loneliness* has not stuck as a historical label. This is unfortunate because this reference to unwilled solitariness importantly aligns a canonical group of films with the archetypal character of international modernist narrative – the loner alienated from family, friends, and culture, writ large and populating much of modern fiction and art cinema, from Camus and Bellow to Antonioni and Godard. Perhaps because A *Cinema of Loneliness* offers only a minimal group portrait of the chosen directors Kolker never anatomizes or contextualizes the loneliness he identifies as the major theme of their filmmaking. It is nevertheless *le mot juste*. The protagonists of many Renaissance films, including a number of those discussed in this volume, are the failing agents of their own destinies. They simply lack the power to achieve any of the forms of success that provide Hollywood films with conventional happy endings. Rootless wanderers on the earth like Travis Bickle (Robert de Niro), the workaholic cabbie in Scorsese's *Taxi Driver*, or the sailors trapped in an unjust military system in Hal Ashby's *Last Detail* (1973), are always in motion but discovering that they have nowhere to go. The American cinema, however, had at other times featured characters similarly *in extremis*, and beginning in the eighties would do so again, contesting any simple model of its functioning as a culture industry purveying mindless entertainment.

POSTSCRIPTUM

As we have said, all of the filmmakers considered by the contributors to this volume, by express intention, are outside the New Hollywood "A List." They form, therefore, something of a lacuna as regards Hollywood of that decade, a conspicuous silence that we are hoping this book will overcome. Yet another coterie hibernates within or beside this group, smaller, often now entirely forgotten, makers of post-1960s films that boldly stated the young generation's frustration with and rejection of establishment practice that had more or less defined American culture in the latter half of the 1960s. Here were films made by filmmakers of extreme creativity and ingenuity, but people also entrenched in the commitment to show some youthful and energetic force in the battle against, and triumph over, staid, predictable, repressive conventions. In many cases here, however, this "youthful force" was metaphorized by means of an older character, old enough, say, to be operating on Wall St. on behalf of the establishment while at the same time being flippy, or cantankerous, or much smarter about social conditions than appearances told. This "old young man" type had the acumen to see where the wires were connected, to know how to disable power, and to evade capture, and was also passionately invoking the attitude younger people clung to (but all too often did not act upon).

In a spirit of remembrance, we end this introduction with three arbitrarily selected but fascinating examples:

They Might Be Giants (1971)

A bizarre enough tale of a man named Justin who takes himself to be Sherlock Holmes (George C. Scott, in a powerfully comic performance flowing in part from his work in *Dr. Strangelove* [1964]). Notwithstanding that he lives the typical enough life of a Manhattan isolate, and that Holmes exists only as a fictional put-up (albeit one with world-scale popularity), our hero is clearly off the mark, even, as we may well suspect, patently insane. Insane, yet also wise. Insane only from the point of view of the system (that also treated young people who wouldn't cut their hair as if they were insane). With a small cluster of similarly disenfranchised friends, living in the dank interstices of the gleamy metropolis, Holmes chases after, and finally in a blazing victory defeats, the nefarious Moriarty (an evil presence we never quite manage to see). Holmes here acts strictly in accordance with the principles of freedom, enlightenment, and civil peace that young people were trumpeting to deaf ears.

When he finished this film early in 1971, Anthony Harvey was just forty, having already edited two major cinematic masterpieces, *Dr. Strangelove* (1964) for Stanley Kubrick and *The Spy Who Came in from the Cold* (1965) for Martin Ritt. His only major directorial achievement prior to *Giants* was the glorious Peter O'Toole/Katharine Hepburn vehicle, *The Lion in Winter* (1968), curiously exploring the tumultuous marriage between two wise old cats (Henry II and Eleanor of Acquitaine) squabbling and wrestling like a pair of randy teenagers over the dispensation of familial power.

The China Syndrome (1979)

Here, the forward-thinking hero in a mature body is Jack Godell (Jack Lemmon), managing operator at a nuclear facility not far from Los Angeles. On the surface of his coffee cup one day he noticed a vague and very brief tremor, but he is experienced, sage, and sensible enough to realize he is seeing the first sign of a "China Syndrome," a core meltdown capable of producing a leak of fissionable uranium that would head straight down and travel all the way through the earth until it hit – on the far side – China. Major nuclear disaster. He attempts to warn the public and the proper authorities with the aid of a local news broadcaster (Jane Fonda) and her wily cameraman (Michael Douglas). Things do not go well for Jack, but in his final moments he is successfully telecast through an uplink so that people across the country can see his heroism, his sincerity, his desperate seriousness in the face of their own too-institutionalized blithe unconcern about capital power and its rapacious attitude toward nature.

Releasing this film, James Bridges was forty-three. He had written *Urban Cowboy* (1980) and numerous scripts for "Alfred Hitchcock Presents." *Syndrome* was his most controversial film project, aimed directly at a burgeoning electrical power movement that was protested often and vociferously by environmental activists. Fonda, herself an anti-Vietnam War and environmental activist known worldwide – she was married to the celebrated activist Tom Hayden from 1973 until 1990 and in 1970 was arrested, she claimed on directions from the Nixon White House – articulated the anti-establishment voice of the film, straining to support the genteel and responsible Godell against all odds. Bridges's earlier major venture was a brilliant film about the confrontation between passionate youth and stodgy old age, *The Paper Chase* (1973).

The Hospital (1971)

Here, based on a script by the genius Paddy Chayefsky (who later wrote *Network* [1976]), is Arthur Hiller's story of Bock, Chief Medical Officer of a major New York hospital. Life is both zany and battle-scarring for this man, advanced in his career, bold in his knowledge, yet carrying in his heart the noble spirit young people of the time craved so uniformly to emulate. He begins to discover that patients in his hospital are dying: not in the normal numbers, as one would find in any hospital, but routinely, in what seems a pattern. They come in basically healthy, with some tiny complaint, and the next thing he knows is that things have aggravated and he has a corpse on his hands. The film turns out to be at once an artful murder mystery – these deaths are not happening by accident – and a scathing social critique, since the hospital with its rigid bureaucratic organization is an apt metaphor for the new Babylon being constructed by global capitalism at the time, Dr. Bock its angry prophet. As the bitterly wearied Bock, George C. Scott gives an indelible performance; as one of his barmy patients, who may well not be so very barmy, the inimitable Barnard Hughes drools and raves. Richard A. Dysart is exquisitely on point as a craven and unfeeling myrmidon of the system who treats his patients like cattle.

Arthur Hiller made seventy-five films, eleven of them in the 1970s. These included comedies like *The Out of Towners* (1970) and *Plaza Suite* (1971), the much talked-of *Love Story* (1970) introducing Ryan O'Neal, *The Man in the Glass Booth* (1975), about the trial of Adolf Eichmann, *Man of La Mancha* (1972) from the Broadway musical based on Cervantes's *Don Quixote* (and with Peter O'Toole in the lead). *The Hospital* stands out in this eclectic mix as a film of brutal critical sharpness (faithfully picking up Chayefsky's trademark critical voice), the protagonist's growing agony produced explicitly by the system's carelessly stifling his every noble effort. Scott plays Bock as an improviser with a built-in social critique, the sort of man who would have developed his medical skills in the Korean War while observing how preposterous systemic arrangements can be. Robert Altman's *M*A*S*H* struck the same chord, in 1970, but with more slapstick and less fidelity to the sort of wise courage young people wanted to admire.

In these cases, and the many others explored in these pages, 1970s directors posed against some of the fundamental social tensions of the time, showing, in effect, an undeclared war: between the aspiring young and the brutal, insensitive system in which they were caught; between idealistic hopes and the cold aggressions of the everyday; between gender traps and communicational

Figure I.6 Women's dissatisfaction with bourgeois marriage, then taking shape in second-stage feminism, was dramatized in a number of Renaissance films such as *Diary of a Mad Housewife* (Frank Perry,1970). Digital frame enlargement. Courtesy of Frank Perry Films.

obstructions; between self-delusions and aspirations for a better future, and more. In the chapters that follow, it is hoped that the discussions of these films and filmmakers will inspire readers to take a look at the cinema of an earlier age in which resistance – psychological, physical, inter-personal, occupational, national, and cultural – was the order of the day. It becomes clear looking at the films of the directors discussed here how keen was their analysis of American culture of the time, how penetrating and incisive. They were secret mavericks, whose films took on, among many other targets, the havoc of the Nixon administration.

WORKS CITED

Balio, Tino. *The Foreign Film Renaissance on American Screens, 1946-73*. University of Wisconsin Press, 2010.

Barattoni, Luca. *Italian Post-Neorealist Cinema*. Edinburgh University Press, 2012.

Berliner, Todd. *Hollywood Incoherent: Narration in Seventies Cinema*. University of Texas Press, 2010.

Borde, Raymond and Étienne Chaumeton, *A Panorama of the American Film Noir: 1941-53*. Translated by Paul Hammond, City Lights, 2002.

Bordwell, David. *Narration in the Fiction Film*. University of Wisconsin Press, 1985.

Bordwell, David, Janet Staiger and Kristin Thompson, eds. *The Classical Hollywood Cinema: Film Style & Mode of Production to 1960*. Columbia University Press, 1985.

Cagle, Chris. *Sociology on Film: Postwar Hollywood's Prestige Commodity*. Rutgers University Press, 2017.

Cook, David A. "Auteurs and the Film Generation in 1970s Hollywood." *The New American Cinema*, edited by Jon Stone, Duke University Press, 1998, pp. 11–37.

Cook, David A. *Lost Illusions: American Cinema in the Shadow of Watergate and Vietnam 1970-1979*. University of California Press, 2000.

Crowther, Bosley. "*Bonnie and Clyde* Arrives." *New York Times*, 14 Aug. 1967, www.nytimes.com/1967/08/14/archives/screen-bonnie-and-clyde-arrives-careers-of-murderers-pictured-as.html. Accessed 28 August 2019.

Debruge, Peter. "*Silence* Review: Martin Scorsese Belabors his Passion Project." *Variety*, variety.com/2016/film/reviews/silence-review-martin-scorsese-1201935391/. Accessed 6 August 2019.

De Man, Paul. *Blindness and Insights: Essays in the Rhetoric of Contemporary Criticism*. 2nd edition. University of Minnesota Press, 1983.

Friedman, Lester D., ed. *American Cinema of the 1970s: Themes and Variations*. Rutgers University Press, 2007.

Gelmis, Joseph. *The Film Director as Superstar: Kubrick, Lester, Mailer, Nichols, Penn, Polanski, and Others*. Doubleday, 1970.

Giovacchini, Saverio. *Hollywood Modernism: Film and Politics in the Age of the New Deal*. Temple University Press, 2001.

Godfrey, Nicholas. *The Limits of Auteurism: Case Structures in the Critically Constructed New Hollywood*. Rutgers University Press, 2018.

Guerrero, Ed. "The Rise and Fall of Blaxploitation." *The Wiley-Blackwell History of American Film Volume 3*, edited by Cynthia Lucia, Roy Grundmann, and Art Simon, Wiley-Blackwell, 2012, pp. 435–69.

Hillier, Jim. *The New Hollywood*. Continuum, 1992.

Jacobs, Diane. *Hollywood Renaissance: The New Generation of Filmmakers and their Works*. Dell, 1979.

Jameson, Fredric. "Reification and Utopia in Mass Culture" (1979), *Signatures of the Visible*, Routledge, 1992, pp. 9–34.

Jones, Mike. "Martin Scorsese Thinks Joker is Cinema." *Screenrant*, 4 Nov. 2019, www.screenrant.com/martin-scorsese-joker-cinema-comments-update/. Accessed 22 December 19.

Kael, Pauline. "The Frightening Power of 'Bonnie and Clyde.'" *The New Yorker*, 21 Oct. 1967, www.newyorker.com/magazine/1967/10/21/bonnie-and-clyde. Accessed 28 August 2019.

Kirshner, Jonathan. *Hollywood's Last Golden Age: Politics, Society, and the Seventies Film in America*, Cornell University Press, 2012.

Klein, Amanda Ann. *American Film Cycles: Reframing Genres, Screening Social Problems, and Defining Subcultures*, University of Texas Press, 2011.

Kolker, Robert. *A Cinema of Loneliness*. Four editions. London: Oxford University Press,1980; 1988; 2001; 2011.

Langford, Barry. *Post-Classical Hollywood: Film Industry, Style and Ideology since 1945*, Edinburgh University Press, 2010.

Lev, Peter. *The Euro-American Cinema*, University of Texas Press, 1993.

Lewis, Jon, ed. *The New American Cinema*. Duke University Press, 1998.

Madsen, Axel. *The New Hollywood: American Movies in the '70s*. Thomas Y. Crowell, 1975.

Martin, Nina K. *Sexy Thrillers: Undressing the Erotic Thriller*. University of Illinois Press, 2007.

Monaco, James. *American Film Now: The People, the Power, the Money, the Movies*. New American Library, 1979.

Palmer, R. Barton, ed. and trans. *Perspectives on Film Noir*. G.K. Hall, 1996.

Palmer, R. Barton. *Shot on Location: Postwar American Cinema and the Exploration of Real Place*. Rutgers University Press, 2016.

Palmer, R. Barton. "The Small Adult Film: A Prestige Form of Cold War Cinema." *Cold War Film Genres*, edited by Homer Pettey, Edinburgh University Press, 2017, pp. 62–78.

Pye, Michael and Lynda Myles, *The Movie Brats: How the Film Generation Took Over Hollywood*, Holt, Rinehart and Winston, 1979.

Sarris, Andrew. *The American Cinema: Directors and Directions 1929-1968*, E.P. Dutton, 1968.

Schatz, Thomas. *The Genius of the System: Hollywood Filmmaking in the Studio Era*, Pantheon, 1989.

Sherman, Eric and Martin Rubin. *The Director's Event*, Athenaeum, 1972.

Wilinsky, Barbara. *Sure Seaters: The Emergence of Art House Cinema*, University of Minnesota Press, 2001.

1. HAL ASHBY, GENTLE GIANT

Brenda Austin-Smith

There is a gentleness coursing through the films of Hal Ashby, discernible in spite of the association of his work with rebellion, and the assumption that the rebel is always a belligerent outsider. But who says outsiders are always ferociously angry? The protagonists of *The Landlord* (1970), *Harold and Maude* (1971), and *Being There* (1979) are certainly not, even though they are very much at odds with their circumstances. More typically, an air of puzzled melancholy arises from the characters in his films, from Badass Buddusky in *The Last Detail* (1973), through George Roundy in *Shampoo* (1975), to Bob Hyde in *Coming Home* (1978). Characters in Ashby's films are men and women (but mostly men) with roles to play in their worlds, expectations and demands to meet and fulfill. But they pause in front of Ashby's camera, captured by doubt, or seized by a frustration that interrupts their bluster or certainty. In those moments Ashby's concern "not to be too harsh" in rendering difficult, unattractive, or just typically confused people on the screen, is palpable.

While not often accorded the status of an auteur – in either the über cool atmosphere of the 1970s in which he did his best work, or in the following decades that saw other filmmakers re-discovered and re-described in those terms – Hal Ashby brought a number of iconic movies to the screen. The titles of his films are immediately recognizable, but without calling Ashby himself inevitably to mind as their director. He is a curious example of someone habitually denied the credit of a coherent oeuvre, whose works are often remembered as a series of stand-alone achievements that nevertheless conjure up for viewers something indelibly specific about the "Me Decade" of the

1970s. Perhaps the topicality of his films fastens them too firmly to the years of their release. Films like *The Landlord* and *Shampoo*, for example, can seem too rooted in the particular, and even limited, concerns of his characters to gain a lasting purchase on the viewer, especially when those concerns are naively self-serving and unironically expressed at the same time. "I don't know what I'm apologizing for," says George (Warren Beatty) half to himself in his final confrontation with Jill (Goldie Hawn) about sleeping with just about all of his clients in *Shampoo*. "Let's face it; I fucked 'em all. I mean, that's what I do." While honest, these justifications by an adorable womanizer neither make us hate him, nor give him a diabolical edge. He's too sweet to be a monster, and too self-indulgent to champion whole-heartedly. That Ashby moves unexpectedly between realism and satire also complicates the search for a through line of vision associated with auteurism. Satire can become dated, wrapped up in debates of very long standing, such as white gentrification in *The Landlord*, or promiscuity in *Shampoo*. Meanwhile, Ashby's perceptive take on military culture and the trauma of war in both *The Last Detail* and *Coming Home* suffuses both films with a quiet compassion at odds with more flamboyant and angry assessments of service life and war.

Ashby's films focus on matters that pre-occupied American society in the 1970s, such as the sexual revolution, race relations, the political influence of television, the cult of celebrity, and the reverberations of the lost Vietnam War, channeling the adjustments of characters (usually white and male) to the upheavals posed by a decade of social change. But while the topics were serious and potentially controversial, the films are thoughtful rather than fiery, though no less shrewd in their assessments of character. Ashby is no rock-throwing iconoclast. Horatio, not Juvenal, is his satiric god. His tone is humorous rather than eviscerating, his protagonists shambolic in their routes to rebellion, missing trains and losing hubcaps rather than shooting up the place.

Hal Ashby appears in all of the films discussed here: at a wedding in the first few frames of *The Landlord*, at an arcade in *Harold and Maude*, in the bar watching Badass Buddusky play darts in *The Last Detail*, passing Sally Hyde and Vi in a sports car, and flashing them a peace sign in *Coming Home*, standing at a filing cabinet in *Being There*. His commitment to film as a deeply communal endeavor seems most apparent in these moments of communion with the worlds he helped create over this decade of cinema wonder.

THE LANDLORD

Ashby's first feature stars a mop-topped Beau Bridges, looking like a blonde Beatle, as Elgar Enders. From one angle, the film tells the tale of a young, wealthy, white man's social conversion from insulated carelessness to an engagement with racial politics. From another, it seems to show the effects of the "eviction powder" tossed through a window of an apartment slated for upgrading by the arrival of rich whites. "What the hell is that?" asks Elgar, staring at the whitish haze that rises from the floor in front of him. "Just a little voodoo," replies the real estate agent, nonchalantly. As a substance intended to drive away the threat of gentrification, the eviction powder eventually works its magic, as Elgar gradually gives up on his plan to drive the black tenants out of the apartment building he has purchased.

In an extended pre-credit sequence to the film comprised of shots juxtaposed through straight cuts, we see a teacher ask a grade school class "Now, children, how do we live?" Several hands are raised, and the teacher calls on one child, "Elgar?" before we cut away to that same character, now in his late twenties. Elgar lounges near a pool, accepting a drink from Heywood, one of his family's black servants. Addressing the camera, the recumbent Elgar announces his vaguely liberal views on the fundamental similarities among people, foremost among them, the desire for territory and a place to live. As he talks, a series of intercut shots show us an increasingly frustrated black man trying to hail a cab, and snippets of an exchange from inside a Brooklyn hairdressing salon. Elgar's cluelessness about the real differences between rich whites and working-class blacks in 1970s America could not be made more obvious.

Ashby's deft and allusive cutting strategy in the opening minutes of *The Landlord* reminds us of his previous award-winning career as a film editor for Norman Jewison on films like *The Russians are Coming* (1966) and *The Thomas Crown Affair* (1968). Elgar, swigging brandy as he talks about his plans to throw "the goddamn tenants" out of the tenement he has just bought, is shot against a background of pure white, as if suspending him in a racial bubble. In the background, we hear the echoes of a handball game, and see over-exposed images of the players, dressed all in white, their white sneakers squeaking against the floor of the court. These images of vigorous leisure underscore Elgar's twinned admissions that he "has never really done anything," and that "money's never been a problem." Brooklyn, then, will be the proving ground for his self-actualization.

Just as action set in the Ender family's world of wealth is bathed in white light (as the characters themselves tend to dress in white), so are the shots of the Park Slope neighborhood in which Elgar has purchased his building tinged with brown, suggesting not only the literal brownstone building Elgar has purchased, but also the contrast between sheltered, moneyed whiteness and unpretentious, downtown grit. The symbolism is insistent, as gradually the darker tones of the Brooklyn scenes become associated with a vibrancy and emotional directness among the residents of Elgar's building that is missing from the repressed life he has known till now. His mother Joyce (Lee Grant) is too busy practicing new dance moves with her instructor to pay much attention to Elgar. She can't remember either his birthdate or the name of her daughter-in-law. Elgar's sister Susan (Susan Anspach) has her own issues: she keeps a roach clip in her hair, and falls downstairs a lot. The family's racism takes a number of forms, both casual and vicious. Susan congratulates Elgar on his interest in his tenants, remarking, "Somebody has to integrate. I can't. I just don't have the stomach for it," while Elgar's father (Walter Brooke), responding to Elgar's provocation – "We are all octoroons" – calls him a "lazy, no-good liberal."

It is soon clear that Elgar has bought a building that comes with a community, one subtly and persistently resistant to Elgar's plans for it. As he shares meals, fixes doorbells, replaces toilets and delays eviction proceedings, he is gradually absorbed into the life of the tenement, where no one has paid rent for as long as anyone can remember. Unsurprisingly, women are central to this reverse integration. Marge (Pearl Bailey) feeds him, Fanny (Diana Sands) flirts with him, and Lanie (Marki Bey), a bi-racial dancer he meets at a bar and starts to date, talks candidly with him about the complexities of race. Ashby's gift for casting is on early display here. In particular, the status of Pearl Bailey and Diana Sands as well-known African American actresses and jazz/pop entertainers at the time, gave the film considerable cultural resonance. Bailey was famous as a singer and entertainer, and had won a Tony Award for her role as Dolly in an all-black production of *Hello Dolly!* two years before the film's release, while Diana Sands had earned similar recognition for her role in both the stage and film versions of *A Raisin in the Sun* (1963).

There is a trace of the "magical Negro" in the unfolding of Elgar's maturation, even a sense that the tenement functions as a through-the-looking-glass space for his Alice-in-Wonderland status. Elgar is naive rather than conniving, and when he gets drunk at his own rent party and ends up in bed with Fanny, the sex is neither adventurous nor cynical. The resulting pregnancy, however, tests the narrative's investment in the tenement as an extended family, with members covering for each other, forgiving each other, and making endless excuses for each other, as they all do for the fugitive renters in the basement, whose presence is indicated only by the occasional lowering of window blinds.

In the midst of the rent party sequence, though, a series of shots of characters testifying to their identification as black people interrupts the flow of the film. It isn't clear if this sequence actually takes place in the world that Elgar inhabits, if it unfolds in his liberal white imagination, or if it exists in an extra-diegetic space in which Elgar and his tenants might face each other over the class and racial gulf that divides them. But the close-ups of black people describing what it is like to deny, suppress, or ignore their own blackness, as if it is an unsightly mole, and then suddenly to realize that moles "are in, baby," confronts Elgar with the enduring reality of blackness in a world in which he thinks it might be just "a fad."

The governing conceit of the sequence – that skin color is like a small

Figure 1.1   Fanny and Elgar come to terms in *The Landlord* (1970). Digital frame enlargement. Courtesy of the Mirisch Corporation.

blemish – makes its own attempt to be progressive deeply uncomfortable, in the same way that Elgar's romance with Lanie ("She's very light," he tells his mother) and his emptying of a soup tureen over the head of Heywood, the Enders' black butler, are uncomfortable, because it accommodates the racism it purports to oppose. This blunts the film's excoriation of white liberalism by appearing to protect Elgar, rather than exposing his timidity as a kinder, gentler version of his father's virulent intolerance. That Elgar and Lanie take up residence in Elgar's building, taking Fanny and Elgar's bi-racial baby as their own, ends the film on a bright note. Elgar quits the job he had given himself as the landlord, and disappears happily into the vivid world of the tenement.

HAROLD AND MAUDE

There are similarities between Harold Chasen (Bud Cort), the protagonist of *Harold and Maude*, and Elgar Enders of *The Landlord*. Both are living at home long after it would have been normal to leave. Both are rich, and have self-absorbed mothers. Both need something to propel them out of stasis and stagnation. But while Elgar stars in a social satire, Harold is the main character in what verges on a caricature. We meet him in a moment that appears to be his last, carefully preparing to hang himself. He kicks over a chair and dangles in the air, just as his mother (Vivian Pickles) enters the room. When she picks up the phone, we expect to hear her call the police or an ambulance, but instead, she calmly cancels an afternoon appointment. The sight of her son struggling with a noose he has fastened around his own neck seems to bother her not a whit. Neither is she flustered in another scene by an encounter with Harold's apparently lifeless body floating face down in the pool. We learn later on that Harold has staged over a dozen of these scenarios of self-mutilation or suicide, and when asked by a therapist if he does this for his mother's benefit he pauses before replying, "No, no – I would not say 'benefit'."

Only once do we see Harold contemplate killing his mother rather than himself. He points a gun at her from a chair while she fills in his questionnaire for a computer dating service, substituting her own preferences for Harold's, oblivious, as she must have been for some time already, to his barely suppressed hatred. But before Harold's many attempts on his own life can succeed – or before he graduates to murder – he meets Maude (Ruth Gordon). Like Harold, Maude enjoys going to funerals and is fond of the juxtaposition of the bucolic and the slightly macabre, like picnics in scrapyards. But in contrast to Harold's methodical deadpan, Maude is the picture of impulsivity and expressiveness. Harold's demeanor is reminiscent of a member of the Addams Family, while Maude is a hippie version of Auntie Mame. While at first Harold stands stiffly, arms at his sides, saying little, Maude is irrepressible and outlandish. She nabs other people's cars, digs up city trees for transport to the country, sings loudly and off-key, and poses nude for a sculptor. That Gordon was seventy-five years old at the time made her depiction of Maude a complicated challenge. Viewers who cheered the life-affirming energy of Maude as "young at heart" weren't necessarily as comfortable with the extension of that energy into the realm of the erotic. The scene of Harold blowing bubbles as he lies naked in bed with a sleeping Maude (presumably after lovemaking) was a shock to many viewers for whom free love was the exclusive privilege of youth.

Ruth Gordon's rendering of Maude has to contend with a character written as almost desperately madcap, who comes across as a senior version of the Manic Pixie Dream Girl, there to teach and inspire an emotionally stunted young man to discover a reason to live, and then to move on without her. We don't get much of Maude's backstory apart from a quiet scene of reminiscence and a brief glimpse of numbers tattooed on her forearm, which seems unpardonably cavalier of the script. As are the tenants of Elgar Enders' apartment building, Maude exists largely as a vehicle through which Harold achieves personal insight and growth. Maude has no need of further development, and indeed hints in her first conversation with Harold that her life will end in the next week. The few days of Harold and Maude's romance play out in a kind of dramatic irony, with one partner fully aware that there is an end in sight while the other is awash in the bliss of beginning.

Though the film bombed upon first release and attracted scathing reviews for its depiction of a love affair between a twenty-year-old man and a

Figure 1.2 Harold and Maude's radical love in *Harold and Maude* (1971). Digital frame enlargement. Courtesy of Paramount Pictures.

seventy-five-year-old woman, *Harold and Maude* eventually found a cult audience, striking a chord with viewers ready to champion those who, like Harold, kick over the traces of middle-American convention. It didn't matter that the character is rich, white, and not immediately interested in leaving the warm, and extremely well feathered, family nest. What mattered was Harold's embodiment of counter-cultural rebellion without the uncomfortable hardship of disenfranchisement and poverty. But the more radical message of Harold's insistently self-destructive performances may be the power not just of obstinacy, but also of refusal. Harold's flamboyant demonstrations of bodily cessation are an affront to patrimony, and his romance with Maude, while often regarded as an embrace of the life force she seems to incarnate, is actually consistent with his thwarting of the forces of legacy. While he stops short of actual self-annihilation each time, Harold's determination to confront his mother with the specter of his death is also, always, the threat of an end to the Chasen line.

These anti-capitalist and anti-patriarchal themes are not as obvious and perhaps not as attractive as the themes of inter-generational love and sex, something that thrilled some viewers and horrified others at the time. But if there is indeed sex between Harold and Maude, it is sex for pleasure only. Quite apart from the scandalized commentary on the sensual unseemliness of this chronologically mismatched pair, the impossibility of Maude's pregnancy acts as a rebuke to the typical cinematic pairing of a fecund woman with a man of just about any age. The romantic and erotic interactions of this couple not only challenge the insistence of some viewers on the aesthetic impossibility of a young man finding an elderly woman a preferred sexual partner but also defy similar assumptions that men always take a woman's fertility into consideration when contemplating the suitability of potential erotic companions.

Sex with Maude offers Harold a way to achieve intimacy while also continuing to frustrate his mother's hopes for him. More than this, Maude's decision to end her life confronts Harold with the example of sincere action rather than attention-seeking stunting. She ups the death ante by really meaning it, a move that calls Harold's bluff. In a literal though fitting response, Harold backs away from that edge.

THE LAST DETAIL

The realist poignancy of *The Last Detail* stands out visually and thematically from Ashby's first two features, both of which rely on exaggeration to convey social criticism. In *The Landlord*, excessive whiteness infects scene after scene of the Enders' family estate. In *Harold and Maude*, there are Mrs. Chasen's ever-changing hairdos, the missing arm that Harold's uncle manipulates into a salute (à la *Dr. Strangelove* [1964]), and the soldiers who stumble and collapse around them as they tour a veterans' retirement home. Characters in both of those films trace a topical and appealing arc of escape from the racial and class expectations of their families. Not so in *The Last Detail*, where Signalman "Badass" Buddusky (Jack Nicholson) and Gunner's Mate "Mule" Mulhall (Otis Young) are Navy "chasers" assigned to take young Seaman Meadows (Randy Quaid, in his second film role) from Virginia to military prison in Maine for trying to steal forty dollars from a charity collection box. The two seamen object to the "chicken-shit detail," but after hearing that they have five days of covered travel, realize that if they hustle the kid to jail in two days, they can split the value of the per diems and enjoy a slow good time on the way back.

The Last Detail is a variant of the buddy road movie, but with a threesome rather than a pair. Instead of the open road, a military prison lies ahead of the travellers, making the end of the journey something to put off for as long as possible. Buses and trains, rather than cars, are the modes of transport. This means that someone else is always driving, which limits the potential for true waywardness. Dally as they might in hotels, bars, and a brothel, Buddusky and Mulhall's orders exert a force that neither of them finally resists, though the cluelessness of the stolid, bovine Meadows works its way into their sympathies over the sheer length of time they spend together. The grace and emotional directness with which Ashby directs this simple story of three men reluctantly traveling north from Norfolk to Portsmouth makes Ashby's third feature a masterpiece, a fiction film comparable to the Maysles' documentary *Salesman* (1969) in its depiction of travel as a form of fate.

Figure 1.3   The "mother-fucking shore patrol," in *The Last Detail* (1973). Digital frame enlargement. Courtesy of Columbia Pictures.

The first leg of the train trip sets up the relational dynamic. Mulhall looks out the train windows, deliberately detached, reluctant to engage with either of his companions. Mulhall tells Buddusky that the Navy is "the best thing that ever happened to me," and he is wary of anything that could endanger his place in it. Buddusky, the Id of the group, stares intently at Meadows, absorbing the fact of his youth, and the outrage of the eight-year sentence he faces. Mulhall discourages Buddusky from probing Meadows about the crime, asking him, "So tell me, how you going to help him?" before turning back to look out at the snow-streaked fields. Channeling his pity for Meadows and his disdain for much of the military ("takes a kind of sadistic temperament to be a Marine," he says), Buddusky decides that giving Meadows a few days of beer-drizzled indulgence in Washington, New York, and Boston is the best answer he can think of.

Almost every scene of Ashby's film reminds us of the coldness of the environment. In the very first scene, a seaman walks with his shoulders hunched against the chill. And at each stop along the trip, the characters blow on their fingers, or stamp their feet, hands jammed in the pockets of their pea jackets. The deepening chill marks the northern progress of the detail, and operates as an inverse index of the men's emotions. Buddusky's determination to prove Mulhall wrong about Meadows ("You said he couldn't enjoy himself") becomes more insistent as they leave New York for Boston. Buddusky is a sparkplug, a coiled spring of cocky bravado, and Nicholson plays him with exuberant volatility, exhibiting what Vincent Canby calls "an anthology of swaggers optimistic, knowing, angry, foolish, and forlorn." Buddusky sees Meadows as a protégé, someone in need of mentoring. In the hotel room they rent after missing the connecting train and downing several beers, Buddusky seems flattered when Meadows asks for instruction in how to be a Signalman, and is silently nonplussed when Meadows mimics his demonstration of hand signals perfectly. Later still, in Boston, Buddusky approves of Meadows's choice of prostitute in the brothel: "He picked the same one I would've." In the first restaurant they go to, Buddusky urges Meadows to insist on the correct order rather than to settle for what he gets from the kitchen, saying to the kid, "It's easy to have it the way you want it." Buddusky wants Meadows to show some backbone, some spirit in the face of the unjust sentence he faces. He is exasperated by Meadows's passivity and acquiescence to rules and authority. "Don't you ever get mad at nobody? Don't you ever want to romp and stomp someone, bite off their ear, just to get it out of your system?" Meadows answers that the guy who nabbed him was "just doing his job."

Meadows's refusal to get angry infuriates Buddusky, but lends credibility to the kid's later adoption of the Buddhist chant, which he repeats for the rest of the film. Praying for deliverance rather than breaking out seems to fit Meadows's accepting nature – "You're too good to believe," says Mulhall of him. This makes the film's penultimate scene of the snowy picnic into a tangle of bad timing and broken trust. Meadows, edging away from the turned backs of the two chasers in a last-minute escape attempt, shows them that he has indeed learned something from his time in this "Navy of three." He does exactly what Buddusky has goaded and dared him to do, but his act of self-assertion coincides with Buddusky's quiet admission that it's time to "get this over with." Meadows makes a break for it over the snow, only to be tackled and badly beaten up by a suddenly out-of-control Buddusky, whose fury is inchoate and complex. Meadows's sudden bolt illustrates Buddusky's comment to Mulhall that the "kid's come a long way in the last few days, ain't he?" It also undercuts Buddusky's judgement of Meadows as someone secretly glad to be heading to jail. Moments earlier, Buddusky had confessed to Mulhall that he likes being at sea, as close to an admission of his own institutionalization as we get from him. But more than anything, by trying to run away, Meadows forces the two lifers to set aside their feelings and deliver him to his fate. In the end, they do their jobs.

Christopher Beach calls *The Last Detail* the "least hopeful of Ashby's films" (2009: 68). Received as it was in the wake of the Vietnam War, the film isn't so much about frustrated American military prowess as about skepticism toward all things martial. The film's focus on the Navy even seems a bit of a front for a character study that narrows in on Nicholson's Buddusky, gripped by the fate of the hapless Meadows but unable to do anything but delay its onset. Keen to show off in the cities they visit along the road, crowing with both rage and righteousness ("I *am* the mother-fucking shore patrol!"), in the end Buddusky is hemmed in by the same hierarchies that have short-changed Meadows, his loser, working-class bluster brought to heel by the commands of a petty Marine (Michael Moriarty).

SHAMPOO

Richard Nixon was a target of Ashby's ridicule as early as 1970, appearing as an image on a television screen in *The Landlord* and then again as a "deified picture" (Dawson 140) on Uncle Victor's office wall in *Harold and Maude*. But in *Shampoo*, the appearance of the caption "November 4, 1968, Election Eve" in the opening scene of a couple noisily making love frames this story of sexual distraction in the larger national context of political inattention. *Shampoo* presents a day in the over-lapping lives of Beverly Hills star hairdresser George Roundy (Warren Beatty) and a number of beautiful and/or wealthy social and political scenesters. They include George's girlfriend Jill (Goldie Hawn), his ex-lover Jackie (Julie Christie), Felicia, his bit on the side (Lee Grant) and Felicia's rich Republican fundraiser husband, Lester Karpf (Jack Warden).

The motif of distraction, embodied in characters who don't listen to the people they are talking to, surfaces often in Ashby's work. Elgar Enders' mother is too pre-occupied to listen to her son's plan for moving away from home, just as Mrs. Chasen is too concerned with the social adornments of her own life to pay attention to Harold, thus validating his theatrical bids for her attention. Flightiness attaches to many of Ashby's female characters in particular, which makes George's combination of good-natured self-interest and daft masculinity unusual and disarming, working its charms on viewers as much as on other characters in the film. As others have remarked, George's character was at least in part based not just on William Wycherley's play *The Country Wife* but on one or two actual hairdressers active in Beverly Hills at the time, as well as Warren Beatty's own amorous history. Lester, the businessman who arranges the first party all of the principle characters attend on the night of the election, thinks George must be gay, as befits his own stereotype of the profession, especially after hearing George talk about having gone to beauty school ("It's an unusual trade," says Lester, inexplicably). Thus, he has no suspicions that George is sleeping with his wife, and even asks George (who has approached Lester for business backing) to pick up Lester's current mistress, Jackie (George's ex), on the way to the event. The farcical construction of the film calls up Wycherley's work, in which the character Harry Horner professes impotence in order to gain sexual access to a number of married women and their daughters.

Pauline Kael calls George a "sexual courier," a sensual democrat who is the only person in the film who isn't completely selfish (87). This is perhaps too kind, for George's "generosity" is usually expressed and enacted in the anticipation of personal pleasure, rather than something that would benefit someone else exclusively. In the first scene, for example we watch him adroitly sidestep Felicia's questions about why he is leaving his own apartment late at night after getting a phone call just after they've finished sex:

FELICIA: I thought you said you weren't going anywhere –
GEORGE: I'm not. I'm just going to see this friend for a few minutes.
FELICIA: Wait – it's one of those girls isn't it? You're going to see one of those girls!
GEORGE: What are you talking about? She's not a girl, she's just a friend of mine.

George's talent for bafflegab here rivals that of Groucho Marx ("Who are you going to believe? Me? Or your lying eyes?"). It also allies him, despite his self-professed disdain for money – he says to Jackie "I don't fuck anybody for money; I do it for fun" – with the realm of politics, where platitudes and doublespeak are the currency of manipulators. George's modus operandi is superficial flattery, tossing the phrase "You're great, you're great!" in the air as a substitute for genuine engagement, getting the sex and star power that he wants, in the world of "heads."

Shampoo isn't critical of the sexual revolution or even George's philandering ways per se. Rather, it presents them as stupefying forces that draw the attention of characters away from the radical shift about to take place from the progressive era of the 1960s to the decade of greed and criminal corruption that follows the election of Richard Nixon. References to the election are sprinkled throughout the film. Jill walks by a poster of Nixon and Agnew, and a woman walks in front of George wearing a hat in support of their campaign. And as in *The Last Detail*, snippets of broadcast media act as a disembodied chorus, Agnew on television commenting on social permissiveness, or Nixon declaring his intention to bring America "together." And of course, a huge framed Nixon portrait hangs at the top of the stairwell of The Bistro, where things begin to fall apart for George.

Chuck Kleinhans sees in this film an upending of the usual triumph of youth and virility over age in the Restoration comedies it takes as partial inspiration. The satiric dig is that, in contrast to the typical victory of the rake over the older, Oedipal father figure, *Shampoo* dramatizes the failure and accumulated losses of the seducer. Wealth, and the "personal power accruing to wealth," trumps free love:

While the initial stages of the action give George the comic triumph of cuckolding Lester by way of both Felicia and Jackie, the action turns out to be ironic, and George ends up losing Felicia to her divorce settlement, Jackie to Lester, Jill to Johnny, and being used in a low-grade revenge by Lorna. Everyone wins except George. (Kleinhans)

As the revelations of multiple betrayals pile up (Felicia learns that both Lester and George are cheating on her; Lester realizes that Jackie isn't faithful to him, and that George isn't gay after all; Jill confronts George's compulsive womanizing) not one of these characters can summon a principle to stand on, even from each other. They are all hypocrites and users, too pre-occupied with temporary pleasures to understand, let alone dread, the shift in US political culture they are about to live through. As Kleinhans puts it, "Nixon was the president these people deserved."

COMING HOME

The second of Ashby's films to treat life in the military as a complicated choice rather than an easy target for mockery, *Coming Home* breaks with Ashby's focus on men as protagonists. The film also showcases Ashby's enduring strengths as a director who favors long takes and allows conversations to occupy considerable screen time. It is remarkable how attentive this film is to what people say to each other, and how respectfully it regards quiet and simple exchanges of dialogue. *Coming Home* is just as profound an analysis of military culture as are any other of Ashby's more stylized works, but in its contrasting portraits of Bob Hyde (Bruce Dern) and Luke Martin (Jon Voight) it also achieves a compassionate depth through the credit it gives these characters for having, or having once had, a genuine belief in what they have done. Each has been injured in some way by the war.

The film opens on a group of wounded vets (apparently in a rehab hospital) playing pool and talking about whether they would go back into combat if they ever could. The talk sounds unscripted, and Voight's character, Luke, is fully integrated into the mix of men. The scene lets us eavesdrop on injured soldiers who are the war's human residue. We hear their frustration, doubt, and anger at being warehoused, as if their injured status were an embarrassment to the military. The credit sequence that follows shows Bob Hyde, pictured running on the base, and the vets in their wheelchairs and aqua therapy pools.

Christopher Beach's discussion of the film notes its path-breaking attention to the experiences of paraplegic vets. Beach also recounts the dismissal of the film's politics by those who, like David James, objected to what they saw as the re-framing of US military aggression in terms of erotic melodrama. But while *Coming Home* does not feature a character who articulates a strident position on the invasion of Vietnam, there is no way to misunderstand the jocular jingoism of Bob Hyde and his pal Dink (Robert Ginty) on the shooting range, talking about heading to "Combat City" or feeling as if they are representing the US at the Olympics, as anything other than critical of the men's arrogance. Ashby's cross-cutting between shots of those heading out to fight and the injured who have returned stresses not just the separation of these two groups of soldiers from each other, but the reliance of the military on this distance in order to maintain the fiction of the successful invasion of Southeast Asia. Nor is there any other way of viewing the shots of planes unloading a cargo of filled body bags, or soldiers on stretchers, but as a bitter comment on the human cost of the US action.

In its depiction of Luke Martin's rehabilitation, *Coming Home* also breaks with the depiction of acquired combat disability as a personal alteration symbolic of national diminishment. Luke's paraplegia is a material condition that shapes but does not fatally determine all of his life choices. He moves back into his previous apartment, starts giving swimming lessons and drives a retrofitted car. We see him at one point in conversation with a sex worker, and learn that these arrangements are routine for him. Luke's disability makes him neither a sensation nor a pity case. And though he tells Bob's wife Sally (Jane Fonda) that in his dreams he can still walk, neither Luke nor the other vets in the hospital are depicted as so devastated by their injuries that they would rather die than live with disability.

The centrality of Sally's story as a conventional Marine wife who, in the absence of her deployed husband, begins to enjoy her own independence, is another way *Coming Home* distinguishes itself from other features about the social effects of the war on the US, such as *The Deer Hunter* (1978), as Beach observes. Through her volunteer work at the rehab hospital and her friendship with Vi Munson (Penelope Milford), Sally grows into the space created by Bob's absence. She no longer straightens her hair, she buys a sports car, and she moves into an apartment on the beach. And as Luke's initial rage gradually becomes a more profound political anger directed at American militarism, so Sally's initial dismay at the dismal efforts made by the military to meet the psychological and social needs of the vets turns her into an advocate and ally.

In his essay "Making Love, Not War," James Conlon argues that the film is a commentary on the conventional "soldier male," intent on dominance both in battle and in sexual intimacy. Conlon zeroes in on the first sex scene between Luke and Sally, infamous at the time of release both because it depicts sex between a disabled and non-disabled person and because that sex involves cunnilingus. The scene is remarkable in its emphasis on the sexual pleasures of sight as well as touch for both partners, as well as for its depiction of non-penetrative sex. Luke asks Sally to turn the light on because he wants to see her. Sally asks Luke what she should do, and how she should touch him. "That's nice," he says, "I'm real sensitive in all the areas that I feel." Conlon's

Figure 1.4 Luke and Sally in *Coming Home* (1978). Digital frame enlargement. Courtesy of Jerome Hellman Productions.

argument that the intimacy between Luke and Sally is by necessity verbal in addition to physical, and that it undoes a notion of masculinity reliant on silence, distance, and self-reliance, draws a line between the sexual politics of the film and its judgment of military aggression.

Despite its consideration of combat disabilities, *Coming Home* leaves the suffering of Bob Hyde somewhat under-addressed. Even before he returns from his tour of duty we see him on furlough with Sally, confessing to her his shock and confusion at the atrocities his own men have committed. By the time he is back home, the symptoms of his PTSD are obvious in his drinking and outbursts of anger. Though the injury for which he is to be decorated, now that he is home, was accidental and self-inflicted, he has no choice but to participate in a ceremony he knows to be completely inauthentic and cynical. Rather than honored, Bob is humiliated by the occasion. His suicide not only contributes to uncertainty about whether and how Luke and Sally's relationship might continue, but more crucially dramatizes the needs of those with mental rather than physical combat injuries who need something more than a ramp.

BEING THERE

The spectacle of an intellectually vacant man being catapulted by coincidence and general gullibility into the highest office of the United States is the (almost) incredible premise of *Being There*, a film whose relevance has never completely waned. The film was an adaptation of Jerzy Kosinzki's 1970 novel and capitalized on Kosinzki's remarkable popularity in the US following the publication of *The Painted Bird* (1965) and *Steps* (1968). The film stars Peter Sellers as Chance, a childlike man whom we meet just as he is about to leave the home of a wealthy man for whom he worked as a gardener, and who has just died, precipitating the sale of the house. In the first few scenes we see Chance awaken and immediately turn on the television. Music from a broadcast symphony concert scores his morning preparations, until suddenly Chance changes the channel and a raucous cartoon takes over the small screen. In an instant, the viewer's reading of the segment alters. This is not, as we have assumed, a portrait of a cultured man's habitual morning ritual, but rather the media-dependent routine of man incapable of articulating anything but a rudimentary inner life, who relies on television to supply him with phrases and instructions on everything from how to prune plants to how to make love. We never discover Chance's antecedents, whether he was a by-blow of his benefactor, a poor cousin, a foundling or a waif. Ejected onto the streets of Washington, wearing dated but good quality middle-class finery, and with an umbrella in hand, Chance wanders aimlessly into the path of the rich and politically well-connected, beginning an upward trajectory through layers of influential Beltway society that, at the end of the film, seem to have transported him to the realms of the otherworldly and perhaps even the holy, as he walks on the surface of a pond in the final frames of the film. Ashby's typical long takes are present here, as are deadpan compositions, as when he frames Chance striding purposelessly along a traffic median to the sound of "Thus Spake Zarathustra" or presents Chance and the magnate Benjamin Rand (Melvyn Douglas) in side by side wheelchairs, the silliness of one and the gravitas of the other cancelling each other out.

On taking her leave of the house on the day of the old man's death, Louise (Ruth Attaway), the black housekeeper, meets Chance in the garden. He is oblivious to his imminent change in circumstance, and still carries out his normal gardening tasks. Louise says goodbye, and urges Chance to find an old lady to live with because he "won't do a young one any good with that little thing of yours. You're always going to be a little boy, ain't you?" Despite these insufficiencies, Chance's luck improves when he steps back in wonder upon seeing his image on a screen in a window shop. He stumbles backward off the curb, where he is hit by a limo owned by Eve Rand (Shirley MacLaine). Eve invites Chance to recuperate at her house, where he meets and becomes a close confidant of her dying husband Benjamin, a friend of the President (Jack Warden). Ensconced in the luxurious estate, and endlessly fascinated by the in-home elevator, Chance begins his unlikely ascent into the highest reaches of domestic and international power.

Christopher Beach writes of *Being There* that it is "a cautionary tale about the power of the media to manufacture reality and thus control the political process" (105). This is a tad incomplete. The threat to social and political life in *Being There* is not just media but also a pervasive impatience in communication that permits the circulation of half-understood words and concepts in a competitive bid for authority and influence. Chance coughs in Eve's car as he tells her his name and occupation, creating the first misunderstanding that he is Chauncey Gardiner, a man of class and status, which appeals to Eve's snobbery. The film is thus a vast cinematic game of broken telephone in which snippets of garbled conversation are passed from character to character. The people who encounter Chance are receptive to the words and images delivered to them by television, but also actively contribute to the distortion and hyperbole that rapidly inflate his reputation. They are not so much media dupes as they are media enablers.

The circles of influence into which Chance wanders are themselves receivers of his broadcast of blankness, crediting Chance's halting and repetitive gardening tips and general platitudes with profundity and significance. The satire here is directed not at television but more pointedly at the neediness and striving of the political and social classes in Washington. Paranoia, greed, and all-around social climbing are rampant in every room Chance enters, and find in him a convenient screen upon which to project their own expectations and desires, from the sexual to the existential. At a reception for the Soviet Ambassador Chance receives a book contract offer, his remarks that he can neither read nor write taken as evidence of his busyness, making him more of a catch than ever. Sexually importuned by a man at the same party, Chance says, "I like to watch," prompting the man to say excitedly, "You wait right here. I'll go get Warren!" Ben Rand, comforted by Chance's equanimity, tells his doctor that having him around will make it easier for him to die. It is even possible to hear Chance's influence in the droning world salad of the President's eulogy of Ben Rand, concluding with Ben's claim that "Life is a state of mind."

At the film's conclusion, it seems likely that Chance will vault over the incumbent to become the preferred candidate for the Presidency. His utter unsuitability seems a guarantee rather than a deal-breaker, making the enduring pertinence of *Being There* deeply chilling.

Works Cited

Beach, Christopher. *The Films of Hal Ashby.* Wayne State University Press, 2009.

Canby, Vincent. "Last Detail: A Comedy of Sailors on Shore." *New York Times*, 11 Feb. 1974, p. 50.

Conlon, James. "Making Love, Not War: The Soldier Male in *Top Gun* and *Coming Home.*" *Journal of Popular Film and Television*, vol. 18, no. 1, 1990, pp. 18–27.

Dawson, Nick. *Being Hal Ashby: Life of a Hollywood Rebel.* The University Press of Kentucky, 2009.

James, David. "Rock and Roll in Representations of the Invasion of Vietnam." *Representations*, vol. 29, Winter 1990, pp. 78–98.

Kael, Pauline. "Beverly Hills as a Big Bed." *The New Yorker*, 17 Feb. 1975, pp. 86–93.

Kleinhans, Chuck. "*Shampoo*: Oedipal Symmetries and Heterosexual Satire." *Jump Cut*, 26 Dec. 1981, pp. 12–18.

2. REMAKING GENDER IN THE EARLY FILMS OF PETER BOGDANOVICH

Douglas McFarland

As much, if not more, than any of the young American filmmakers of the late sixties and early seventies, Peter Bogdanovich was immersed in film history. His Howard Hawks retrospective at MOMA, his documentary film on John Ford, and his interviews with Orson Welles attest to this. Moreover, in his own early work the influence of classical American film is palpable. *The Last Picture Show* (1971) is informed by Ford's interest in the precarious status of communal culture. *What's Up, Doc?* (1972) is a remake of a Hawks screwball comedy, and *Paper Moon* (1973) is a classic American road picture focusing, again as Ford did so often, on the fragility of family. But in the social and political context of second-wave feminism, Bogdanovich's interrogation and re-fashioning of gender roles marks these films out as his own. A bevy of women, some entrapped in traditional social roles, others complicit in their enforcement, orbit the periphery of *The Last Picture Show*, entering into and then receding from the ostensibly masculine-centered narrative. In *What's Up, Doc?* Barbra Streisand redefines Katharine Hepburn's thirties screwball persona, and in *Paper Moon*, the independence and strength of a nine-year-old girl supersedes that of her male counterparts. Perhaps because of his own very public history with women, culminating in his affair with a former Playboy bunny, Bogdanovich's testing of contemporary gender assumptions in traditional generic forms has been largely overlooked. In a recent discussion of his early work, Bogdanovich comments that "Men don't understand women" (Malone). The three films I here analyze suggest that this could not be said of him.

GOD'S LONELY WOMAN

It seems odd that in Robert Kolker's seminal 1980 study of the filmmakers of the American Renaissance of the late 1960s and early 1970s, *A Cinema of Loneliness*, Peter Bogdanovich's *The Last Picture Show* should have no mention whatsoever. Bogdanovich is himself mentioned only once, and only in a parenthetical aside (Kolker 186). And yet loneliness circulates throughout *Picture Show* as much as through any other film that Kolker analyzes. In his assessment of Martin Scorsese's characters and their environments, Kolker describes a world remarkably similar to the one Bogdanovich shaped in *The Last Picture Show*: "Scorsese's films all involve antagonism, struggle, and constant movement, even if that movement is within a tightly circumscribed area that has no exit ... all his characters lose to their isolation" (Kolker 189). The landscape of Bogdanovich's film is populated by lonely figures who struggle with one another, with themselves, within a town that seems on the verge of dying. Only one character finds an exit from that small Texas town of the early 1950s. But a war fought thousands of miles away on the Korean peninsula offers little chance of alleviating a sense of alienation and a lack of purpose. In *The Last Picture Show* communal spaces are in recession, familial connections are tenuously held together or simply lost, and entropic failure seems inevitable.

Bogdanovich, however, differs from Scorsese and other second-wave American filmmakers with respect to one very important issue: the portrayal of the subjective loneliness of women. Kolker recognizes a generalized absence of meaningful depictions of women in the films of this period. At best he can bestow only faint praise onto Scorsese for his one attempt: "Scorsese ... managed an almost creditable film about a woman in *Alice Doesn't Live Here Anymore* (1974) by avoiding psychology" (Kolker 411). Scorsese, in short, fails to project through cinematic means the subjective consciousness of his main character. Henry James, with his proclivity for depicting a range of women in his novels, is helpful in understanding this shortcoming. In the "Preface to the New York Edition" of *The Wings of the Dove*, James describes a passage in the novel "where all the offered life centres, to intensity, in the disclosure of Milly's single throbbing consciousness" (James xlii). While Scorsese is able to portray a woman oppressed by a patriarchal culture, he neglects to represent the "intensity" of her inner life. He testifies to the oppression and eventual freedom of a woman but does not enter into the sphere of her – as James puts it so well – "throbbing consciousness." In *The Last Picture Show*, however, Bogdanovich crosses the boundary dividing the simple objectification of loneliness from a genuine projection of the interiority of loneliness.

Before I address the particular woman in Bogdanovich's film to whom I have been obliquely referring, let me first attend to her narrative counterpart. Jacy

(Cybill Shepherd) stands out in the gray landscape of material need in *Picture Show*. She is the daughter of the wealthiest family in the oil town of Anarene, Texas. Jacy drives a fancy convertible, wears the fashionable teenage clothing of the period, and understands and exploits her ability to project herself as an object of male desire. Cybill Shepherd began her career as a beauty pageant winner and magazine model. She seems to draw on those experiences for her portrayal of Jacy, a young woman who embraces her objectification rather than questions it (McFarland 156). The first appearance of Jacy is appropriately located in one of the town's few communal sites: the movie theatre. Bogdanovich shows her "making out" with her boyfriend (Jeff Bridges) against the backdrop of *The Father of the Bride* (1950) featuring Elizabeth Taylor as the daughter and Spenser Tracy as the father. Taylor's onscreen presence, her status (particularly in this film) as a Hollywood fantasy of the American Girl on the cusp of becoming a woman, hovers both literally and figuratively over the real-life couples in the theatre. In the first shot of Jacy in the film, Bogdanovich chooses to bestow upon her a cinematic aura as if she herself had merged with the images of Taylor on screen. The camera looks down at Jacy and Sonny's pal Duane from behind and somewhat above. In a medium close-up, Jacy's face is aglow with soft lighting. Eschewing the gritty black and white realism that otherwise informs the film, Bogdanovich romanticizes Jacy's face, as if she were the reflection of what concurrently appears in the film on the screen. Bogdanovich cleverly uses the shot to reveal what the audience needs to know about Jacy's character and what will be born out in the remainder of the film: she comprehends male desire, she embraces it, and she uses it to her advantage.

Figure 2.1   Jacy Farrow (Cybill Shepherd) embraces Duane Jackson (Jeff Bridges) in The Last Picture Show (1971). Digital frame enlargement. Courtesy of Columbia Pictures.

Jacy's proclivity for staging herself is strikingly emphasized in two later scenes. At a traditional Christmas gathering of the local population, Jacy is invited to a pool party in the larger and more sophisticated town of Wichita. The requirement that all participants must swim and cavort about in the nude does not deter her from accepting the invitation. Newcomers to the gathering must stand on the edge of the diving board, as if it were a platform or a stage, and with everyone watching strip naked and then dive into the pool. At first Jacy hesitantly removes her garments, performing a kind of strip tease, but then strips away what is left of her clothing and climactically enters the pool. Later in the film, having decided it is time she lose her virginity, she invites her boyfriend to meet her in a motel room where the act might take place. She has also invited several friends from high school who have congregated outside in their cars facing the motel room entrance, as if it were a drive-in theatre. Although her boyfriend fails to perform, Jacy exits the motel room playing the role of one who has just lost her virginity. Her titillated friends demand that she tell them all about it. In a semi-swoon she fabricates the details of what has become a quasi-theatrical event. Jacy seems, in short, less interested in the act itself than in its staging. But while we are privy to how she fashions herself, she remains an object before the camera. The Jamesian sphere of consciousness, in short, does not absorb the narrative. Bogdanovich ironically grants her no more than what she herself desires: to be looked at.

Ruth Popper (Cloris Leachman), the marginalized wife of the high school football and basketball coach (Bill Thurman), is sharply contrasted to the narcissistic Jacy. Ruth is ignored and isolated, and leads a life devoid of love and intimacy. She has no children, is married to a husband more interested in his student athletes than in her, and seems unable to participate in the world outside the narrow confines of her house. At the Christmas gathering I mentioned earlier, she serves refreshments in the kitchen rather than participate in the dancing. Later in the film, her husband asks Sonny (Timothy Bottoms), a senior in high school, to take Ruth to a doctor's appointment. We never learn the malady that she suffers, but because she avoids talking about it and because multiple trips to the doctor are required it feels as if it might be as physically debilitating as her psychological condition. Although Ruth is old enough to be Sonny's mother, they soon become lovers. One would be tempted to delve into the Freudian implications of their relationship, especially since Sonny doesn't seem to have a living mother (his father is an alcoholic), and Ruth is childless. But this critical approach, however convenient it might be, does not speak to Bogdanovich's real interest: the absence of intimacy in his characters' lives and its consequences. For much of the film, Sonny provides the most prominent subjective point of view. He is the first person we see in the film and subsequently occupies more minutes by far than any other character. However, when Sonny abandons Ruth in favor of the manipulative and shallow Jacy, the audience pulls back, compelled to pass judgment on him. As the marginalization of Ruth becomes more and more pronounced, and as the abandonment of her not simply by Sonny but also by her husband and the town in general grows more acute, her own "throbbing consciousness" supplants Sonny's. In the aftermath of Jacy's abandonment of him, the deaths of his young friend Billy (Sam Bottoms) and Sam the Lion (Ben Johnson), who owned the movie theater, and the departure of Duane for the Korean War, Sonny abjectly returns to Ruth. When she opens her door, we see that she is still not dressed by the middle of the day, nor has she cleared away the morning dishes. She grudgingly allows him to enter for a cup of coffee. Having once felt the touch of a lover, she now feels even more acutely its absence. She is perhaps less bereft of Sonny than of love itself. She turns the angry contortion of her face onto Sonny, berating him for his betrayal. He is reduced to adolescent self-pity. The judgment she hurls at him goes to the heart of the film: "You didn't love me." The ultimate betrayal is the withholding of love. Ruth is portrayed at this climactic moment not as a victim of that betrayal but instead as one who understands through her own pain, and in a more expansive, almost existential degree the loneliness that informs the film. As the two sit at the kitchen table facing one another, Sonny will not look up, but stretches his hand towards Ruth's across the table. She then finally encloses it within her own two hands. The "throbbing consciousness" in this scene is hers. The audience is privy to these few moments when she passes from anger to forgiveness, or to put it differently, from the intimacy of desire to the intimacy of absolution. The closing credits of the film are set against the voice of Hank Williams singing, "Why don't you love me like you used to do?" The voice we hear is a man's, but the allusion is to a woman; for it is Ruth whose own lament has an intensity and depth that the popular country singer cannot emulate.

I Am Woman

Bogdanovich followed his much admired *The Last Picture Show* (nominated for Best Picture and winning Oscars for both Ben Johnson and Cloris Leachman) with the screwball comedy *What's Up, Doc?*, essentially a remake of Howard Hawk's *Bringing Up Baby* (1938). As I mentioned earlier, Bogdanovich had organized the Hawks retrospective at MOMA in 1962 and was well versed in the body of his work. As much as any of the second-wave American filmmakers, Bogdanovich's early career followed the pattern set by Truffaut, Godard, and others who began as critics writing for *Cahiers du Cinéma*. But *What's Up, Doc?* is more than an homage to a much-admired director of a previous generation. The film reflects Bogdanovich's ongoing interest in the representation of women onscreen. The casting of Barbra Streisand in the lead role and the relocation of the film to the cultural context of San Francisco of the 1970s are the significant elements in Bogdanovich's refashioning of what Shakespeare called the "woman's part" (*Cymbeline* 2.5.20).

In *Bringing Up Baby* Katharine Hepburn plays what Maria DiBattista calls a "fast talking dame" of the American comedies of the 1930s:

> The classic American comic heroine – the dame attained her majority with the birth of sound – became a fast-talker not just to keep up with the times, but to run ahead of them. She paved the way for a new class or sort of woman who finally would answer to no one but herself. (DiBattista 11)

In Hawks's film this new woman exercises her freedom to snatch her male object of desire (Cary Grant) away from another woman, and in the process to convert him from a narrowly focused paleontologist into a mate worthy of her, a mate whose identity is multifaceted, fluid, and yet fully integrated. In the screwball environment into which Hepburn leads Grant, the scholar learns how to become a lover.

In *What's Up, Doc?* Barbra Streisand takes Hepburn's place and plays Judy, a young woman who is clever, playful, witty, sexy, adept at improvisation, master of the one-liner, and hip. It's love at first sight when she glimpses a professor of music (Ryan O'Neal) in the hotel lobby where a convention of musicologists is being held. Howard teaches at a college in Iowa and is vying for a grant from the sponsor of the event. He believes that he can hear musical notes emanating from ancient stones but seems unable to keep up with the fast-talking Judy. The film takes place in one of the centers of the 1970s counter-culture movement: Haight-Ashbury, the Fillmore Auditorium, the Free Speech Movement across the bay in Berkeley, The Grateful Dead, and so on. Judy is perhaps the lone figure in the film who seems to reflect this contemporary environment. She wears bell-bottomed pants and a 1960s Carnaby Street mod hat. In contrast to the narrowly focused college professor of musicology, Judy is a self-confident free spirit who is able to improvise, play different parts, and move into and out of whatever environments she encounters.

Judy can also sing. After all, she is Barbra Streisand. And herein lies the overarching joke of the film. She will teach a musicologist about music; she will convert him from a devotee of the sounds made by rocks to the captivating sounds of a flesh and blood woman. She will show Howard, in short, how they can make beautiful music together. Bogdanovich makes this evident in the opening and closing credits. They are accompanied by Streisand's rendition of Cole Porter's witty and sophisticated *You're the Top* (who else would rhyme Mahatma Gandhi and Napoleon Brandy?). The composer, the song, and the singer offer a world far removed from Howard's faculty office in Ames, Iowa. The virtuosity of Streisand's performance is enhanced by the playfulness, the sassiness, the utterly confident style of her singing. And after all of the comic chases, chaos, and fun in the body of the film, Bogdanovich concludes with an important variation on the singing that accompanies the closing credits. It's still Streisand's voice singing Cole Porter, but now Howard accompanies her. And herein lies another joke: Ryan O'Neal can't carry a tune. He starts off tentatively, following Judy's musical lead, but by the time they arrive at the end of the song, their voices have blended into a duet. They finally make the beautiful music together that we have anticipated since the beginning of the film. This ending was foreshadowed earlier when Howard wanders into a room under construction in the hotel where he is staying. He finds a piano that has been covered with a painter's tarp, and as he begins to fiddle with the keyboard suddenly there is Judy, hiding under the tarp. She immediately begins to sing "You Must Remember This" and goads Howard into accompanying her on the piano. Judy's alluring ash blonde hair comes undone so that Howard seems doubly seduced, by the music and the flowing strands of hair. When they tumble off the piano bench and become entwined on the floor, Howard is transported into a private and intimate world inhabited only by himself, Judy, and the music. But as they begin to kiss, they are interrupted by a painter and this magic moment vanishes. There is still work to be done in teaching the musicologist the joys of music and the liberation of falling in love.

By 1972, after a decade of activities that included the Equal Pay Act of 1963, the founding of the National Organization of Women in 1966, and the publication of the first issue of *Ms.* Magazine in the same year as the release of *What's Up, Doc?,* the so-called second-wave feminist movement had firmly

Figure 2.2   Judy (Barbara Streisand) alluringly reclined in *What's Up Doc?* (1972). Digital frame enlargement. Courtesy of Warner Bros.

established itself. Judy's possibilities are, therefore, much broader that those of Hepburn's character in *Bringing Up Baby*. Judy is not simply a pretty face with a great voice. She is also a polymath who is conversant in almost any discipline, from music theory and paleontology to higher mathematics and quantum physics. Her linguistic facility, the speed of her wit, and the breadth of her expertise run ahead of all the other characters in the film.

However, Judy's intelligence is qualified early in the picture. "Don't you know the meaning of propriety?" asks Howard's fiancée, Eunice (Madeline Kahn), a very unhip pre-feminist stereotype of the domineering woman. Judy decides to show off and to squelch her rival by responding with an exact quotation from the Webster's Dictionary. She provides no meaning of her own, no thoughtfulness about the complexities of what might be proper, little interest in how the proper identity for a woman had changed from the 1950s to the 1970s, all issues with which she should be concerned and which Eunice's question have implicitly raised. At best she is being flip and ironic, demonstrating her intellectual and linguistic superiority over Eunice. But because her response is taken verbatim from a dictionary, her apparent intellectual sophistication might be nothing more than a photographic memory. We are left with the suspicion that everything she knows, she had to memorize. Judy has a gift, not necessarily a set of accomplishments. Moreover, as the film progresses we learn that Judy is knowledgeable in so many fields because she has changed majors so many times. And each change of major is accompanied by a change in institution. She cannot settle down. She cannot find a discipline that will challenge her talent, or one might even say that Judy leaves just when that talent is challenged. It may even be that the clever patter and playful irony that she relies on are a cover for her failure to engage in a meaningful way the materials she so effortlessly memorizes.

In the courtroom at the end of the film, where the comic confusion and misunderstandings are ready to be dispelled by a stern and exasperated male judge (borrowed from *My Favorite Wife*), Judy conceals herself under a blanket, hiding in plain sight. As it turns out the judge is, in fact, her father. When her identity as the prodigal daughter is uncovered, she has the look of an adolescent child caught in some transgression. The revelation raises the question of her finances: has this perpetual student been dependent on her father all this time? Money never seemed to be the problem for the upper-class Hepburn, who knows her way around a country club. But how free is Streisand's modern woman who seems not to care about money? Bogdanovich offers us a new kind of woman, but this new kind of woman finds herself in a new kind of world. Can Judy have it both ways? Can she be the modern independent woman and concurrently be a paternal dependent. In the early 1970s, Gloria Steinem told an audience of young women at Smith College that in order to be liberated one should be knowledgeable and in charge of one's own finances. In a very subtle manner, Bogdanovich suggests to his audience that freedom brings its own set of responsibilities, and this fast-talking dame of the early 1970s provides the subject of a cautionary tale.

The foil to Judy is Howard's Midwest fiancée, Eunice. In *Bringing Up Baby*, Cary Grant's domineering future bride informs him in the opening scene that there will be no honeymoon. But she is subsequently banished from the screwball world into which Hepburn drags Grant. In Bogdanovich's remake, however, this figure is given a prominent role. Like her counterpart in *Baby*, she doesn't seem to consider marriage as anything other than her duty to arrange her husband's life for him. One almost ritualistic pleasure of comedy is the elimination of a so-called "blocking" figure (usually a father) who stands in the way of the sexual energy of a younger generation. Eunice is a version of this blocking figure. Her domineering ways deny the liberation that love might bring. Bogdanovich undermines the pleasure of the elimination of Eunice by bestowing on her a depth of character that traditional comedy would avoid. On the one hand, she is the butt of the joke, mocked relentlessly by the thoroughly modern Judy. On the other hand, she is a sympathetic woman trying to negotiate the changing gender roles of the 1970s. At the beginning of the film she is the stereotypical dominatrix, confusing her independence as a woman with ordering the lives of others. After their arrival at the airport in San Francisco, Eunice scolds Howard as if he were a child wandering off from his parents. Howard can reply to her commands and admonitions only by repeating, "Yes, Eunice." The first joke in the film occurs when she orders the skycap to take their luggage to a taxi; he too has no other response than a "Yes, Eunice." She suppresses language, rejects play, orders grown men about, and generally must have her way. She is the enemy of comedy. At the opening banquet for the convention, Judy arrives early pretending she is Eunice, Howard's fiancée. She usurps Eunice's place and brings her own energy, humor, and sexiness to the event. Everyone loves her, especially the head of the foundation that will fund the grant Howard hopes to win. When the real Eunice shows up, she is blocked from entering the hall and told that Howard's fiancée has already arrived. After she physically forces her way in, Eunice is unceremoniously dragged away lest she break the spell that Judy has generated. Howard is given the chance to correct matters but when he is asked if he knows this woman, he responds, "I never saw her before in my life." There is an element of cruelty in comedy. That cruelty can be harsh if the butt of the joke begins to take on an interiority. Once Shylock rails against the injustice of what is being done to him, once he delivers the speech that begins, "Hath a Jew not eyes," once the audience is drawn into his own perspective, once he ceases to be a one-dimensional scapegoat, *The Merchant of Venice* ceases to have its comic design. A few scenes after the removal of Eunice from the feast, back in Howard's hotel room, she reveals her competitive nature, as well as her insecurities. She asserts to

Howard, "You know I am a woman too." He responds that he never thought of her "as a woman." It might be too facile to point out that in the same year the film was released, Helen Reddy recorded her enormously popular anthem of woman's pride, *I Am Woman*. In a deft reversal of her role as a blocking figure, the butt of the joke, Eunice now becomes a woman who is denied her identity as a woman. Perhaps this demonstrates the cost of her need to dominate others, but for this short instance Eunice becomes, as Shylock does at that pivotal moment in Shakespeare's play, something almost tragic. A final twist comes at the end of the film. Upon Howard's departure from the airport back to Iowa, Eunice informs him that she will not be going with him. She has a new partner, the diminutive head of the foundation sponsoring the convention (Austin Pendleton). The irony is, of course, both geographic and cultural. Eunice will be staying in San Francisco, while the liberated Howard and the liberating Judy are heading for the Midwest where the newly emerging gender roles of the 1970s have quite probably not had time to catch on and where Judy runs the risk of becoming a "faculty wife." In some way, Eunice emerges as the most compelling character in the film as she finds herself caught up in a screwball world where, to quote another Cole Porter song, "Anything Goes."

It Wouldn't Be Make Believe If You Believed in Me

If *What's Up, Doc?* is a remake of *Bringing Up Baby*, then we might think of *Paper Moon* as a prequel to Preston Sturges's *The Lady Eve* (1941). The latter features a father and daughter team that has been on the road for many years, successfully supporting themselves as "card sharks." *Paper Moon* tells the story of how that relationship might have begun. In *The Lady Eve* the heroine goes "legit" by leaving her father, giving up her unscrupulous ways, and marrying a wealthy and clueless bachelor. On the other hand, for the nine-year old Addie of *Paper Moon* (Tatum O'Neal) legitimacy depends on finding her father and taking up rather than rejecting his unscrupulous ways. Bogdanovich's film opens at the graveside funeral ceremony for Addie's mother. A late attendee arrives with flowers that he has snatched from a nearby headstone. Unaware of her death, Moze (Ryan O'Neal) has come with the intention of renewing an intermittent sexual relationship, not of paying his last respects. "Are you my father?" the clever and intuitive Addie asks him almost immediately. He is thrown off balance and gives a very nervous negative response. This is the question that underlies the picaresque narrative that follows. With the prospect of monetary compensation and admitting no blood relationship, Moze is talked into taking Addie to St. Joseph, Missouri to live with her only known relatives.

While the absence of a parent casts a shadow over *The Last Picture Show* and *What's Up, Doc?*, in *Paper Moon* that absence is foregrounded, informing the first as well as the final scene of the film. Stanley Cavell has argued that the absence of a mother in many of the comedies of the 1930s and 1940s has an antecedent in Shakespeare's romances, especially *The Tempest*, in which a paternal lineage supersedes a maternal one. In *The Lady Eve*, the daughter frees herself from that lineage by "playing a role and manipulating the cards to insure a happy outcome for herself" (Cavell 57). In *Paper Moon*, the happy outcome for the protagonist combines the legitimacy of a paternal bond with the freedom that the father's way of life on the road bestows. *Paper Moon* is a classic road picture, one in which the road itself takes on meaning. Like Arden Forest in *As You Like It* or the woods outside of Athens in *A Midsummer Night's Dream*, the road provides a space in which Addie might hone her skills and prove herself to be her father's daughter. Her Aunt's world in St. Joseph threatens Addie with the confined space, both literal and figurative, of a traditional role for a woman. Life with her father, on the other hand, imparts to Addie the open-ended possibilities of the road.

Addie is the most sophisticated, strongest, and smartest of Bogdanovich's women. Moze's most reliable flimflam is to sell Bibles to recently widowed wives. He goes through the obituaries, finds the name of a widow, goes to her residence, and claims that before his death her husband had ordered a Bible for her, payment upon delivery. The irony seems lost on him that he preys on households without a patriarch as he ardently flees his own paternal role. Addie quickly proves she is able to play this game at a much higher level than Moze. In one encounter with a bereft widow, she comes up behind the unsuspecting Moze, quickly ascertains that the widow is very well off, and sets an inflated price on the Bible. Moze looks at her in astonishment and irritation. The woman, however, not only happily pays the amount but also gives Addie a bonus. But unlike Moze, Addie is able to make moral and ethical decisions. When they arrive at the porch of a poor widow surrounded by a roomful of children, straight out of a Walker Evans photograph, Addie intervenes not to raise the price but to tell the widow that the Bible has already been paid for. She understands, in a way that Moze does not, that to live outside the law, as one poet of the road put it, you must be honest (Dylan).

Addie's independence is reflected in her broad cultural awareness, which other characters in the film lack. She is cognizant of the economic collapse of the 1930s, the consequential social diaspora, the political leadership of the period, and the new mass media. One of the few possessions she takes with her on the road is a radio. Each night she listens to Fred Allen and Jack Benny; her references to Frankie Roosevelt suggests that she may have listened to a fireside chat or two. That she calls him "Frankie" rather than Franklin gives the impression that she is after all still a child, but also that she feels a familiarity with the figure who led the nation during the Great Depression. This suggests to me a maturity, and an understanding of oneself as part of a larger cultural identity, that Moze lacks.

Figure 2.3   The strikingly aware Addie (Tatum O'Neal) in *Paper Moon* (1973).
Digital frame enlargement. Courtesy of Paramount Pictures.

Because she has not yet reached puberty, Addie's identity as a woman is incomplete. However, Bogdanovich provides the audience with traits and characteristics, an understanding of self and the world that will become part of her as an adult. Almost counterintuitively, because she is not fully formed, she is Bogdanovich's most nuanced representation of a woman. The uncertainty of how the elements of her pre-adolescent personality will finally take shape requires that the audience imagine her as a woman and thereby dig deeper into her character. After a barber has finished cutting Moze's hair, he asks if the little boy might want his done. With her short hair, bib overalls and defiant attitude this might seem a reasonable assumption to make. She responds with indignation and defiantly asserts that she is a girl. When another woman (Madeline Kahn) enters the picture and competes for Moze's attention, Addie sabotages her through a clever trick but also shows herself capable of understanding her rival. In an attempt to stop Addie from undermining her, Trixie confesses that relationships for her are inevitably short-lived. She speaks to Addie privately outside the hearing of Moze. There is an intimacy between them, the intimacy between two sophisticated and knowing women. Later Addie will clumsily dowse herself with perfume: a girl comically demonstrating her awkwardness and inexperience. But then again, she uses her childlike innocence as a persona in her own flimflam. She tricks a shop girl and store manager by crying like a little girl at the mercy of the adults. As a result, she leaves the emporium with more money than when she entered. Rather than a finite representation of a woman, we are left with ambiguities, questions, possibilities, contradictions, hopes, and fears. Will other women threaten her; will she use or misuse her extraordinary talents at reading others; will she have a sense of ethical social responsibility; how and at what point will she leave her father; will her vulnerability and her aggressiveness somehow complement one another; will her gender prove more liberating than constraining; and will her zealous insistence on her independence become merely a defiance? Bogdanovich's achievement is to demonstrate through Addie how precarious can be the process whereby a girl becomes a woman.

When they finally do reach St. Joseph and Addie is delivered over by Moze to her aunts, her facial expression and her body language tell us that she will not be long for this conventional woman's domain. She is too sophisticated, too worldly wise even at nine years old, to abide life in the sequestered realm of her aunt, along with the expectation that at some point in the future she will marry, have children, and care for the home. The road, with its risks, its rewards, its possibilities for improvisation and quick thinking, and its sense of comradery, suits her. In less than an hour with her aunt, she has run away, chasing and then catching Moze as he heads off to his next experience. During the closing credits, the camera looks out at the road winding its way through the vast Midwestern landscape that lies ahead. This final shot alludes both visually and thematically to John Ford's *My Darling Clementine* (1946). As Wyatt (Henry Fonda) rides off, Clementine (Cathy Downs) remains behind, watching him recede into the distance. She will become the schoolteacher in Tombstone and await Wyatt's return. Ford uses variations of this ending in *The Grapes of Wrath* (1940) and *The Searchers* (1956). In the former, Tom Joad (Henry Fonda) leaves his mother behind as he goes off into the world in order to change it; in the latter, Ethan Edwards (John Wayne) leaves his family behind to wander in the world. In Bogdanovich's film there is no separation, no solitary figure either left behind or going ahead. There is no single sphere of consciousness expressed, but rather the expectation that Addie and Moze, like Walter Burns (Cary Grant) and Hildy Johnson (Rosalind Russell) in *His Girl Friday* (1940), will continue on together, squabbling, sharing tricks, and experiencing the intimacy of the road.

Works Cited

Cavell, Stanley. *Pursuits of Happiness: The Hollywood Comedy of Remarriage.* Harvard University Press, 1981.

DiBattista, Maria. *Fast-Talking Dames.* Yale University Press, 2001.

Dylan, Bob. "Absolutely Sweet Marie." *Blonde on Blonde*, Columbia, 1966.

James, Henry. *The Wings of the Dove.* Oxford University Press, 2009.

Kolker, Robert. *A Cinema of Loneliness.* 1980. Oxford University Press, 2011.

Malone, Alicia. "A Conversation with Peter Bogdanovich." *Filmstruck*, June, 2017.

McFarland, Douglas. "Translating Daisy Miller." *Nineteenth-Century American Fiction on Screen*, edited by R. Barton Palmer, Cambridge University Press, 2007, pp. 146–60.

3. IN EXTREMIS: JOHN BOORMAN'S CINEMA OF DISLOCATION

Ina Rae Hark

The fortuitous timing of John Boorman's first feature *Catch Us if You Can* (US *Having a Wild Weekend*, 1965), released just when Hollywood producers, as Boorman later reflected, "were camping out in London, trying to make pictures, because there was this feeling that somehow the younger European directors knew how to attract an audience"(qtd. in Cowie 228–9), led to MGM signing him to make the adaptation of a pseudonymous Donald E. Westlake novel *The Hunter* with Lee Marvin, a star fresh off an Oscar-winning performance. The resulting film, *Point Blank* (1967), positioned Boorman among the first New Hollywood directors alongside Americans Arthur Penn, Mike Nichols, Robert Altman, and Stanley Kubrick, as well as fellow Europeans Richard Lester, John Schlesinger, Ken Russell, and Roman Polanski. It told a standard story of crime and revenge in a style that drew comparisons to the art cinema of Alain Resnais and Michelangelo Antonioni. It starred a former character actor not in the pretty boy mold of the new male stars of the fifties. It had a downbeat, ambiguous ending.

Michel Ciment notes how: "[Boorman] expresses himself exclusively through codified cinematic genres, whose strict formal parameters he will subsequently be free to subvert or enrich" (9). The director rang changes both brilliantly and disastrously upon the war movie (*Hell in the Pacific*, 1968); the western, with the conflict between savagery and civilization transplanted to the contemporary South (*Deliverance*, 1972); the science fiction film (*Zardoz*, 1974); and horror (*Exorcist II: The Heretic*, 1977). He capped the era with the epic Arthurian fantasy, *Excalibur* (1981). Often shot harrowingly on location, the films feature characters transported into unfamiliar landscapes or otherwise seeing their once familiar surroundings transformed. These landscapes turned dreamscapes confront them with the threat of imminent death and the immanent presence of spiritual powers from the primitive, mythic past. The Englishman who dislocated himself to come to Hollywood filled his films with, in Adrian Danks's words, "a character (or often set of characters) let loose in an environment – modern or primeval – they can barely comprehend and plainly don't belong to."

With an abiding interest in Jungian theories of myth (see Ciment and Hoyle), Boorman constructed a monomyth of his own that recurs throughout his career. He suggests the origins of this narrative in *Hope and Glory* (1987), in which a young boy modeled on Boorman finds his quiet English upbringing completely reoriented as German bombs drop from the sky, tidy neighborhoods become burned out rubble, yet the exhilaration of these threats of extinction spurs the imagination of the children and liberates the adults from social norms that prevailed before the Blitz. Here the dislocation occurs without a journey. In his other films, however, the protagonists, sometimes representing the primitive, at others the modern, undertake journeys to unfamiliar, difficult to access enclaves; once in, they labor under threat of death to get out, all the while illustrating through their interactions with those they encounter there, the conflicts between lush nature and sterile technology and the inextricable link between virility and violence. Frequently a shaman figure stands at the threshold to the hard-to-breach realm. Few of his protagonists conclude their journeys with a clear-cut victory or defeat, as the pre-industrial, natural world Boorman obviously prefers cannot shake off the homicidal violence its phallic energy too often devolves into. This monomyth isn't confined to his New Hollywood films, but three of them portray its major permutations and combinations: *Point Blank*, set in the concrete canyons of Los Angeles; *Deliverance*, taking place in the forested hills surrounding a wild river in Georgia; and *Zardoz*, presenting a dystopia that is a hodgepodge of urban ruins, medieval-era country villages, and a futuristic society powered by psychic energy.

POINT BLANK: AN AVENGING SPIRIT

Point Blank disorients both its protagonist and its audience via the extended title sequence that begins the film. Under the studio and producer credits, an image of Walker (Lee Marvin) appears in closeup, a red filter and shadows of foliage overlaying it. There is a cut to a medium shot in which the shadows have disappeared and sweat (or water) glistens on his face. Two shots ring out as he backs away from his assailant and falls prone as the film's apposite title appears. His fingers and legs twitch; then he focuses on the ceiling and

Figure 3.1 *Point Blank* re-stages film noir in a modernistic, dystopian L.A. Digital frame enlargement. Courtesy of Metro-Goldwyn-Mayer.

speaks in voiceover: "Cell, prison cell. How did I get here?" A series of brief flashback scenes follow, revealing, in a sort of temporal matryoshka doll, that Walker encountered an old friend, Mal Reese (John Vernon) at a crowded social gathering and implored him for help to get out of trouble with a criminal organization whose money he had lost.

The sequence returns to this encounter several times, intercutting it with scenes that sketch out the plan Mal has hatched. He and Walker will knock out the men who collect illicit cash profits at the deserted Alcatraz prison to transfer to the organization's money launderers and steal the money. The robbery goes south immediately, as Mal is forced to shoot the men and then the amount of money is insufficient to pay back the organization while giving Walker his share. So Mal guns him down in one of the cells and leaves with Walker's wife Lynne (Sharon Acker), with whom he has been having an affair. The film returns to Walker's POV on the cell's ceiling as he ponders, "Did it happen, a dream, a dream?"

At this point the rest of the titles play out over scenes both moving and freeze-framed[1] of Walker pulling himself to his feet, reaching the shoreline of the island on which Alcatraz sits and striking out for the shore as he battles the strong current. With his plunge into San Francisco Bay, a woman's voice starts up on the soundtrack, explaining the many attempted escapes from Alcatraz, every one futile because the waves drowned them all. This narration continues uninterrupted while the visual abruptly cuts to Walker, now nattily dressed in a suit and tie, on the observation deck of one of the tour boats that take visitors out to the island. A man, who will introduce himself as Yost (Keenan Wynn), approaches him, and asks how he managed to escape. Walker assumes he is a police officer when Yost explains that he wants to take down "the organiza-tion" that has Walker's $93,000 and to enlist him in the effort in exchange for helping Walker obtain the money. As his first gesture, he gives Walker the address where Mal and Lynne are living in Los Angeles.

This prologue in large part defines the various dislocations that characterize *Point Blank*'s *modus operandi*. It transfers ontological uncertainty from its protagonist to its audience as it, too, wonders whether this is reality or a dream. The ellipsis between Walker entering the bay and reappearing a year later with Yost by his side is typical of dream logic; is this a pre-planned rendezvous or the result of Yost's surveillance? Disconnections between image and sound continue in the first third of the film. Walker strides through a corridor at the LA airport, the sound of his footsteps greatly amplified, and that implacable Lee Marvin stride provides the soundtrack for a montage of Lynne's day until Walker reaches her door, flings her to the side in slow motion, and shoots up the bed in which he (erroneously) assumes Mal is sleeping, as if the corridor led directly there. At other points the score cuts out and only the sounds picked up by the microphone can be heard. Overnight Lynne kills herself and, in an apparent dream within a dream, Walker awakes to the house stripped bare. As the film goes on, the audience may wonder if all the dreaming occurs in the mind of a dying man, an interpretation advanced by many (see Hoyle; Thomson) and endorsed as possible by Boorman himself: "One should be able to imagine that this whole story of vengeance is taking place inside his head at the moment of death" (qtd. in Ciment 79).

Whether Walker is actually dead or not, he functions more as a relentless spirit of revenge than a fully rounded character. No one ever learns his first name, as if to stress his incompleteness. Indeed, Boorman sold the role to Marvin by describing him as someone who "had been emotionally and physically wounded to a point where he was no longer human," a condition that made him "frightening, but also pure" (Boorman 127). Danks believes Boorman played a significant role in allowing Marvin to develop "his patented and expressly physical and gestural mode of performance." Boorman's admiration for Marvin as an actor[2] reveals that he did not value the Method-acting interiority or hints of neurosis/psychosis typical of many New Hollywood stars such as Dustin Hoffman, Al Pacino, Jack Nicholson, or Gene Hackman.

As a tool of Yost's war on the organization, Walker suggests a sort of Golem. His mission of vengeance is from the outset subsumed in the larger aims of his handler. Walker gets to Mal in the middle of the film, only to have him accidentally fall to his death, and in the end vanishes into the night without his money. Neither event produces either satisfaction or frustration, again illustrating that human emotions have died in Walker, even if he is technically neither dreamer nor ghost. The conclusion of the film reveals that Yost is actually the organization's chief financial officer, Fairfax, who wants to move from writing the checks to pocketing more of the proceeds. As a trickster who directs Walker's quest, Yost/Fairfax is a naturalized manifestation of the shaman/magician Hoyle notes as so common in Boorman's work, a figure that culminates in *Excalibur*'s Merlin.

Although the disjunctive flashbacks and asynchronous sound diminish as Walker gets to work gaining access to and threatening the various organization middlemen, *Point Blank* remains visually committed to its common Boormanian intersection of the primitive with the modern. Danks says: "Walker is something of a 'natural man' who is made to encounter totally synthesised surroundings." Flashbacks associate him with the ocean; he apparently worked on a boat and enjoys surfing with Lynne. Free-flowing water is a central symbol of the natural and the primitive for Boorman (Ciment 22–5), who never discounts its violent, destructive properties but contrasts it to the sterile constructions of contemporary society.

In Los Angeles, a succession of distinctive, artificial spaces define Walker's assault on the organization. Instead of ocean waves or fast-moving streams, he must arrange a money exchange in the concrete storm run-off culverts of the LA River. The changing *mise-en-scène* includes the mirrored walls of Lynne's apartment, filled also with glass bottles and decanters; her sister Chris's (Angie Dickinson) nightclub, The Movie House, a maze of screens with alternating projections of women from Renaissance art and pin-up photos, underscored by a jazz singer whose lyrics are variations on a primal scream; the spaces beneath the intersecting overpasses of the freeways; a well-appointed corporate office in a commercial high-rise; the penthouse of a luxury hotel; and a sprawling ranch home in the hills, whose ultramodern appliances and systems Chris activates all at once in an effort to penetrate Walker's emotional armor. All of them, Thomson notes, reflect "Boorman's mixed feelings about modern designed space," as if *Point Blank* "is sometimes a little like an Antonioni film reassessed by Samuel Fuller" (Thomson 16). The director further demarcates the sites' constructedness by filming each in a specific color palette. The film's action centerpiece, Walker's breach of Huntley Hotel security in order to confront Mal, for example, is a carefully designed mélange of yellows and oranges, down to Dickinson's strawberry blonde hair.

Although Walker seems to be waging a successful war against a modern, corporatized crime syndicate, this success is illusory, as the revelation of Yost as Fairfax emphasizes. Walker never gets his money and never himself kills any of those who betray him. He merely sets them up to be picked off by the sniper hitman (James Sikking), who admires Walker's professionalism and can be seen as his alter ego in a dream scenario. *Point Blank* illustrates that modernity has no purpose for the natural and primitive except its co-optation.

Figure 3.2   The banjo virtuoso in *Deliverance*, deconstructing a national stereotype. Digital frame enlargement. Courtesy of Warner Bros.

Deliverance: The Return of the Repressed

Deliverance, adapted from the best-selling novel by James Dickey, turns *Point Blank* inside out. Its action takes place in rural north Georgia, most of it on the untamed, fictional Cahulawassee River and filmed on the actual Chattooga. Its four protagonists are modern men from Atlanta who intrude upon this natural space only to find themselves in conflict with the primitive mountain people, about to be displaced by a massive hydroelectric dam that will flood their valley and turn the raging rapids into a placid lake. The directorial style is realistic, absent almost all the stylistic flourishes seen in *Point Blank*. (Boorman did desaturate the color, however, turning vibrant blues and greens of sky, forest, and water into more ominous shades of slate and olive.) Nevertheless, the brute force of primitives is in the end no match for organized modernity, what the would-be survivalist Lewis calls "the system," even if modernity wins by out-primitiving the primitives.

Deliverance's generic roots derive from the colonialist adventure and more precisely narratives in which uninitiated members of the colonial order venture out into territory still under the sway of indigenous peoples, guided by one of their own who has considerable experience in the ways of the natives. Usually these indigenous populations comprise people of color, as is the case with other Boorman primitives such as the Amazonian Indians in *The Emerald Forest* (1985) or the Africans in *Exorcist II: The Heretic*. Racial difference does not complicate *Deliverance*, however, as all the mountain people are white. The homogeneity of a cast of characters who are all of European descent makes all the more striking the dislocation the Atlantans feel upon encountering the few inhabitants who have yet to evacuate.[3]

Each of the four men experiences a different sort of disjuncture as they leave their cars behind with a few of these holdouts. Lewis (Burt Reynolds), who serves the guide function, claims to champion the river and those living along it as he rages against the power company and the modernity it sacrifices nature to fuel:

> They're gonna stop the river up. There ain't gonna be no more river. There's just gonna be a big, dead lake . . . You push a little more power into Atlanta, a little more air-conditioners for your smug little suburb, and you know what's gonna happen? We're gonna rape this whole god-damned landscape!

At the same time as he bemoans the power company's hegemony, he also predicts that modernity will fail and only those who preserve the skills of the pre-industrial age will survive the system's collapse. Yet for all his professed identification with the locals, he condescends to them and attempts to substitute his own, inevitably mistaken, knowledge of the wilderness for theirs. He perhaps actually wishes to displace them and lead a purer life in nature in their stead rather than as their ally. As Anil Narine points out:

> Lewis is, after all, the most driven of the men to conquer the river and master, if not beat, its unforgiving currents. In this way, he embodies the very will to master and manipulate nature that he despises in its modern, technological form. Although he works to be the least modern of the men – the least comfortable with technology, and the least willing to accept his own identity as a capitalist urbanite – his designs are surprisingly consistent with those of the power company whose project he deplores. (457)

The crass Bobby (Ned Beatty), a glad-handing insurance salesman for whom the back seats of rusting cars or an air mattress summon up reveries of sexual gratification, expresses only contempt for the rural locale and its people. "Talk about genetic deficiencies – pitiful," he says when they encounter a physically and mentally challenged young boy (Billy Redden). His polar opposite, Drew (Ronny Cox), a believer in the principles of American democracy and its laws, accepts the mountain folk as equals, symbolized by his "Dueling Banjos" duet with the very boy Bobby has denigrated. Ed Gentry (Jon Voight), the narrator of the novel, operates comfortably within the system of modernity but also feels the pull of untamed nature that Lewis advocates. He looks upon the suffering of the rural people with empathy, rather than disgust.

The fateful encounter with two mountain men collapses the safe distance each Atlantan believes allows him to experience the primitive without sharing in its violence and desperation. In the infamous "squeal like a pig" sequence, the hinterlands rape back. One man sodomizes Bobby and the other intends to force Ed to commit fellatio on him until Lewis sneaks up from behind and shoots the first man (Bill McKinney) with an arrow. While he dies a slow, agonizing death, Ed chases off the second (Herbert "Cowboy" Coward). Although many a film would treat this outcome as a triumph for its action hero, as in *Point Blank*, the death of adversaries provides little satisfaction and only creates new threats and conflicts. Drew sees the situation as clear-cut self-defense and thinks they should call in law enforcement. But Lewis questions whether a jury made up of members of the in-bred, clannish population would see it that way. For their own reasons, Bobby and Ed also agree that they should bury the body and let the coming flood efface their act of violence. This instinctual self-protection strips the men of their privilege within the legal machinery of the modern city and leaves none of them unscathed as they rush to traverse the river rapids and exit in the town of Aintry downstream.

The punishments are condign, beginning with the sexual violation of the self-gratifying Bobby. Next, Drew falls from his canoe and drowns, his body broken on the rocks, a death that the film variously attributes to his suicidal despair at their failure to acknowledge the killing, a gunshot by the surviving assailant, or mere accident. As in the novel, this indeterminacy is never resolved. The event, however, precipitates the other wounds the men suffer as the boats capsize and hurl them into the rushing water. Lewis, who was going to tame the Cahulawassee, is instead shattered by it, suffering a compound leg fracture that reduces him to a bleating, wounded animal for the rest of the journey. Ed must scale a cliff and vanquish the "toothless man," which he does despite his instinctive resistance to killing another living being. He manages to fall on one of his own arrows and wound himself in the process, however.

Given the themes of the novel, these woundings are refracted through the lens of masculinity. Their drive to overcome the primitive results in and reveals the emasculation of the Atlantans. Loss of certainty unmans Drew; his rapist characterizes Bobby as feminine and casts him as non-human (Welling 24–5); and while Lewis may suffer permanent loss of his leg, his own arrow penetrates Ed. This dovetails with the repeated Boormanian idea that the primitive is the only space in which untrammeled virility holds sway. The director confirmed the strong hints at erotic attraction between Mal and Walker in *Point Blank* (Ciment 29). Mal's first appeal for Walker's help takes place in an all-male crowd as he leans over his friend, who is inexplicably lying prone on the floor. When Walker accesses the penthouse, he pulls Mal from the bed as if about to ravish him. The two men double the homosocial triangle with their mutual involvement with sisters Lynne and Chris. In the scene where Walker and Chris finally have sex, they roll over and over on the floor, morphing into the four heterosexual couples the quartet have formed but also underlining by its absence the Mal–Walker coupling. Thomson credits the director here as "ahead of just about everyone" catching "the homosexual fascination/loathing between gangsters" (16). I would suggest rather that Boorman is implying that no procreative bonds spring from the union of primitive and modern.

Modernity's anti-natural sterility, represented by *Point Blank*'s glass, steel, and concrete or the earth stripped bare of vegetation by the power company's bulldozers at the beginning of *Deliverance*, has its own answer to the exercise of phallic violence. Lewis is wrong about what the system is doing to the landscape. It does not rape; it neuters. The mountain men can't make good on their threat to cut off their captives' testicles, but the company castrates that vigorous river into a still body of water suitable for city dwellers' weekend getaway cabins. This is not a clear-cut conflict between primitive and modern but a merging that reveals "how inextricably entangled 'human' concerns have become with 'the natural' in our postmodern condition – how inseparable, in fact, the discourses and tangible realities of 'wilderness' and 'civilization' have *always* been" (Welling 27). In *Deliverance* at least, civilization will subsume wilderness.

Therefore, as Welling asserts, Boorman rejects "Dickey's dangerous fascination with the regenerative possibilities of sexualized violence and violent forms of sexuality" (25). He portrays Lewis's and Ed's killings as anything but triumphs by their macho impulses over the urban environment that constrains them. Both deaths lead to uncertain, grueling, and destructive efforts to hide the evidence and the bodies, the filming of which is slow and deliberate, deflating any sense of catharsis or climactic action. Just as Bobby will bear lasting scars of his sexual violation and humiliation, and Lewis may be disabled, guilt and fear of retribution will haunt Ed, as his dream of the dead hand emerging from the lake illustrates. He may be a *paterfamilias* with a loving wife, a son, and another child on the way, but the foundations of his manhood remain forever shaken.

ZARDOZ: GUNS AND PENISES

Based on novels and set in the contemporary US, *Point Blank* and *Deliverance* fail to open a space in which pre-modern nature and a potent masculinity can survive castration by the systems that organize industrial capitalism without surrendering to violence. So Boorman next developed a film about a futuristic society, an original concept that he would write, direct, and produce. The result, *Zardoz*, is pseudo-profound and laughable, overwrought in both senses of the word. Hoyle calls it "a critical and commercial disaster, but one that nevertheless merits careful attention" (91). And he is right. For all its many flaws, this seemingly incoherent hodge-podge of 70s science-fiction tropes nonetheless makes crystal clear how Boorman imagines a resolution of the contradictions inherent in his two previous films. It also foregrounds the necessary link between living an authentic human life and the proximity of its extinction.

In *Zardoz* Lewis's prediction in *Deliverance* that the system will collapse and take society down with it comes true. A small number of "the rich, the powerful, the clever," benefiting from the technological advances of an alien race, wall themselves off from a dying planet in a place called the Vortex. They attempt to preserve the best of both worlds, living in a natural setting, sustaining themselves through pre-industrial farming techniques and artisanship, and maintaining a collection of crucial cultural artifacts from throughout human history. Meanwhile, a type of psychic energy, based on refracted light and centered in a crystal called the Tabernacle, provides them with immortality and a group consciousness. Set design of the interiors, with naked bodies shrink-wrapped in plastic, goes overboard in depicting a world of prismatic glass and kaleidoscopic mirrors, images that signal modernity gone awry in so many Boorman films.

Like many such utopias, of course, the Vortex and the Eternals who inhabit it fall prey to unintended consequences. With procreation unnecessary, all the men become impotent. Consuella (Charlotte Rampling), one of the leaders of the matriarchy that has emerged in the absence of the phallus, points out that the violations of women that this erect organ inflicted for millennia makes its detumescence a moral good. Boorman is no feminist, however, and the lack of both penetrative coitus and death – or rather the Tabernacle's ability to restore the dead to life, an ability with no off switch – has led to a purgatorial and purposeless existence. As befits a crystalline society, the Eternals have begun to fracture. Those who want to change things, called Renegades, are punished by being aged and sent to an old folks' home where they participate in an endless party; others, called the Apathetics, fall into near catatonic depression. Beyond the Vortex lie the Outlands, a Hobbesian charnel house where life is nasty, brutish, and short. There a giant flying head, the image of an angry God named Zardoz, intones that "the gun is good" and "the penis is evil" because the one spews bullets to end life while the other spews seeds to create it. Zardoz has created a death cult called the Exterminators, well-armed, scantily clad men on horseback charged with a genocidal campaign against the so-called Brutals who struggle to survive in the wasteland outside the Vortex. The Renegades and Apathetics dropping out of the labor force has led to a modification of this dynamic; Zardoz now commands enslaving the "Brutals" to grow crops rather than just whittling down their numbers.

Removing the inherent phallic violence that previously kept Boorman's primitive worlds from receiving his full endorsement does not allow the Eternals to blend pre- and postmodern as they had hoped. Without phallic energy, their immortal society collapses upon itself into a never-ending entropy. Meanwhile, in the Outlands, phallic energy channeled only into violence forfeits any of the fertile potential of a primitive assault upon sterile modernity. Having laid out this schema, Boorman uses one of his trademark shamans, an imaginative, artistic Eternal named Arthur Frayn (Niall Buggy), to explode it. In a brief prologue Boorman added after test audiences responded with bafflement, Frayn identifies himself as false god and true magician, an admirer of Merlin, who has written the narrative about to unfold. He thus acts within the diegesis – he is in charge of administering the Outlands – and as an avatar for the filmmaker himself. Their joint plan is to introduce an Exterminator, Zed[4] (Sean Connery), unknowingly bred and educated for the purpose, into the Vortex as both Messiah of Death and source of new life, uniting the dual functions of the film's bifurcated masculinity, violence and fertility, gun and penis.

By projecting his mind into the psychic community of the Tabernacle, he severs that connection and destroys the technology that keeps the Eternals eternal. ("You have penetrated me," the voice of the Tabernacle laments, Boorman's dialogue too on-the-nose as usual.) Other Exterminators he has enabled to breach the Vortex barrier rush in to massacre most of the Eternals, who plead for extinction. Two men, Frayn and his ally Friend (John Alderton), engineer this convoluted suicide pact. Some of the women, on the other hand, had already lobbied for procreation to begin again in the Vortex. Zed's primitive masculinity is potent enough to arouse the female Apathetics from their stupor with just a sniff of his sweat[5] and he bargains with Consuella's rival May (Sarah Kestelman) to exchange his seed for help in defeating the Tabernacle. She and her followers flee the slaughter to start a new generation.

Although *Zardoz* provides Boorman's primitives with the chance to annihilate emasculating modern culture rather than being neutered by it, their triumph does nothing to solve the fundamental problem of phallic masculinity's inevitable surrender to violence. The film does, however, offer a tentative

Figure 3.3   Zed returns phallic masculinity to the sterile Vortex. Digital frame enlargement. Courtesy of 20th Century Fox.

antidote: love. Consuella has consistently branded Zed a danger who must be terminated, but when she takes the matter into her own hands, approaching him with an upraised knife while he is linked to the Tabernacle, she cannot strike. Zed informs her that she loves him, so cannot kill; he likewise finds himself unable to fire a gun at a willing Eternal because his mutual love for Consuella has extinguished his violent impulses. The two retreat to a cave where they have a son and, in a montage sequence, in which the family stares into the camera as if having a series of posed portrait photographs taken, grow old and die, their skeletons holding hands until they crumble into dust. One half expects the Beatles' "All You Need is Love" to fire up on the soundtrack. Stephanie Goldberg asserts the tenuousness of this resolution: "The fundamental Utopia that Boorman appears to be championing is nothing more than an idealized version of the traditional nuclear family, with patriarchal values intact" (8). This is a fair assessment of Boorman's masculinity-obsessed cinema.

CODA: LEAVING THE SCENE

Zack Stentz, twenty-first-century screenwriter and admirer of *Excalibur*, once tweeted: "John Boorman: the humanist Stanley Kubrick? Discuss." Putting aside the matter of Kubrick/humanist seeming an oxymoron too extreme to hold, identifying Kubrick as the New Hollywood director most comparable to Boorman has merit. Ciment makes the same comparison, distinguishing the two along the axis of Boorman's Jungian dialectics vs. Kubrick's Freudian analytics (19). Both directors give visuals predominance over dialogue and narrative, work across a broad range of genres, and use characters to represent ideas in action rather than as unique individuals with fully developed inner lives. Kubrick employs these methods to dissect and expose, while Boorman does so to diagnose and (possibly) to heal. However, their most significant likeness, I would assert, is that they left Hollywood for the bulk of their careers.

In reconfiguring the old Hollywood conventions, the New Hollywood implicitly sought to open up American history and culture to inquiry. Kubrick, headquartered in England from the early 60s on, still threaded the idea of an American militarism fueled by castration anxiety from *Dr. Strangelove* (1964) to *Full Metal Jacket* (1987). A vivid sense of a particular place and its inhabitants characterizes Penn's rural Texas in *Bonnie and Clyde* (1967), Coppola's New York Italian enclaves in *The Godfather* films, Scorsese's many films also set in that city, or Altman's *Nashville* (1975). Even émigrés like Schlesinger and Polanski showed intimate understandings of the seedier precincts of Manhattan or the dark heart beneath the swimming pools and orange groves of Southern California. Boorman, on the other hand, with his commitment to myth and Jungian archetypes, makes all his far-flung shooting locations mere backgrounds for universal human actions. America did not speak to him except in generalities. "The decadence of American society makes it very vulnerable to more primitive forces," he told Ciment (76).

Unwilling to raise his family in the US, Boorman found a home in rural Wicklow, Ireland. Unmarked by industrialism, it represents that mythic place Boorman's protagonists strive, usually in vain, to reach in order to achieve a balanced life. He had long tried to film Tolkien's *The Lord of the Rings* but, as the New Hollywood era was ending, explored another fantasy green land in *Excalibur* by chronicling the rise and fall of King Arthur and the machinations of the Merlin so many of his other shaman figures evoke. Arthur ends between life and death on another of Boorman's special islands. Although for the next two decades the director would continue to go on location to dislocate Westerners in *The Emerald Forest* or *Beyond Rangoon* (1995) or with *The Tailor of Panama* (2001), *Excalibur* marks a full circle from the beginning of *Point Blank* when its spectral hero emerges from Alcatraz. It also demonstrates that Boorman was just passing through the New Hollywood on his way to Camelot.

NOTES

1. Some of the still shots have symbolic valence, such as a sparrow perched on the razor wire, suggesting both freedom and imprisonment.
2. Boorman cast Marvin in his next film, *Hell in the Pacific*, always looked for roles to offer him in subsequent films, and made a TV documentary honoring Marvin in 1998.
3. One might argue that the "degenerate" effects of in-breeding function as a marker of difference similar to that of race. The guitar-playing boy who suffers from these effects stands on a bridge the canoes pass under on their way down river, marking the quest threshold and giving him a rudimentary shamanistic power.
4. Named after the final letter of the alphabet and the first and last letters of Zardoz's own name, Zed represents the culmination of Frayn's planning, which depends on triggering Zed with a copy of *The Wizard of Oz*, the story of another fake god who hides behind a big head and a loud voice.
5. The casting helps Boorman (barely) carry off this potentially offensive and ludicrous idea of no woman being able to resist Zed because the rough sexual magnetism Connery brings to James Bond manifests itself here as well, despite his having a long braid down his back and wearing only a bright red loincloth tied with an enormous bow.

WORKS CITED

Boorman, John. *Adventures of a Suburban Boy*. Faber and Faber, 2003.

Ciment, Michel. *John Boorman*. Translated by Gilbert Adair, Faber and Faber, 1986.

Cowie, Peter. *Revolution: The Explosion of World Cinema in the 1960s*. Faber and Faber, 2004.

Danks, Adrian. "A Man Out of Time: John Boorman and Lee Marvin's *Point Blank*." *Senses of Cinema*, vol. 45, Nov. 2007.

Dickey, James. *Deliverance*. Delta, 1970, rpt 1994.

Goldberg, Stephanie. "*Zardoz*: Boorman's Metaphysical Western." *Jump Cut*, vol. 1, 1974, pp. 8–9.

Hoyle, Brian. *The Cinema of John Boorman*. The Scarecrow Press, 2012. Kindle file.

Narine, Anil. "Global Trauma at Home: Technology, Modernity, *Deliverance*." *Journal of American Studies*, vol. 42, no. 3, 2008, pp. 449–70.

Palmer, R. Barton. "Narration, Text, Intertext: The Two Versions of *Deliverance*." *Struggling for Wings: The Art of James Dickey*, edited by Robert Kirschten, University of South Carolina Press, 1997, pp. 194–203.

Thomson, David. "'As I Lay Dying': Lee Marvin's Walker in John Boorman's *Point Blank*." *Sight and Sound*, vol. 8, no. 6, 1998, pp. 14–17.

Welling, Bart H. "'Squeal Like A Pig': Manhood, Wilderness, and Imperialist Nostalgia in John Boorman's *Deliverance*." *Green Letters*, vol. 6, no. 1, 2005, pp. 24–38.

4. JOHN CASSAVETES:
IN YOUR FACE AND OFF THE GRID

Rebecca Bell-Metereau

Cassavetes, who provided the impetus of what would become the independent film movement in America . . . "spent the majority of his career
making his films 'off the grid' so to speak" . . . unfettered by the commercial concerns of Hollywood. (Fine 99).

Without necessarily intending to, John Cassavetes captured the zeitgeist of an
era in which segments of American society yearned for sexual and social liberation. He revolutionized American movie making through films and techniques
that forecast larger trends in everything from documentary and melodrama
to horror and comedy genres. *Faces* (1968), *Husbands* (1970), *Minnie and
Moskowitz* (1971), *A Woman Under the Influence* (1974), and *Opening Night*
(1977) enjoyed varying degrees of success, prompting extensive commentary,
with critics trending toward either worshipful admiration or utter disdain
for his work. Cassavetes's treatment of the physical bodies of the men and
women who enacted hard-drinking, tobacco-fueled lives mirrored aspects of
his own off-screen life, which ended with his death in 1989 from cirrhosis
of the liver at fifty-nine. The brilliance of his work lies in his ability to reflect
America's social struggles of the 1960s and 1970s through a raw depiction
of the inner lives of his characters – in all their rebelliousness and revolutionary spirit – taking viewers off the grid of Hollywood production and into
uncharted and often painful psychological territory. Cassavetes exhibits occasional unwitting and seemingly oblivious celebration of white male privilege,
even though he claimed to sympathize and identify with his female characters.

Using hand-held, up-close camera work, his innovative take on both film and gender performance epitomizes the lived experience of men and women of his era in a visceral way that prompts anger, humor, shocked recognition, and deep artistic engagement for thoughtful viewers.

HUSBANDS

When Cassavetes opens *Husbands* with a series of still armpit shots, edited in rhythmic montage set to low-key drums and a bass playing a cool-jazz rendition of "When Johnny Comes Marching Home," he instantly captures all that is hilarious and disturbing about modern masculinity. Sweaty T-shirts and bare hairy chests appear in photos of men comparing their biceps at a gathering of families looking on with mild amusement or otherwise occupied. These stills reveal most subjects looking off to the side, but one chubby man breaks the fourth wall, gazing into the photographer's lens, leaving viewers to piece together who this is as the film progresses. In an abrupt dialectic shift, Cassavetes switches to a more somber event, captured with a handheld camera shooting from inside a car, passing rows of limousines, cutting to a shot of a very old woman dressed in black emerging from a yellow cab. Cassavetes wanted a catchy introduction to his story, asking his male actors, "What's the most cumbersome thing you could bring to a funeral?" and answering his own query: "A grandmother!" (Staff Writers 56).

Greeting this grandmother, the hairy-chested men from the stills are now impeccably dressed in funeral garb, but their dialog quickly undermines any

Figure 4.1   Both hilarious and disturbing: men compare their biceps in *Husbands* (1970). Digital frame enlargement. Courtesy of Columbia Pictures.

reverence for grandma or the occasion. Walking toward the grave, Archie (Peter Falk) claims a newly discovered truth: that "lies and tension will kill you" before alcohol or cigarettes. Gus, played by Cassavetes, insists, "Don't believe truth," and then asks him for a cigarette and a light. When Archie yells up ahead for a match from his friend, Harry (Ben Gazzara) and the old woman slowly turn back to look at them, creating a jarring moment of comedy. The scene cuts to shots of mourners not looking particularly mournful, listening to a priest's backhanded compliments about the self-centered deceased that explain why no one looks very sad. This opening typifies Cassavetes's genius, both in its form and wryly cynical substance. If a scene acts as a kind of locational grid, Cassavetes constantly pushes viewers off that grid before they achieve balance, leaving them to wonder how the previous location relates to the present moment – in a modern American embodiment of Eisenstein's deliberately challenging intellectual montage.

Cassavetes uses post-funeral scenes to catalogue what men stereotypically do for fun: get extremely drunk, talk sports, cavort playfully through city streets, play basketball, swim, drink some more, and try to hook up with women. This montage reveals three men mourning the loss of one of their buddies through self-indulgent and narcissistic regression to a blatant display of male bravado. When they join some female mourners at a local bar, a singing spree ensues, and Harry insists, "Look at me!" as one woman sings "I Dream of Jeannie." Harry, Archie, and Gus grow increasingly abusive as they interrupt one woman and force her to begin over and over, insisting she lacks real emotion, a ritual that seems to mimic Cassavetes's own methods for obtaining authentic performances from actors. Far from relying on improvisational techniques, as many claimed he did, Cassavetes required nearly as many takes as Kubrick to elicit the emotional intensity he wanted. Viewers may find the scene variously puzzling, pitiful, or infuriating until Cassavetes lightens the moment as Archie insists, "I'll take off my clothes if you do it better," and he undresses, unexpectedly causing the woman to burst out laughing. Gus contributes some sexist psychobabble: "You don't like us; you know why, because you've got some bitterness in your heart, because you've been told by your mother," and Harry piles on with his own query: "Where's the warmth?," a characteristic expected of women.

As in most of Cassavetes's work, the film plays with contrasts between sensitivity – associated with effeminacy – and toxic masculinity. Harry calls Archie "insensitive" and he replies that Harry is "phony," an accusation that prompts him to respond with the castrating suggestion: "Bite his finger!" All the while, Harry's rants are rendered ridiculous by his wearing an absurd-looking red and black plaid tam appropriated from a woman at the bar. The suggestion of homophilic desire surfaces when he confesses, "I've been telling my wife for years, aside from sex (and she's very good at it), God damn it, I

73

like you guys better." He kisses each one and says, "I love you," and when they call him a fairy he laughingly chants, "Fairy Harry," admitting, "I wouldn't be surprised. Might be better off." Cassavetes refuses to point the audience toward any conclusion about their exchange.

In a pivotal role as odd man out in the threesome, Harry swings between moody emotional displays and aggressive expressions of toughness, while the film's tone also vacillates from slapstick humor to visceral abuse. Harry barges in on Archie and Gus in a horrendously long restroom vomiting scene, and later wants to go home to shower, but Archie insists: "If I wanna stink, I'll stink. That's my privilege," telling Harry, "You have to be free. You have to be an individual." At home, Harry's mother-in-law calls him a "bad boy" and shoos him out, but he returns to accuse his wife of not loving him, adding, "I just don't like being in a closet," another allusion to possible suppressed homosexuality. The scene devolves into screaming, hitting his wife and trying to strangle her mother, until his friends rescue him, and he swears: "I only lived there because of a woman. You know – the legs, the breasts, the mouth." With its violence and blunt objectification of the female body, this sequence is an emotional assault for many female viewers, but Cassavetes was surprised that women "loathed the picture, with such a passion that it was unbelievable" (Fine 241). The scene is equally disturbing for some men, who may view it as a nightmare spectacle of impotent fury and emasculation.

The narrative shifts like quicksand as Harry proposes an escape to London, a decision taken from an unexamined position of privilege. With an ease typical of affluent white males, his friends readily accompany him, asking one of the wives to deliver their passports. The compliance of the wives and the ease of their departure have a dreamlike quality, but their alcohol-drenched flight ends abruptly when they exit down the steps into a torrential downpour that seems to last the entire visit. They improbably locate a bevy of women who drink with them and participate in varying degrees of sexual play, from disastrous slurpy kisses with an Asian woman dressed as a schoolgirl to the near rape and asphyxiation of a 6'3" woman who unpredictably enjoys the encounter. Claustrophobic close-up shots with a handheld camera deny viewers full view of the action, which seems to be captured practically in real time, in drawn-out jump-cut shots. Cassavetes wanted his film to be three and a half hours, but his contract restricted it to two (Cassavetes and Carney 244–5), so after showing one comical preview edit to studio executives to ensure production he kept editing a grimmer cut until 1970.

The final version ends with no clues on Harry's whereabouts, following Cassavetes's pattern of long unresolved scenes that end abruptly. The only character whose sexuality is in question manages to have what seems like a satisfying sexual experience, but it is difficult to pin down what happens. The rather matronly woman who takes him to bed bats her artificial eyelashes at him as he grins sheepishly and says, "After all those years of being married, I never . . .," leaving the audience to wonder whether he refers to cheating, having performance issues, or experiencing great sex. The viewer never finds out. In a similarly benign conclusion, Gus returns home with what looks like a genuine smile, even though he is greeted by wailing children. The last line of the film, screamed by the eldest boy to his mother – "Hurry up and come out, why don't you?" – is ironic, given that the wayward father should be in the parenting dog house, not the mother, who has patiently cared for their brood on her own. Characters' disparagement of women or racial groups in the film reflects Cassavetes's effort to capture a reality, but in this subtle critique of stereotypical American masculinity he does not tip his hand, assuming that the "truth" of his subject will speak for itself. Although Cassavetes endorses equality, neither he nor his admiring critics may fully recognize the biases inherent in his narratives.

A Woman Under the Influence

If the title of *Husbands* suggests a film that features married men, *A Woman Under the Influence* promises to focus on at least one important female. Ray Carney argues that Cassavetes's narratives exhibit "his democratic equality of treatment of the various characters – his abandonment of star-system photographic and narrative hierarchies in his scenes" (Carney 114). However, this democratic impulse applies more to male actors than to females. Although Mabel (Cassavetes's wife, Gena Rowlands) – the "influenced" woman – has more screen time than the female actors in *Husbands*, this film still privileges the words and actions of men, particularly those of her husband, Nick (Peter Falk). The title encourages viewers to think Mabel simply has a drinking problem, but other characters question her sanity, even as the film neglects any scenes showing her confinement in a mental institution. Instead, *A Woman Under the Influence* opens with a crew of men trapped by their work, waist-deep in water, expected to continue their shift through the night to fix a broken water main. Crew chief Nick wants to refuse, because he has promised a "love night" with Mabel, but he ends up breaking that promise. When his co-worker and friend Eddie (Charles Horvath) comments that he should call her or she might tear up the house because she is a "sensitive delicate woman," Nick insists she is "not crazy," automatically making viewers wonder. His proof of her sanity is that she "cooks, sews, makes the bed, and washes the bathroom." Nick's failure to communicate prompts Mabel to go on a binge and bring home a strange man for an unintentional and ambiguous one-night stay. Later, she arranges a disastrous play date for the neighboring Jensen children, trying to create madcap fun that devolves into cross-dressing and child nudity. Nick's mother (Katherine Cassavetes) insists this is grounds for committing Mabel.

Cassavetes poignantly depicts Nick's betrayals, first when Mabel resists being institutionalized and asks Nick what is happening with psychiatrist Dr. Zepp (Eddie Shaw): "I get the idea there's some kind of a conspiracy going on here. I mean, you've been looking at me so quiet-like and, uh, he's got something in that bag." Instead of admitting his plan, Nick questions her sanity: "One, you're acting crazy . . . Why are you so insecure? Hmm? Everybody loves you." The only validation Mabel receives is when Zepp tells her, "I have a piece of paper here that says . . .," trailing off to imply that Mabel will be institutionalized. Cassavetes abruptly cuts to the construction site, where Eddie, a sane and loyal minority figure, becomes his next target for betrayal. Eddie says nothing about Mabel, but Nick yells, "You're a silent son of a bitch. Don't give me that shit. From the moment I got here that's all anybody's been talking about – Mabel. Don't say you didn't know when you know." Eddie specifies, "I didn't say I don't know," and walks away, infuriating Nick, who yells after him, "You Goddamn Mexican Indian! Don't you walk away from me!" Eddie goes to scale down a steep grade and Nick yanks upward on his climbing rope in a gut-wrenching shot that shows Eddie flailing and rolling to the quarry below. Nick's next emotional spree shows him yanking his three children out of school to visit a miserable cold beach and sharing a six-pack of beer with them on the way home. The children stumble and spin in the front lawn, too drunk to eat or do anything but stagger off to bed. If Cassavetes intends this final scene to bring home Nick's lack of parenting skills, it is interesting to note how biographer Marshall Fine omits this incident from his analysis, perhaps in unwitting sympathy for Nick's character.

Cassavetes creates erasure of Mabel's time in the mental hospital by cutting to a black screen with a white intertitle, "SIX MONTHS LATER," followed by a shot of Nick and two construction buddies scurrying home for her homecoming party. By this point in the narrative, most viewers grasp that Mabel's real problem is being under the influence of Nick, whose own sanity is increasingly questionable. A painfully comic scene shows guests showing up as Nick enters the house, where a woman kisses him and comments that there is "no wine, no beer, no coke, nothing." His mother yells at him, "Have you gone out of your mind?" so he asks Eddie's wife, Nancy (Ellen Davalos), what she thinks. When she replies, "You really want to know what I think? You're a shit. You sent her away, you could have picked her up," he turns again to his mother to rescue him: "I can't do it! Can't tell 'em not to go – to go. You do it." Torrential rain soaks the departing guests and Mabel as her car pulls up. Avoiding even getting wet, Nick waits for her on the porch.

Cassavetes creates an agonizing scene as Mabel enters and faces the people who sent her to the mental institution six months earlier. Her mother-in-law clings to her and Dr. Zepp apologizes for committing her, but Nick's mother says not to talk about the past. When Mabel wants to see her children, Nick says, "Why don't you wait a minute? You go in there, they're gonna start to cry and you're gonna start to cry, and everybody's gonna get so emotional." Mabel insists on seeing them, and when she returns, her father says it is time to leave. Nick urges him to stay, but Mabel repeats, "Dad, . . .Will you please stand up for me? Will you just stand up for me?" Throughout the painful homecoming, Nick tells her to just "be yourself" when she is subdued and then reverses his instructions, saying, "It's your first day and you're letting yourself go, and you know that's not good.. . .Relax. Be calm." When she finally insists that she wants to go to bed with her husband, everyone leaves, and they say goodnight to their children. The film's closing scene seems endless, as Mabel asks Nick, "Do you love me?" to which he lamely replies, "I, uh. I, uh. Now let's go clean up that crap." When Mabel complies and starts cleaning, he changes his mind again and tells her, "Let's just leave it," offering a tiny sliver of hope.

By the end of the film, some viewers may arrive at a conclusion about the prospects for Mabel's future distinctly different from that of actor Falk, who describes Nick's character and the narrative's resolution in terms of masculine primacy: "It's that guy's incredible primitive commitment to Mabel that's gonna save them both, he's crude, unknowing, but he would put his head through concrete for her" (Burke 44). In analyzing the actor's claim, David Degener adds this addendum to Falk's statement: "As long as the dishes get washed" (12). This says it all. Some males, both in the narrative and in the audience, may consider it a happy ending if the woman returns to what they view as her appropriate female function. The director and his male actors have good intentions for their "influenced" woman, but they are all more

Figure 4.2   Nick (Peter Falk) and (Mabel) Gena Rowlands in *A Woman Under the Influence* (1974). Digital frame enlargement. Courtesy of the Criterion Collection.

invested in exploring the male role of managing or rescuing Mabel than in understanding a woman's experience or showing her engineer her own escape from the restraints of gender.

Attempting to step outside of stereotypical gender restrictions and evade the commercialism and control of the Hollywood system, Cassavetes avoided many conventional Hollywood requirements, from script design to marketing, but he exploited the system when he could, first by radio crowdsourcing $2000 for *Shadows* (1959). Winston Wheeler Dixon describes how his early film *Faces* (1968) "would eventually cost $200,000 and force Cassavetes to accept five acting jobs in three years to complete the film" (89). Imagine the actors who would have loved to be "forced" to take five acting jobs. The ambitious and creative Cassavetes took advantage of being a handsome, talented white male – a privileged position that he was unable or unwilling to fully recognize. He exploited the various talents and resources of family and friends, and he acknowledged the effects of gender when he explained his sense of identification with the position of women:

> ... it was a difficult time for today's woman to be left alone while somebody goes out and lives. I know when ... Gena was working for me ... I stayed home and took care of the baby and I was a pretty good housewife and all that. But I didn't have really the same reactions as a woman would have, mainly because I didn't have to think into the future of when I'd get older or when my attractiveness would fade or ... kids would grow up or when the baby would cease to cling to you. All those things are more interesting than what they're making movies out of. (LoBianco)

With his next important film, Cassavetes turned his attention to the notion of performance, emphasizing the collaborative nature of filmmaking and the nature of role-playing.

OPENING NIGHT

> When Myrtle delivers her lines as Virginia in *Opening Night*, we are never entirely certain who speaks, finally: the character Virginia, the actress Myrtle, the playwright Sarah, or ultimately, the actress Gena Rowlands or the writer/director Cassavetes. (King 4)

Opening Night exemplifies the power of communal effort in multiple narratives that begin *in medias res* with a shot of Gena Rowlands taking a shot of liquor and a drag from a cigarette before stepping on stage as the actress Myrtle Gordon, playing a character named Virginia. Rowland's husband plays

Virginia's fellow actor, Maurice, sitting above her, unnoticed at first, but descending the stairs to ask where she has been. Virginia confesses to having stopped for a drink, a co-mingling of life and script that creates a startling self-reflexive impression. The film creates a narrative *mise-en-abîme*, meandering back and forth between actions of the stage-play characters and behind-the-scenes interaction of the professional actors. Typical of Cassavetes's home-movie feel, the film features a cast of his usual actors and family members. The theme of aging reflects Cassavetes and Rowlands's artistic maturation and life circumstances, with Myrtle describing her discomfort with her role as an aging actress, a performance she claims will restrict her to older roles in the future. Mourning the loss of youth, she confesses, "When I was seventeen, I could do anything . . . I'm finding it harder and harder to stay in touch." This statement establishes a common motif in Cassavetes's films – an aging woman on the verge of collapse, even madness.

In this context, the film takes a swipe at the phenomenon of celebrity through scenes of fans frantically grabbing for the star's attention. In a sinister turn, a young woman follows Myrtle out to her limousine, repeating, "I love you" and crying, soaked by one of Cassavetes's frequent filmic downpours. Blowing kisses to Myrtle and banging her hand on the window, the young woman is suddenly hit by a speeding car, seemingly out of nowhere. Like Eddie's unexpected brutal fall down the mountain in *A Woman Under the Influence*, this hit-and-run sequence serves as a visual and narrative gut punch that prompts viewers to wonder what just happened, who is at fault, and what the incident means. In typical Cassavetes form, the film refuses to provide answers, instead shifting immediately and intentionally to a near-miss sex scene. As if to ward off her own sense of guilt, Myrtle turns to the solace of a bottle and an attempted seduction of her leading man, who rejects her over-tures with a practical excuse: "I have a small part. I can't afford to be in love with you." Meanwhile, her director Manny (Ben Gazzara) tries to boost her sense of sexual prowess – for his own financial gain – by telling her repeatedly, "You're the most exciting woman I know . . . There's no one I love more than you at this moment."

It becomes clear that Myrtle's issue is larger than insecurity over her powers of seduction, as she balks when the director insists that she rehearse how to get slapped. She finds it demeaning, but he counters: "There's nothing humiliating about getting slapped. It has nothing to do with being a woman. It's a tradi-tion; actresses get slapped." Although Myrtle makes a legitimate point about the overall violence of the play, the film ends up playing the rehearsal scene for laughs, as her stage husband goes to slap her and she falls down prematurely. Maurice shakes his head and Manny, watching from the auditorium, says, "That was, uh, all right." When Maurice does manage to slap her she laughs hysterically and playwright Sarah (Joan Blondell) asks, "You expect to be funny in this? Perhaps I could write a funny line for you?" Rowlands's next line, "I always wanted to say something that made sense," seems to speak for Myrtle and for Rowlands herself, called on so many times to play a crazy woman, a woman under the influence. When Sarah asks the actress "what this play doesn't express" and Myrtle replies, "Hope," the word encapsulates a key concept of the entire film, indeed, of Cassavetes's entire career – the desire for optimism.

As he explores the theme of hope in the face of aging and death, Cassavetes employs various techniques, in a visual and stylistic nod to – or innovation in – practically every film genre. For example, the unfolding story of the death and apparent haunting of Myrtle's young fan passes from melodramatic moments – think *A Star Is Born* (1976) – to shock editing that presages the horrific bathroom scene of *The Shining* (1980). Cassavetes uses jump-cut profile shots of Rowlands looking to the side and seeing, through an out-of-focus extreme closeup, the eyes of the young girl. At first, both women's faces mirror each other in expressions of hope and wonder, as Myrtle raises her hand to touch the girl's hand. This tight shot is interrupted when she hears a sudden knock at the door and the girl disappears. In an abrupt transition, Sarah talks to Myrtle about retirement and their possible future friendship, but Myrtle says, "I don't think we'll ever be friends," followed by a quick cut to a shot of the marquee for their play, *Second Woman*. The film portrays characters' inability to understand the point of view of others by juxtaposing perspectives throughout. As an older playwright, Sarah observes this irony when she complains, "Oh, I hate actresses. She tried to talk to *me* about age." When Myrtle goes to visit the mourning Jewish family of the girl, they observe: "You don't have children; if you had, you wouldn't have come here."

During the course of the film, bits of *Second Woman* emerge, offering a plausible rationale for discussing aging, performance, art, and love. The character Virginia tells her husband, "I'm not good enough for you," but he answers, "Before you, I was a drunk. I was W. C. Fields without a nose . . . I thought art was bullshit," in lines that suggest a self-reflexive comment on the part of screenwriter Cassavetes. When Maurice's character Marty slaps Virginia and tells her to get up, the scene foreshadows Myrtle's opening night performance, when Manny insists that she get up on her own, telling her, "Everybody loves you. You're a super high-priced professional." Expressing her anxiety about the character, with whom she identifies so intensely, Myrtle asks him, "Does she win or does she lose?" and then articulates his stake in the matter: "You're afraid that somehow my behavior is going to undermine you."

The film's next segment veers into what looks for a moment like psychological horror. After Myrtle finds herself practically paralyzed when she tries to perform, Sarah asks if she has seen the girl who died. Myrtle confesses that she has but insists that the apparition is part of her acting technique, a figure she can conjure or dismiss at will. Sarah takes her to a spiritualist, but Myrtle leaves abruptly, and upon their return – with no musical soundtrack – Myrtle enters a darkened penthouse in a sort of dreamscape. The silence builds horror-film tension as she wanders around the apartment, gradually hearing distant music and talking to herself until she is suddenly attacked by the girl. She runs out to the playwright's penthouse, where she proceeds to hit her own face against a door jamb, claiming she has done this to herself, as Sarah watches in horror.

In echoes of *A Star Is Born*, Myrtle's character continues to spiral downward, as Manny's jealous younger wife (and Myrtle's understudy) smiles in the background. After several people offer her drinks that she refuses, she finds herself alone, when a startlingly loud bass piano thump sounds and the girl suddenly reappears. To a non-diegetic musical soundtrack, the girl approaches, saying, "I like to turn people on, and that's what the theater is; it's like getting laid." Myrtle strikes the girl, throws a glass vase at her head and races back to confront her co-star, Maurice. She asks if he loves her, but he counters that she just wants to him to "make an ass" of himself. On opening night tension builds as an impatient audience claps rhythmically for the curtain to open, no Myrtle in sight. The producers debate whether to cancel the performance, and then she shows up falling-down drunk. Backstage, Manny tells actors to take their places, and insists that no one help her. After a quick makeup job, she stumbles down the hallway, falling down right before her entrance onstage. Struggling up and entering to applause, her co-star soon swoops her up in his arms when she is about to fall again, but from that point on, she manages to soldier on to the end of the first act. Meanwhile, Manny goes out for a double scotch. As difficult as it is to watch the scene, viewers and future actors may take a lesson from the performance, which points to the notion that – like the actor on a stage – people must stand or fall on their own strength of will. As Bobby (John Finnegan), the stage assistant, walks Myrtle onstage for the final act, he says, "I've seen a lotta drunks in my day, but I've never seen anybody as drunk as you and still able to walk." Throughout, Myrtle repeats variations on a line she speaks toward the end of the play: "I am not me; I used to be me. I'm not me anymore," as if reflecting on the disorienting experience of living in an aging alcoholic body, a line alluding to words Rowlands speaks as a character in Cassavetes's early film, *Faces*. Veering unexpectedly toward a semi-comic conclusion, the play within a play finds the two main characters reconciling their differences. Fooling both the audience and the other character, Cassavetes as Maurice and Rowlands as Myrtle go to shake hands, then thrust their thumbs over their shoulders and pretend to hit each other, until he finally closes by asking if she wants to see something wonderful. He starts to take off his coat, mugging lewdly at the audience. In the final comedic gimmick, they rehearse a trick where they walk forward to shake hands but then bend

I've seen a lot of drunks in my day,

Figure 4.3   The aging actress Myrtle (Gena Rowlands) in *Opening Night* (1977), as a stagehand commentates on her condition. Digital frame enlargement. Courtesy of the Criterion Collection.

and grab each other's ankles. As is customary for Cassavetes's narratives, men rescue women – sort of – calling final shots that never quite reach the goal.

FACES

The open-ended, unexpectedly upbeat endings of *Husbands*, *A Woman Under the Influence*, and *Opening Night* both contrast with and originate in the mood of Cassavetes's early work, *Faces*. Revisiting this film reveals roots of the characters and motifs that would resurface in later films. Filmed in 16 mm, *Faces* captures the masculine rituals of corporate America in dialogue that prefigures the *Mad Men* television series (2007–15), economically establishing the world of Richard Forst (elegant white-haired John Marley), a spoiled male executive surrounded by men vying for his approval as women hover in the background, acting as handmaids. Once the title *Faces* appears, Cassavetes rockets the narrative abruptly from business to nightlife, in a tight closeup of Gena Rowlands's flawless face. Her character, Jeannie, exits a bar called "The Loser" with Richard and his pasty-looking sidekick Freddy (Fred Draper) passing a flask. *Faces* offers an interesting case study, in light of Cassavetes's stated concern over the gender paradigm prevalent in American society in the sixties and seventies:

I'm very worried about the depiction of women on the screen. It's gotten worse than ever and it's related to their being either high- or low-class concubines, and the only question is when or where they will go to bed, with whom, and how many. (*Cassavetes on Cassavetes*)

He paints a clear picture of this dynamic, but viewers may wonder whether his treatment critiques or merely naturalizes such behavior.

Cassavetes depicts mating in slyly cynical terms, and when Jeannie goes into the bedroom in her apartment to change her clothes it throws Freddy into such a paroxysm of anticipation that he wistfully asks Richard, "Remember when we didn't have to worry about our wives?" Freddy sings at her bedroom door, "I Dream of Jeannie," an old-fashioned song that resurfaces later on in *Husbands* and *A Woman Under the Influence*. The disconnect between the sentimentality of this song and the carnality of Freddy's fantasies is muddled by associations with the popular 1960s sitcom of the same name, perhaps referring to men's desire for Barbara Eden's magically compliant Genie, a prototype of manic pixie dream girls who would proliferate in the next century. Jeannie dances alternately with the two men until Freddy snidely asks, "What do you charge? I know I have to pay," to which she counters, "What you meant to say was you had a very good time and you liked my house and you liked me." Undaunted, Freddy treats her like a hooker until she finally says, "You're crude," and he stumbles out the door. When Richard tells her she is lovely, she replies, "I'm too old to be lovely, and I haven't got a heart of gold," demonstrating her awareness of her diminishing shelf-life and presumed status as a prostitute. As a promise to return, he plants a passionate kiss on her before leaving.

Once home, the seemingly guilt-free Richard embraces his wife Maria (Lynn Carlin) as she tries to disentangle herself from a phone call with their friend Louise (Joanne Moore Jordan), who complains that her husband Freddy talks about other women in his sleep. Richard scoffs and says women will soon have "everything – the house, the bills, etc." and she answers, "Oh, I'm so sorry, do we emasculate you?" After exchanging barbs, they end up rolling in bed, laughing, but the next morning, out of nowhere, he says he wants a divorce. Maria giggles, the camera zooming in on her face, and he adds, "That's the only thing to do, isn't it?" slamming his hand down and phoning Jeannie in front of his shocked wife. Arriving at Jeannie's place, domination is the name of the game, as Richard finds younger men who cede the field when they learn he is chairman of the board. Once they leave, Richard admits, "I like you . . . I'm just a mild success in a dull profession, and I've got a bad kidney," perhaps warning her not to expect money or performance. He says, "You're a lovely girl, but you talk too much," announcing that he is spending the night, which prompts her reply: "You're a son of a bitch, . . . because you get to me." He swats her and she puts on music, the scene closing with her dancing as soft piano music plays.

In what looks like a tit-for-tat, the scene shifts abruptly to Richard's wife, sitting with her friends at a disco. A zoom shot shows Maria refusing young Chet (Seymour Cassell), who wants to dance with her, followed by a quick cut to her house, where he has joined her and her friends, Florence (Dorothy Gulliver), Louise, and Billy Mae (Darlene Conley), who tells him in a southern drawl, "Our husbands are scared of you – your youth, and your spirit. They think they're the kings of the earth and they do not want you taking their place." When Louise dances with him he says they are making fools of themselves, and she bursts out, "I take care of a family of five and I have a college degree, and I don't need you to tell me I'm making a fool of myself." She slaps him and storms out, followed by Billy Mae, who says this incident "is going to put her back on the couch for another twenty-five years."

Cassavetes modulates the comic tone as Florence muses about lost youth, admitting that "these wild crazy dancers have succeeded where science has failed." She embraces Chet and falls on top of him, and he kisses her tenderly on the lips, then sweetly on the nose. In a risky decision, Maria gives Chet her keys to drive Florence home, and Cassavetes shifts moods again. She walks through the house, turning out lights, the camera following from behind, a sequence that resembles modern stalker films. Music and lights suddenly go off, and Maria screams as Chet grabs her and chases her up to the bedroom, laughing hysterically. In a harshly lit profile shot the two grow silent, a hand-held camera closing in as he gently kisses her shoulders, nuzzles down to her chest, picks her up, kisses her mouth, and lowers her to the bed. He laughs and rests his hand on his hip, a shot through the crook of his arm framing her face as she says, "Let me change," an echo of Jeannie's statement. Removing his sweater, he wails, "Mama's little baby," breaking the sensuous heat of the moment. With no rights to music, Cassavetes used improvised music snippets to create a sense of immediacy and cut costs. The impression of realism is underscored as Maria returns wearing a frumpy flowered house robe. Extreme close-ups in the bright bedroom emphasize every pore, and when she says she dislikes the lights he simply pulls the bedspread over their heads. Cassavetes presents a parallel scene with Richard wanting to conceal his body. Jeannie opens the door on him shirtless and he screams, bursts out laughing, and covers himself. She says, "You know you have a beautiful body," even though he looks like an embarrassed old woman covering her sagging breasts. In a series of tropes that resurface in *A Woman Under the Influence* and *Opening Night*, Jeannie and Richard exchange insults until he says, "Don't be silly anymore. Just be yourself." She says, "But I am myself. Who else would I be?" The trope of identity resurfaces throughout Cassavetes's films, urging viewers to ask themselves the same question.

Although the parallel structure suggests Cassavetes's even-handed impulse, he paints a grimmer picture of female infidelity when Chet discovers Maria comatose from an apparent overdose. After calling for rescue, he resorts to the remedy Cassavetes would use in *Opening Night*: black coffee. Here, Chet drags around a woman who cannot walk, slaps her, performs sounds and jumps like a monkey (as Manny and Maurice do in *Opening Night*). With the typical slapstick of Cassavetes's endings, *Faces* shows Richard running into his house singing, clicking his heels, and shouting, "I'm ready," only to see out the bedroom window a shirtless Chet running across the roof and jumping off. Cassavetes made Cassell repeat this stunt until exhaustion – just for "fun" – although he had the take he wanted – a dark example of Cassavetes's vaunted sense of humor. Inside, Richard immediately attacks Maria, ignoring his own behavior of the night before: "You want to be rewarded. Adultery. Beneficiary who is the adulteress gets paid off. All I have to do is find that ten-year-old rapist and kill him, and you get paid off." He then asks, "You want violence?" pushing and slapping her until she slaps him back, saying, "I hate my life." Sitting on various stairsteps, they smoke and cough until he puts on music with the words, "Hold me in your arms." Silent, they shift positions and the film leaves viewers wondering where they will settle.

Examination of *Faces* reveals numerous paradoxes inherent throughout Cassavetes's work. He wanted spontaneity and authenticity, captured through a communal artistic effort, but he shunned unions – designed to empower and unify film laborers – as cramping his individual style. In the Whisky-a-go-go scene of *Faces*, Haskell Wexler, one of the camera operators, was "worried to death the union's gonna shows up and find he's shooting

Figure 4.4   Gena Rowlands as Jeannie in *Faces* (1968), the entitled male executive Richard Forst (John Marley) standing behind her. Digital frame enlargement. Courtesy of the Criterion Collection.

a non-union film" (*Faces* Extra). Cassavetes refused to direct actors, saying, "You own it," but in making *Faces* he had strict rules. No actor was allowed to speak about his or her part, requiring "tremendous in-depth study" to be the person rather than act a role (Rowlands, *Faces* Extra). Cassell describes how George Sims did most of the camera work, but sometimes handed it over to an actor to get in close, giving actors "utmost freedom." (*Faces* Extra). Cassavetes wanted the camera in actors' faces for the aptly named film, *Faces*, a style he maintained throughout his career. Having them wear body microphones allowed greater range of movement, although it compromised sound quality. Rowlands describes his "musical approach, sometimes with a jazz tempo, at other times romantic and languid" (Extra), as he shot in sequence, a rarity in American filmmaking, where the cost-effectiveness of grouping scenes by locale and actors dictates shooting schedules. Cassavetes wanted actors to experience character lives unfolding – but with endless repetitions. His films involve actors getting slapped or dragged – which happened much more often to women than to men – yet Rowlands credits him with being "one of very few directors who paid attention to 'women of a certain age,'" noting the stunning performance of Gulliver, who passionately kisses Chet. At the same time, as director of *Faces* Cassavetes seemed unconcerned about the physical well-being of his two leading women – both of whom were in early stages of pregnancy – being slapped, manhandled, and stressed to the point of tears. His actors and characters suffer and survive, with no final revelations or redemption, just a wry possibility of uncertain hope. Like *Faces*, all of Cassavetes's films leave his viewers hanging, considering a multitude of possibilities, laughing with relief or sighing with frustration or bewilderment, perhaps outraged by depictions of "in your face" sexism, racism, or even insanity, but thinking furiously – probably considering the nature of reality from some location beyond common sense. Cassavetes challenges viewers to venture off the grid into the unknown, along with his actors and characters.

WORKS CITED

Burke, Tom. "Falk in 'Falk Talk'." *Rolling Stone*, 24 April 1975, pp 40–44.
Carney, Ray. "The Adventure of Insecurity: The Films of John Cassavetes." *The Kenyon Review*, vol. 13, no. 2, 1991, pp. 102–21
Cassavetes, John and Ray Carney, eds. *Cassavetes on Cassavetes*. Farrar, Straus and Giroux, 2001.
Degener, David. 'Director Under the Influence.' *Film Quarterly*, Winter 1975, vol. 29, pp. 4–12.
Dixon, Wheeler Winston. 'Review of *The Films of John Cassavetes: Pragmatism, Modernism and the Movies*.' *Journal of Film and Video*, vol. 48, nos. 1–2, pp. 88–94; University Film and Video Association, 1996.
Fine, Marshall. *Accidental Genius: How John Cassavetes Invented American Independent Film*, Miramax Books, 2005.

Flaubert, Gustave. "Letters about *Madame Bovary*." *Madame Bovary*. Translated by Eleanor Marx Aveling and Paul de Man, W. W. Norton & Company, 2005, pp. 300–312.

Jenkins, Chadwick. "*Faces*: The Authenticity of Discomfort." *Pop Matters*, Mar. 2009, https://www.popmatters.com/70500-john-cassavetes-faces-the-authenticity-of-discomfort-2496059614.html. Accessed 12 May 2020.

King, Homay. "Free Indirect Affect in Cassavetes's Opening Night and Faces." *Camera Obscura: Feminism, Culture, and Media Studies*, vol. 19, no. 2, 2004, pp. 105–39.

LoBianco, Lorraine. "*A Woman Under the Influence*." *Turner Classic Movies*, www.tcm.com/this-month/article/138056%7C0/A-Woman-Under-the-Influence.html. Accessed 1 January 2019.

Staff Writers. "Husbands on the Run." *Life*, 19 May 1969, pp. 53–8.

5. "LET ME LOVE YOU": AMBIGUOUS MASCULINITY IN MICHAEL CIMINO'S MELODRAMAS

I-Lien Tsay

When Michael Cimino died in July 2016, film historian Peter Biskind penned an obituary for the *Hollywood Reporter* which contained the following:

> At the risk of being struck down for speaking ill of the dead . . . it's worth musing on Cimino's career because it was such an instructive one, illustrative of the best and worst of the so-called New Hollywood, the directors' decade of the '70s. (24)

Cimino's first three films, *Thunderbolt and Lightfoot* (1974), *The Deer Hunter* (1978), and *Heaven's Gate* (1980), fit neatly within the New Hollywood period. Written by Cimino, *Thunderbolt and Lightfoot* has been dubbed "one of the great directorial débuts of the New Hollywood era" (Brody 12). Cimino's second film, *The Deer Hunter*, cemented his reputation as a New Hollywood auteur when the film garnered five Academy Awards, including Best Picture and Best Director. What followed then was the historical epic and box-office flop *Heaven's Gate* (1980), which led to the end of the excesses of New Hollywood (Biskind 24). As film critic Manohla Dargis writes,

> Widely reviled and feverishly admired, *Heaven's Gate* holds one of the most contested places in American movie history. It has been called a disaster and a disgrace, yet also anointed a masterpiece. In unsympathetic accounts of its making, it is a $44 million object lesson in directorial ego and executive incompetence – the film that torpedoed both a legendary studio [United Artists] and New Hollywood. (AR10)

This is no mere hyperbole, as the financial excesses and the studio's bungled management of the film did, in fact, lead to significant implications for the film industry. Most of the analysis on Cimino has dwelled on the political economy of the film industry, perhaps in part due to *Heaven's Gate* producer Steven Bach's juicy tell-all memoir *Final Cut: Art, Money, and Ego in Heaven's Gate, the Movie that Sank United Artists*. However, Cimino deserves more examination within the context of New Hollywood films, not just within the political economy of the film industry, and closer scrutiny of Cimino's New Hollywood films provides insight into the shifting pressure on American masculinity during this time. Cimino's films share in the brutal realism, frank sexuality, and cynical attitude of New Hollywood, but they are also intent on exploring the boundaries of masculine intimacy. In each of the films, the homosocial bonds between men are the primary focus. *Thunderbolt and Lightfoot* is a buddy crime caper that depends on the unlikely but genuine affection between the titular characters. *The Deer Hunter* features three friends from a Pennsylvania steel town who serve in the Vietnam War, and their acute disillusionment after the war. *Heaven's Gate*, a historical epic set during the Johnson County Wars of 1892, demonstrates how two Harvard classmates wind up on opposite sides of a class conflict between Eastern European immigrant settlers and wealthy cattle owners on the Western frontier. Despite the differences of genre and setting, all these films are preoccupied with masculine intimacy. On what basis do men forge friendship? What happens when male friendships are put under duress? How do men experience and express intimacy within a friendship? Cimino's New Hollywood films can be described as masculine melodramas that examine the tension between violence and emotional vulnerability within a morally ambiguous world.

In her analysis of Cimino's films, Naomi Greene identifies a "new kind of cinematic melodrama" that reflects "the traumatized social/political climate of post-Vietnam, post-Watergate America" (38). Melodrama has been broadly theorized as a genre that attempts to assert a legible social order during a moral crisis. As defined by Peter Brooks, the characteristics of melodrama include "the indulgence of strong emotionalism; moral polarization and schematization; extreme states of being, situations, actions; overt villainy, persecution of the good, and final reward of virtue; inflated and extravagant expression; dark plottings, suspense, breathtaking peripety" (11–12). In Cimino's films, the protagonists are pitted against an exaggerated enemy (the Viet Cong in *The Deer Hunter*, the wealthy cattle barons of the Wyoming Stock Growers' Association in *Heaven's Gate*), but unlike that of traditional melodrama the resolution of dramatic conflicts in these films offers no clear sense of a winner, with no moral high ground captured. Instead, Cimino's films emphasize the struggle experienced by the individual attempting to make sense of society's moral contradictions. Without the clarity usually provided by melodrama,

Cimino shows the uneasy energy of male intimacy, fraught with pleasure and pain.

Cimino's films both present the grand visual and emotional spectacles typical of melodrama and reflect the political cynicism and loss of innocence which characterize the post-Vietnam period. For Greene, Cimino's films depart from previous melodramatic forms in that "the mood of these films gently persuades us that all idealism is empty, all action futile, history and historical awareness unimportant" (36). Instead of being moved by passion to take action, or reaffirming a sense of social order, Greene posits that Cimino's melodramas instead "encourage us to lament the past, to forget history, and to luxuriate in spectacle for its own sake" (37). While we may be momentarily moved by the elaborate staging of social events, the sweeping cinematography, the deep-focus shots, and detailed mise-en-scène, the overall effect can be hollow. In conventional melodrama, visual spectacle often equates to a significant emotional experience, but in Cimino's films, spectacle seems to serve a different purpose. Instead of providing stability, Cimino's melodramas blur moral certainty by highlighting emotional unpredictability, particularly in moments of masculine intimacy.

Todd Berliner offers a view of New Hollywood that relates this unpredictability to the narrative structure of the films from this period. Berliner identifies New Hollywood films as narratives marked by "perversities" such as "ideological incongruities, logical and characterological inconsistencies, distracting and stylistic ornamentation and discordances, irresolutions, ambiguities and other impediments to straightforwardness in a film's narration" (10). Cimino's New Hollywood films demonstrate many of these characteristics, in that none of them fit neatly into a single film genre, nor do they provide an easily digestible reflection of the tumultuous socio-political tensions of the 1970s. These narrative "perversities" allow Cimino to reveal the contradictory nature of masculinity. *The Deer Hunter* and *Heaven's Gate* use violence as a means of "cloaking a mood of existential uncertainty," much like other New Hollywood films like *Bonnie and Clyde* (1967), *The Godfather* (1972), *Mean Streets* (1973), and *Chinatown* (1974). While violence and power are consistently associated with masculinity, the resulting impression is ambiguous. The hero may be deliberately callous and turn a blind eye to suffering (Michael in *The Deer Hunter*, Averill in *Heaven's Gate*), or the villain/rival may demonstrate emotional sensitivity and an affinity for domesticity (Nathan in *Heaven's Gate*). Instead of providing a coherent and normative version of male behavior, Cimino's characters are unreliable and uneasy in expressing masculine intimacy, thus highlighting the struggle to determine what masculinity actually means. Despite the risks or costs of doing so, the male characters seem compelled to attempt a genuine expression of intimacy with each other. What assuages this masculine thrust in Cimino's films is his use of sublime natural landscapes as a backdrop for narrative and character development. How the men in Cimino's films approach the wilderness represents their attitudes to each other and their ability to navigate the social order. Cimino returns again and again to the rugged and majestic landscape of the American frontier, as if to remind us visually that no matter what brute ugliness is enacted by man, no matter what political cynicism or social anxiety exists, there is no explicit judgment meted out by these implacable and majestic landscapes. The American West, the Pennsylvania mountains or the tropics in Vietnam are landscapes that frame the difficulties of masculine intimacy. One of Cimino's gifts as a director is his ability to capture this natural beauty in what feels like an offering of visual consolation for the gritty and grubby depictions of masculinity.

Thunderbolt and Lightfoot pairs taciturn Korean War veteran John "Thunderbolt" Doherty (Clint Eastwood) and baby-faced, loose-limbed Lightfoot (Jeff Bridges) as partners in a bank robbery. If *Thunderbolt and Lightfoot* was merely a heist movie, the action would be incredibly languorous. The film devotes its first forty-five minutes to the developing friendship between Doherty and Lightfoot, and the bank heist seems secondary to the fulfilment of intimacy between these characters. Cimino signals the theme of friendship early in the film. When Doherty takes his leave of Lightfoot at a bus terminal, he attempts to give Lightfoot a watch in gratitude for rescuing him from his pursuers. Lightfoot pushes the proffered watch back to Doherty and says, "I don't want your watch, man." Lightfoot hesitates, then confesses his true object of desire: "I want your friendship! Goddamnit, I like you, that's all. I thought we were getting to be friends." Laughing ruefully, Lightfoot declares, "We're good together." Doherty pauses, as if considering the honesty of Lightfoot's emotions, but continues on his way. However, when Doherty spots a member of his former gang at the bus station, he returns back to the safety of Lightfoot's car and companionship.

Part of the charm of *Thunderbolt and Lightfoot* is found in the unlikely partnership between the two criminals. The film begins with Thunderbolt Doherty in his disguise as a Pastor Reverend, delivering a Sunday sermon at the small community church in Spirit Lake, Idaho. Doherty stands behind a pulpit, in the center of a symmetrically composed shot lined by church pews, providing a sense of serene stability. Doherty gently extols his parishioners to "remember that we are all imperfect . . . as under the redeemer's gentle reign, the wolf shall dwell with the lamb and the leopard shall lie down with the kid." The serenity of the church is upended, and the film cuts immediately to Lightfoot, connecting him visually with "the kid" mentioned in Doherty's sermon. In the next shot, Lightfoot is loping easily across railway tracks. As he approaches a used car lot, he adopts a limp and gets into a white Trans Am with a blue spread eagle on the hood. The salesman hails him as "kid" and "boy," and questions Lightfoot's masculinity, saying, "I don't know if you're man enough to take on a car like this." Lightfoot replies, "I don't know – I have a wooden leg," as if a physical disability brings his masculinity into question. (Later on, the film shows Doherty wearing a leg brace for an injury sustained during the Korean War.) The salesman nervously says, "Aw, you wouldn't kid about a thing like that, would you?", uncomfortable with questioning the authenticity of Lightfoot's limp but willing to raise doubt, however tentatively, about Lightfoot's veracity. For the salesman, pretending to have a wooden leg goes well beyond the pale of what is tolerable in a used car negotiation. The audience, privy to Lightfoot's deception, understands that Lightfoot has transgressed this moral boundary without hesitation. To seal the deal in his con of the salesman, Lightfoot gleefully revs the engine, as if to demonstrate his virility, and triumphantly pulls away with tires squealing.

The film cuts back to Doherty's sermon, delivering the wisdom that "A true Christian, like his divine master, is of meek and forgiving temper. *He owes no man anything but to love one another*, and he overcomes evil with good" (emphasis added). A stranger enters the church, pulls a gun and fires at Doherty, who flees, running from the back of the church into the fields. Enter Lightfoot in the stolen muscle car, who accidentally hits the mysterious pursuer. Doherty, desperate for an escape route, throws his body through the passenger window, but winds up half in and half out, clutching the roof of the car and dislocating his shoulder in the process.

Thus, Doherty and Lightfoot are brought together, shown to be capable of conning ordinary people, but with different strategies for doing so. In his disguise as a pastor, Doherty's strategy is to avoid detection by following the conventions of his position. Lightfoot, on the other hand, flaunts the existing codes of decency in order to commit a crime in broad daylight. Yet both Doherty and Lightfoot are knowledgeable about the wilderness, and their versions of masculinity are linked with an ability to navigate nature that allows them to evade and survive. After the opening car chase, Doherty jerks his dislocated shoulder back into place by strapping Lightfoot's belt around a tree trunk for leverage. When another stolen car is wrecked, Lightfoot knows the unsigned spot on Snake River where the Hell's Canyon delivery boat will stop to take them up river. The two friends are shown as evenly matched in an affectionate partnership, and the film ends by emphasizing their bond (see Fig. 5.1). After retrieving the proceeds of a bank robbery, Doherty fulfils Lightfoot's dream of paying cash for a white Cadillac, and he and Lightfoot head back on the road. Lightfoot, who is losing consciousness from a vicious and fatal head wound, congratulates Doherty: "Hey, you know something? I don't think of us as criminals, you know? I feel we accomplished something, a good job. I feel proud of myself, man. I feel like a hero." The camaraderie expressed here is genuine and tender, and the poignancy of Lightfoot's death underscores that the job accomplished was the achievement of intimacy

Figure 5.1 Criminals-in-arms Lightfoot (Jeff Bridges) and John 'Thunderbolt' Doherty (Clint Eastwood) celebrate their recovery of the bank loot with cigars in Michael Cimino's *Thunderbolt and Lightfoot* (1974). Digital frame enlargement. Courtesy of MGM.

between two distinct versions of masculinity. As Brody suggests, "With its mix of spectacle and intimacy, exuberance and tragedy, 'Thunderbolt and Lightfoot' points ahead to the radical extremes of Cimino's 1980 masterwork, 'Heaven's Gate'" (Brody 12).

In his second film, Cimino left behind the breezy escapades of *Thunderbolt and Lightfoot* for more serious and darker matters. Released three years after the fall of Saigon, *The Deer Hunter* tells the story of three friends, Michael (Robert DeNiro), Steven (John Savage), and Nick (Christopher Walken), who leave a Pennsylvania steel mill town to serve in the Vietnam War. Instead of the complementary masculinities of *Thunderbolt and Lightfoot*, *The Deer Hunter* portrays different versions of masculinity that arise from a shared class and ethnic background, within a broader social context in which the Americans are losing the war as well as shedding traditional markers of masculinity. According to Pauline Kael, the film gives the "fullest screen treatment so far of the mystic bond of male comradeship" (800). Michael's masculinity is established by his ability to survive the industrial workplace, the uncivilized wilderness, and the Vietnam War. The "deer hunter" of the title, Michael follows a strict moral code, symbolized by his insistence on allowing himself only "one shot," to honor prey and hunter equally with a demonstration of individual restraint, even if it comes at the cost of alienating his friends. When the friends embark on a hunt the day after Steven's wedding to Angela, Michael is shown ready for the expedition, while his friends are in various hungover stages of undress from formal tuxedos to outdoor gear (see Fig. 5.2). Michael takes pride in his masculine code but also takes offense when his friends do not follow his example. Stanley, who has forgotten thermal socks and hunting boots, asks to borrow Michael's spare pair, and Michael flatly refuses, saying, "You gotta

Figure 5.2   Michael (Robert DeNiro) takes aim in *The Deer Hunter* (1978), while his friends, Stanley (John Cazale), Axel (Chuck Aspegren), Nick (Christopher Walken), and John (George Dzundza), look on in varying states of readiness. Note the Cadillac still festooned with "Just Married" decorations from the previous night's wedding. Digital frame enlargement. Courtesy of Universal Pictures.

learn, Stanley . . . no more, no way." When Stanley protests and continues to ask for the boots, Michael explodes and draws the line with Stanley: "This is this. From now on, you're on your own." Nick intervenes by handing the spare boots to Stanley and gently reproves Michael, asking him "What's the matter with you?" Frustrated, Michael fires a shot into the air, to punctuate his emotional outburst.

While Michael is shown to possess an unyielding mental and physical fortitude, his friends are shown as less sure and more vulnerable to their surroundings. In an early scene when the friends leave the steel mill after their shift, Michael decides to race his Cadillac against a truck, barely managing to overtake the truck on the inside lane. Michael crows triumphantly, "One shot against a sure thing!", to which Nick responds, "There's no such thing as a sure thing." This exchange establishes a rupture in a traditional notion of masculinity, wherein conflict can be resolved through competition or physical effort. Anxiety about masculine intimacy exists in *The Deer Hunter* because instead of winning the fight or the hunt or the war, masculinity is shown to be insufficient and flawed, no matter how prepared one might be. Part war film, part melodrama, Cimino describes the film as "about friendship and courage and what happens to those qualities under stress" (*The Deer Hunter*).

Much like *Thunderbolt and Lightfoot*, Cimino spends the first portion of the film capturing quotidian details in order to set up the dramatic action that follows. The first hour of *The Deer Hunter* shows the intimate details of the entire town of Clairton preparing and celebrating Steven and Angela's ornate Ukrainian wedding, from Steven's mother bewailing the marriage, to the bridesmaids running through the streets carrying weddings gifts to Angela and staining her wedding dress with a single drop of red wine. Vincent Canby acknowledges the importance of these sequences in emphasizing social rites of passage:

> No sensible director would have allowed that early wedding-feast sequence to go on as long as it did, but as 'The Deer Hunter' evolved, it became obvious that the length and detail of that wedding feast were vital to our appreciation of everything that happened afterward. ("Culling Gems" A15)

The social rituals here are shown to be overwhelmingly raucous, almost stifling in the presence of human bodies, and ominously violent. Nick's girlfriend Linda (Meryl Streep) is backhanded by her drunk father as she brings him dinner in her bridesmaid dress; she attends the wedding with a fresh bruise on her face. At the wedding feast, Stanley watches his date dance with the band leader whose hands begin to roam, and Stanley intervenes by savagely hitting his date who immediately drops to the floor. After being restrained from going after the band leader, Stanley picks up his girl from the floor, and they kiss and make up. The women in Cimino's films tend to be distractions or casualties quickly glossed over in the focus on male friendship.

While the men are thoughtlessly violent or inept with the women in the film, Cimino shows the men being both affectionately crude and disarmingly honest with each other. For example, he includes not one but two scenes where the friends sing along to Frankie Valli's "Can't Take My Eyes Off You." In the first scene, the men are playing pool at Welch's Lounge after their shift ends at the steel mill. When the song starts playing, the friends spontaneously sing along, delightfully boozy and unrestrained in their bar stool camaraderie. The same song is played during the wedding feast at Veteran's Hall, where the men once again serenade each other, variously crooning and belting out the lyrics. Reading against the grain, the lyrics suggest that the men find solace and joy not in romantic love but in homosocial intimacy with each other: "can't take my eyes off you / you'd be like heaven to touch / I want to hold you so much / at long last love has arrived / and I thank God I'm alive." While "at long last love has arrived," the men are unable to "let me love you." The whole enterprise, that of fulfilling masculine intimacy, seems "just too good to be true."

The expression of this intimate masculine look, shared over beers and a pool table at Welch's Lounge, is turned on its head when the film shifts to Vietnam. In the environment of an exoticized ethnic enemy, intimacy has been superseded by violence. When Michael, Steven, and Nick are being held by the Viet Cong and forced to play Russian roulette, Michael begs Steven to play the game, or face being tortured in the water pit. Michael entreats Steven, who has dissociated from his situation: "Look in my eyes, Stevie. Look at me!"

Michael attempts to coach Steve through the process by the power of his gaze, but only partly succeeds. Steve loses his nerve, takes his eyes off Michael, and when he pulls the trigger the shot grazes his head. Similarly, towards the end of the film, attempting to rescue Nick from Saigon where he has been playing Russian roulette for money, Michael relies on the power of his gaze to focus Nick's traumatized mind. In a last, desperate effort, Michael challenges Nick at the Russian roulette table, surrounded by bettors in a high-stakes gambling den. Michael entreats Nick to remember his Clairton past. Michael begs Nick to look at him, begs him not to pull the trigger. "Look at me," Michael pleads again and again, asking if Nick remembers the mountains. As their eyes finally meet, Nick has a momentary flash of recognition but too late to stop his finger from pulling the trigger. In that moment, masculine intimacy confronts the violent impulses of masculinity, with deadly consequence.

While the film provides a confronting (and fictionalized) depiction of the Vietnam War, the effect is intended to feel emotionally real. Cimino considers the war as "incidental to the development of the characters and their story." The film does not address the political justification for US involvement in Vietnam, instead focusing on the effects of wartime trauma and the alienation faced by veterans. Cimino explains that the closing scene of *The Deer Hunter*, with characters singing a tenderly tentative rendition of "God Bless America" around a kitchen table, was "not meant to be a political statement" but was intended to represent the overwhelming grief after Vietnam (Abramovitch 135).

While the emotional impact of *The Deer Hunter* was acclaimed by audiences and critics, Cimino's third New Hollywood film, *Heaven's Gate*, failed to resonate with audiences at the time of its release. Cimino's epic about the Johnson County War in Wyoming was highly anticipated and despite "every initial indication that Cimino's film would participate in the cultural rebuilding of American ideological confidence" (Keathley 305), *Heaven's Gate* was panned by film critic Vincent Canby as "something quite rare in movies these days – an unqualified disaster" ("Heaven's Gate" C29). When a shortened version of *Heaven's Gate*, from 219 minutes to 149 in length, was re-released in April 1981, Canby relented by calling the film "no longer an unqualified disaster" but simply "a desperately muddled compromise" ("Shorter 'Heaven's Gate'" C10).

Unlike his first two films, where the conventions of melodrama are used to unsettle dominant ideologies of masculinity, Cimino's third film is a more straightforward melodrama. *Heaven's Gate* is set at a time when wealthy ranchers undertook a brutal campaign to wipe out immigrant settlers. The protagonist, James Averill (Kris Kristofferson), is a Harvard-educated federal marshal who helps to organize the immigrants in resisting the monopolistic Wyoming Stock Growers Association, with whom Averill's college friend

William Irvine (John Hurt) casts his lot. Like Michael in *The Deer Hunter*, Averill is positioned as the masculine ideal, and romances whorehouse madam Ella Watson (Isabella Huppert) in a love triangle with hired gun Nathan Champion (Christopher Walken).

In *Heaven's Gate*, Cimino again shows the workings of male intimacy, but this time the conflict is overtly about class privilege and ethnicity. The film begins with the 1870 Harvard commencement, with formal festivities that include a marching band processional and a vertiginous outdoor waltz. As intoned by the university scholar to the tittering graduates, their (white) privilege entails moral responsibility: "If it be not a mere farce you are enacting in these sacred valedictory rites . . . they have for you a mandate of imperative duty." He continues the lesson: "It is not great wealth alone that builds the library, bounds the college. It is to diffuse the higher learning culture among the people. It is the contact of the cultivated mind with the uncultivated." What follows this solemn view of privilege is, in fact, a farce of a commencement oration by Irvine. With raised eyebrow and sophomoric humor, Irvine excuses himself and his class from any moral obligation: "We disclaim all intention of making a change in what we esteem."

At the end of the commencement sequence, when the graduates are gathered around the oak tree in the Yard, Averill slings his arm around Irvine and grins at him affectionately (see Fig. 5.3). As the men drunkenly sing, "Let our friendships be forever / let our care perish never / when we're parted, stick together / heart to heart, bold and true / never fear, then for '70!", Irvine turns to Averill and whispers, stricken, "It's over, James. Do you realize? It's over?"

Heaven's Gate demonstrates, indeed, that the gilded age is over. The film cuts to twenty years later, when Averill is a federal marshal in Johnson County,

Figure. 5.3   In *Heaven's Gate* (1980), John Irvine (John Hurt) and James Averill (Kris Kristofferson), members of the Harvard Class of 1870, participate in commencement festivities. Digital frame enlargement. Courtesy of United Artists.

Wyoming. Eastern European settlers are in conflict with the landed gentry of the Stock Growers Association, who have the backing of the US government. Cimino is unflinching in showing the casual violence experienced by the immigrants, who persevere despite the wealthy landowners' efforts to prevent foreign otherness from infringing on their American privilege. Within this context, Averill is sympathetic to the struggles of the laboring class, and the dissolute Irvine becomes more and more downtrodden, any semblance of his previous insouciance blurring into an alcoholic haze. While Irvine is incapable of following the principles of a cultivated Harvard man, Averill uses his education to mobilize the immigrant settlers in the final battle between the settlers and the Stock Growers Association's hired guns, based on Roman military strategy. The two friends are shown irrevocably on opposite sides of class conflict.

In producer Steven Bach's view, *Heaven's Gate* evinces a "callous or uncaring quality about the characters" that contributed to a sense of the characters and narrative being "sacrificed to the filmmaker's love of visual effect and production" (416). Bach muses that

> there was something else there that aroused antipathy . . . That something else, I think, is a pervasive nihilism that runs through the film from its advertising – 'What one loves in life are the things that fade' – to its climatic and violent reworking of history. (ibid)

This "pervasive nihilism" that Bach identifies echoes what Greene refers to as the empty idealism and futile action in Cimino's films (36). While audiences may have appreciated *The Deer Hunter* as a means of processing the social trauma of Vietnam, perhaps they were not yet willing to question the class ideologies raised by *Heaven's Gate*. As Christopher Sharrett proposes,

> it may be a tiny bit possible that *Heaven's Gate* was sabotaged because it is the most politically radical Western ever made in the United States, surpassing the revisionist Westerns of the Sixties and Seventies. It fits within the 'Marxist operas' of the era, including *The Damned, Once Upon a Time in the West*, and *1900*. (58)

Heaven's Gate's recent revival suggests that today's audiences are more willing to engage with the film's critique of American class ideology.

After the success of *The Deer Hunter*, Cimino was able to secure the right of "final cut" in his contract for *Heaven's Gate*, with an initial budget of $7.5 million and a projected release date of Christmas 1979. By the second week of filming, Cimino had already spent half of the budget and fallen behind schedule one day for each day spent shooting. He was spending $200,000 per day for only 90 seconds of usable material (Thompson 50). And yet, Cimino insisted on taking his time. Obsessively protective of his film, Cimino refused to show studio executives a rough cut, and when he finally presented them with a five and a half hour version of the film executives "reportedly were taken with the film's visual beauty, but shocked at its length" (Pollock R1). Cimino fought the studio's demands for a film that would not exceed three hours (ibid).

The film's costs totaled over $40 million and were created by Cimino's insistence on painstaking historical detail. As Cimino describes, "There is no building and no interior that has not been inspired in one way or another by a picture. Every single costume, from leads' to extras', has been designed based on specific photographs" (Vallan). The cost of recreating authentic period costumes for the 1,200 extras was vastly underestimated and contributed to the budget blowout. Cimino demanded the top hats in the Harvard graduation scene be procured from England (Griffin), the locomotive used in the Johnson County sequences be an authentic working nineteenth-century locomotive, and that 80 wagon trains were necessary for the final battle scene (Harmetz C8). *Heaven's Gate* "swiftly became a symbol for Hollywood excess" (Thompson 50) for its exorbitant production costs and Cimino's refusal to compromise his artistic vision. As one executive reflected, the studios "were afraid to say, 'Oh God, we can't tell these auteurs they're crazy.' Well, let me tell you, that dance has ended'" (Pollock R1). Biskind views the spectacular failure of *Heaven's Gate* as marking "a sorry end to New Hollywood, which finally foundered on the egos of auteurs like Cimino" (26). After box-office takings of barely $3 million, *Heaven's Gate* caused the sale of United Artists by its parent corporation Transamerica to MGM, and studios began wresting the reins back from brash, young directors like Cimino.

As Guilia D'Agnolo Vallan points out, *Heaven's Gate* was released into the environment of popular successes such as *The Empire Strikes Back* (1980), *Raiders of the Lost Ark* (1981), and *E.T.* (1982):

> Seen today, in its stark contrast to the Manichaean spirit of those two space sagas and Indy's anti-Nazi comic-book adventure, Cimino's dark, very untriumphant epic looks like a beautiful anachronism. And there is no doubt that the film paid dearly for its disconnect from the contemporary zeitgeist.

Yet Cimino's ability to showcase elaborate social rituals, shot in deep focus and with sweeping camera movements, cannot be dismissed. In addition to the Harvard commencement, Cimino includes a rollicking dance sequence (on roller skates, no less) in the titular Heaven's Gate hall in Sweetwater. The scope of these scenes is stunning. Cinematographer Vilmos Zsigmond worked with Cimino on both *The Deer Hunter* and *Heaven's Gate*, and their collaboration demonstrates a fluid sense of movement, carefully wrought with intricate choreography. The detailed mise-en-scène and deep focus allow the viewer to be immersed in the sensory experience of these sequences, features of melodrama that translate "character into action . . . and action into gesture and dynamic space" (Elsaesser 78). What Cimino reveals in these sequences is that these social rituals assert a moral code of behavior, but that masculinity struggles to maintain this code as a victim of its own human weakness. Power and strength are at odds with emotion and vulnerability, but there remains an unflinching view of how masculinity struggles to express itself. While the social rituals may be highly legible in custom and tradition, these sequences show the arbitrariness of Manichean good and evil, however strong the desire for intimacy and moral legibility may be.

Christine Gledhill states,

> Melodrama's survival rests in the fact that its conflicts are not tied to a particular moral outcome or content . . . thus whether melodrama takes its categories from Victorian morality or modern psychology, its enactment of the continuing struggle of good and evil forces running through social, political and psychic life draws into a public arena desires, fears, values and identities which lie beneath the surface of the publicly acknowledged world. (32–3)

While other directors who made their mark during the New Hollywood period continued to work in the film industry, Cimino's career was indelibly derailed by *Heaven's Gate*. In reverting to a more clearly melodramatic form for *Heaven's Gate*, perhaps the director lost the ambiguity and complexity that made *Thunderbolt and Lightfoot* and *The Deer Hunter* so compelling. Should Cimino be remembered as a cinematic savant, capable of capturing exquisitely choreographed and emotionally draining spectacles, or should he be remembered as an inhumane perfectionist who single-handedly brought down the legendary United Artists? As the above suggests, Cimino's gift as a director is in his ability to offer audiences a glimpse of the inner workings of masculine intimacy and male friendship in a way that feels authentic, despite knowing that the truth has been embellished and deliberately overwrought.

WORKS CITED

Abramovitch, Seth. "The Deer Hunter, the Director and a Decade in Seclusion." *Hollywood Reporter*, 27 Feb 2015, pp. 134–6.

Bach, Steven. *Final Cut: Dreams and Disaster in the Making of Heaven's Gate.* Newmarket Press, 1985.

Berliner, Todd. *Hollywood Incoherent: Narration in Seventies Cinema.* University of Texas Press, 2010.

Biskind, Peter. "Implosion of a Reckless Auteur." *Hollywood Reporter*, 22 July 2016, pp. 24–6.

Brody, Richard. "On the Wild Side." *The New Yorker*, 3 July 2017, p. 12.

Brooks, Peter. *The Melodramatic Imagination: Balzac, Henry James, Melodrama and the Mode of Excess*. Yale University Press, 1976.

Canby, Vincent. "Shorter 'Heaven's Gate', With Voiceovers, Tries Again." *New York Times*, 24 Apr. 1971: C10.

Canby, Vincent. "'Heaven's Gate,' A Western by Cimino." *New York Times*, 19 Nov, 1980: C29.

Canby, Vincent. "Culling Gems." *New York Times*, 5 Apr. 1981: A15.

Dargis, Manohla. "The Second Coming of 'Heaven's Gate.'" *New York Times*, 17 Mar. 2013: AR10.

The Deer Hunter. Directed by Michael Cimino, Universal Studios, 1978.

Elsaesser, Thomas. "Tales of Sound and Fury: Observations on the Family Melodrama." *Imitations of Life: A Reader on Film and Television Melodrama*, edited by Marcia Landy, Wayne State University Press, 1991, pp. 68–91.

Gledhill, Christine. "The Melodramatic Field: An Investigation." *Home Is Where the Heart Is: Studies in Melodrama and the Woman's Film*, edited by Christine Gledhill, British Film Institute Publishing, 1987, pp. 5–39.

Greene, Naomi. "Coppola, Cimino: The Operatics of History." *Film Quarterly*, vol. 38, no. 2, Winter 1984/1985, pp. 28–37.

Griffin, Nancy. "Last Typhoon Cimino Is Back." *Observer*, 11 Feb. 2002, www.observer.com. Accessed 12 May 2020.

Harmetz, Aljean. "Behind the Fiasco of 'Heaven's Gate'." *New York Times*, 21 Nov. 1980: C8.

Heaven's Gate. Directed by Michael Cimino, United Artists, 1980.

Itzkoff, Dave. "Michael Cimino, Director of 'The Deer Hunter' and 'Heaven's Gate,' Dies at 77." *New York Times*, 2 July 2016.

Kael, Pauline. "*The Deer Hunter*: The God-Bless-America Symphony." *For Keeps: 30 Years at the Movies*, Plume, 1994, pp. 800–7.

Keathley, Christian. "Trapped in the Affection Image: Hollywood's Post-Traumatic Cycle (1970-1976)." *The Last Great American Picture Show*, edited by Thomas Elsaesser, Alexander Horwath, and Noel King, *Film Culture in Transition*, Amsterdam University Press, 2004, pp. 293–308.

Pollock, Dale. "'Heaven's Gate' Analyzed: Hollywood Searches Its Soul." *LA Times*. 30 Nov. 1980: R1, pp. 6-7.

Sharrett, Christopher. "Heaven's Gate." *Cineaste*, 9 Feb. 2013, pp. 58–9.

Thompson, Anne. "And Now, the Unkindest 'Cut' of All." *Film Comment*, Nov./Dec. 1985, pp. 48–50.

Thunderbolt and Lightfoot. Directed by Michael Cimino, MGM, 1974.

Vallan, Guilia D'Agnolo. "*Heaven's Gate*: Western Promises." *The Criterion Collection*, 20 Nov. 2012, www.criterion.com. Accessed 12 May 2020.

6. DE PALMA'S EMBATTLED RED PERIOD: HITCHCOCK, GENDER, GENRE, AND POSTMODERNISM

Linda Badley

Robert Kolker's dismissal in *A Cinema of Loneliness* (1988), repeated in subsequent editions, could not have been more unconditional or influential: Brian De Palma had "made a career of the most superficial imitations of the most superficial aspects of Hitchcock's style, worked through a misogyny and violence that manifest a contempt for the audience exploited by his films" (161). This is no wonder in view of Kolker's investment in modernism and condescension for what succeeded it. De Palma was the first of the "Movie Brats" to show flagrant signs of postmodernism, which Kolker has continued to view reductively as facile or cynical parody and/or nostalgia. While critics like Pauline Kael and David Denby defended De Palma's work through what is called his "Red Period" (from 1973 to 1984), dominated by Hitchcockian erotic thrillers, Kolker's has until recently remained the standard view.

This is remarkable especially in light of the New Hollywood auteurs' engagement with Hitchcock, genre revisionism and an aestheticized violence that has become a kind of group signature. Viewed from such a perspective, De Palma is no outlier but at the center of the movement, and two recent studies and a documentary film have contributed to a reclamation of his reputation. Chris Dumas recovers the Godardian whose political vision has been obscured by controversy, and David Greven explores De Palma's deconstruction of heteronormative homosocial masculinity. *De Palma*, a documentary by Noah Baumbach and Jake Paltrow, reintroduced De Palma as a charming, articulate narrator-raconteur and inspired at least four summer 2016 retrospectives at theatres in New York City, Toronto, Miami Beach, and Nashville.

As for the charge of misogyny, this chapter will venture that De Palma was the only New Hollywood figure to consistently foreground the gender politics inherent in the language of cinema – while targeting contemporaneous feminist hot-button issues with the instincts of a provocateur. A post-postmodern perspective reveals that his "Red Period" films were *about* misogyny among other things; flamboyantly analytical reworkings of the Hitchcock legacy, they exposed the technologies of the scopophilic regime and frequently spoke through female protagonists – doing so through controversial adaptations of stigmatized genres and character types.

THE DE PALMA HYSTERIA: 1980–84[1]

Kolker's write-off reflected the radical shift in reception in 1980 with the controversy surrounding *Dressed to Kill*. The films of the early 1970s, *Sisters* (1972) and *Carrie* (1976) in particular, had been welcomed as the marks of a major new talent, a technical virtuoso and satirist with a wicked sense of humor. But the rise and convergence of feminist film theory with radical feminism and anti-pornography movements (where radical feminists and the "moral majority" became uncomfortable bedfellows) created a very different cultural environment. When the June 1978 *Hustler* cover depicted the naked body of a woman being fed head-first into a meat grinder next to the caption "We will no longer hang up women like pieces of meat," thousands of feminists refused to get the joke. Several anti-pornography groups united in protest against images that eroticized the degradation of female bodies, adopting Robin Morgan's slogan "Pornography is the theory, and rape the practice" (139). Two years later they found *Dressed to Kill*'s "Joshing Jack-the-Ripper approach to women" (Denby 67) even less funny as the debate over pornography, violence, and censorship peaked. Promos had featured a *Vogue*-style stiletto-heeled leg and the caption, "What happens to Kate [Angie Dickinson] in the shower is the latest fashion . . . in murder." The allusion was to the film's opening shower sequence, which De Palma explained as "a woman's erotic fantasy" of being "attacked by a faceless stranger" (Bonavoglia 26). Women Against Pornography corrected him: "The idea that . . . [Kate] likes what's going on is a decidedly *male* fantasy." Or was it? Such essentialist assertions alienated many women while uniting them in their opposition, documented by Varda Burstyn's *Women Against Censorship* (1985), to having their sexual expression proscribed.

If the protests turned the film into a box-office sensation, *Dressed to Kill* confirmed De Palma's reputation as a superficial visual stylist whose self-defense – "I can give all the answers Hitchcock gave. Like, What is the content of a still life? *Nada!*" (Hirschberg 80) – did not improve matters. *Esquire's* Lynn Hirschberg described how De Palma "put his wife [Nancy Allen] in lingerie, sent a razor-wielding transvestite schizophrenic after her, and filmed the scene, knowing it would be shown to millions of people" (80). Reviewing *Blow Out* when it came out in 1981, Andrew Sarris found De Palma still dedicated to the "thesis" that "all women are hookers and bimbos, and deserve to be punished for their sinfulness and stupidity" (qtd. in Kapsis 210). The reaction was exacerbated by a backlash against horror films led that same year by Roger Ebert's denunciation of the post-*Psycho* "women in danger" movies with which De Palma's were often lumped. De Palma in turn proclaimed his next film would be "*Dressed to Kill II*": "I'm sick of being censored. . . . [I]f they want an X, they'll get a *real* X. . . . I've been thinking about this for years: BRIAN DE PALMA'S *BODY DOUBLE*!" (Hirschberg 83). Before its release, Susan Dworkin's "exclusive on-the-set profile" *Double De Palma* appeared, and *Body Double* (1984) dominated two Fall 1984 issues of *Film Comment*, but there were no marches, and the hype buried the film. De Palma had become a "bad object" for Hitchcock loyalists and feminists alike; his flamboyant sensibility, laced with "adolescent" humor, and affinity with exploitation genres vulgarized what remained implicit in the master. The political climate had changed, and he shifted to making "A"-list movies written by other people.

MULVEY'S HITCHCOCK = DE PALMA'S POSTMODERNISM

De Palma's back story illuminates much. A surgeon's son and science nerd who, like Peter Miller in *Dressed to Kill* (Keith Gordon), won science fair prizes and majored in physics at Columbia before undertaking graduate studies at Sarah Lawrence in theatre and film, he brought technical expertise and an analytical approach to filmmaking that merged with a radical left-wing political sensibility. Long before he became a confirmed Hitchcockian, he was prone to statements like, "My films are about the obscenity of the white middle class" and, "If I could be the American Godard that would be great" (Dumas 87). His "Godardian" films were ambitious, anarchic, sprawling political satires like *Greetings* (1968) and *Hi, Mom*! (1970), and he adapted the thriller perfected in Hitchcock's "testament" films *Rear Window* (1954), *Vertigo* (1958), and *Psycho* (1960) to provide a cinematic structure and "language" – a way of telling a story visually that exposed cinema's inherent subtexts. Bringing Godardian montage and Brechtian alienation effects to an already self-referential Hitchcock "genre," the voyeuristic thriller concerned with gender and power, his films updated Hitchcock by becoming provocatively metacinematic. Hence Robert Kapsis notes that to critics like Pauline Kael who were "practicing a nascent form of postmodern criticism" De Palma was "the prototype of the postmodern artist; out of the junk heap of our pop culture . . . he forged a rich, satirical, and highly reflexive art whose real subject was art itself" (200). It was also, however, about "the obscenity of the white middle class."

From this politicized, proto-postmodern perspective, De Palma's oeuvre ended up playing off and exposing the same processes that Laura Mulvey outlined in her epoch-making "Visual Pleasure and Narrative Cinema" (1975). With Freudian and Lacanian premises, Mulvey approached classical Hollywood cinema as a language in which male and female were signs subordinated to the psychic processes of identification and the "gaze." Quintessentially male, the gaze was limited to patriarchal heterosexist oppositions, and the female gaze was non-existent except as a kind of "transvestism" in which the female spectator shifted between male- and female-coded viewing positions (Mulvey, "Afterthoughts"). For her key supporting examples (of narcissistic identification, fetishistic scopophilia, and sadistic voyeurism), Mulvey looked to Hitchcock's *Rear Window* and *Vertigo*, regarded as the filmmaker's most confessional and self-reflexive works that unpacked their own psychic processes. They inspired many of her insights, as they had already (by 1970) inspired De Palma's – to the extent that *Body Double* according to Dumas is "a Ph.D. thesis on Hitchcock" (76).

To provide a "political weapon," Mulvey called for a kind of filmmaking "already undertaken by radical film makers" (Godard et al.) that would deconstruct the gaze, expose the apparatus, and alienate the audience "into dialectics and passionate detachment," destroying "the satisfaction, pleasure, and privilege" of the spectator while "highlight[ing] how film has depended on voyeuristic active-passive mechanisms" ("Visual" 68). De Palma's "Hitchcockian" films outdo Mulvey; they test and validate, but also dispute or extend both Hitchcock's and her arguments and much second-wave feminist film criticism to follow. His Red Period coincided with or anticipated many of the concerns of the work of Linda Williams, Barbara Creed, and Carol Clover as well, while *Dressed to Kill* and *Body Double* challenged radical and anti-porn feminist movements. Instead of abandoning the politics of De Palma's early satires as is often thought, these "guilty pleasures" incorporated politics into the film's form and focused on the key issue of the late 1970s and early 1980s, the relationship between gender, sexuality, and power.

But whilst Mulvey wanted to destroy visual pleasure (and cinema itself), flamboyant (and violent) visual pleasure was De Palma's métier. In this respect, his films represented one tendency in postmodern popular culture, ludic postmodernism, which celebrates the play of simulacra, intertexuality, and the subversion of distinctions between high and low art. Another strain, however, is what Hal Foster in 1983 called an "oppositional" (xi) or "resistance" postmodernism (xxii) which Teresa L. Ebert and others claimed for feminism (129–80). This "seeks to question rather than exploit cultural codes, to explore rather than conceal social and political affiliations" (Foster xxii). In De Palma's films, these two tendencies may work alternately or simultaneously and sometimes problematically. In any case, his Red Period is far more female-centered than most of the canonical New Hollywood films and has commonalities with various post-modern feminisms: a concern with gender as a function of cinematic language and relative to the nuances of film genre; an emphasis on social construction and performativity under patriarchal capitalism; and sex positivism.

BEFORE AND BEYOND THE MALE GAZE

More than five years before Mulvey's "Visual Pleasure" appeared, *Hi, Mom!* (1970) spun off *Rear Window* in a series of films within the film, as cynical, politicized wanna-be revolutionary Jon Rubin (Robert De Niro) makes reality-based porn, filming his unsuspecting neighbors. These cinematic experiments culminate in "Be Black, Baby!" a Situationist guerrilla troupe theatre production that removes the fourth wall, subjecting a group of white Village liberals to the "black experience" and reversing the white male gaze. The audience is painted with blackface, beaten and raped as the black characters (in whiteface) look on, revelling afterwards in the masochism of liberal guilt. Approaching Guy Debord's "Society of the Spectacle" from the perspective of race as well as a stance one might call proto-performativity, De Palma was thinking far ahead of Mulvey's white heterosexist male gaze.

His next feature funneled an equally political satire into the Hitchcockian voyeuristic thriller. *Sisters* opens with a racially and sexually charged film-within-the-film called *Peeping Toms* (an obvious reference to Michael Powell's *Peeping Tom* [1960]), a *Candid Camera*-esque television show in which a handsome, upwardly mobile black man, Phillip Woode (Lisle Wilson) is set up as a voyeur (Fig. 6.1). When a nubile French-Canadian "blind" girl, actress-model Danielle Breton (Margot Kidder), begins disrobing in the frame's center front, available simultaneously to the camera and to Phillip's gaze, he discreetly turns and leaves. The host proclaims him "chivalrous" and the players are awarded prizes – Danielle a cutlery set (an important plot point) and (a wincing) Phillip two tickets to the "African Room," a club decked out in a gorillas-in-the-jungle motif.

Sisters establishes a proto-postmodern, feminist motif that runs throughout De Palma: the film multiplies gazes, offering black and female perspectives while demonizing or undermining the white male look and refusing closure. Danielle (Mulvey's "fetish," whose function is to be looked at) is doubled by her (dead) conjoined twin Dominique (also Kidder), now her jealous and murderous alter ego, and also by Grace Collier (Jennifer Salt), a feminist activist journalist who witnesses Phillip's murder through the window and seeks justice. Reversing the terms of *Psycho, Rear Window,* and *Vertigo* to update and politicize Hitchcock, *Sisters* proposed an "oppositional" gaze of resistance against the repression of the black person's right to look, together with a progressive female gaze.

Figure 6.1   *Peeping Toms*: Margot Kidder posing as a voluptuous blind girl to entrap Lisle Wilson, *Candid-Camera* style, in *Sisters* (1973). Digital frame enlargement. Courtesy of American International Pictures.

The villain, Danielle's ex-husband and psychiatrist Emil (William Finley), a caricature of the mad scientist as the medicalizing gaze, Dominique satisfyingly dispatches with his scalpel – in a flashback we learn that he surgically separated the twins to possess Danielle, resulting in Dominique's death. The flashback, delivered to Grace under hypnosis, is conveyed through mock-sensational horror tropes including a surrealistic freak show sequence that refers not only to twins' exploitation but also to the male understanding of women's "grotesque" bodies as requiring institutionally sanctioned "correction." The film culminates in an elaborate (political) joke: the black male gaze is suppressed and the female investigator, who writes and speaks out against oppression, is silenced through hypnosis, made to parrot the line, "There is no body because there was no murder." The film ends on a darkly humorous note as a detective (Charles Durning), realizing that the missing black body is in Danielle's white foldout sofa, tracks it to a train stop in rural Quebec. Peering through binoculars from a telephone pole, he waits for it to be picked up by perpetrators who are, ironically, either insane (Danielle) or dead (Emil). If the film's revolutionary perspectives are posited only to be crushed, its ending, in which the key terms of a classical thriller – the perpetrator, the body, and the white male protagonist – are all missing, serves up a savage postmodern irony.

In *Sisters* and each of his subsequent films, and in contrast to Mulvey's Hitchcock, whose protagonists – Jeffries, Scotty, Sam, and Dr. Richmond – represent patriarchy and the law, the male subject position is either defeated, missing, eradicated, or, as in *Obsession* (1976), exposed as an uncomfortable space from which to gaze. Set in Florence and New Orleans and replete with Madonnas, restorations, and pedestals, *Obsession,* written with Paul Schrader and scored by Hitchcock composer Bernard Herrmann seemed like an uncharacteristically "tasteful" and humorless homage to *Vertigo* by way of Dante's *La Vita Nuovo.* But the narrative is reinforced by a melancholy score and soft-focus sequences all the better to "out" the psychic/cinematic process that Mulvey called fetishistic scopophilia (the substitution of a fetish for a real woman), exposing it as necrophiliac, pedophilic, and incestuous, while pointing out its heritage in patriarchal capitalism, the idealized nuclear family, Roman Catholicism, and courtly love. Dante fell in love with Beatrice when she was eight years old and idolized her after her early death; the revered object of *Obsession* is similarly represented at a beatifying, memorializing distance. When his wife (a virginally lovely Geneviève Bujold) and daughter are kidnapped and murdered (in a plot engineered by his business partner), Cliff Robertson as New Orleans real-estate mogul Michael Courtland (nick-named "Court," a triple reference to courtly love, property, and law) devotes a swath of prime land to a massive funeral monument shaped like the basilica Miniato al Monte. Fifteen years later he spots his wife's seemingly miraculous double, Sandra Portinari (also Bujold, named for Dante's Beatrice) elevated on a scaffold, where she is restoring a Madonna. In the original version of the film's conclusion, after he marries and sleeps with Sandra she reveals that she is Court's daughter (who was brainwashed into seducing and framing him, somewhat like *Vertigo*'s Judy). The film ends as she cries out "Daddy!! Daddy!!" and in a perverse blend of ecstasy and horror they embrace and achieve what might be called the incestuous sublime (Fig. 6.2). Had it included De Palma's usual humor it would have ended in a cackle.

Blow Out is similarly about the failure of the male gaze to uncover the truth and save the girl. In a reversal of Hitchcock's predominantly visual

Figure 6.2   Courtly love or incestuous sublime?: Geneviève Bujold and Cliff Robertson embrace in *Obsession* (1976). Digital frame enlargement. Courtesy of Columbia Pictures

artistry and Antonioni's *Blow-Up* (1966), the film privileges the aural voyeurism inherent in the role of movie sound recordist Jack Terry (John Travolta), who tapes a murder disguised by an automobile accident. Like Coppola's *The Conversation* (1974), it is about American politics, conspiracies, and suppressed voices, referencing Watergate, Chappaquiddick, the Bicentennial, and the political assassinations of the 1960s. Like De Palma's other films, it is also about the deadliness and moral culpability of voyeurism, and ends in a pointed reference to snuff cinema when the death scream of the heroine (Nancy Allen, the witness to a political assassination whom Jack fatally endangers, wiring her and using her as bait) is buried in the soundtrack for a sleazy slasher flick.

Shower Scenes, Split Screens, and Spectatorial Performativity

In her landmark essay of 1984, "When the Woman Looks," Linda Williams excoriated *Dressed to Kill* as a "male fantasy in drag" whose "attention given to the expression of women's desires, [was] directly proportional to the violence perpetrated against women" (34). In 2000, in "Discipline and Fun: *Psycho* and Postmodern Cinema," with second-wave feminism behind her, she returned to the issue from the perspective of distribution, reception, and performativity. "Disciplining" audiences by refusing late entrances, Hitchcock's roller coaster ride of suspense and successive shocks elicited what Williams calls "spectatorial performances" of gendered terror. Hence, "a film that is itself about the performance of masculinity and femininity," *Psycho* "represent[ed] a new level of gender play and destabilization that [she] took to be a founding moment of the greater awareness of the performativity of gender roles increasingly ushered in by a postmodern, 'post-classical' reception of cinema" (195). In contrast, her critique of *Dressed to Kill*, limited by second-wave psychoanalytic theory, had completely missed out on De Palma's address to audiences presumed to be educated in spectatorial performativity. If his Red Period preceded Judith Butler's "Performative Acts and Gender Constitution" (1988) and *Gender Trouble* (1990) by more than a decade, his Godardian and techno-cinephilic proclivities had already resulted in an approach to the pressing 1970s issues of the gaze, identity, and gender in terms of their potential for performative play with the cinematic apparatus, genres, and roles.

Hence, beginning with *Carrie*, four of these films either opened or closed with a set up – a prologue, epilogue, or cheesy film-within-the-film – that winkingly re-enacted *Psycho*'s shower scene as a fantasy. Like *Sisters*' "Peeping Toms," each is an elaborately staged performance that propels the film's narrative while taking on very different meanings from the original. For instance, *Dressed to Kill*'s notorious opening draws out the *Psycho* quote to an absurd length, staging it as soft-core pornography (with an obvious body double, Dickinson seductively front and center before the camera, pouting, stroking herself) until, interrupted by choreographed violence, the whole is revealed as Kate's fantasy and a self-reflexive joke.

In *Carrie*, adapted from Stephen King's first novel (1974), the (almost) opening shot is the ultimate steamy adolescent male fantasy as the camera penetrates the fortress of the girls' high school locker room, gliding in slow motion before closing on Carrie (Sissy Spacek) showering. The close-up resembles an autoerotic soap commercial complete with a phallic shower head, until the shock of Carrie's period, with its connotations of castration, abruptly cuts off the visual pleasure. The bleeding woman survives, and blood becomes associated with female rage and power. From then on, as the film meshes the Hitchcockian thriller with horror, the high school film, and woman's melodrama, women rule. The telepathy of the novel's heroine is represented viscerally and indicated clumsily in the text by the word "FLEX"; in the film her powers are a bravado reconfiguration of the gaze. In her climactic revenge scene at the prom, having spent her (oppressed) life looking down, Carrie stands erect, her eyes wide and blazing, sweeping the crowd below her. At first beyond her control, her look has become a conscious act, a demonstration of the meaning of the gaze as total domination. In the novel she avenges her mother's treachery by inducing a heart attack; in De Palma's grand finale she turns a series of kitchen implements (women's tools) into phallic projectiles.

De Palma's trademark split screen, enhanced by contrasting primary colors, intensifies affect and accentuates the sense in which Carrie's gaze is performed by showing it and the devastation it causes simultaneously (Fig. 6.3). Yet in multiplying perspectives, it is also an alienation effect; it ruptures the illusion

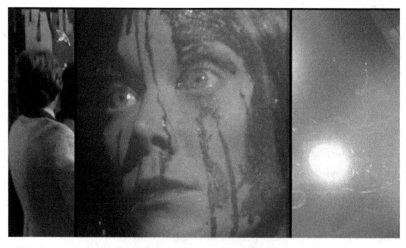

Figure 6.3   Split screen: The female gaze is unleashed by Sissy Spacek at the prom in *Carrie* (1976). Digital frame enlargement. Courtesy of Red Bank Films.

that the frame is a seamless vision of reality, undermining any sense of a universal or monolithic gaze. Hence in *Sisters*, it depicts two actions simultaneously, building suspense, with Danielle primping in the bathroom mirror as Grace confronts the police. More importantly, it underscores characterization and theme; contrasting the narcissistic woman with the woman who uses the investigative gaze to seek justice; it literalizes the motif of dual identities.

SPECTACLE, DEPTHLESSNESS AND "WANING OF AFFECT"

"Film lies all the time, 24 times a second," De Palma is fond of saying, and by 1980 his films were reveling in their unreality. Telling stories cinematically while repeating sequences and motifs from his previous films, he turned the psychological thriller into what Tom Gunning has deemed a "cinema of attractions" prioritizing spectacle and affect over narrative. Inflected by the giallo's propensity for surrealistic incoherence, De Palma's films confuse reality with fantasy to lead inevitably to the point that cinema is the superior dream – or nightmare. Further, *Dressed to Kill* and *Body Double* exhibit what Fredric Jameson called a "waning of affect" or emotional and psychological "depthlessness." This was a "liberation from every other kind of feeling as well, since there is no longer a self present to do the feeling." Such feelings as exist are "free-floating, impersonal, and tend to be dominated by a peculiar kind of euphoria" (15–16) induced by a mass-mediated consumer society and the shift from the modernist understanding of the "deep" psyche to the simulacrum in which distinctions between fantasy and reality collapse. Together with postmodern "schizophrenia," depthlessness helps explain De Palma's fixation on aesthetics and what Thomas Leitch calls his "sovereign disdain for characters" (268) who became increasingly cartoonish and intertextual.

In one of his favorite tropes, De Palma updated and "flattened" Hitchcock's pop-Freudian psychology into a literalization of Dissociative Identity Disorder in which the self is revealed through performance and gender play. Within a dreamlike mise-en-scène that externalizes the "deep" psyche, the self splits cinematically into different characters, and the performative nature of identity becomes visible. After their surgical separation, Danielle and Dominique are literalized into a "split" personality, and the biological origin of their condition is effaced by an emphasis on their institutional construction. In *Dressed to Kill*, De Palma multiplies the identity confusion that *Psycho* centers on Mrs. Bates by making the psycho the psychiatrist Dr. Elliott (Michael Caine) and casting Susanna Clemm as his trans alter-ego Bobbi as well as the policewoman who tracks both Bobbi and Liz – creating a bewildering surplus of tall blondes with big hair (Fig. 6.4). The film's succession of shocking revelations, accentuated by doubling and dressing up, becomes ludic as gender turns into play with wigs, costumes, and mistaken identities; it engages audience with the

Figure 6.4   Blonde confusion: Nancy Allen confronted with Susanna Clemm in *Dressed to Kill* (1980). Digital frame enlargement. Courtesy of Filmways Pictures.

danger, fun, and fluidity of gender as performance. (De Palma's magnum opus in this regard would be the neo-Red Period *Raising Cain* [1992], in which John Lithgow plays five different roles.)

De Palma's tour-de-force in depthlessness is *Body Double*, on one level a self-parodic dirty joke in retaliation against the protest against *Dressed to Kill*. Set in Hollywood, the first half is a pastiche of motifs from *Rear Window* and *Vertigo* in which the characters are nearly all actors performing Hitchcockian or other film references. A claustrophobic, cuckolded, out-of-work actor Jake Scully (Craig Wasson) is duped by a "friend" (Gregg Henry) into witnessing his wife Gloria's (Deborah Shelton) murder, setting him up in a voyeur's paradise, a ridiculously phallic edifice on a tower overlooking the city, providing him with a telescope, and paying a porn actress, Holly Body (Melanie Griffith) to put on a window show of undulating autoeroticism. Sharing his complicity we watch Jake perform the act of watching through a series of zooms, reaction shots, and cross cuts, his face a clownish mask of desire, guilt, and shame. After tracking Gloria in time to observe her death, staged by Henry disguised as a grotesquely costumed "Indian" wielding an outsized power drill, Jake consoles himself by watching adult movies, recognizes Gloria's double in "Holly Does Hollywood," and sets off to find her on a nocturnal journey into the porn world, where "acting" and "watching," the film's primary metaphors, are literalized in gender/sexual performativity. In contrast to *Vertigo*, where Judy is punished for her performance, the porn industry "saves" Jake by giving him a role, and Holly becomes the film's unlikely heroine.

CAPITALISM AND POSTMODERN FEMINISM

In a *Film Comment* interview, De Palma commented on how in Hollywood where "you have to use tremendous sums of money to do what you want to do, you're dealing with a huge capitalistic structure. And capitalism exploits. You become corrupted" (Smith 31). *Body Double* is especially telling in relation to De Palma's satire, often mentioned in regard to *Scarface* (1983), on capitalism and consumerism. Hollywood, presented as a culture of acquisition and exploitation equated with the postmodern scene, is a glittering pleasure-drome enhanced by the sensual gliding and circling of De Palma's first-person camera, a media-saturated environment in which everyone is a voyeur and an exhibitionist. Jake tracks Gloria through the Rodeo Collection mall, a dazzling maze of brick, marble, and glass surface; in the complementary world of porn, he tracks Holly – after auditioning for a porn movie that explodes into a campy rock video with the refrain, "Relax. . . . Relax. . . . When ya wanna cum" – (Fig. 6.5) by acting his way through a maze of films within the film. Both realms exude the curious euphoria of consumption and information overload.

Despite his "inveterately dark sense of humor" and "determination to push the envelope of censorship," De Palma has "a surprising sympathy for the problems of women," as Leitch observes (268); yet, as the critics complained, his female characters were (increasingly) either victims or prostitutes. Like the gangsters in *Scarface*, however, they should be understood within a postmodern and satirical critique of capitalism; they portray women dying or surviving within a sexual economy in which they will be subjugated as long as late capitalism continues. The prostitutes and porn stars function as a shorthand for the extent to which women's roles are constructed and performed within this environment. Converted into commodities, they utilize and relish their power as images to manipulate the gaze.

Figure 6.5 Film within the film: Greg Wasson auditions for a porn movie with Melanie Griffin in *Body Double* (1984). Digital frame enlargement. Courtesy of Columbia Pictures.

Dressed to Kill's Liz works as a Park Avenue call girl in order to play the stock market and invest in art. Kate Miller's young, unneurotic opposite, she becomes the film's survivor along with Kate's geeky-brilliant adolescent son Peter. Where Kate is driven by sexual frustration, Liz is a savvy, no-nonsense sex worker whose "real" sexuality is never visible (she wears shapeless pajamas at home). For Liz, sexuality, like her role as an amateur detective, is a performance in the scene in which she strips to arouse Dr. Elliott in order to access his records. Interested in sex as a means of achieving her goals, or intellectually, as in her technical discussion of sex-change surgery with Peter, she is in this respect like Peter, whose sexuality is ambiguous or nonexistent.

Despite or because of her titular circumscription, *Body Double*'s Holly becomes the film's single character to transcend her role, achieving a limited authenticity with powerful affect. Holly is "intelligent," Griffith told Dworkin, "a woman who has made a choice." She is "flamboyant about what she does because she does it well. . . . She doesn't want anybody to fuck her over. . . . She's not a whore. She's a businesswoman" (92). A butch-cut platinum blonde in studs and black leather, Griffith is as vulgar, lively, and outspoken as her double, the rich, sleek, dark-haired Shelton, is stylized, passive, and silent. In the scene in which she tells Jake (posing as a producer) what kinds of sex she will and will not perform, she is funny and self-possessed as are no other characters in the film. The narrative ends when Holly, shoved into a freshly dug grave by Gloria's murderer, pops out and yells: "Don't touch me! Corpse fucker! I've seen your type on those horror movies on late night TV, you're a necrophiliac! Yechhhh! Unconscious is good but dead is better, right? Well. . . . I'm not dead yet." When she steps out of the narrative and into the closing film-within-the film – a shower scene whose actress is replaced by a gum-snapping body double who admonishes, "Be careful. My breasts are very tender. I got my period" – Holly has the last line and the last gaze. Watching the body double perform, she whispers her appraisal to the actress: "I'll bet you get a lot of dates after this one." In this appropriation of the male gaze by the female who is simultaneously object and subject of the gaze, Holly stands for the contradictions inherent in the social construction and performativity of the female viewer. In contrast to their richer, sleeker doubles, Liz and Holly are survivors within a world circumscribed by capitalism, consumerism, and the simulacrum. To say, like Sarris, that they are punished for their sin and stupidity misses the point. In the one exception, *Blow Out,* which ends spectacularly and tragically when she is assassinated to cover up a political conspiracy, the feisty call girl becomes the film's martyr (Fig. 6.6).

Figure 6.6   John Travolta is devastated by the assassination of Nancy Allen in *Blow Out* (1981). Digital frame enlargement. Courtesy of Filmways Pictures.

CONCLUSION

The idiosyncratic, nascent postmodernism of Brian De Palma's Red Period was poorly understood during the volatile era in which both the Hollywood Renaissance and second-wave feminism were born. From a perspective that includes postmodern, third-wave, and "post" feminism, De Palma's critique of gender under a capitalist sexual economy in an increasingly mediated and visual culture becomes visible. Two recent neo-noirs, *Femme Fatale* (2002) and *Passion* (2012) pick up where the earlier critique left off. They focus on alliances among twenty-first century femme fatales within a postfeminist capitalist environment where women are commodities and/or predators in a corruption of feminism's quest to shatter the class ceiling. In *Femme Fatale*'s re-envisioning of the noir narrative, female bonds transcend violence and mercenary norms; in *Passion* they provoke the lethal weaponry of corporate "frenemies" constructed within our current audiovisual culture. None of this means that Brian De Palma is a feminist; his real target is the international capitalist environment in which he is trapped, like the rest of us, except in our dreams.

NOTE

1. "The De Palma Hysteria" and the discussion of *Body Double* draw briefly on Chapter 4 of my book, *Film, Horror, and the Body Fantastic* (Greenwood, 1995).

WORKS CITED

Bonavoglia, Angela. "Protesting Chic Porn." *Ms.*, vol. 9, no. 6, Dec. 1980, p. 26.
Burstyn, Varda, ed. *Women Against Censorship*. Vancouver: Douglas & McIntyre, 1985.

Denby, David. "The Woman in the Window." *New York*, 5 Nov. 1984, pp. 67–9.

Dumas, Chris. *Un-American Psycho: Brian De Palma and the Political Invisible*. Intellect Books, 2012.

Dworkin, Susan. *Double De Palma: A Film Study with Brian De Palma*. Newmarket, 1984.

Ebert, Roger. "Why Movie Audiences Aren't Safe Anymore." *American Film*, vol. 6, no. 5, March 1981, pp. 54–6.

Ebert, Teresa. *Ludic Feminism and After*. University of Michigan Press, 1996.

Foster, Hal. "Postmodernism: A Preface." *The Anti-Aesthetic*. Bay Press, 1983, pp. ix–xvi.

Greven, David. *Psycho-Sexual: Male Desire in Hitchcock, De Palma, Scorsese, and Friedkin*. University of Texas Press, 2013.

Gunning, Tom. "The Cinema of Attraction[s]: Early Film, Its Spectator, and the Avant-Garde." *Cinema: Space Frame Narrative*, edited by Tomas Elsaesser, BFI, 1990, pp. 56–62.

Hirschberg, Lynn. "Brian De Palma's Death Wish." *Esquire*, vol. 101, no. 1, Jan. 1984, pp. 79–83.

Kapsis, Robert. *Hitchcock: The Making of a Reputation*. University of Chicago Press, 1990.

King, Stephen. *Carrie*. Doubleday, 1974.

Kolker, Robert. *A Cinema of Loneliness*. Oxford University Press, 1980.

Jameson, Fredric. *Postmodernism, or, the Cultural Logic of Late Capitalism*. Duke University Press, 1991.

Leitch, Thomas M. "How to Steal from Hitchcock." *After Hitchcock: Influence, Imitation, Intertexuality*, edited by David Boyd and R. Barton Palmer, University of Texas Press, 2006, pp. 251–70.

Morgan, Robin. "Theory and Practice: Pornography and Rape." *Take Back the Night: Woman on Pornography*, edited by Laura Lederer, Morrow, 1980.

Mulvey, Laura. "Afterthoughts on 'Visual Pleasure and Narrative Cinema'." *Feminist Film Theory*, edited by Sue Thornham, New York University Press, 1999, pp. 122–31.

Mulvey, Laura. "Visual Pleasure and Narrative Cinema." *Feminist Film Theory*, edited by Sue Thornham, New York University Press, 1999, pp. 58–69.

Sarris, Andrew. "*Blow Out*." *Village Voice*, 29 July–4 August 1981.

Smith, Gavin. "Dream Project." *Film Comment* Nov./Dec. 2002, pp. 28–31.

Williams, Linda. "Discipline and Fun: *Psycho* and Postmodern Cinema." *Alfred Hitchcock's Psycho: A Casebook*, edited by Robert Kolker. Oxford: Oxford University Press, 2004. pp. 165–201.

Williams, Linda. "When the Woman Looks." 1984. *The Dread of Difference: Gender and the Horror Film*, edited by Barry Keith Grant, 2nd edn, University of Texas Press, 2015, pp. 17–36.

7. ESCAPE FROM ESCAPISM: BOB FOSSE AND THE HOLLYWOOD RENAISSANCE

Dennis Bingham

Amid the widely acknowledged youth boom of the New Hollywood, a trio of men in their forties broke through as film directors. Robert Altman (1925–2006) labored throughout the 1950s and 1960s directing television episodes; Hal Ashby (1929–88) worked his way up as a film editor; and Bob Fosse (1927–87) was immersed in dance, vaudeville, and musical theatre, but above all a devotion to cinema.

Fosse was an electrifying dancer in his youth, as evidenced by his few film appearances as an MGM contract player. But MGM only wanted to turn him into "the next Gene Kelly," as can be seen in one of his movies, *Give a Girl a Break* (1953). The studio system was crumbling, and there would be no "next Gene Kelly." Fosse broke his contract after a year. His career breakthrough occurred on Broadway, courtesy of Hollywood. Producer-director George Abbott saw *Kiss Me Kate* (1953), which included a spectacular extra-narrative 45-second dance at the end of the film that Fosse was permitted to choreograph and perform. Abbott hired Fosse to choreograph his latest musical, *The Pajama Game*. The sensational "Steam Heat" number introduced the Fosse style, derby hats, movements down and in rather than up and out, as well as finger snaps and jazz hands. Choreography on Abbott's *Damn Yankees* teamed him with Gwen Verdon, the play's star, and eventually his third wife, muse, and professional partner.

Broadway was his lifeblood for the next dozen years. His choreography for the back-to-back film versions of *Pajama Game* (1957) and *Damn Yankees* (1958), would be his only forays to Hollywood during this period. By 1969, when the forty-one-year-old Fosse directed his first film, the adaptation of his 1966 show, *Sweet Charity*, he owned five Tony Awards for Best Choreography and had been nominated three times for Best Director. The film's star, Shirley MacLaine, started as a dancer in *Pajama Game* and pushed Universal, which bought the film rights, to hire him to direct.

Charity got lost in the musical roadshow glut of the late 1960s. After its failure, Fosse turned down offers to direct Broadway shows. He resolved that he was a film director, and vowed not to go back to the stage until he proved it. *Cabaret* (1972) overturned nearly all the conventions that had doomed the film musical in the 1960s. It introduced a realistic style to a genre which, previously, could not get past its family-friendly frivolity. *Cabaret* proved that Bob Fosse was a film director.

About Bob Fosse as New Hollywood auteur, however, much remains to be proved. In his own time, however, recognition of his vision and creativity as a film artist were widespread. Fosse is the only person to win – or even be nominated for--an Academy Award (for *Cabaret*), a Tony (*Pippin*), and an Emmy (*Liza with a Z*) – all in the same season, and all as Best Director. Fosse's dazzling "triple crown" of 1972–73 may blind film scholars to the importance of what he accomplished in *Cabaret*. For most of its history, the film musical, a genre born with the sound film, had married popular music, dance, and romantic comedy to striking mise-en-scène and camera movement. In *Cabaret* Fosse reinvented the musical as a conceptual montage form; the film's visual and sound juxtapositions brought Fosse closer to Sergei Eisenstein's concepts of conflict in editing than to Vincente Minnelli's lush mise-en-scène-based approach to musicals. Each Fosse film is more defined by editing than the last. In 2012, when the Motion Picture Editors Guild asked its members to vote for the 75 best-edited films of all time, "considered in terms of picture and sound editorial as opposed to just the former," *All That Jazz* (1979) ranked fourth,[1] and *Cabaret* thirtieth.

Overall, however, Fosse is rarely recognized as part of the Hollywood Renaissance. His film directing is seldom acknowledged as being on the same level as his contributions to dance and the Broadway musical. Two of his films are musicals, two are biopics, and one, *All That Jazz*, is both, a musical film à clef. "Musicals have the auteur strike against them going out of the gate," writes Nick Barrios. "The directors who really took off in musicals," such as Fosse, "do not always earn the respect of the serious-minded, never mind that they usually should" (9).

There is the ongoing debate over what constitutes the Hollywood Renaissance auteur. Like most of the widely acknowledged New Hollywood directors, Fosse made revisionist genre movies, and was intoxicated with cinephilia, especially postwar European art cinema. The cinematographers on his last two films, *All That Jazz* and *Star 80* (1983), were Guiseppe Rotunno and Sven Nykvist, veterans of films by Federico Fellini and Ingmar Bergman, respectively. Fosse directed only five movies, but an output consisting of a handful of films does not keep Sergei Eisenstein, Jean Vigo, Jacques Tati, or Sergio Leone from casting a giant shadow, and should not obscure Fosse's contributions to cinema either.

SWEET CHARITY

Sweet Charity tries to be several contradictory things: a touching adult story, and an avant-garde but expensive family musical. One sees an inventive direc- tor tangled in his own web of conventions. As a stage show, *Sweet Charity*, which Fosse conceived for Verdon, was the first musical comedy based on a European art film, Fellini's *Le notti di Cabiria* (*Nights of Cabiria*) (1957). Played by Giulietta Masina, Fellini's wife and muse, Cabiria is more a female version of Chaplin's Little Tramp than a realistic prostitute. Cabiria walks the streets, but never seems to meet a john. Fosse's interest in the sleazy underbelly of showbiz feeds *Sweet Charity*, as it would compose fundamentally the sub- jects of all his later shows and films. His research took him to the seedy dance halls of Times Square where he saw "dance hostesses available in every flavor, some sixteen, some forty-two, . . . none with talent" (Wasson 197).

While the ambiguity and formal discontinuity of art cinema fascinated Fosse, he chose a work that would not essentially disrupt the whimsy and escapism of musical comedy. Thus Charity drifts aloof from the other hardened dance hall girls – she's absent from the "Hey, Big Spender" number in which the taxi dancers offer themselves up for the dispiriting prospect of making a living.

Figure 7.1   Fosse dance moves: down and in. Suzanne Charney and "The Aloof" dancers in "Rich Man's Frug" in *Sweet Charity* (1969). Fosse may not have realized it yet, but his eventual preference in film musicals would be for numbers performed on a stage. Ostensibly a five-and-a-half-minute series of POV shots, in its widescreen glory, its deadpan wit, and its application of the "Fred Astaire rule", the sequence is cinematic in spite of itself. Digital frame enlargement. Courtesy of Universal Pictures.

The movie's Charity Hope Valentine (MacLaine), like Cabiria, tags along behind a glamorous male movie star (Ricardo Montalban) who treats her like one of his fans. She follows a religious procession ("The Rhythm of Life," sung by Sammy Davis Jr., in a prime example of the "guest star" appearance in the late musical roadshow cycle). Charity falls in love with a dubious Mr. Right (John McMartin), a neurotic type from the pen of the prolific Neil Simon, who was brought in to "save" a book drafted by Bert Louis (as in *Robert Louis* Fosse) and a young (uncredited) writer, Martin Charnin. The failure of *Sweet Charity* on film can be attributed to a number of decisions that track back to the Broadway original. There the combination of Fosse's razzle-dazzle and the charm and electric talent of Verdon, covered over a narrative that was episodic and, away from Fellini's magic (neo-) realism, rather aimless.

This is where the star performance in the film of *Sweet Charity* takes on a sense of ventriloquism. Hollywood continually gave Shirley MacLaine in her peak star years roles as prostitutes (*Irma La Douce* [1963], *Two Mules for Sister Sara* [1970]) and waifish victims (*Some Came Running* [1958], *The Apartment* [1960]). Charity Hope Valentine would seem in her wheelhouse. However, the character was conceived for and developed by Verdon, perhaps the greatest female dancing and comedy actress of Broadway in its Golden Age. If Verdon were having her career now, she probably would be in demand for voice work; if Pixar needed to find, say, Dory's sister, Verdon's vocals, expressively warm and scrunchy, might fill the gills. As heard on *Sweet Charity*'s original cast album, Verdon makes a line like "Wow. This place sure is crawling with celebrities. I'm the only person in here I never heard of," funny and adorable. Spoken on film by a world-famous movie star, however, the line is jarring, pulling the film out of itself for a moment. In Fosse's film, the handsome movie star in New York takes Charity to a Romanesque night club where precision Fosse dancers perform a "radical chic" conception of "groovy" dance moves. With lead dancer Suzanne Charney and a pre-stardom Ben Vereen in the dance platoon, the number gives American cinema its first look since the mid-1950s at full-out Fosse choreography, and in 2.35: 1 Panavision yet. The "Rich Man's Frug" serves the generic purpose of spectacle for this 1960s roadshow. The number detaches from the narrative and its protagonist, however, for five-and-a-half minutes. This is typical of the way the film's highlights, some of the most impressive in musicals, also point out its problems, particularly its point of view. Are we in Charity's mind, or observing her from a distance?

With cinematographer Robert Surtees, a versatile artist who was capable of shooting *The Graduate* and *Doctor Dolittle* in the same year (both 1967), *Charity* shows none of the dull, pale gloss of Universal movies in the sixties, an achievement in itself. The staging and cutting of MacLaine's "If My Friends Could See Me Now," with jump cuts matched to dance moves, mark the first opportunity to see Fosse at play with the affinities of dance and film editing.

He explores these with far more success in *Cabaret*, *Lenny* (1974), and *All That Jazz*.

CABARET

Cabaret is a disciplined film, hard as agate and black as onyx, with a tight narrative line punctuated by songs that parallel and comment upon the action. All the numbers, with one highly justified exception, are performed on the dinky, grimy stage of the fictional Kit Kat Klub in Berlin. *Cabaret* subverts its genre as thoroughly as *McCabe and Mrs. Miller* (1971) unravels the western or *Chinatown* undoes the film noir. Perhaps because it stands as a star-making vehicle for Judy Garland's daughter – its one bow to genre tradition – *Cabaret* has never been accorded its due as a Hollywood Renaissance musical. Fosse took the show, with its score by John Kander and Fred Ebb, and shook it until almost nothing was left of the film musical conventions observed since the genre began. Without the look of repugnant razzle-dazzle he designed with British cinematographer Geoffrey Unsworth and West German production designer Rolf Zehetbauer, and a firm refusal of the candy-box Freed Unit luster that producer Cy Feuer is said to have favored, *Cabaret* might well be one more item in the dustbin of film musicals, rather than a film that needs to be understood in the context of the Hollywood Renaissance.[2]

Figure 7.2   The antics of the Emcee (Joel Grey) are probably best taken only in small doses from odd angles. In *Cabaret* (1972) Fosse manages, among other feats, to become a montage documentarian. He captures glimpses – snapshots – of the Nazification of the Berlin cabaret, from the point of view of an outsider, probably Brian's (Michael York). They add up over the course of the film. Digital frame enlargement. Courtesy of Allied Artists.

Some decisions, such as the elimination of most of the plot from playwright Joe Masteroff's and director Harold Prince's 1966 Broadway musical, and the retrieval of alternative stories from the original sources, *Goodbye to Berlin* (1939) by Christopher Isherwood and *I Am a Camera* by John Van Druten (1951), were made before a director was hired. Jay Presson Allen wrote a first draft script that scuttled the show's secondary plot concerning Frau Schneider and her aborted romance with a Jewish fruit vendor, and opted for a youth-film emphasis, with Liza Minnelli attached. Sally Bowles, based upon a nineteen-year-old runaway English heiress named Jean Ross whom Isherwood met in Berlin, would be American for the first and, to date, only time in a major production of *Cabaret*. "Christopher," Isherwood's avatar, was renamed Brian Roberts (Michael York) and once again became an Englishman (in the show he is a writer from Harrisburg, Pennsylvania).

In their first scene together Sally tells Brian, "I do think one ought to go to the man's room if one can. I mean it doesn't look so much as if one expected it. Does it?" Far from the affected Sally of most of the other versions, Minnelli's Sally speaks with a confidence associated with masculinity, coming down on the ends of sentences, rather than going up tentatively. Kander and Ebb's new song, "Mein Herr," is in the "Ramblin' Man," "Don't Fence Me In" genre of song traditionally sung by a male singer.

The fragmentation and vamping of the end of the song's introduction is matched by Fosse's editorial cubism, the dancers' bodies draped backwards over chairs, a physical movement on each cut. The severe, mechanical movements of the expressionless dancers – starkly different from the smiling hyperkineticism of conventional show biz numbers – makes the cramped square stage evoke the chokehold Germany feels from the Nazis, taking it in as entertainment. *Cabaret* is not organic; the songs don't grow out of the story, or do they? It might be more accurate to say that the story grows out of the songs. Kander and Ebb's score creates incisively the plot and characters. For example, after meeting Max von Heune (Helmut Griem), the multimillionaire, there is a sudden close-up of Sally and an eyeline match to Max's Rolls Royce. Cut again to Sally, backstage applying makeup and intoning "Money," then to the Master of Ceremonies (Joel Grey) onstage in close-up repeating "Money," and then, in a jump cut, to their comic cabaret duet, "Money Makes the World Go 'Round." This is a modernist show musical. The plot could move forward without the number, but the song instantly burlesques Sally's attraction to Max as the shallowest materialism. The film's only mature love may be that which transpires between Max and Brian, with Sally in the *Suddenly Last Summer* role of the woman who brings closeted gay men together. Fosse wrote in notes on the script, however, that Max, the film's representative of the decadent German aristocracy that profits from the country's social, moral, and political collapse,[3] "dumps them" because "he's already gotten what he wants" (*Cabaret*, Box 16B).

There are no establishing shots showing the Klub from the outside. The Emcee's opening spiel contrasts "inside" with "outside," as if the outer edifice of the cabaret were Germany itself. The Emcee, in Fosse's conception, is a burlesque Mephistopheles, delivering his audience to the Nazis while inviting them to forget their troubles, a devilish reconception of songs like "Get Happy," that Garland sang in her films. In the way that other film genres examined their assumptions amid the Hollywood Renaissance, so *Cabaret* can be considered an anti-musical, systematically demolishing the genre's nostalgia for the past by inducing the spectator to imagine the future for its characters. For instance, the marriage of Fritz and the Jewish heiress Natalia, which can take place once he confesses to her that he has been a Jew trying to pass for Gentile, is chillingly poignant here, since we know what horrors this couple will face together.

The cabaret debases women and reduces human values to brutalism. Early in the film, the cabaret manager ejects a Nazi leafleteer, while on the stage the Emcee sprays water onto female mud wrestlers. As the audience howls, the Emcee smears a Hitler moustache in mud onto his upper lip and thrusts out his right arm. The manager smiles weakly, nervously loosening his collar. The triumph of the Nazis foretold by these gestures soon plays out. Sally stands underneath an elevated train, instructing Brian on how to release tension by screaming just as the train passes. On Sally's cue, "Now!," Fosse cuts to the beating of the manager by Nazi thugs, intercut onstage with the Emcee and five female dancers clad in traditional lederhosen performing a "slap dance," seeming to match the two events. Much later, the killing of Natalia Landauer's little dog by a Nazi mob chanting, "*Juden*" is parallel-edited with dancers doing a "Tiller-style" precision dance.[4] As Nazi goons jump over the Landauer fence, and Natalia discovers her murdered pet, Fosse cross-cuts with the dancers, whose headwear has been transformed into combat helmets, and whose Tiller dance has become the goosestepping of storm troopers, led by the Emcee in drag. Thus are dehumanization and indoctrination disguised as burlesque, with the cabaret entertainment becoming the soundtrack of real-life violence.

The "folk musical," one of Rick Altman's subcategories for the genre, has great faith in the people. When the common people sing a song in *Cabaret*, however, it isn't "Edelweiss"; it's "Tomorrow Belongs to Me." When the common people speak in *Cabaret*, they spread poison, not folk concepts such as optimism and the promise of the future. The number, moreover, is documentary-style, sung by total strangers to us, ordinary folk, and led by a young man who, we realize, represents the Aryan ideal. The scene is even shot in the style of Leni Riefenstahl, with low angles that draw us in and then overwhelm us.

After failing to become "Bob Fosse, Cinematic Auteur" in his own property, he needed to go outside himself in one way, to find the film artist he
was. Following *Cabaret*'s triumph and the Triple Crown that set him atop
the show business world, Fosse was now a seventies auteur. The films *Sweet
Charity* and *Cabaret* were projects that others launched and Fosse joined. The
three films that ensued were conceived by Fosse, then shepherded through
the process with producers and studios who believed in him. Increasingly, he
put his personal stamp on his films, co-writing *All That Jazz* and then solely
scripting *Star 80*.

LENNY

Lenny marks a departure from the musical genre, but not from Fosse's fascination with lowdown showbiz milieux. Dustin Hoffman plays the beatnik
comedian Lenny Bruce (1925–66), known for his iconoclastic satires of racial,
sexual, and religious hypocrisies. As tightly assembled a film as *Cabaret*, *Lenny*
is nonetheless denser, less a chronicle of Bruce's life than a film essay about the
comic and his effect on the culture and those who knew him. Only ten years
after a relentless series of obscenity arrests crushed Bruce's career, comedy
bits that Bruce was arrested for performing in front of consenting audiences
in small venues late at night could be projected with no objections over movie

Figure 7.3 Young Lenny Bruce (Dustin Hoffman), onstage in the Borscht Belt with
bigtime comic Sherman Hart (Gary Morton, a semi-retired comedian whose full-time
job was being Mr. Lucille Ball, until her death). The character was reportedly based
on Milton Berle. Fosse poured his encyclopedic knowledge of show business into the
story of Bruce, which, in his hands, seems a lot like the story of Bob Fosse. Digital
frame enlargement. Courtesy of United Artists.

theater speakers around the world, in an R-rated prestige film released by a major Hollywood studio.

With *Lenny*, Fosse leads the conversion of the biopic from a producer's showpiece to an auteur's means of expression. Fosse's identification with his subject is made obvious. Fosse, a Norwegian American in a largely Jewish business (his closest friends were well-known Jewish writers: Paddy Chayevsky, Herb Gardner, and Neil Simon), explores the life and times of a comic who displayed his Judaism openly. No comedian before Bruce wove Yiddish so thoroughly through his act; the more conservative Chayevsky blasted Bruce, as well as Julian Barry's play, on which the film is based, as "helpful to the anti-Semite" (Gottfried 265). The film pivots around an unseen interviewer who is heard questioning three subjects, Bruce's mother Sally Marr (Jan Miner), his manager, a fictional character played by Stanley Beck, and his ex-wife Honey (Valerie Perrine). Fosse himself is heard as the interviewer, as well as seen out of focus, in corners of the frame, thus insinuating himself into the infrastructure of his film. One of the few post-1966 films made in black-and-white, *Lenny* marks the only time Fosse ever worked in the format, not counting a few early-TV segments. The film cuts among three distinct black-and-white modes as rendered by cinematographer Bruce (son of Robert) Surtees: brilliant high-contrast for scenes showing Lenny's nightclub act; low-contrast documentarian photography of the sort that Wheeler Winston Dixon characterizes as "drab" for the interviews, and for the flashbacks to Lenny's day-to-day life the melodramatic noir look familiar from films such as *Sweet Smell of Success* (1957) and *I Want to Live!* (1958) (18).

Brilliantly edited though *Cabaret* is, it was on *Lenny* that Fosse learned that the cutting room is where a movie really learns to dance. With Alan Heim, whom he met on *Liza with a Z* (TV, 1972) and who remained his film editor for the remainder of his career, Fosse creates a biopic in the form of the dialectical montage mosaic. *Lenny* wants to be, like *Citizen Kane* (1941), a critical investigation and atomization of its subject. In the film's first half, Honey tells the interviewer about her courtship and marriage to Bruce, to the extent where their six-year marriage, which ended shortly before Bruce rose from raw young comic in low-class dives and striptease joints like those where Fosse started, to standup beatnik icon to, finally, the object of legal censorship battles around the US, over what was still called in the early-1960s, "public indecency." The Lenny–Honey marriage takes on more significance than it may have actually had, bearing noticeable similarities to the Bob–Gwen relationship. Lenny's standup monologues function similarly to the Kit Kat Klub songs in *Cabaret*, the stage soundtrack often overtaking the dramatic mise-en-scène. The film's second half covers the rise to fame with which biopics are conventionally concerned.

This is perhaps the only biopic ever filmed that doesn't end with a validation of the subject. No one emerges to testify to Bruce's lasting contribution to comedy; no homage is paid to Bruce as a fighter for the First Amendment. *Lenny*, like *All That Jazz* and *Star 80*, ends with a blunt shot of the subject's corpse. (So does *Cabaret*, if one counts the deadly state, literally, to which the Kit Kat Klub delivers Germany after conditioning it to be a culture that condones genocide.) The reviews by Pauline Kael and Vincent Canby stressed the film's supposed resemblance to the "suffering artist" hagiographic biopics of the studio era, selling extremely short Fosse's innovative biographical montage. Ultimately, however, it is true that *Lenny* cannot move past the limitations of the warts-and-all subgenre, itself the product of the compromise of postwar cinematic realism with hagiography. Warts-and-all had been since the 1950s the genre's dominant biopic story type, especially in entertainer and sports biographies.[5] Despite its formal originality and brilliance, *Lenny* averts its gaze from some of Bruce's self-destructive behavior, especially the epic drug addiction that might have taken him down and brought on an early death, even without all the censorship of his act.

ALL THAT JAZZ

After *Lenny*, Fosse put a screenwriter, Robert Alan Aurthur, to work on a film version of the 1974 novel, *Ending*, by Hilma Wolitzer. *Ending* is about a young

Figure 7.4   "If you need me, I'll be in the cutting room." Joe Gideon (Roy Scheider) in *All That Jazz* (1979) exiting the Palace on Broadway and 46th, a former movie palace that reopened as a legitimate stage house with *Sweet Charity* in 1966. The Embassy movie theater next door is playing *Animal House* (1978), the youth comedy whose blockbuster success explains perfectly why the Hollywood Renaissance ended. Digital frame enlargement. Courtesy of Columbia/20th-Century Fox

woman whose husband is dying of multiple myeloma. Fosse, as he dramatizes in *All That Jazz*, experienced his own brushes with death. He suffered two heart attacks while juggling *Lenny*'s final editing with the start of rehearsals for *Chicago*. After emerging from the hospital and mounting *Chicago*, whose opening was delayed from January to June 1975, and interviewing numerous doctors and specialists on death, Fosse began to eclipse *Ending* with thoughts of an autobiographical docu-comedy and surrealistic musical, based upon the events surrounding his own heart attacks in the fall of 1974.

Fosse and Aurthur interviewed everyone who had been in Fosse's orbit at the time, casting many of them in the film. Dancer Ann Reinking essentially plays herself, as do the film editor Alan Heim, dancer Kathryn Doby as Joe Gideon's assistant choreographer, and actress-turned-journalist Chris Chase as the TV reviewer who pans *The Standup*. A number of actors important to Fosse, among them Ben Vereen from *Pippin*, play prominent roles here. Cliff Gorman, who played the title character in *Lenny* on Broadway, gets to play a close facsimile of Lenny Bruce here. Gwen Verdon is played by stage actress Leland Palmer. Fosse and Verdon never were divorced, though she separated from him due to his countless affairs. They were lifelong partners professionally; he actually died in her arms outside the National Theater in Washington DC, on the opening night of a new *Sweet Charity* revival. When I, then a PhD student, heard that Fosse died, my sick-joke response was that I'd seen that movie already. Lenny Bruce couldn't have said it better. Verdon lived to oversee the curation of both their papers for the Library of Congress.

Fosse appears to have adhered to the creative writing axiom: "When writing about someone else, pretend you're that person. When writing about yourself, pretend it's somebody else." This allows him to be somewhat honest, turning himself into an anti-hero, with the tough-tender Roy Scheider cast against type as Gideon/Fosse.

Burlesque finds its way into much of the film. The movie producer of *The Standup*, as *Lenny* is retitled for this film, is relentlessly caricatured, and so are the trio of producers of the stage musical. There is an older man whose fatherliness seems a thin coating for duplicity, and two younger men, one straight and one gay. Both of them seem to be in the business for all the attractive young women or men it puts them in contact with (not that Gideon/Fosse doesn't use his proximity to vulnerable, ambitious dancers for the same thing). The excruciating cross-cut sequence between the insurance company accountants who tell the producers that "You could become the first show on Broadway to turn a profit without really opening" and Gideon's open-heart surgery is a different form of burlesque – a sick joke in which Fosse indulges himself, with no basis in actuality.

In *All That Jazz*, perhaps of all his films, we see how Fosse thought like a dancer in his filmmaking. Fosse regarded temporality as the least important of the editing relations. Fosse edits for motif (as in music), for theme and variation, for rhythm, and for point and counterpoint, as well as more conventional establishment/breakdown/re-establishment of scenes (including musical numbers). His disregard for linearity was so great on some films that his staff coined a term, "Fosse Time." For Fosse and Heim, this was a concept of "time as a jazz standard, there to be riffed on . . ., a network of asynchronous pieces of picture and sound" (Wasson 374). The film starts in fairly conventional chronology – the show musical's story of how a show is put on – before other elements take it in unanticipated directions.

One of the film's main themes with variations is the repeated sequence in which Antonio Vivaldi's "Concerto Alla Rustica for Strings and Continuo in G Major" is heard on an audio cassette player, accompanied by coughs, as Joe Gideon begins his day with a shower, an Alka-Seltzer, and a Dexedrine. This sequence ends, "It's showtime, folks!" It is seen and heard, though hardly repeated exactly, five times up until the episode that culminates in Joe's first heart attack. In the final "showtime," which takes up the second half of the film, the "A-Number-One games-player," as TV host O'Connor Flood (Vereen) introduces Joe, makes "his final appearance on the great stage of life." Either it's no longer showtime and it's life for real, or it's "the final curtain" to which all of his behaviors have been leading.

While this film cannot with exactitude be called a musical, it includes scenes, especially the series of numbers that Joe hallucinates directing, which take on conventions of movie musicals. The number that Fosse takes the most seriously is "Everything Old Is New Again," a song danced "offstage" by Katie (Reinking) and Michelle, to a record by Peter Allen; the song seems to signal a new beginning, a new appreciation for life, in opposition to "Air-otica," the ballet that points up everything dehumanizing about the sexual revolution. *All That Jazz* is as personal, and as formally complex and cinematically beautiful, as any film made in the Hollywood Renaissance. Like *Lenny*, it creates a dialectic between its narration – Joe's life as he tells it to Angelique (Jessica Lange) – and its drama. The film's central relationship is the courtship between Joe and Angelique, the angel of death.

Fosse's final three films greatly deepen the pattern set in *Cabaret*. Angelique's deathly but seductive anteroom, with stark black background and luminous white foreground, furnished with many of the personal effects we have seen in Joe's apartment, serves a similar function to the Kit Kat Klub. "Outside" is Joe's life in all its glorious creativity, its self-destruction, and its latticework of relationships. The time is impossible to ascertain, until the heart attack, when cutaways to Angelique show her letting her hair down and preparing for the final seduction. Joe struggles to hold onto his "chastity," while doing things like sneaking cigarettes and holding parties in his hospital room, which give him away as "easy."

This is one New Hollywood film without an open ending, to put it mildly. Its ambiguity comes from the questions it raises. "If *All That Jazz* is Bob Fosse's version of his own life," asks Fosse biographer Martin Gottfried, "why does he die in it?" (384). It gives new meaning to the idea of the director's having the final cut. Fosse will seemingly always be associated with death. Of Fosse's two biographies, one is subtitled *The Life and Death of Bob Fosse* and in the other the chapters move backwards (Twenty Years, Five Years, One Year and so on), in a morbid countdown. The great irony, however, is that Fosse's cinematic dances of death keep on living. The letter that writer Pete Hamill wrote to Fosse, inspiring him, apparently, to transform *Ending* into *All That Jazz*, laid down "a hell of a challenge to you as a choreographer to design a film that *feels* like death. I want to see a Fosse film about a death that makes me feel what it will be like to die" (Hamill 1). Fosse's films, ironically, are animated with life, while locked in a staring contest with death. The final shots of his last three movies are of dead bodies. The zipping of the body bag that bluntly rings down the curtain on Joe Gideon's life is followed by Ethel Merman's lusty rendition of "There's No Business Like Show Business" over the end credits. There's no better example of rebirth and revision. Fosse changes the context and the meaning of Irving Berlin's anthemic song for *Annie Get Your Gun*, which conveys resilience, power, glitter, and the appeal of the comeback. Unlike Berlin's song, Bob Fosse's films kept refusing the resilience of showbiz. Like the song, however, Bob Fosse won't stay dead. But at the same time, he conveys the precariousness of life – a man who dances, who glamorized women who dance, and whose film shots dance and flicker unpredictably.

STAR 80

Having staged his own fictional demise, Fosse still appeared determined to explore death. *Star 80* stands with troubling final films such as *Lola Montes* (1955) and *Eyes Wide Shut* (1999). Formally, it's nearly flawless, a confrontation with the consequences of the values of popular culture, his theme since *Cabaret*. A film about the murder of 1980 Playmate of the Year Dorothy Stratten by her estranged husband-promoter Paul Snider, who then killed himself, it was based on Teresa Carpenter's Pulitzer Prize-winning *Village Voice* cover story, "Death of a Playmate." The structure of Fosse's screenplay is starkly simple. Paul Snider (Eric Roberts) is a Vancouver hustler who "manages" his young wife, Dorothy Stratten (Mariel Hemingway), into as semi-big time as a *Playboy* Playmate gets and then goes mad as she slips into the tawdry inseam between exploitation and what passes for entertainment. Snider is called a "pimp" by none other than Hugh Hefner, who is played by Cliff Robertson, the square-jawed actor who once played JFK.

While the Stratten/Snider murder/suicide was reenacted in Fosse's film,

Figure 7.5 *Star 80* (1983): Innocence corrupted. Filmed at the very same Dairy Queen in Vancouver where Paul Snider met Dorothy, Paul (Eric Roberts) takes his first look of Dorothy Hoogstratten (Mariel Hemingway), whom he will promote to *Playboy*. Digital frame enlargement. Courtesy of the Ladd Company.

American movies and the Great White Way that Fosse had conquered were turning into carefully scrubbed precincts resembling the rides at Disney World. Reagan Era culture seemed intent upon developing amnesia as far as the previous two decades were concerned. Fosse thought he could make the world look at the sexual revolution's appalling underside, but his own film becomes a part of it; like Hefner with many of his models, Fosse indirectly spurred Hemingway, who badly wanted the part, to have breast implants before he would cast her. The world refused to look. Critics, by and large, rejected *Star 80*; audiences stayed away. The film is as hard and honest as any of Fosse's films; however, without the clear object of Nazism in *Cabaret*, censorship in *Lenny*, or life and death itself in *All That Jazz*, *Star 80* implicates the entire culture, Fosse included. "You're playing *me* if I wasn't successful," the director stormed at Roberts on set (Wasson 526). The idea of a dazzling creator making art out of his fears of failure is not new. One can always regret that this angry dissection of damnation and the crushing of innocence was Bob Fosse's final film, but this director's signature blend of darkness and bedazzlement has never been so corrosively felt. It is also an all-too-fitting epitaph to 1970s auteur cinema.

The heart of *Star 80* is in Vancouver, British Columbia, the kind of flyover town that Fosse's films, with their trajectory of "NY to LA" (the original title of the show being put on in *All That Jazz*), had never before considered. Filming in the very same Dairy Queen where Paul first spotted Dorothy working behind the counter, Fosse cross-cuts from the murder scene in the depths of Los Angeles to the elusive but dubious heights from which Snider is repeatedly turned back. Whereas Fosse's Sally Bowles is hardly talentless, and Lenny Bruce and Joe Gideon have uncommon gifts, Paul Snider is a sub-ordinary guy in a celebrity culture that exaggerates the extraordinary. Paul promotes wet t-shirt contests, which Fosse stages with no less degradation than he devoted to the mud wrestling in *Cabaret*. Desperate to impress, Snider practices smiling and introducing himself in a mirror; before long, his frustration turns to hatred. His discovery, Dorothy Stratten, née Hoogstratten, is a *Playboy* Playmate, a male fantasy of supposedly exceptional beauty, albeit one recreated by Hefner's magazine twelve times annually for over sixty years. Fosse defies the spectator to disregard the content and look purely at form – and discovers that this probably cannot be done. The opening credits take us back to the title sequences of *Bonnie and Clyde* (1967) and *Mean Streets* (1973): photographs taking up part of the frame surrounded by a black background. Dorothy's "Oh gosh, me – a *Playboy* centerfold" interview on the soundtrack is uncomfortably at odds with her nude shots; "*Playboy*'s motto is the girl next door. They look for girls who are fresh and wholesome and naive. They look for all that." Dorothy on the layout (in voiceover): "It took me five months to shoot my Playmate of the Year layout. I took over twenty thousand pictures. They don't go for just great nude shots. They go for art, perfect art. And I'm very proud of that. And I'm happy to share that with someone who can appreciate it."

Right away colliding ideas clash. The prurience, the masturbatory aspect of Playmate "appreciation" are the least of the monsters that dare not growl their names. The images of Hemingway as Stratten confront the spectator with an undraped "Body Too Much," reflecting Jean-Louis Comolli's concept that the actor who plays a well-known person in a biography competes with our knowledge of the actual person. The tensions – Should this actress be playing this part? Should this film have been made? – squirm uncomfortably on the screen.

The idea of the auteur molding the actress to meet his design, like the *Playboy* photographers and editors refining the model into "perfect art," tussles with Stratten's ownership of her image. Dorothy's use of the first person pronoun. "*They* look for this . . ." becomes "it took *me five months to shoot . . . my layout*" (emphasis mine). The woman's ownership of her image cannot be allowed. This is what drives Snider around the bend. Dorothy's fetishized images gaze back at the spectator. Her last line, "And I'm happy to share that with someone who can appreciate it" is so counterintuitive when the topic is, finally, softcore porn, that the film crawls with contradictions even before Fosse thrusts us into its main conflict, which arrives soon enough.

The Eisensteinian montage collision, the Fossean dance steps, "not up and out, but down and in" become metaphors for Snider's covetous rage which, gruesomely, Fosse is "happy to share with someone who can appreciate it." *Star 80*, perhaps more than any Hollywood Renaissance film, is still "looking for" the appreciation it has never received. Perhaps in the Trump Era, we might be finally ready for a film that faces the consequences of the culture's fixation on celebrity worship at any cost.

NOTES

1. Significantly, three of the top four were released in a seventeen-month period at the climax of the Hollywood Renaissance. Ahead of *All That Jazz* (released December 1979) were *Raging Bull* (November 1980) at Number 1 and *Apocalypse Now* (August 1979) at 3. Only *Citizen Kane*, no less, crashes this late-New Hollywood party, at Number 2 (Brevet).
2. To see the crucial difference Fosse makes, one need look no further than the only two other film musicals Cy Feuer produced, the movie versions of *A Little Night Music* (1978) and *A Chorus Line* (1985), famous fiascos both.
3. He is a dissolute American millionaire in the Isherwood original.
4. The Tiller Girls were a British troupe of high-kicking precision dancers, led by their choreographer, John Tiller (1854–1925). Their popularity led to many other troupes in the "Tiller style," notably Radio City Music Hall's Rockettes. The Tiller Girls were big in Weimar Germany. There's a reference to them in the great film *Varieté* (1925), starring Lya De Putti, the German movie star of whom *Cabaret*'s Sally Bowles is so envious. Fosse's film is richer with references than any of the other versions, even Isherwood's.
5. See Bingham, *Whose Lives Are They Anyway?*, 17–18.

WORKS CITED

Allen, Jay Presson. *Cabaret*. Script draft with Bob Fosse annotations. N. D. Bob Fosse andGwen Verdon Collection. Library of Congress. Washington, D.C. *Cabaret (Fosse)*, Box 15B.

Barrios, Nick. *Dangerous Rhythm: Why Movie Musicals Matter*. Oxford University Press, 2014.

Bingham, Dennis. *Whose Lives Are They Anyway? The Biopic as Contemporary Film Genre*. Rutgers University Press, 2010.

Brevet, Brad. "Editors Guild Selects 75 Best Edited Films of All Time." *ComingSoon. net*, 4 Feb. 2015. Accessed 15 May 2017.

Canby, Vincent. "*Lenny*, With Dustin Hoffman, Is One-Fourth Brilliant." *The New York Times*, 11 Nov. 1974, http://www.nytimes.com/movie/review?res=9404E4D91 33BE63BBC4952DFB767838F669EDE&mcubz=0. Accessed 17 August 2017.

Carpenter, Teresa. "Death of a Playmate." *The Village Voice*, 5–11 November 1980: 1+.

Comolli, Jean-Louis. "Historical Fiction: A Body Too Much." *Screen*, vol. 19, no. 3, 1978, pp. 41–52.

Dixon, Wheeler Winston. *Black & White Cinema*. I.B. Tauris, 2015.

Gottfried, Martin. *All His Jazz: The Life and Death of Bob Fosse*. 1990. Da Capo, 2003.

Hamill, Pete. *Letter to Bob Fosse.* 25 April 1976. Bob Fosse and Gwen Verdon Collection. Library of Congress. Washington, D.C. *Endings (Fosse):* Box 14B.

Hornstein, Scott. "The Making of *Lenny*: An Interview with Bob Fosse." *Filmmakers Newsletter.* February 1975, pp. 30–34.

Kael, Pauline. "When the Saints Come Marching In" 18 November 1974. *Reeling.* Atlantic, Little, Brown, 1976, 371–77.

Kennedy, Matthew. *Roadshow!: The Fall of Film Musicals in the 1960s.* Oxford University Press, 2014.

McWhorter, John. "Razzle Dazzle." *The New York Times Book Review*, 6 December 2013.

Shalit, Gene. Interview with Bob Fosse. 1986. *All That Jazz.* Special Features. Blu-ray. Criterion Collection, 2014.

Wasson, Sam. *Fosse.* Houghton, Mifflin, Harcourt, 2013.

Wolitzer, Hilma. *Ending.* Morrow, 1974.

8. THE LITTLE DEATHS OF JOHN FRANKENHEIMER

Daniel Varndell

> The storyteller is the figure in which the righteous man encounters himself.
>
> – Walter Benjamin

It is often in the smallest of moments, observes Murray Pomerance ("Moment of Action," 5), that some of the most overwhelming, affecting, and indelible images in film can be found. Pomerance sees such moments in cinema as emerging like "riddles" from the great performances and the great movie scenes that perturb our thoughts long after the credits have finished rolling. For David Thomson, something like this "riddling" effect was often all one had to cling to when leaving the picture houses of the 1970s, since filmmakers presented us with "unfamiliar shapes" that "switched course," which "didn't stick to the rules" and sometimes "broke off in your hands or your mind" – Al Pacino recognizing his authority in *The Godfather* (1972) when he notices his hands aren't shaking; Harvey Keitel at the end of *Fingers* (1978) crouched naked in the corner of the room ("The Decade," 74). Such moments echoed and even "haunted" other, more dominant, images from those films (Pacino's powerfully impassive stare as he exercises that authority; Keitel's recognition of his instinct for violence).

Three such moments stand out for me in the early films of John Frankenheimer. The first, from *The Manchurian Candidate* (1962), when Ben Marco (Frank Sinatra) is confronted by a wave of guilt after realizing that he has been unable to save his friend from committing a horrific murder, to the extent that, reading the headline in the newspaper, he assumes responsibility for the act ("In a way it was me," he says, echoing his nightmare of the brainwashing sequence in which he really was complicit in murder). The second, from *Seconds* (1966), when Antiochus "Tony" Wilson (Rock Hudson) – a depressed middle-aged banker who, through a radical surgical procedure, has been transformed into a handsome young artist living a dream life – is mortified as his girlfriend playfully responds to his sexual advances by calling him a "dirty old man." The third, from *The Fixer* (1968), when Yakov Bok (Alan Bates), a Jew living incognito in anti-Semitic Czarist Russia, spies a row of sleeping children which triggers the memory of an argument he once had with his estranged wife about their childless marriage ("Without children," he asks, "who can a man look in the eye?")

With falling shoulders and sagging faces, their eyes glaze over as they stare into a personal abyss only they are contemplating. It is, in many ways, a subjective image of the kind Roland Barthes described as having the ambiguous quality of the "little death" (*petite mort*[1]) in which an "abrupt loss of sociality" leads to a point where "*everything* is lost, integrally" (39), even while the consistency of the individual seems otherwise intact. The world falls away in such moments as these, marking a loss of the kind that none of these men, despite having been "through the ringer," seemed to be expecting.

This image of the "little death" is, I want to argue, also key to understanding the power of Frankenheimer's moral questioning in his 1970s films. I make this claim despite the fact that Thomson dismissed Frankenheimer's late-1960s and early 1970s films as abandoning the "intimate portraits" (*Birdman of Alcatraz* in 1962, for example) and sharply defined political dramas (such as *Seven Days in May* in 1964) for "glossy production values, a speculative eye on subject matter and a flashy, insecure style." Frankenheimer's career, feared Thomson, was "hopelessly lost" ("Biographical Dictionary," 190). The view was not uncommon among critics of Frankenheimer's work, yet, while some of his 1970s films seem to confirm Thomson's prediction (*99 and 44/100% Dead* in 1974, or *Prophecy* in 1979) others refute it (*Impossible Object [Story of a Love Story]* in 1973 and *Black Sunday* in 1977). More recently, Frankenheimer scholars have attempted a serious revaluation of his work. R. Barton Palmer and Murray Pomerance defend him as a director whose thoughtful vision of contemporary America "quickly became an art generally lost in a 1970s film culture captivated by generic gigantism" ("Introduction," 9), while Stephen B. Armstrong celebrates the "dark dramas" cut through with the pessimistic fatalism (2) characteristic of this period in Frankenheimer's oeuvre.

By looking at three "little deaths" – three moments in three of Frankenheimer's 1970s films – this chapter will enter into the same spirit as these scholars who are reclaiming Frankenheimer as a director whose work is every bit as riddling as that of his better-known contemporaries. It will focus on moments that

Figures 8.1a–c   Three "little deaths": Sinatra in *The Manchurian Candidate* 1962), Hudson in *Seconds* (1966) and Bates in *The Fixer* (1968). Digital frame enlargements. Courtesy of MGM/United Artists, Paramount Pictures, and United Artists.

reveal a director committed to exploring the difficulty of subjective freedom, a director whose vision of modern man sees in the crisis of the individual a microcosm of the crisis of "individuality" itself. It is also, in many ways, a response to Richard Combs's question about why, in a career he describes as having been "combustible" and filled with "dead-ends," Frankenheimer remains a director who tells us "what an impossibly spiky, unpossessable object cinema is, how chaotic and liable to fall to pieces in anybody's grasp" (46). One might say *especially*, perhaps, in Frankenheimer's grasp, since here was a man who seemed to understand the Barthesian sense of the "little death" only too well, who often blamed his struggle for consistency in the 1970s on circumstances beyond his control – such as poor casting choices (often imposed by producers) and production issues[2] – yet whose work seems to have been every bit as affected by deeply felt personal tragedies, including the assassination of his close friend, Robert F. Kennedy.

Yet, while Gary D. Engle attributed "Frankenheimer's slide" to personal issues – to "marital problems, an intense perfectionism that was frequently seen as arrogance, [and] the myopic misjudgments that all too commonly attend early, meteoric success" (50) – what the films themselves reveal, in little moments, is the ongoing struggle we all have in facing ourselves. It is, by definition, a personal battle, and the "little deaths" of John Frankenheimer are the "moments of action," as Pomerance puts it, that disrupt the ordinary course of a life when some riddle, some disruptive force, involuntarily breaks the surface, disturbing the "face" one shows to others. Such moments are almost overwhelming in such films as *The Horsemen* (1971), *The Iceman Cometh* (1973) and *French Connection II* (1975). They are moments suffused with an existential ambiguity, which raise questions that cannot be easily forgotten, which cause ripples that refuse to be stilled. Hence, despite having been hailed in the late 1960s as "probably the most important director at work in the American cinema today" (Pratley 14), Frankenheimer fell short of this expectation precisely because his films provoked questions about what it means to be, and not just do, right in the world; to grasp – sometimes feebly, uncomprehendingly – for what is ungraspable in modern life. Such moments define our collective failures and, hence, continue to speak to us in riddles.

An Unexpected Exposure in *French Connection II*

"I'm naked." That's how Jimmy "Popeye" Doyle (Gene Hackman), eyebrows raised, sardonically summarizes his condition as he desperately tries to orientate himself in Marseilles in order to pursue drug kingpin Charnier (Fernando Rey) – his nemesis, who at the end of William Friedkin's *The French Connection* (1971) escaped justice. Doyle is naked not just because his French counterpart, Henri (Bernard Fresson), has denied him the right to carry a gun but because he has neither the language skills – Doyle (like Hackman) makes *zero* effort to speak French – nor the geographical knowledge to be effective in what is for him foreign territory. Doyle's inability to establish a "cognitive mapping" of this new environment led Roger Ebert to criticize what he saw as

Frankenheimer's reduction of the New York detective to "a clown . . . being used for comic relief and stripped of his dignity" (1975). In Frankenheimer's hands, Doyle has lost his edge and his ability to run on instinct and "native" understanding. His famous hunches – nearly always correct but often ethically questionable in the first film – no longer yield results and the explosive violence that made him so successful on the streets of New York is now misdirected. He has become an even bigger liability to his fellow officers than to himself.

Another way of looking at it, however, is that the first movie ends with Doyle so blinded by his obsession that he loses sight of the clear perspective needed to capture Charnier. Instead, he accidentally shoots and kills a fellow cop, Mulderig (Bill Hickman). Friedkin ends his movie with the single gunshot of a frustrated Doyle who, off-screen chasing shadows, is lost. The decision to explore how Doyle copes in unfamiliar territory is thus fully consistent with how Friedkin left him. The final gunshot in the first movie (fired in frustration at nothing) carries an echo of Mulderig's earlier swipe at Doyle's claim to be "dead certain" about a line of enquiry to which Mulderig replied, "the last time you were dead certain we had a dead cop." In Frankenheimer's sequel, this line about "dead cops" is repeated when, in an early scene, Doyle accompanies Henri on a drug raid and in his confusion chases down a black suspect who turns out to be an undercover officer and who, because Doyle has exposed him, is subsequently stabbed to death in the street. When Doyle attempts to be bullish about the mistake Henri turns on him, deflating his ego: "You don't help us outside. You just fuck up! What do you know about Marseilles? You think it's Harlem, just kicking blacks around the streets?" In addition to being

Figure 8.2   Gene Hackman as "Popeye" Doyle in *French Connection II* (1975). Digital frame enlargement. Courtesy of 20th Century Fox.

naked without his gun, Popeye is exposed here in another sense altogether: his steel gaze softens as Hackman – brow furrowed – lowers his eyes in a rare moment of introspection.

The moment is doubly haunted, perhaps, by another line from the first film – Doyle's notorious "Never trust a nigger" statement – since the "dead certainty" with which he pursues this "criminal" is clearly framed by his racist vision of the world.

A Breed Apart in *The Horsemen*

Pride is the central flaw at the heart of *The Horsemen*, in which riders called *Chapandaz* compete in the traditional sport of *Buzkashi*[3] to become legends so that, like Shelley's Ozymandias, they might survive death through the celebration of their victories in tales passed on through generations. Tursen (Jack Palance) is a former champion of the *Buzkashi* who, even in his crippled old age, adheres to a strict and rigid tradition that has left him somewhat estranged from his son, Uraz (Omar Sharif), who spends his time gambling his money away and drifting from one event to the next. When a Royal *Buzkashi* is announced, Tursen publicly names Uraz as one of the riders he chooses to represent their clan and proclaims that should he win he will have the privilege of owning the horse, Jahil (the finest in Tursen's royal stable), on whom he is expected to ride to victory. Uraz warily thanks his father for such an honor, but this moment of recognition is soon broken when Tursen carelessly states (before the entire clan), "If you cannot win on Jahil, you cannot win on any horse." Uraz hardens and bitterly observes that while the royal *Buzkashi* will be no trifling matter, the "*horse* will win," leaving Tursen to reflect on the scathing implication – that it is the horse, not his son, who will define the legend of his victory. Eager not just to win but also to prove his worth, Uraz rides recklessly and, thrown from his horse, breaks his leg. His humiliation is complete when another *Chapandaz* from Tursen's clan rides Jahil to victory.

With both body and pride wounded, Uraz seeks comfort in a tavern as he contemplates the long ride home to face his father following his defeat. However, his face falls when he overhears a merchant storyteller regaling a crowd with the tale of Tursen, "the greatest *Chapandaz* who ever lived," thereby inflicting a much deeper wound on Uraz than his damaged leg and failure in the *Buzkashi*. "It was a different time, remember," proclaims the storyteller, "a time that produced a different breed of men. The *Chapandaz* of that time, huh! – yesterday's Royal *Buzkashi* would have been a mere *preliminary exercise*." As the storyteller speaks of this old, superior breed of horsemen, Frankenheimer lingers on and slowly zooms into a close up on Uraz's face as he contemplates, for the first time, a deeper crisis. It is not

THE OTHER HOLLYWOOD RENAISSANCE

Figure 8.3   Omar Sharif as Uraz in *The Horsemen* (1971). Digital frame enlargement. Courtesy of Columbia Pictures.

simply that he has failed to live up to his father's mark but that he never could. Immortality will elude him as he languishes in the shadow of Tursen's formidable legend; a legend which, galvanized over years of successive retellings in darkened taverns on sultry nights, opens up an irrecoverable distance between the modern individual of the present day and "*that* breed of man" living in "*those* days," that is, the past.

As Sharif's eyes slowly fill the frame, the storyteller's words trigger a dissolve[4] – a memory from Uraz's childhood of a *Buzkashi* from long ago in which he helped his father (commanding, powerful, imposing) secure the prized goat before riding off to win the event. The merchant's story seems to confirm for Uraz what he has long feared: that it is in the stallions bred at his stud that Tursen will find his champion, not in his own bloodline.

Grave Thoughts in *The Iceman Cometh*

Pipe dreams underpin the illusions of all who drink in Hope's Saloon, and when they aren't passed out or slugging back shots of whiskey, the soused down and outs in Frankenheimer's *The Iceman Cometh* spin yarns to one another on the subject of their bright tomorrows. One dreams of opening a gambling joint while another fancies marrying his sweetheart; a pair of war veterans wistfully speak of returning home while another idly discusses a return to work. Such empty grandstanding is fueled by cheap liquor and masked by self-deception since, like the characters waiting for Samuel Beckett's Godot, every "I will" resolves into a "tomorrow" which inevitably never comes. The *agent provocateur* of this back-room drama is Hickey (Lee Marvin), a reformed hell raiser who, with a sinister secret lurking beneath his cheery salesman's facade, arrives at the bar on a mission to "save" the barflies by exposing their pipe dreams to the harsh light of reality. Hickey's Mephistophelian act is performed under the cynical gaze of former anarchist Larry (Robert Ryan), who glibly passes comment on the irony of the barflies' "tomorrow philosophy" while, at the same time, acting as their "foolosopher" by flattering and nurturing their chimerical dreams of "tomorrow." Hickey observes that Larry will be the toughest nut to crack since his ironic play covers up his own pipe dream: not the difficulty of living, but a denial of death, since Larry cannot accept the basic fact of mortality (a time of *no* tomorrows.)

One by one, Hickey's provocations cause the barflies to flee his salesman's pitch about the absurdity of life, to prove to him (if not to themselves) that they are capable of living "tomorrow" today. Finally moved to anger by Hickey's sermonizing (exacerbated in Frankenheimer's adaptation of Eugene O'Neill's play by Marvin's more robust, unsympathetic performance of the role), Larry confronts his old drinking buddy with an ironic counter-logic:

> LARRY: "I'm afraid to live, am I? – and even more afraid to die! I just sit here with my pride drowned on the bottom of a bottle, keeping drunk so I won't see myself shaking in my britches with fright, or I hear myself whining and praying: Beloved Christ, let me live a little longer at any price. If it's only for a few days more, or a few hours even, have mercy, Almighty God, and let me still clutch greedily to my yellow heart this sweet treasure, this jewel beyond price, this dirty, stinking bit of withered old flesh which is my beautiful little life. You think you'll make me admit this to myself?"
>
> HICKEY: "But you just did admit it, didn't you?"

Figure 8.4   Robert Ryan as Larry Slade in *The Iceman Cometh* (1973). Digital frame enlargement. Courtesy of American Film Theatre.

Larry is rendered speechless with the realization that he has demonstrated Hickey's thesis that he is only "playing dead," that his liquor-fueled grand-standing is really a disavowal of the "Iceman" (Death), in all its finality.

By ironically parroting Hickey's own "lying" words back to him, Larry finds himself suddenly speaking, almost as if he were possessed by it, the truth about his lusterless condition.

<h2 style="text-align:center">UNTURNED KEYS</h2>

The momentary stunned silence in each of these examples echoes what Stanley Cavell called the "creative limitation" of the philosopher-teacher who, by following the logic of a point to the end, eventually reaches an impasse which, by virtue of the meaning of the point exceeding the teacher's ability to finally say it, risks the misfortune of his exposure in/to the world ("Philosophy the Day after Tomorrow," 320). Silence, in this regard, conveys what the characters' unthinking "talk" conceals, whether it is Doyle's bullish overzealousness, Uraz's arrogant self-regard, or Larry's haughty self-conceit; each ends up confirming the thesis of the man who confronts him. These are moments of intense vulnerability in men for whom any show of weakness – especially in front of other men – can seem fatal.

This manner of speaking exposes the subject in much the same way as a tool is "exposed" when it breaks in our hands or an occupation when a worker suffers an injury preventing them from working more. Such moments accentuate, as Cavell puts it (quoting Heidegger), "the conspicuousness, obtrusiveness and obstinacy of things" since what is ordinarily concealed by an object's silent functioning is revealed by its non-functioning – what Heidegger called the "worldhood of the world announcing itself" ("What Becomes of Things on Film," 2). What is crucial for Cavell is that not all cinematic images have this effect; that is, it is not simply the effect of filming things, but a sudden change (or charge) given to those things by a shift in the way we relate to them, as when Buster Keaton registers an interruption with his "extraordinary gaze." What I have been calling the moment of the "little death" in John Frankenheimer's 1970s films is one such exposure of the hero to the conspicuousness, obtrusiveness and obstinacy of that knot at the core of his being, the "announcement" of which has the effect of disturbing his activity as a "matter of course."

This philosophical description of such an announcement – or to use Heidegger's word, "disclosure" – of the authentic self as it is covered and obscured by the disguises we wear, is directly articulated in *Seconds* when Nora (Salome Jens) wonders "what kind of a man" Wilson really is, surmising that "there is grace in the line and colour but it doesn't emerge pure, it pushes at the edge of something still tentative, unresolved, as if somewhere in the man there is still a key unturned." When Wilson warily responds that this is "quite an analysis," Nora, perhaps realizing she has pushed his buttons, reassures him that "When you come to think of it, it sort of fits everybody, doesn't it?" The image of the "unturned key," and what it discloses about an individual, is at the heart of these key moments in Frankenheimer's films. It is an image that recalls the question identified by Michael Levenson as lurking in the modernist literary works of the early twentieth century: "This thing we name the individual, this piece of matter, this length of memory, this bearer of a proper name, this block in space, this whisper in time, this self-delighting, self-condemning oddity – what is it? who made it?" (xi). Such a question makes it no longer possible to make a claim to self-transparency or self-authorization and any pretension as such echoes with the ironic hollowness of the statement Nietzsche made just before he went mad – "*ecce homo!*" (Behold the man!). "Popeye" Doyle, the Great Lawman; Uraz, Descendant of the Legendary Tursen; Larry Slade, Activist and Philosopher: all are exposed in the moment of the "little death" and, try as they might, they find they cannot live otherwise. "We *revenge* ourselves on life," wrote Nietzsche, "by means of the phantasmagoria of 'another,' a 'better' life" (49); such phantasms work, then, to raise our defenses once more, to cover up any difficult and potentially humiliating insights.

So, when Doyle, Uraz, and Larry each dismiss this uncanny feeling and return instead with renewed vigor to their activity (or inactivity, in the case of Larry), they suffer a second, much more devastating blow. Doyle, already conspicuous, obtrusive, and obstinate on the streets of Marseilles, is easily captured by Charnier whose thugs get him hooked on heroin in order to interrogate him until, satisfied that he has learned nothing of their operation, they inject him with an overdose and dump him back at police headquarters. Henri and a team of doctors save his life but Doyle, now a junkie, must battle his addiction (an addiction that manifests itself in a manner curiously reminiscent of his obsessive personality). Uraz, determined not to ride the easy road back home to confront Tursen, takes a deadly mountain path known as the "old road of long ago," a "road for dead men" (read: road of the past). The resulting journey leaves him requiring an emergency amputation of his damaged leg when a farmer recognizes a life-threatening gangrenous infection. And finally, his cage rattled by Hickey, Larry finds his true reckoning in a confrontation with an adolescent, Parritt (Jeff Bridges) – a member of Larry's old anarchist movement – whose arrival stirs up memories in the old "foolosopher" of a lost fidelity both for the political cause he abandoned and for the woman he once loved. The woman is Parritt's mother who, Parritt informs him, has been arrested after a tip-off by a traitor that Larry begins to suspect, but refuses to believe, might have been the young Parritt himself.

Each of these men is derailed, forced once more to confront the riddle first exposed in the "little death". What none of Frankenheimer's protagonists finally manage, however, is to turn the "unturned key" described by Nora. Rather, the enigma at the heart of their condition becomes a guiding principle to orientate themselves around their chaotic and unstable worlds. Rather than being riddles themselves, Frankenheimer's tortured heroes ultimately reveal their relation to the idea of the riddle "as such," suggesting that, to quote Levenson (in words that might have been written of Frankenheimer's protagonists), "subjectivity . . . cannot be captured in a mark on the body, in a mental scar, in the 'lumpish past,' in the literal event, in a verbal tic, in an emotional obsession" (71). Rather, the endeavor to find "moral poise in an endlessly changing world" becomes the discovery, and embracement, of the *type* of relation that "allows him to have, not a fixed view, but a constant angle of vision" (73).

A Constant Angle of Vision

To arrive at such an "accord," Frankenheimer stages a second encounter between these men that establishes an enduring relationship based on their recognized mutual vulnerability. To help Doyle overcome his heroin addiction, go "cold turkey," Henri strikes up a brandy-fueled conversation about baseball that stumbles on the fact that he, a Frenchman, hasn't a clue about it. As Doyle attempts to explain the sport (even demonstrating a pitch using a chicken leg and apple for props), his suffering from the withdrawal overtakes his ability to speak and his words become guttural noises. Finally, fully exposed before Henri, Doyle breaks down and buries his face in his hands as Frankenheimer cuts to a graphic match of him washing his face in the shower, having come "clean" (in every sense). In *Horsemen*, Uraz finally returns home and enters Tursen's quarters as he is dressing, catching him "naked." The father briefly rebukes his son, who uses the opportunity to reveal the truth about his amputated leg ("Forgive me for looking upon your nakedness," he says, revealing his stump, "look upon mine.") As R. Barton Palmer and Murray Pomerance put it, this moment in *Horsemen* is "a perfectly shot, perfectly lit, perfectly poised rendition not only of interpersonal tension but of cultural and traditional mores, value structures, and belief, not to say filial love" (9). This filial love is echoed in a conversation in *Iceman* when Larry finally confronts his past and accepts some responsibility for Parritt. By acknowledging and indeed condemning the boy for betraying his mother and the cause, Larry sentences Parritt to the death he himself craves, but is too cowardly to take. For Parritt, Larry's judgement unburdens him of his shame and is received as a momentous source of relief; it is a revelation of the paternal moral authority sorely lacking in his life.

Such moments convey something of the "sometimes cruel intensity" (12), as Gerald Pratley terms it, of Frankenheimer's desire to expose the struggle

– clearly present in both the director himself and his work – to *be*, not just do, right in the world. "Being right," writes Levenson, is not just a case of "raising a general point about moral rules or ethical principles or even norms of etiquette," but is an appeal to a rigorous perception that will "allow him [the hero] to be right, as a line in a drawing or a phrase in a sonata is right" (62). This is what Levenson means by a "constant angle of vision," one that "changes with the changing scene." It is what I am suggesting is exemplified in Frankenheimer's films through his embrace of a type of relation between an individual and his or her "unturned key," whatever the devastating consequences might be for the ego.

One encounters this kind of phrasing in a number of commentaries on Frankenheimer's work. For Pratley, Frankenheimer directed movies akin to "social documents stated with a strong point of view," brought to life "with extreme formal and thematic continuity" (14–15). For Armstrong, meanwhile, it was his emphasis on "the constancy of [his] point of view, his persistent interest in existential scenarios and the ambiguity of morality in the modern world" (5). In his interview with Evans Evans (Frankenheimer's wife), Murray Pomerance describes Frankenheimer as "among a small number of film-makers who always know exactly where to be. His camera is not only in a good place, his camera is in the *only* perfect place, in *every* shot." "What was he like in life?" asked Pomerance, "Did he always come into a room and sit in a certain chair, get the perfect point of view?" Yes, Evans Frankenheimer enthusiastically affirmed – he had a perfect point of view (237).

"That's the main thing a director has to have," Frankenheimer himself stated, " – a point of view" (qtd. in Pratley 203), and this "point of view" amounts, as he rearticulated it many years later, to the need to be "a great storyteller" (qtd. in Rhys and Bage 128). This, above all else, mattered to Frankenheimer, since a great storyteller is one who can convey the enigma of the individual without such an enigma collapsing our connection to the drama. To have a "constant angle of vision," then, refers to a certain kind of fluid movement in the way a storyteller, like Frankenheimer, frames his hero. It demonstrates an ability to move with the moving horizon of a hero who suffers an existential shift whereby, as his own framing of the world changes, so does the storyteller's frame change with him. Such movements turn on moments like the "little deaths," but also on the moments in which a flicker of love and mutual recognition changes a relationship – between two hard and cynical men in *French Connection II*; between a father and his estranged son in *The Horsemen*; between a parentless adolescent and a childless old man in *The Iceman Cometh*. Such moments amount to a *modus vivendi* in Frankenheimer's stories about vulnerable men struggling to orientate themselves in the modern era.

Hence, when Palmer and Pomerance describe Frankenheimer as a director whose approach to storytelling was "lost" in a 1970s culture captivated by "generic gigantism" (e.g. *Star Wars* and *E.T.*), one perhaps hears echoes of David A. Cook's description of the 1970s as the decade of "lost illusions," during which movies about the margins were themselves being marginalized. What such movies about the margins reveal, however, is a new depth to the cliché that it is only by first losing ourselves that we discover what it means to be. Equally, it is only through such a loss that one can become a great storyteller. This is certainly how Walter Benjamin understood the paucity of great storytellers in the modern age, when he commented that storytelling as a "practice," as an art, could find its home only in someone who knew how to "let the wick of his life be consumed by the gentle flame of his story" (107). Such an "artistic observation" of life, he wrote (quoting Paul Valéry), comes "exclusively from a certain accord of the soul, the eye, and the hand of someone who was born to perceive them and evoke them in his own inner self" (106). Hence, the "great, simple outlines" of the consummate storytellers of our times can no longer be seen directly – they require an "angle of vision" (83), that is, *some distance*. This is why the Frankenheimer "moment" is one in which his heroes are first provoked and then exposed by the disclosure of a concealed aspect of themselves which must later be *recognized* (without being fully fathomed) and accepted as a guiding light for their "being right" in the world, not to say in their relation to others. This need for distance is also why, perhaps, it has taken us so long to regard Frankenheimer as one of cinema's great storytellers.

NOTES

1. Barthes is playing on the multiple meanings of "*petit mort*" in the French language which, like *jouissance*, can mean both orgasm and a brief loss experienced as a sudden confrontation with death.
2. From miscasting Rock Hudson in *Seconds* (1966) and Gregory Peck in *I Walk the Line* (1970) to not getting the casting he wanted (that is, Steve McQueen for *Grand Prix* (1966); he blamed struggles with locations on *The Fixer* (1968), falling out with the producers of *The Gypsy Moths* (1969) and the bankruptcy of the company responsible for financing *Impossible Object* (1973). For more, see interviews with Frankenheimer by Roberts (89), Macklin (196) and especially Engle (50–5).
3. Popular in Afghanistan, *Buzkashi* (literally "goat-pulling") is a violent variant on the Persian sport of Polo in which the players – horsemen called "*Chapandaz*" – must fight over an animal carcass weighted with sand before riding to victory. The sport is a bloody, no holds barred contest, and there can be only one champion.
4. A dissolve similar to that in *The Fixer* when Bok mentions "Passover" as the old Jew breaks unleavened bread.

WORKS CITED

Armstrong, Stephen B. *Pictures About Extremes: The Films of John Frankenheimer.* McFarland & Company, 2008.

Barthes, Roland. *The Pleasure of the Text.* Translated by Richard Miller, Hill and Wang, 1998.

Benjamin, Walter. "The Storyteller: Reflections on the Works of Nikolai Leskov," 1936. *Illuminations*, edited by Hannah Arendt and translated by Harry Zorn, The Bodley Head, 2015.

Cavell, Stanley. "Philosophy the Day after Tomorrow." *Cavell on Film*, edited by William Rothman, SUNY, 2005, pp. 319–32.

Cavell, Stanley. "What Becomes of Things on Film." *Cavell on Film*, edited by William Rothman, SUNY, 2005, pp. 1–9.

Combs, Richard. "Impossible Cinema." *Film Comment*, vol. 38, no. 6, Nov./Dec. 2002, pp. 46–7, pp. 49–52.

Cook, David A. *Lost Illusions: American Cinema in the Shadow of Watergate and Vietnam 1970-1979.* University of California Press, 2000.

Ebert, Roger. 1975. "French Connection II," www.rogerebert.com/reviews/french-connection-ii-1975. Accessed 5 May 2017.

Engle, Gary D. "John Frankenheimer: An Interview (1977)." *John Frankenheimer: Interviews, Essays, and Profiles*, edited by Stephen B. Armstrong. The Scarecrow Press, 2013, pp. 49–62.

Levenson, Michael. *Modernism and the Fate of Individuality.* Cambridge University Press, 2004.

Macklin, F. Anthony. "John Frankenheimer (2000)." *John Frankenheimer: Interviews, Essays, and Profiles*, edited by Stephen B. Armstrong, The Scarecrow Press, 2013, pp. 191–211.

Nietzsche, Friedrich. *Twilight of the Idols and The Anti-Christ.* Translated by R. J. Hollingdale, Penguin, 2003.

Palmer, R. Barton and Pomerance, Murray. "Introduction: Why Don't You Pass the Time by Playing a Little Solitaire?" *A Little Solitaire: John Frankenheimer and American Film*, edited by Murray Pomerance and R. Barton Palmer, Rutgers University Press, 2011, pp. 1–12.

Pomerance, Murray. "'He Loved What He Did So Much!' An Interview with Evans (Evans) Frankenheimer (2010)." *John Frankenheimer: Interviews, Essays, and Profiles*, edited by Stephen B. Armstrong, The Scarecrow Press, 2013, pp. 229–45.

Pomerance, Murray. *Moment of Action: Riddles of Cinematic Performance.* Rutgers University Press, 2016.

Pratley, Gerald. *The Cinema of John Frankenheimer.* A. Zwemmer Limited, 1969.

Rhys, Tim, and Bage, Ian. "Hollywood Survivor John Frankenheimer (1996)." *John Frankenheimer: Interviews, Essays, and Profiles*, edited by Stephen B. Armstrong, The Scarecrow Press, 2013, pp. 125–34.

Roberts, Jerry. "Frankenheimer Says Casting Is the Key (1986)." *John Frankenheimer: Interviews, Essays, and Profiles*, edited by Stephen B. Armstrong, The Scarecrow Press, 2013, pp. 87–92.

Thomson, David. *A Biographical Dictionary of the Cinema.* Secker and Warburg, 1975.

Thomson, David. "The Decade When Movies Mattered." *The Last Great American Picture Show: New Hollywood Cinema in the 1970s*, edited by Thomas Elsaesser, Alexander Horwath and Noel King, Amsterdam University Press, 2004, pp. 73–82.

9. WILLIAM FRIEDKIN: FRAYED CONNECTIONS

Dominic Lennard

As my father said to me when he died in my arms, "I don't understand any of it. I never did."
— Michael (Kenneth Nelson) in *The Boys in the Band* (1970)

At the conclusion of his 2013 memoir, William Friedkin, citing cinema's collaborative nature, dismissively writes that he "[doesn't] give much credibility to the auteur theory." But then he seemingly hesitates: "A director's intelligence *can* inform a film" (473), he concedes, before citing several of his own influences. This reticence is strange (even comedic) in the final pages of a book that catalogues the endeavors of a director notorious for his willfulness, audacity, and even brinkmanship in the service of having things his own way. Indeed, Friedkin's 1970s work demonstrates several distinctive and developing stylistic features: a mode of distanced observation carried over from his earliest documentary work, use of cryptic cutaways, a willingness to subordinate strict narrative continuity to the emotional force of the events onscreen, and often a focus on strenuous physical action. In the majority, these films are also conspicuously male-focused, centered especially on men at or beyond the fringe of normativity and troubled in their own isolated identities. Released in 1970, Friedkin's adaptation of Mart Crowley's play *The Boys in the Band* signaled this theme early: a group of gay male friends gather for a birthday party, the jovial atmosphere of which is disturbed by the unexpected arrival of a straight and rather naive college buddy unaware of the others' sexuality. Already filled with resentments, the young men needle at each other, revealing a suite of insecurities, symptoms of self-loathing compounded by the culture around them. Viewers are thus invited first as guests to an exclusive world of marginalized masculinities, and eventually as spectators to the men's turmoil. In this chapter, however, I focus on the turbulent masculinities of Friedkin's more recognized films from this era, including *The French Connection* (1971), *The Exorcist* (1973), *Sorcerer* (1977) and *Cruising* (1980), examining their depictions of men pushed into various states of crisis and disconnection.

THE FRENCH CONNECTION

Following the release of *The Boys in the Band*, William Friedkin was dating Kitty Hawks, daughter of Howard Hawks. On first meeting Friedkin, the senior filmmaker gave him a few words of advice concerning *Boys* that, by Friedkin's admission, "really stayed with [him]" (qtd. in Biskind 203). The story goes that Hawks was dismissive: "People don't want stories about somebody's problems or any of that psychological shit," he said, "What they want is action stories." Friedkin's penchant for experimentation, moodiness, obscurity and – in short – "psychological shit," would never be properly suppressed; yet the seriousness with which the young director took Hawks's advice would certainly explain the marked shift in style and content between *The Boys in the Band* and his next film, police thriller *The French Connection*. Whereas *Boys* was emotionally rather than physically turbulent, and the drama housebound, *The French Connection* is brutal and energetic, and employed numerous outdoor locations, its police protagonists followed (often frenetically with handheld camera) through wintry New York City streets. Abrupt cutting around violent action demonstrates the director's French New Wave influences (especially *À bout de souffle* [1960]): *The French Connection*'s violence is slicing, instantaneous – without pause for breath or reflection. Given its theatrical source, *Boys* is dialogue-heavy, and begins with a lavish modern rendition of Cole Porter's bouncing "Anything Goes" as the various boys prepare for the party; in *The French Connection* dialogue is kept to a spare and desultory minimum, music is rare, and in general the film maintains a documentary preference for diegetic sound. We are observers: what happens onscreen may provoke our curiosity, urgency, or even outrage, but it is not aestheticized.

Yet for all *The French Connection*'s difference from *Boys*, troubled masculinities remain a key point of focus. At the center of the film is New York City detective "Popeye" Doyle (Gene Hackman). Unlike the masculinity of the eponymous *Boys*, Popeye's manhood is bluntly heterosexual. Moreover, whereas theirs was self-loathing and socially oppressed (and in some cases repressed), Popeye's manhood is predatory, careless, and propelled by an infantile enthusiasm and entitlement. He begins the film dressed as Santa to the amusement of a gaggle of grinning black kids, his partner "Cloudy" Russo

(Roy Scheider) posing nearby as a hotdog vendor. Popeye has the paternal power but none of the responsibility, is only playing the child-friendly figure: the kids are forgotten as the two cops leg it in pursuit of a black suspect as he runs from the bar, eventually falling on him in an abandoned lot with a hail of punches and kicks. After a couple of blows, Cloudy's moral sense kicks in; Popeye's does not. His nickname Popeye (never explained within the film) underscores his macho style, while his actions contradict the noble moral simplicity of his cartoon namesake. The rogue cop's propensity for surveillance and aggressive pursuit of his targets is linked with his sexual appetite when, having clocked off, he begins surveilling a female bicyclist on his way home, sizing her up for a sexual encounter. This same sexual intensity triggers investigation of the "French connection" from which the film takes its title. As Popeye suspiciously eyes the table of a local small-timer and his girlfriend at a club, criminal activity is not the only action on his mind: "You wanna play hide the salami with his old lady?" Cloudy asks him. Popeye and Cloudy follow the crook on a hunch, yet the trail leads all the way up to suave French heroin-importer Alain Charnier (Fernando Rey), known as "Frog One" to the cops, and his right-hand man ("Frog Two"), Pierre Nicoli (Marcel Bozzuffi), against whom the detectives range themselves in frequently hectic pursuit.

The French Connection has been seen by some commentators as endorsing the brutal policing it depicts, especially from the hyper-masculine Popeye. *TimeOut*'s Geoff Andrew (without a single positive word for the film that won Friedkin the Oscar for Best Director) refers to *The French Connection* as "maintain[ing] no critical distance from (indeed, rather relishes) its 'loveable' hero's brutal vigilante psychology" (382). Several moments of the film indeed invest us in Popeye's actions: when Frog Two takes a shot at the detective from a rooftop with a sniper rifle, he misses his mark but shoots dead a woman pushing a pram nearby. Popeye's subsequent chase thus immediately acquires urgent retaliatory purpose, and a hair-raising car chase amplifies our identification with him through its focus on physical vulnerability but also through the thrill of police power and recklessness. Yet the charge of conservatism and an absence of critical distance loses significant traction in the context of the film more broadly. Friedkin's documentary use of handheld camera, especially during scenes of police brutality, holds us at a troubled observational remove. After Cloudy and Popeye run down their black suspect early on in the film, we expect the apprehended crook to be taken to the station; instead, from a distance we see the two cops, clutching their battered charge, approach an abandoned lot to turn up the violence beyond public view. Here and elsewhere, Doyle's racism is on obvious and alienating display: "Never trust a nigger," he schools his partner after the encounter. Also there to cast doubt on Doyle in our eyes is Mulderig (Bill Hickman), the federal agent assisting the investigation, who begrudges Doyle's involvement in the death of a cop on a previous case.

Figure 9.1 "Mulderig! You shot Mulderig . . .": Cloudy (Roy Scheider) is stunned by his partner Doyle's (Gene Hackman's) insane recklessness; the frenzied Doyle cares only about readying his revolver to fire again. Digital frame enlargement. Courtesy of 20th Century Fox.

The details of this past event are unknown to us although, at least according to Mulderig, the death was the result of one of Doyle's previous "hunches."

However, it's at the film's conclusion that the critical distance becomes a veritable gulf, as Doyle chases Frog One into the dark and grimy labyrinth of an abandoned warehouse: he negligently shoots Mulderig dead and, apparently indifferent to his shocking error, darts away to fire another shot, indicative of his by now insane recklessness, as the film closes. Cloudy signals and enacts the viewer's shock, enforcing the film's moral center: "You shot Mulderig!" (Fig. 9.1). The transgression upsets the film's rhythm substantially: sinister atonal whining dominates the soundtrack, complementing the almost horrific location. No longer is the film merely about cops and criminals, as we watch the moral and psychological decay of a man consumed by his own audacity and power. Several big-timers are killed, and underlings captured, yet the biggest fish in the French Connection case dissatisfyingly escapes. Popeye has repeated his error of getting a cop killed – definitively and outrageously. At this point in the film, the detective is, in a way we cannot recuperate, overcome by his own macho bravado, leaping off madly into the dark.

THE EXORCIST

The domestic sphere is not a safe retreat in William Friedkin's films. Even in *The Boys in the Band*, largely confined to a domestic setting, a party is the scene for spectacular psychological and communal breakdown. Nor do Friedkin's films generally feature children; typically, autonomous and/or emotionally isolated men, the director's protagonists are elsewhere all notably childless. It is unsurprising, then, that the domestic environment of *The Exorcist*, and the child at its center, should be subject to such stunning subversion, but also that the film's characterological and emotional focus remains primarily on the male priest who comes to her aid.

Friedkin's documentary style is again engaged in an opening prologue set in and around an archaeological dig in Northern Iraq, where an aging priest, Father Merrin (Max von Sydow), unearths a small idol of an Assyrian demon, a sign of trouble to come. Later, an average twelve-year-old in Washington DC's Georgetown section, Regan MacNeil (Linda Blair), begins manifesting various symptoms both bizarre and belligerent, such as spontaneous urination and sudden eruptions of aggression, leading to speculation of demonic possession. Father Damien Karras (Jason Miller) is called to attend, a priest who is also psychiatrist for his seminary (and first glimpsed discussing with another priest shared feelings of fraudulence). With no experience of the arcane rites of exorcism, Karras is assigned the aging expert Merrin to lead the ritual, and in this way the old man will finally face his nemesis from the prologue.

Despite this foreshadowed confrontation, and despite the now-iconic image of the possessed Regan – scarred, empurpled, and vomit-smeared, not to say foul-mouthed and flagrantly masturbatory – the troubled Father Damien is the film's most central and developed character. And the possession, with its spectacle of childhood made monstrous and unholy, has powerful resonance for him in particular. Racked with doubt, Damien's anxiety is especially focused around his elderly and ailing Greek mother, who lives in a rundown neighborhood, and whom Damien cannot afford to provide with any great luxury. On his way to visit her, he rides the nearly empty subway (shot by Owen Roizman like a modern, metropolitan Hades), where a slumped and filthy homeless man asks him for money: "Can you help an old altar boy, Father? I'm a Catholic." The priest frowns downward in near distress at the sight. In this derelict ex-altar boy, the doubting priest sees his religion's failure, a glimpse of a world without warmth and redemption (Fig 9.2). Moreover, Damien is surely horrified by this image of the decay of romanticized childhood innocence. Increasingly senile, his mother is eventually committed to a stark sanatorium; upon visiting her there, Damien's uncle smirks that had his nephew not joined the priesthood and practiced psychiatry privately instead, she would be living in a penthouse. His once-loving mother harrowingly compounds his guilt, shirking his touch as he leans over her: "Why you do this to me, Dimmy?" she cries. She dies shortly thereafter, and Damien's self-blame deepens. As Carol Clover has observed, "*The Exorcist*, for all its focus on Regan's excrescences, turns on Father Karras's tortured relation to his mother" (85). Indeed, the degradation of Regan's treasured innocence and affection is precisely the degradation that Karras feels he has himself enacted, and the film's editing several times couples Damien's increasing anxiety with the worsening of Regan's condition, as if she manifests the priest's own inner turmoil. In the revolting Regan we see explosively metaphorized the young priest's feelings of self-loathing, inherited from a confused mother who virtually curses him for his autonomy and perceived abandonment of her. While he is hardly the rogue of *The Exorcist*, the film's crisis circles around Damien's autonomy, a sense of self troubled by feelings of isolation and rejection. In his devotion to and rejection by his mother we see a conflict between his desire to always be the idealized, doting good son and his self-initiated role in the priesthood. At the end of *The French Connection*, Popeye darted off into the darkness of his own amoral disorientation, leaving viewers to recognize and recoil from his corruption; the doubt-filled Damien, however, already acutely feels himself to be morally disgraced and abandoned.

The Exorcist also sees Friedkin's work assume the stylistic "incoherence" attributed to several other American directors of the era. Writers such as Todd Berliner, Bill Krohn, and Robin Wood (52–62) have highlighted the logical and narrative fissures in Friedkin's style. Adrian Martin refers to the director's work as characteristic of a "cinema of hysteria" associated with films of the New Hollywood: "a mode of filmmaking that actively cultivates incoherence: structured upon moment-to-moment spectacular effect, it aims for the sudden gasp, the revelatory dramatic frisson, the split-second turn-around

Figure 9.2   Anguished priest Damien Karras (Jason Miller) seems unable to reconcile his religion with the world around him, as he gazes on a homeless former altar boy in *The Exorcist* (1973). Digital frame enlargement. Courtesy of Warner Bros.

of meaning or mood." There are certainly gaps in *The French Connection*: how did Doyle's hunches initially "[get] a good cop killed"? – and what is the meaning of the dramatic final gunshot, since closing titles tell us that Frog One escaped unharmed? Yet *The Exorcist*'s disconnections are more prominent still. For instance, around the middle of the film a crucifix has been placed under Regan's pillow, much to her mother's aggravation, although the culprit remains unclear. Just before she famously urinates on the carpet, Regan tells a guest at her mother's party, "You're gonna die up there." The announcement may ring ominously for readers of William Peter Blatty's source novel, which tells us that this guest is an astronaut, but his occupation is not signaled in the film and Regan's meaning is thus left unclear. More obviously, the film is founded on a spatial/narrative disunity that is never properly resolved: what precisely is the connection between Merrin's foreboding experience in Iraq and this particular girl in Washington DC? The film is exemplary of Friedkin's tendency to subordinate strict logical continuity to the sensory and emotional power of filmic rhythms and moments. Since the possession itself is not, of course, a "logical" event, the film's supernatural subject alleviates the need for very strict causal relationships. Yet also, if we read the film's events as somehow a chaotic reflection of the internal anguish of Damien, its main male character, its narrative leaps and fissures might be seen as an additional expression of emotional turbulence and disorientation.

SORCERER

Early in *Sorcerer*, a loose remake of Henri-Georges Clouzot's *The Wages of Fear* (*Le salaire de la peur,* 1953) with a screenplay by Walon Green, Parisian investment banker Victor Manzon (Bruno Cremer) dines in an upmarket restaurant with his wife and her friend. Unbeknownst to his present company, Victor and his brother-in-law Pascal (Jean-Luc Bideau) have recently been discovered by the President of the French Stock Exchange fraudulently misrepresenting their collateral on a multi-million-dollar deal. Victor is attempting to enjoy this lavish luncheon during the twenty-four hours the President has given him to return the missing sum before he will be arrested and face a lengthy jail term, and after having instructed Pascal to plead with his wealthy father to loan them the money. Mid-meal, a waiter informs Victor that Pascal is waiting outside. Pascal's father has refused, and Victor anxiously urges him to call again before leaving to rejoin his companions. Pascal does not comply: he gets inside his golden Citroën sedan and shoots himself in the head. Victor turns back to the car, stunned, as his partner's blood trickles down the shattered rear-windshield. The music repeats a light, almost jaunty *pizzicato* melody that earlier accompanied shots of the decorous, chatter-filled dining room, evoking not so much the moment's sadness as its inane incongruity. Evidently no one inside the restaurant has heard the shot, so Victor paces politely inside and does something just as unexpected. He calls stealthily on the *maître d'hôtel* to advise his wife that he has been called away suddenly on business. Then he leaves – the restaurant, the city, the continent – and for good. And he leaves having received from his wife that morning a watch touchingly engraved in commemoration of their ten-year anniversary together: *Pour ces 10 années de notre éternité.*

Victor flees to a remote South American village where, along with a motley group of male misfits, he tries out for and receives the hair-raising job of trucking packages of highly volatile nitroglycerine hundreds of miles across hazardous jungle terrain so that the material can be used to blow up a flaming oil well. Victor's back story, detailed above, is just one in a series of vignettes explaining the men's origins and showing how each is concealing some past of secret criminality. Along with Victor is an Arab terrorist, Kaseem (Amidou); the driver for an Irish gang in New Jersey, Jackie Scanlon (Roy Scheider); an assassin from Veracruz, Nilo (Francisco Rabal); and a mysterious German, "Marquez" (Karl John), presumably a former Nazi. They are all exiles, men who have thrown themselves into a radical (possibly lethal) autonomy, disa-vowing emotional comfort, connection, and belonging. Yet this is an amplifi-cation of their already-existing tendency toward isolation: for instance, when Victor receives the watch, his wife isn't even sure he likes it, such is his habitual emotional reserve – "I can never tell with you," she remarks.

The mission necessitates from the men an extreme recklessness with their own lives, and the film contains scenes of agonizing suspense as trucks roll along the edge of sheer cliffs and across a raging river. As its director has emphasized in numerous interviews, the existential threat of sudden and unpredictable death is a pressing thematic concern. Yet this is expressed, again, specifically through male isolation and emotional disavowal. Victor's own death is one of the most intriguing in this regard. His truck, having rounded cliffs with its wheels virtually overhanging the edges, seems now on steady ground, so its driver begins chatting to Kassim beside him: "I'm from Paris – you know Paris?" Victor speaks wistfully of his life at home, the wife he met there. He shows his new friend the watch: "The day she gave me this was the last day I saw her." He glances at the time, pondering: "It's five minutes before nine, in Paris." (Fig. 9.3). The truck's front tire blows out and the vehicle lurches heavily. The nitro in the back tumbles forward and the truck explodes instantly. Some distance away, Scanlon and Nilo watch smoke pour into the sky above. Victor is centralized more than Kassim, the focus of an emotional connection rare within this grimy, hardboiled film. Like so many of Friedkin's characters, he is overloaded with guilt and secrecy. It is at the point that he recalls the life he has disavowed, with all its emotional resonance (the gift, his wife's love, a place where still at this very moment she exists) that the explosion occurs, as

Figure 9.3 "It's five minutes before nine, in Paris," Victor (Bruno Cremer, right) tells Kassem (Amidou, left) in *Sorcerer* (1977). The comment that wistfully recalls the life he has drastically deserted is the last thing Victor will ever say. Digital frame enlargement. Courtesy of Paramount Pictures.

if the detonation and death somehow reflect Victor's inability to sustain this massive repression.

Not dissimilarly to *The French Connection*, *Sorcerer* pushes male isolationism and autonomy into a kind of psychosis. Scanlon is the only man to complete the mission: dazed and haunted by his experiences, he steers the truck through a desolate, lunar-like landscape, then stumbles madly toward the inferno, attempting to deliver his box of nitro by hand. Friedkin's framing of the film as a meditation on the randomness of existence threatens to short-circuit any critical search for symbolic meaning; yet what we see in *Sorcerer* are also highly autonomous male identities pushed to a state of internal crisis, the outcome of which is either psychosis or the trauma of emotional destitution exploding (much as in *The Exorcist*) within the narrative itself – and in this case exploding literally.

Cruising

Expensive, time-consuming and occasionally life-threatening to put on film, the bleak and grimy *Sorcerer* nevertheless failed in a culture embracing the nostalgic, film-serial style adventure of *Star Wars* (1977). Yet despite the film's critical and box-office failure, Friedkin's next film did not involve any shift to more commercially appealing or audience-friendly filmmaking – if anything, the reverse. In *Cruising*, Friedkin's focus on obsessive and increasingly disconnected male protagonists was amplified through an erosion of the boundaries of heteronormative sexuality: in *Cruising*, "male obsession" becomes "male-obsession." Moreover, the film retained its director's interest in experimentation with its disconnected approach to narrative.

With body parts washing up in the Hudson River, NYPD Captain Edelston (Paul Sorvino) gambles on their connection to a series of slayings of gay men in the underground leather bar scene. Edelston calls police officer Steve Burns (Al Pacino) to his office, and after quizzing him indecorously about his sexual preferences (Burns is straight) offers an undercover assignment in promise for speedy promotion, since – dark-haired and dark-eyed – Steve appears to be this killer's "type." Clad in denim and leather, Burns ventures into the underworld far outside "the mainstream of gay life," where men engage in various (individual and group) sexual adventures in bars like the "Ramrod" in New York's meatpacking district.

Ten years after *The French Connection, Cruising* was thus a return for Friedkin to the crime-thriller genre, an apt precinct for critical interrogation of the functioning – and malfunctioning – of hardboiled men. Early on, the film confuses the boundaries between normative and "deviant" sexualities (thus masculinities) as two police officers cruise the bar district in their radio car, muttering disgust at the neighborhood's decay in a scene that strongly recalls Scorsese's *Taxi Driver* (1976). Yet moments later, they bully two crossdressers to fellate them. Their targeting of these figures is indicative of their socially sanctioned feelings of entitlement to harass queers, but their sexual coercion specifically is also reflective of their deep misogyny: moments earlier, one cop had cursed his "bitch" wife while the other concurred: "They're all scumbags." As R. Barton Palmer notes, in this scene "the distinction between queer and straight worlds blurs, making a central point about rigid cultural assumptions of 'homosexuality'" (94). More broadly, the heavy-leather community parodies the traditionally "rigid" masculinity associated with the police force; at one point, Burns even stumbles in on a "Precinct Night" in which bar patrons dress as police officers. The term "cruising" itself, ostensibly used to describe the search for anonymous gay sex, applies also to the police, patrolling in their "cruisers."

Burns is himself powerfully yet ambivalently fascinated by this hidden world of erotic desire. The undercover detail is secret (not even his wife knows), setting him loose with an isolation typical of Friedkin's protagonists. The assignment naturally leads him into amorous contact with other men, and it becomes clear that the role is affecting him both emotionally and sexually, straining his marital life. His wife Nancy (Karen Allen), sensing her husband's emotional and sexual disconnection from her, eventually leaves him. Startled at his own transformation, the revelation of previously suppressed homoerotic fascination or desire, Burns grows edgier and more volatile in his actions. At one point he aggressively threatens the partner of his gay neighbor, an

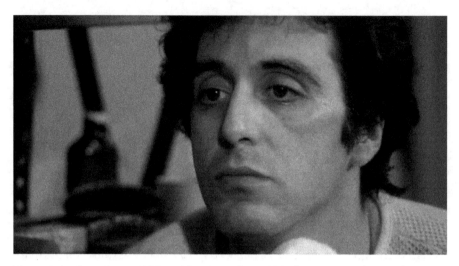

Figure 9.4   Steve Burns (Al Pacino) peers at himself in the mirror at the conclusion of *Cruising* (1980), his identity peculiarly uncertain even to him. Digital frame enlargement. Courtesy of Lorimar/United Artists.

internalized homophobia boiling to the surface to challenge this deep immersion in a world that questions the coherence of his (at least putatively) straight identity (Fig. 9.4).

Meanwhile, the killings continue: we see a man stabbed to death in a peep show, and another in a park pickup spot. "You made me do that," the killer intones to his dying prey. Friedkin's characteristic "incoherence" intrudes when the film allows some focus on the killer beyond the scene of his violent deeds. Stuart Richards (Richard Cox), a grad student at a local university, doesn't speak in the low and raspy tones we know from earlier to characterize the murderer. This discrepancy is to some extent resolved when we discover that Stuart is obsessed with the approval of his dead father (Leland Starnes), whose continued existence he periodically hallucinates and who speaks in a voice we recognize as the killer's. Our view of the murders, then, has been mediated by Stuart's psychosis, and the acts themselves are an attempt by Stuart to disavow his homosexuality and brutally appease his father through grotesque over-performances of paternal discipline ("You made me do that"). Yet the riddle is still not disentangled: Friedkin has arranged that in each of the murder scenes, and while clad in identical aviator sunglasses and a leather cap, the killer is actually played by a different actor; furthermore, the film implies there may be multiple killers by depicting one such suspicious character's return to the Ramrod club at the conclusion of the film. Each man is seen speaking, but the voice in every case is dubbed in as that of Stuart's father, and utters the same words. Such flourishes clearly breach the (even graphic) realism suggested by the bar scenes, with their documentary observance of heavy-leather culture and gay sex, steering the film far beyond the lean cut-and-thrust of *The French Connection* and producing a text that is narratively abstract and logically irresolvable.

Protested by gay rights groups during its production for its suspected connection of homosexuality and violence, and received poorly by critics, *Cruising* was instrumental in the waning of Friedkin's directorial star into the 1980s. However, the film has since undergone significant reappraisal, during which there has been much discussion of the effect and intention (or lack thereof) of these experimental touches. The key forerunner to this revisionism was the work of Robin Wood, who not long after the film's release offered an analysis interpreting the film's internal confusion as a suggestion that the killer was not individuated but part of a culture of homophobia. The father's voice dominates, suggests Wood, because "the film's real villain is revealed as patriarchal domination"; Stuart's father is symbolic of a broader patriarchal, homophobic masculinity: "his demands ... are enacted in the brutality and corruption of the police, and parodied in the sadomasochism of the leather bars" (7). According to such a view, this homophobia, latent in the structure of straight macho masculinity, is finally enacted by Burns, who, the film strongly implies, murders his gay neighbor at the end of the film, violently reacting against the confusion of his own identity. Despite being protested by activists, the film suggests not that homosexuality leads to violence but instead, as Palmer points out, that "homosexuals are the victims of a homophobia that has its roots in the repression of homosexual urges" (93). In this sense, the film's incoherence seems to work to fragment and abstract guilt: homophobic violence is pervasive, symptomatic, ever-present, not contained by an individual killer, but instead social – hence its eventual emergence in the repressed Steve Burns.

Through the implication of Burns himself, *Cruising* engages the well-worn cop-film trope – also explored in *The French Connection* and Friedkin's later *Killer Joe* (2011) – of the similarities between those who commit crimes and those who catch them. In *Cruising* this is conveyed as a gradual erosion of the boundaries between Burns and the killer, who aggressively overreacts to the perceived threat to his masculinity and the "closeness" of homosexuality. In the climax of *The Exorcist*, Damien Karras invites the demon into himself, before hurling himself from Regan's upstairs window to his death. In this invitation, the tormented priest seems to forward himself as the true target, identifying the real "demon" – his obsessive self-loathing over his mother's death – where it seems to have been lurking all along. In *Cruising*, a questioning of one's identity and sexual affiliation also culminates in a breakdown of one's governing identity: the terrible Other is identified as part of oneself. Although *Cruising* lacks the supernatural vocabulary of *The Exorcist*, the killer's internalized homophobia might be said to have similarly "possessed" Burns.

Friedkin's films throughout the 1970s were concerned with the boundaries of normative identity, and with male identities specifically. Friedkin regularly deals with "tough guys"; even the moody and introverted Father Karras of *The Exorcist* is a former prizewinning amateur boxer who still likes to lace up the gloves. Yet they are men whose isolation and autonomy, rather than reinforcing their identity threatens either to undo their sense of self or to consume them. Released ten years after *The Boys in the Band*, we can see that *Cruising* represents a powerful – and darker – re-examination of masculinities on the fringe of social acceptability. *Cruising* also represents a deep problematizing of "accepted" (straight) masculinities. Environments and events both thrilling and exotic are a mainstay of Friedkin's films (the world of drug-trafficking, demonic possession, jungle adventure and, in *Cruising*, underground gay clubs). Friedkin may indeed have taken Howard Hawks's urging toward action and entertainment seriously, and indeed he models the New Hollywood era's continued emphasis on genre. Yet *Cruising*, especially, also reflects Friedkin's seemingly irrepressible desire to drift from the logical coherence expected of commercial Hollywood filmmaking. More even than the fragmentation of *The Exorcist*, it exemplifies Bill Krohn's observation that "a Friedkin film is a collage rather than the execution of a sketch or plan whose unity gives a priori unity to the work." In the director's final film of this period we see a text that, like the male identities that inhabit it, cannot be comfortably clarified – one that only recourse to "psychological shit" can begin to explain.

Works Cited

Andrew, Geoff. "Rev. of *The French Connection*." *TimeOut Film Guide*, edited by John Pym, Time Out, 2011, p. 382.

Berliner, Todd. *Hollywood Incoherent: Narration in Seventies Cinema*. University of Texas Press, 2011. Kindle file.

Biskind, Peter. *Easy Riders, Raging Bulls: How the Sex 'N' Drugs 'N' Rock 'N' Roll Generation Saved Hollywood*. Bloomsbury, 1999.

Clover, Carol J. *Men, Women, and Chainsaws: Gender in the Modern Horror Film*. Princeton University Press, 1992.

Friedkin, William. *The Friedkin Connection: A Memoir*. HarperCollins, 2013.

Krohn, Bill. "Friedkin Out." *Rouge*, vol. 3, 2004, www.rouge.com.au/3/friedkin.html. Accessed 12 May 2020.

Martin, Adrian. "*Cruising*: The Sound of Violence." *Fipresci*, vol. 4, 2008, www.fipresci.hegenauer.co.uk/undercurrent/issue_0407/martin_cruising.htm. Accessed May 2 2020.

Palmer, R. Barton. "Redeeming *Cruising*: Tendentiously Offensive, Coherently Incoherent, Strangely Pleasurable." *B is for Bad Cinema: Aesthetics, Politics, and Cultural Value*, edited by Claire Perkins and Constantine Verevis, State University of New York Press, 2014, pp. 85–104.

Wood, Robin. *Hollywood Cinema: From Vietnam to Reagan... and Beyond*. Columbia University Press, 2003.

10. SIDNEY LUMET AND THE NEW HOLLYWOOD

David Desser

For all of the social movements – the rebellion, the protests, the counterculture – of the late 60s, little of that made a mark on the younger filmmakers of the Hollywood Renaissance. The movie brats, save for the early works of Brian De Palma, were a particularly apolitical cohort. Growing up in the safety and prosperity of postwar America, their concerns were moving pictures not protest and politics. Unlike the movie brats who went to film school, the previous generation of filmmakers who bolstered the Hollywood Renaissance got their education in the proverbial school of hard knocks, frequently overseas during the Second World War. While the movie brats gleefully explored the freedom of film form brought about by the elimination of the restrictive Production Code in 1966, older directors took aim at the society that promised equal rights for all but continued racist policies under the guise of law and order and delivered more sexual than civil freedom, more right to party than the right to vote. No filmmaker of the 1970s (and after) had been more politically inclined, more incisive about social ills and injustice than Sidney Lumet, not even the acerbic Robert Altman (one year Lumet's junior). Although Lumet had something specific in mind other than politics, his assertion that "I think you can draw a solid line between the directors who were brought up on television – who spent their childhoods watching television – and those who didn't" (qtd. in Rapf 126–7) applies to politics as much as to film style.

Lumet was always a figure more respected within the industry itself than by the dominant film critics of the 70s. The movie brat who dominated both the mainstream industry and the culture industry was Francis Ford Coppola (also the oldest of the bunch). His unprecedented Best Picture and Best Director Oscar wins and nominations along with his box-office clout put him on top of the critical heap. His major films from *The Godfather* (1972) through to *Apocalypse Now* (1979) garnered an astounding eighteen major Academy wins and nominations. Few remember that in the same categories Lumet's films of the decade captured twenty-five nominations (though no Best Picture or Best Director wins). That *Network* (1976), nominated in every major Oscar category, a total of ten nominations in all categories, did not win Best Picture remains one of those Oscar mysteries (discussed in more detail below).

Though box-office takings are no indication of quality, it does say something about popular appeal. Thus, it is worth noting that Lumet's three most important films of the decade – *Serpico* (1973), *Dog Day Afternoon* (1975) and *Network* – grossed a total of $104 million; compare this to Martin Scorsese's three best-remembered works of the era, *Mean Streets* (1973), *Alice Doesn't Live Here Anymore* (1974), and *Taxi Driver* (1976), whose total gross is only $49 million; the total for De Palma's top three barely crosses $40 million and most of that belongs to *Carrie* (1976). (Of course, Lumet's box-office cannot compare to Coppola's, or to the pop sensations Spielberg and Lucas.)

Still, outside of the industry, where Lumet, in fact, spent much of his time (he did not make his first film in Hollywood until 1986), he never found as much favor as many in the Hollywood Renaissance. The two most influential critics – both, like Lumet, based in New York – Pauline Kael and Andrew Sarris, feuded throughout the 60s and 70s. Yet, as one interviewer pointed out, they agreed on at least one thing: "they both dislike [Lumet's] films" (Rapf 111). The knock on Lumet, before his apotheosis toward the end of his career when, in 2005, he was given an honorary Academy Award for his "brilliant services to screenwriters, performers, and the art of the motion picture" (*The Guardian*), was that he had a televisual aesthetic. On the one hand, this is not a great surprise considering the years he spent working in, and helping to create, the 1950s "Golden Age of Television." Similarly, he is often called an "actor's director" (as witness the number of times his cast members have received nods and wins from the Academy Awards). Again, no surprise from someone who was an early member of the Actors Studio. On the other hand, Lumet is often thought of as merely an adapter of theatrical, literary, and original scripts by powerful writers. Not only is it hard to argue this point, it is one with which Lumet himself would agree. He said that the notion of the auteur director embarrassed him and that to claim the label for himself was "pretentious" (Rapf 113). He also said plainly that, "[I]t's my job to serve the writer" (Rapf 124). Frank Cunningham, author of an intelligent monograph on Lumet, even subtitles his study, "Film and Literary Vision."

Yet Lumet was certainly an auteur, drawn to specific projects that allowed him to express his social conscience and humanistic instincts. As he explained,

"[A]t the risk of appearing cynical, I'll say that I like questioning things, people, and institutions and in general, everything that passes for 'good behavior.'" (Rapf 105) It is possible to define one of Lumet's premier concerns as "the little guy against the system" (Rapf 112) where the system is corrupt and the little guy almost overwhelmed. The system for Lumet is not some generalized status quo or the function of bad people mucking up the works. The system is very specific and very much identifiable: the police, the courts, the government, and certain social attitudes.

Writing in the *New York Times* in 1974, Stephen Farber noted with some dismay that,

> In the last couple of years . . . with only a few exceptions, our movies have nervously avoided social themes. Among the latest films only *Serpico* has tried to attack the failures of American society, and it had to be financed by an *Italian* producer [Dino De Laurentiis]. (Farber 127; emphasis original)

He goes on to say:

> Whereas the last generation of important American filmmakers (including Arthur Penn, Sidney Lumet, John Frankenheimer and Martin Ritt) had and continue to have strong social concerns, many younger writers and directors have little or no interest in social issues . . . Some of them come from film schools in which the auteur theory has been enshrined as gospel and where courses of study concentrate on arcane meanings in the melodramas of Alfred Hitchcock, Howard Hawks, Don Siegel and Douglas Sirk. When they enter the industry, these young filmmakers want to remake the simple-minded genre movies that they loved as children and that the academics have finally made respectable. (Farber 127)

Though it will doubtless come as a surprise to most that Hitchcock, Hawks, and Siegel made melodramas, more to the point is the overall cringe-worthy complaint Farber makes. This is exactly the sort of thing the *Cahiers* critics dealt with two decades earlier (and with mostly the same directors as examples!). *Cahiers du cinéma*'s "politique des auteurs" would win the day while Lumet would go blithely on his way making socially conscious, commercially successful, and (outside of Sarris and Kael) critically acclaimed films.

"COULDN'T I PAY FOR IT AND GET WHAT I WANT?": *SERPICO*

Writing for TCM, Sean Axmaker calls *Serpico* "the first major American film to seriously and unflinchingly confront police corruption as a systemic issue," and notes Lumet's "documentary-style approach to shooting." Indeed, there are many instances where the combination of location shooting, available light, and handheld cinematography strongly imbue this biographical drama with an air of documentary authenticity. Frank Serpico, the NYPD cop who blew the lid on endemic and widespread police corruption and had to flee to Switzerland to find both safety and respite after his fellow officers failed to help him during a drug bust and almost got him killed, is portrayed in the film (by Al Pacino) as driven by righteous indignation. One could, in fact, begin to feel as his girlfriend Laurie (Barbara Eda-Young) does, that his obsession with police corruption and his fear of his fellow officers is beginning to wear. Of course, we side with Serpico and find it ironic that when he is posted to a precinct in the Bronx, his fellow plainclothes detectives insist he take part in their graft, and claim, "Who can trust a cop who don't take money?" They even offer to give Serpico's cut of their scheme to charity!

The film is insistent in demonstrating how the corruption of the police force expresses itself in many ways: free food in exchange for looking the other way when delivery trucks are double-parked; refusing to answer a rape call because it is not in their sector; beating a suspect with a telephone book so it won't leave marks; lazily checking finger prints in a case file; and divvying up literally thousands of dollars from drug busts. Serpico will have none of it and although he doesn't want to testify in court, he is finally convinced to do so. But even there he sees a kind of corruption on the part of the District Attorney, who refuses to allow him to testify about the top brass, only the little guys on the street. Yet, like Serpico himself, Lumet castigates this corruption with a white-hot fervor, carried by Pacino's intense performance and the propulsive narrative. As Guy Flatley notes, "there is something old about *Serpico* – that same old moral fervor, the same cry of social protest that sounds not too far below the surface of virtually every Lumet venture." (Flatley 111).

The film opens with the sound of a police siren and a heartbeat heard under the sparse credits. As the narrative begins we see Serpico being rushed to the hospital with a gun-shot wound to his face. A brief montage shows different cops being informed, one noting that he knows six cops who would have liked to put a bullet in Serpico. Thus, we are apprised of Serpico's problematic relationship with his fellow men in blue. As he is put on a gurney, the film flashes back to his graduation from the police academy with a sound bridge from the hospital to the graduation. This first flashback is only a brief one of thirty-five seconds or so until we return to the present. Here we see Chief Green (John Randolph) rushing into the hospital, obviously concerned for Serpico. We then see Serpico wheeled into an operating room in a long-take follow shot. After almost two minutes of activity in the hospital we flash back again to the graduation ceremony with another sound bridge.

This intercutting pattern of present-past-present-past has little of the shock

Figure 10.1   The haunted face of Detective Frank Serpico as he tries to fight corruption in the NYPD in *Serpico* (1973). Digital frame enlargement. Courtesy of Paramount Pictures.

value and graphic matching that Lumet and editor Ralph Rosenbloom brought to the use of flashbacks in *The Pawnbroker* (1965). The use of flash cuts to exteriorize the process of Nazerman's (Rod Steiger) memories of his experience during the Holocaust brought to him unbidden and unwelcome by some action or image in the present, was then highly innovative. Cuts of just a few frames from the past gradually get longer and replace the images in the present, with matches on action, such as a woman taking off her wedding ring in the pawnshop leading to a shot of Nazi guards removing the rings of Jewish women as they line up against a fence. We should note that *The Pawnbroker* is heavily – and very successfully – indebted to the filmmaking of Alain Resnais (an "older brother" to the young guns of *Cahiers*). Although Sarris and Kael were enthusiastic about the New Wave connections of other seventies filmmakers (perhaps most notably Arthur Penn), they never managed to respect Lumet, who, early in the period, followed the stylistic and thematic path laid out by Resnais, including the foregrounding of the Holocaust as a primary subject for political cinema. The cuts from present to past in *Serpico* show far less of the Resnais influence. These edits are smoothed over by the sound bridges, but there is otherwise no graphic match and they simply function as typical flashbacks of someone remembering. Indeed, after the second flashback the film proceeds chronologically through Serpico's experiences with police graft and corruption for almost two hours until we return to the present with Serpico recovering from his wound.

The narrative is driven by Frank's experience and dismay at the corruption he sees around him. As his career progresses from a patrol car to plain clothes, the corruption becomes more severe and less acceptable before he feels forced to make official complaints and launch an intensive investigation. Lumet is given to narrative ellipses, so the passing of time is indicated by changes in Serpico, such as his growing a mustache and his rise in the ranks from patrolman to the BCI (Bureau of Criminal Investigation). At each level his integrity and refusal to cut corners become more apparent. By the time he is in plain clothes, working his way up – he hopes – to detective, Serpico has a full beard and long hair. Lumet has described the character of Frank Serpico as "the hippie dressed as a cop" (Rapf 83) and this characterization of Serpico is important, of course, in enabling the film to connect with the youth audience that the New Hollywood discovered in the key year of 1967 and tried not to let go of. The film is structured like a *Bildungsroman*, an education-novel, as Frank moves from naive rookie cop to crusading avenger.

Serpico's naivete as a rookie cop is revealed when he goes to a neighborhood diner with an older cop. The cop asks for "the soup of the day" but Serpico asks for a roast beef sandwich, much to the obvious chagrin of the counterman. Serpico is equally chagrined when his roast beef is fatty. The older cop informs him that he should just take what is offered as it is on the house. Serpico replies, "Couldn't I pay for it and get what I want?" This should be seen as something of the film's theme. What Serpico wants is a graft- and corruption-free NYPD. What he gets is a bullet in the face.

For Vincent Canby, the influential critic for the *New York Times*, *Serpico* moves beyond the issue of police corruption. For him the film also castigates "the sort of sleaziness and second-rateness that has affected so much of American life, from the ingredients of its hamburgers to the ethics of its civil servants and politicians" (Canby, "The Screen: Serpico"). Though one is not sure where or how the film hammers the beloved hamburger, ethics are always on Lumet's plate. In fact, beginning with *The Offence* (1973), the film Lumet released a few months before *Serpico*, he set out on his path to a cinema intimately, although not exclusively, concerned with social justice, societal problems, and the decision to do right or wrong amidst widespread corruption and moral decay.

"TELL THE TV TO STOP SAYING THERE'S TWO HOMOSEXUALS IN HERE": *DOG DAY AFTERNOON*

Lumet reteamed with Al Pacino to make *Dog Day Afternoon* following the now-little known *Lovin' Molly* (1974) and the fun frivolity of the box-office hit *Murder on the Orient Express* (1974). Pacino, meanwhile, was fresh from the unprecedented triumph of *The Godfather: Part II* and yet another Oscar nomination. *Dog Day Afternoon* would go on to out-gross *Murder on the Orient Express* and garner, among other accolades, six major Academy Award nominations. Vincent Canby called *Dog Day Afternoon* "the most accurate, most flamboyant [and] best film [Lumet] has ever made, with the exception of *A Long Day's Journey into Night* . . . (Canby, "Lumet's Quintessential" 129). The film is based on a real-life bank heist that occurred in Brooklyn in the summer of 1972, when two amateur crooks attempted to rob a small branch of the Chase Manhattan bank. The robbery quickly went south and while hundreds of police officers and FBI surrounded the bank, along with numerous onlookers, the hapless thieves held eight hostages inside for over fifteen hours. The drama came to an end at Kennedy International Airport when one of the robbers, Salvatore Naturelle, was shot in the chest by an FBI agent, while the other bank robber, John Wojtowicz, surrendered unharmed.

During the hostage stand-off, it came out that Wojtowicz was gay. The homosexual aspect of the actual incident was of major interest at the time. For instance, the *Lewiston Morning Tribune* in Idaho used a headline which read "Homosexual Robs Bank, Asks Release of 'Wife.'" *The Bulletin* of Bend, Oregon, has a less tendentious headline, but refers to a "dead gunman and his homosexual accomplice" in the first paragraph of their coverage. In the second paragraph the as-yet unnamed robber is referred to as "a homosexual who at one point demanded a reunion with his unwilling former male 'wife.'" Again, in the fifth paragraph we learn that "the homosexual threatened to shoot the hostages . . ." Compare this to the *New York Times* of this date: "2 Hold 8 Hostages in a Bank in Brooklyn." The treatment of homosexuality is also rather different. John is allowed to mention his sexual preference himself: we read that he says, "I'm gay," over the phone during the initial stand-off. Way down in the ninth paragraph we learn of a "bizarre train of events, which included visits to the scene of homosexual friends of the gunmen who kissed them in the bank doorway to the cheers of the huge crowd" (Prial 1).

Lumet and screenwriter Frank Pierson, who won an Oscar for his work, stay close to the basic facts of the story but, naturally, must invent dialogue for the bank robbers, the cops, the FBI, and the hostages. More to the point, whereas newspaper coverage at the time could not resist the homosexual angle, Lumet keeps it from the audience for over one hour. This builds sympathy for the increasingly harassed, desperate, but still likable Sonny Wortzik (played by Pacino, and with a name change from the actual John Wojtowicz). We already know that Sonny is married with two children, so that when he is told that his wife has arrived on the scene we and the characters in the film are surprised, and some are taken aback, when Leon (Chris Sarandon) arrives. One cop is heard to remark, with a bit of a sneer, "He's a queer?" When Leon explains to the (seemingly) sympathetic Sgt. Moretti (Charles Durning) that a psychiatrist told him he was a woman trapped in a man's body it seems that it is all anyone

Figure 10.2   Robbing a bank proves more troublesome and difficult than the robbers can imagine in *Dog Day Afternoon* (1975). Digital frame enlargement. Courtesy of Warner Bros.

on the scene can do to keep a straight face. Sonny's primary motivation for robbing the bank turns out to be to finance gender-reassignment surgery (what was then called a sex-change operation) for Leon.

At this point, Lumet further demonstrates his own sensitivity to Sonny's plight when he shows how the news coverage of the robbery now shifts, like the actual newspaper coverage at the time, to exploit the homosexual angle. First, we learn that the priest who has performed Sonny and Leon's wedding has been de-frocked – gay marriage was certainly anathema to the Catholic Church at that time and doubtless few Americans could envision a moment when such a thing would become both legal and common. Next, we see how the television anchorman refers to the bank robbers as "two homosexuals [who] are holding hostages." It is a tribute to both Lumet and co-star John Cazale that Sal's dismay at being labeled a homosexual and his plaintively asking Sonny to "tell the TV to stop saying there's two homosexuals in here" is far more pathetic than it is funny. Sal asks this more than once, not just of Sonny but later of FBI Agent Sheldon (James Broderick). When gay activists arrive on the scene shouting the gay liberation slogan, "Out of the closet and into the streets," it appears that many in the crowd who had supported Sonny so strongly are beginning to turn against him. In fact, when the bus arrives to take Sonny, Sal, and the hostages to the airport, it is pelted with fists, stones, and shouts.

Here we may realize that Lumet has no fewer than three corrupt institutions on his mind. The first is the FBI. Durning's NYPD sergeant Moretti is frenetically trying his best to keep the situation under control. Compare his sweaty, hoarse attempts with the buttoned-down, eerie, cool, scary, and calm demeanor of Broderick's FBI Agent Sheldon. His suit is impeccable; not a drop of sweat beads on his face; and there is always a hint of a smirk on his lips. There is something very mysterious and disturbing when he assures Sonny that they will "take care of Sal." Just what he means is unclear at the time, but in retrospect it is chilling and horrifying, for at the film's climax Agent Murphy (Lance Henriksen) does indeed take care of Sal, putting a bullet in the middle of his forehead. Of course, we do not expect the FBI to allow Sonny and Sal to jet off scot free to Algeria, but the cold efficiency with which they dispatch Sal and capture Sonny seems somehow heinous.

The second institution Lumet castigates is the press, especially the television coverage. Roger Ebert notes how "Criminals become celebrities because their crimes provide fodder for the media."(Ebert, *Dog Day Afternoon*) In this respect the 1975 hit looks forward to *Network* a year later. Indeed, eerily looking forward to the later film, at one point, Sonny tells the news anchor that he and Sal are going to die on TV as "entertainment." We have already seen how the bank robbers are transformed into nothing more than objects of derision by labeling them homosexuals. The anchorman implies that Sonny and Leon's marriage was nothing more than a charade, a joke, mentioning that the bridesmaids were all men. Yet the anchorman can count on his audience being on his side, for this is the third institution Lumet decries, the fusion of binary sex roles, knee-jerk homophobia, and a profound lack of understanding of the role of gender in life and society. As critic Robin Wood observed at the time, *Dog Day Afternoon* broke new ground as "the first American commercial movie in which the star/identification figure turns out to be gay" (Wood 33). As Sam Roberts reported in 2014, Sidney Lumet recalled that Pacino "was the one at greatest risk," because "no major star that I know of had ever played a gay man" (Macias 46). In a crawl at the end of the film we learn that Sonny is serving twenty years in prison; his wife Angela lives on welfare with their two children; and Leon had his sex change surgery and lives as a woman in New York. Lumet's sympathies clearly extend to all three of them.

Interestingly, in *Dog Day Afternoon* Lumet downplays what many films of the immediate era were beginning to latch on to, and that is the Vietnam Vet. It was in 1973 that America withdrew from Vietnam, and on 30 April 1975 Saigon fell, with those haunting and lasting images of the last helicopter taking off from the US Embassy likely still fresh on people's minds. *Dog Day Afternoon* opened exclusively in New York in September of 1975 and went into wide release on Christmas Day. Both Sonny and Sal apparently served in Vietnam, something that is mentioned only twice. (There is no reason given to doubt this in the film. Both men, for instance, are familiar with weapons and Sonny even teaches one of the hostages the basics of close-order drill.) Sal is also an ex-con who pleadingly tells Sonny that he can't go back to prison. Though perhaps unintentionally, the film reminds us of just who it was serving in Vietnam – the working class, like Sonny, and those who did not or could not attend college, like Sal. Lumet left off exploring any significance of Vietnam, except by implication, in favor of a sympathetic eye toward homosexuality and non-binary gender.

Lumet knew that audiences would have a hard time identifying with a gay character and his transsexual lover:

> Working with 'material that was sensationalist by its nature,' Lumet created 'a naturalistic film ... as close to documentary filmmaking as one can get in a scripted movie' to avoid a negative 'audience reaction' toward 'something they've never confronted before. (Macias 45)

As Lumet elaborated to Dan Yakir:

> Every event in *Dog Day* was true, I shot at a total truth: there was no artificial light. I shot many of the scenes with many cameras, so it was absolutely spontaneous. I improvised about seventy percent of that movie, because I needed an involvement from the actors to make their reality so overwhelming that you wouldn't be able to fight it in any way. And the only way to get the actors to that degree of involvement was to even let them make the words their own. The idea was to make a movie whose climax has a married, gay bank robber talking to his lover, a transvestite who wants to have a transsexual operation – to make this movie work for a truck driver in Brooklyn on a Saturday night who's had a couple of beers. So everything had to be honest, real, naturalistic. (Yakir 53)

The documentary-like elements work well as biopic, but, paradoxically, keep the film lively despite its major setting inside the bank. Lumet relies on a number of moving-camera follow shots and the occasional odd angle to provide both the sense that the camera cannot anticipate where the characters will go, and so must follow, or the sense that the camera must confine itself to an angle that captures the dialogue even if other characters or parts of the set are in the way. Of course, the Oscar given to New Hollywood editor-extraordinaire Dede Allen reminds us that this is no documentary but a film that makes powerful comparative statements along with its naturalistic mise-en-scène.

Let us give the last word on this extraordinary film to Anthony Macias, who expresses just how unique and important Lumet's film was, and remains:

> Yet the real news is that both Sonny and Leon express no guilt about their sexual orientations. Beyond any class-based, anti-establishment, counter-cultural underdog theme, and against the difficult history of gay and lesbian images on the silver screen, including the 1960s cinematic

representations of loveless homosexuals who killed themselves or died violently because of their sexuality, *Dog Day Afternoon* remains significant because the main character is *unashamedly* bisexual, and the supporting character is *unapologetically* transgender. (Macias 46; emphasis original)

"I JUST RAN OUT OF BULLSHIT": *NETWORK*

The most surprising element of *Network* is that it marked the first, and only, time that Sidney Lumet worked with writer Paddy Chayefsky. Born eighteen months apart, the former in Philadelphia, the latter in The Bronx, both were Jews who served in the army during World War II and then worked in the heady atmosphere of live television in New York in the 1950s. Chayefsky is often credited as being one of the major figures, along with Reginald Rose and Rod Serling, of what has been called The Golden Age of Television. Lumet brought Rose's greatest work, *12 Angry Men*, originally a television drama, to the big screen as his directorial debut in 1957. Chayefsky, meanwhile, had scored a huge success in 1953 with the original television play, *Marty*, turned into the Oscar-winning Best Picture of 1955. From that point on Chayefsky turned to the cinema. Like Lumet, one of his major concerns was with powerful institutions that had a mythic hold on American life, including Hollywood, with *The Goddess* in 1958, and the medical establishment, with *The Hospital* (1971).

Though *Network* is clearly about the corruption of the most powerful medium then known, Lumet felt it was more than that. He noted,

Paddy found the perfect image for talking about America. The television medium says more about this country than anything else, even the automobile! ... TV is used as a babysitter and a pacifier. It is in the home, unrestricted. And this is where it begins to dovetail with American behavior. It is a perfect excuse for the lack of personal responsibility. And this is what our picture is about. (Rapf 71)

Network is the most conventionally shot of Lumet's major films of the 70s. Though filmed in New York there is little of the streets, of the boroughs and sidewalks of the city. No surprise, here, however, as the film is set among the high-rises of the high-rollers of the media. We can say that Lumet was truly serving Chayefsky's words, for words dominate this film as few others of the era, a throwback to Classical Hollywood. One exception is the sequence in which company president Arthur Jensen (Ned Beatty) puts magnetic newscaster Howard Beale (Peter Finch) back on the straight-and-narrow path of American capitalism ("The world is a college of corporations, inexorably determined

Figure 10.3 *Network*. Ned Beatty's "face of God" explains the real working of the world in *Network* (1976). Digital frame enlargement. Courtesy of Metro-Goldwyn-Mayer.

by the immutable bylaws of business," Jensen declaims to him.) To be sure, Beatty delivers what amounts to a theatrical monologue in fine fashion, but the highly dramatic lighting and the use of the long take endow the performance with an otherworldly power. In fact, Howard Beale is stunned at the end of the speech, declaring, "I have seen the face of God." Beatty's Best Supporting Actor nomination came due to this scene (the only significant one he has in the film), in which he speaks no more than 400 words. Alternately, the two scenes of Best Supporting Actress winner Beatrice Straight are done, well, straight, with melodramatic emoting, even if convincingly acted. In this privileging of dialogue, Lumet is, overall, content to play second fiddle to Chayefsky.

Yet seen today, at a time when television has achieved a status that is difficult to define, available in a variety of formats that broadcast, narrowcast, stream, and await one's pleasure in cyberspace to an extent unimaginable in 1976, Chayefsky's satire seems almost quaint, though still relevant. For all of the satire and anger that Chayefsky wrote into the script, what remains is the humanity that Lumet brings to the film, the performances from William Holden and Peter Finch that bespeak of good, intelligent people left behind in a brave new world. And as for Lumet's idea that the film is about the lack of personal responsibility: what could be more prescient in a universe of cyberbullying and trolling?

At the Academy Award ceremony held in 1977 to honor the best film of 1976, the smart money may well have been placed on *Network* to garner the statuette for Best Picture; or else the equally serious examination of the corruption of American institutions, *All the President's Men* may have pleased the odds-makers. For cineastes the favorite was likely *Taxi Driver*, though certainly Martin Scorsese's down-and-dirty view of New York City might have been a tough sell to the Academy's aging membership. With no nominations for Best Director for the latter two films, *Network* was the odds-on favorite. As the Academy Awards ceremony proceeded it sure looked like *Network* was living up to its status as the favorite. With ten nominations in all, it certainly was the most honored film of the year in that respect. And it began racking up the wins. The film secured a posthumous win for Peter Finch as Best Actor (and a nomination for William Holden in the same category); a win for Faye Dunaway as Best Actress; and a win for Beatrice Straight as Supporting Actress. A win for Paddy Chayefsky for original script seemed to seal the deal. Yet Lumet lost the Best Director statuette to John G. Avildsen, and when it came time to announce the winner of Best Picture it was also not *Network*, but Avildsen's feel-good, underdog, up-from-nowhere story of an inarticulate, good-hearted lunk named Rocky Balboa. The gasps from the intelligentsia must have been as audible as Howard Beale's "I'm as mad as hell and I'm not going to take it anymore!," but whatever the lasting impact of *Network* – and it is considerable – the Academy actually got it right with *Rocky*. Five direct sequels to this film would follow, along with two re-imaginings devoted to Apollo Creed's son in the form of *Creed* (2015) and *Creed II* (2018). Still, we could easily say that the work of Aaron Sorkin, the most articulate and respected screenwriter of his generation, seems a direct descendent of Chayefsky's entertaining diatribe, particularly *The Newsroom* (2012–14), HBO's eloquent drama that plowed the same territory as *Network*, if on a more realistic level. And *Network* did give us a meme in that line of Howard Beale's: "I'm mad as hell and I'm not going to take it anymore." It is still the go-to film in any discussion of the impact and failure of television to live up to its potential. Sadly, Paddy Chayefsky died of cancer just six years after the success of *Network*, at the age of 58. He and Lumet had been friends for years, but unfortunately never worked together again.

"Oh, here we go again. You get me so worked up that I'm beginning to sound like a Jewish mother": *The Wiz*

By 1978, when Lumet released *The Wiz*, the New American Cinema was beginning to resemble the Old American Cinema. Oscar-winners included the feel-good phenomenon *Rocky*, the sparkling rom-com *Annie Hall* (1977), and the intense and intensely pro-American *The Deer Hunter* (1978), films that could be understood as the return of the repressed of Classical Hollywood. As the counter-culture itself moved to the middle of the political spectrum (as shortly thereafter the country as a whole moved further to the right), so, too, did the Renaissance became a Reformation. This was accompanied by a return to genre filmmaking as an expression of respect for the old ways and a nostalgia for a time before the shockwaves of the counter-culture and the Vietnam War. Of course, a new business model was just as significant, with the invention of the summer blockbuster. This new old wave began with Spielberg's monster hit *Jaws* (1975), an unprecedented and unexpected smash. This was followed up by the even more unprecedented and out-of-this-world success of *Star Wars* as well as *Close Encounters of the Third Kind* (both 1977). *Saturday Night Fever* (John Badham, 1977) showed there were still legs to the venerable musical, while *Grease* (Randal Kleiser, 1978) hit the right notes despite a weak cast, slipping and sliding its way to become one of the most successful live-action musicals in history. Even Martin Scorsese joined the bandwagon with his off-beat drama *New York, New York* (1977), an original musical set in the era of the classical musical. Into this mix came Lumet and *The Wiz*, a loose adaptation of the hit Broadway show of 1975 that is itself a Black-themed adaptation of *The Wizard of Oz*.

Lumet had never directed a musical before (or since). Perhaps that enviable track record of adapting theatre to film (the year before Lumet tried his hand at *Equus*, but it was a flop and remains little seen and discussed) made him a possible choice. Given its setting in New York, *The Wiz* might have seemed right in his wheelhouse. Or maybe even the presence of the luminous Lena Horne – his mother-in-law at the time – brought luster to Lumet's adaptation. Whatever the case, *The Wiz* was a box-office flop, failing to make back its cost; even the soundtrack album only reached #40 on the Billboard Top 100 chart. All kinds of claims are made in the wake of the film's failure – that it ended the film career of Diana Ross; that it halted the production of Black films until the work of Spike Lee. It is also claimed that its $23 million budget made it the most expensive musical ever made. Lumet disputes that aspect. He notes,

> I don't know where all this nonsense got started. Even back in the Sixties, *Hello, Dolly* cost $26 million; *Paint Your Wagon* cost $27 million; as simple a musical as *On A Clear Day* was $17 million. Musicals are expensive. As soon as you get involved with musicians, that's money. Same with choreographers. And in *The Wiz*, there have never been so many dancers on the screen, ever. The smallest number, other than the quartet of crows, was eighty. In Emerald City, it goes up to 400. All of them had to change costumes three times, so it's 1200 costumes in only one sequence. And that includes shoes, hats, even eyelashes – everything! Jewelry too. (Yakir 52)

It is often easy to pick apart a film failure, harder to account for success. In the case of *The Wiz* it is likely that the problem began right from the get-go with the casting of Diana Ross. She had starred in only two films – *Lady Sings the*

Blues (1972) and *Mahogany* (1975) – in the first as a singer, in the second as a model, roles close enough to her real life. In *The Wiz* she was asked to play a naive twenty-four-year-old kindergarten teacher. Ross was far from naive and a full decade older than her role. The original Broadway production was significantly closer in spirit to the classic 1939 musical with an eighteen-year-old Stephanie Mills appearing as Dorothy, far closer in age than Ross to the seventeen-year-old Judy Garland.

Reviews were generally unkind at the time, though there was the occasional bit of praise, this from Roger Ebert, for instance: "The movie has great moments and a lot of life, sensational special effects and costumes, and (Diana) Ross, (Michael) Jackson, and (Nipsy) Russell" (Ebert, "The Wiz"). However, most reviews then as now comment on the essential miscasting of Ross and the failure of the film to spark.

Lumet did put his imprint on the film beyond its New York setting. Talking to Dan Yakir, Lumet noted, "Another thing I didn't realize until I looked at the first rough-cut was that every scene was a scene of liberation: that somebody always starts stuck or immovable and then makes a progress" (Yakir 51). That's an important theme for an African American story, but it might be that only Lumet was able to tease that out; too many things apparently got in its way.

Lumet has had the last laugh with *The Wiz*. Respect for the film and its wonderfully reimagined New York-as-Oz has increased tremendously, outside of critical circles, since its disappointing run in 1978. For instance, the Laemmle chain of art theaters in Los Angeles devoted its "Throwback Thursdays" series to Black History Month in 2019, including *The Wiz* along with the likes of *Stormy Weather* (1943), *School Daze* (1988), and *Dreamgirls* (2006) – not bad for a movie that supposedly put an end to Black films.

While the film careers of Lumet's demographic cohort, including such crucial members of the New Hollywood cinema as William Friedkin and Arthur Penn, petered out after the 1970s, Lumet would go on to direct numerous critical and commercial successes. Still, it is fair to say that never again would he make films as powerful and popular as *Serpico, Dog Day Afternoon,* and *Network*. But then again, the same is true of most filmmakers, from the 70s, or any era.

WORKS CITED

Axmaker, Sean. "Serpico." TCM Film Article, www.tcm.com/this-month/article/276957%7C0/Serpico.html

Blake, Richard A. *Street Smart: The New York of Lumet, Allen, Scorsese, and Lee.* University of Kentucky Press, 2005.

Canby, Vincent. "The Screen: 'Serpico,' Disquieting Drama of Police Corruption." *New York Times*, 6 December 1973, p. 61.

Canby, Vincent. "Serpico, the Saint Francis of Copdom." *New York Times*, 16 December 1973, p. 155.

Canby, Vincent. "Lumet's Quintessential New York Film." *New York Times* 28 September 1975, p. 129.
Canby, Vincent. "Chayefsky's 'Network' Bites Hard as a Film Satire of TV Industry." *New York Times*, 15 November 1976, p. 39.
Cunningham, Frank R. *Sidney Lumet: Film and Literary Vision*. University Press of Kentucky, 1991; 2001.
Ebert, Roger. "*Dog Day Afternoon*," www.rogerebert.com/reviews/dog-day-after noon-1975. Accessed 12 May 2020.
Ebert, Roger. "*The Wiz*," www.rogerebert.com/reviews/the-wiz-1978. Accessed 12 May 2020.
Farber, Stephen. "Where Has All the Protest Gone? To Television." *New York Times*, 31 March 1974, p. 127.
Flatley, Guy. "Lumet – The Kid Actor Who Became a Director." *New York Times*, 20 January 1974, p. 111.
Lewiston Morning Tribune, "Homosexual Robs Bank, Asks Release of 'Wife.'" 23 August 1972, p. 3,
Macias, Anthony. "Gay Rights and The Reception of *Dog Day Afternoon* (1975)." *Film & History*, vol. 48, no. 1, Summer 2018, pp. 45–56
Prial, Frank. "2 Hold 8 Hostages in Brooklyn Bank." *New York Times*, 23 August 1972, p. 1.
Rapf, Joanna E. *Sidney Lumet: Interviews*, University, MS: University Press of Mississippi, 2005.
The Guardian, "Sidney Lumet Gets Honorary Oscar," https://www.theguardian.com/film/2004/dec/16/awardsandprizes.news. Accessed 12 May 2020.
Wood, Robin. "American Cinema in the '70s: *Dog Day Afternoon*." *Movie*, no. 23, Winter 1976–77, pp. 33–6.
Yakir, Dan. "Wiz Kid." *Film Comment*, Nov./Dec. 1978, pp. 49–54.

11. TERRENCE MALICK'S EMERGENT LYRICISM IN *BADLANDS* AND *DAYS OF HEAVEN*

Rick Warner

In critical discussions of Terrence Malick's two landmark films from the 1970s, the word "lyrical" occurs as a frequent, almost inevitable description, and yet commentators have applied this adjective in a variety of ways. For some, it alludes in general to a poetic quality in Malick's filmmaking, a strong proclivity for fragmentation, digression, and ambiguity that deviates from plot-based action to explore a more ecstatic register of poignancy (Michaels 13, 29, 40, 48). For others, a lyrical mode asserts itself more specifically through certain techniques – be it voiceover narration, camera movement, elliptical cutting, or orchestrations of natural light – that embroider his films with their signature moments of beauty and sensation, as well as with a tenor of reflective thought (Petric 38–41, 44; McCann 77–8).

My sense is that the term "lyrical" indeed speaks to something primary in Malick's first two features as director – something, however, that calls for more sustained critical attention than it has thus far received. In this chapter I will attempt to offer a precise description of Malick's lyrical style as it emerges in both *Badlands* (1973) and *Days of Heaven* (1978). I will take into account the above techniques, in addition to matters of sound, landscape, and characterization, but I will press beyond the generalized view of lyricism as more-poetic-than-narrative filmmaking.

Lyricism, whether taken in its literary, painterly, or filmic forms, is notoriously resistant to systematic definition. Derived from the Greek *lyrikos*, "singing to the lyre," the term usually refers to an outpouring of artistic energy, a spontaneous and rhythmic acuteness of feeling and perception that overwhelms the figure who dispenses it, enrapturing the audience in turn. In the case of Malick, such lyrical intensity surfaces through a handling of atmosphere around the edges of the unfolding drama, that is, through a certain "delicacy of mood" and vibrant feel for rural landscape (Elsaesser "*Auteur* Cinema," 237–8) that enacts and provokes contemplation. Moreover, Malick's lyrical style involves an elaborate play of irony that conditions the films' structures of communicability – those configured within the dramatic fiction, as well as those that arise between the film's expressive operations and the audience. Malick's lyricism often uses the impairments of the characters as a foil for the sensory and reflective potentialities of the viewer. Looking into how this lyrical contrast materializes will not only shed light on the poetic dimensions of Malick's early films but will also unearth a novel understanding of his relation to the American "Auteur Renaissance" of the era, a movement to which his films are less tangential than tends to be suggested.

Lyric Horizons Between and Beyond Two Humans

Badlands displays a number of traits roughly in keeping with New Hollywood tendencies circa 1967 to 1975. A road film that moves across the American Midwest, its young-lovers-on-the-run tale engages a classical, nationally specific motif of the journey, but, as with other road films of the era (such as Bob Rafelson's *Five Easy Pieces* [1970], Barbara Loden's *Wanda* [1970], Monte Hellman's *Two-Lane Blacktop* [1971], Hal Ashby's *The Last Detail* [1973], Peter Bogdanovich's *Paper Moon* [1973], and Jerry Schatzberg's *Scarecrow* [1973]), it displaces this motif's built-in notions of progress and discovery by focusing on two characters who lack the "goal-directedness" of their classical antecedents (Elsaesser 225–7). Kit Carruthers (Martin Sheen) and Holly Sargis (Sissy Spacek) are loosely based upon Charles Starkweather and Caril Ann Fugate, who killed eleven people in Nebraska and Wyoming in 1958. *Badlands*, which shifts the setting to South Dakota, Montana, and Saskatchewan, follows Kit's murder spree as Holly accompanies as an observer. Malick's film also self-consciously reworks an earlier, exemplary New Hollywood production, Arthur Penn's *Bonnie and Clyde* (1967), but whereas Penn's two drawn-from-life protagonists still have a more or less legible purpose that grants their criminality a subversive edge, Kit and Holly are more opaque, just as Malick's approach to the subject is less sharply politicized. The teenage Holly narrates the film in a retrospective voiceover delivered in a mostly flat and canned tone, as if reciting a personal narrative she has written for her high school English class, but her account does little to explain her and Kit's deeds, and it often comically stands at odds with the events pictured, making for a sly game of irony by which, as Brian Henderson puts it, the film's "implied author" communicates with the viewer at the narrator's unwitting expense. In this way, the film's treatment of Holly's unfitness as narrator throws into relief, for us, greater "awareness and perspectives that are well beyond her capacities" (1983: 41).

But this conflict between Holly's vocal narration and the onscreen action is compounded (more than allayed) by curious opacities in Malick's communication with the audience. In discussions of modern poetry, lyricism typically names a circumstance of the poet making his or her solitary reflections available to an audience of overhearers (Culler 186–7). Extant accounts of lyrical film, such as P. Adams Sitney's study of its avant-garde tradition (155–87), keep this stress on first-person expressivity, but Malick's work is less grounded in the rhetoric of the filmmaker's individual perspective. In *Badlands*, Malick briefly appears in the role of an architect who pays visit to the wealthy man's home that Kit and Holly have temporarily taken over. Puzzled by the situation, his character writes a note for Kit to give to the homeowner, but Kit, after shutting the door, deposits this note into a large urn, where it will likely go undiscovered. This quirky scene correlates with the film's diegetic theme of messages from which sender and receiver are both partly alienated: we also have, for instance, Kit's two voice recordings made for posterity, the balloon carrying assorted "tokens and things" that he releases ceremoniously into the sky, and Holly's unvoiced thoughts spelled out with her tongue on the roof of her mouth "where nobody could read them." Kit's discarding of the architect's note also comments on Malick's authorial presence and guidance, which makes itself felt indirectly, obscurely, and with no small measure of communicative difficulty.

The film's lyricism emerges in part through a running tension between the equivocal, at times obtuse main characters and the environments they inhabit while trying on and testing out different identities for themselves. Enlisting Martin Heidegger's concept of poetic "dwelling," Steven Rybin points out how, in the first half of the film especially, Kit and Holly never productively adapt to the "codified spaces" they live in, constrained as they both are by severe disaffection, which Malick's imagery counterpoints by suggesting a more vibrant and poetic way of experiencing the world. As Rybin explains, it is rather the spectator who learns how "to dwell" in Heidegger's sense, thereby compensating for the characters' contemplative shortcomings (41–53). I would add that Malick charmingly riffs on this tension through music that evokes not so much Kit and Holly's alienation as their half-conscious need to transcend it, and their faint, albeit limited, capacity to do so. Carl Orff and Gunild Keetman's "Gassenhauer," a modest and gradually building ensemble of marimbas, xylophones, and drums taken from the composers' *Schulwerk Volume 1: Musica Poetica* (1933) recurs at pivotal junctures in the film and is surely one of the most indelible uses of already existing music in post-classical American cinema. The recording Malick samples is performed by children, as the piece was conceived as a developmental exercise for young students learning the basic principles of musical creativity. This feeling of playful experimentation supplied by the music in *Badlands* colors our introductory views of Kit and Holly as a couple-in-the-making, from her baton-twirling on her front lawn to his balancing bit with a broom in an alleyway, through to the first composition they share when he steps into a wide shot of her house, just as BADLANDS letters the screen. The piece returns the morning after Kit's murder of Holly's father (Warren Oates), when the fugitive couple drive out of town and head for the forest.

This music thus imparts a rhythm that lyrically balances the film's drama between tragic and comic tones, between the protagonists' blankness and their charm, between the detachment they exude and its possible overcoming. At the same time this lyricism pitches our engagement as viewers between distance and empathy (Rybin 43–4), between the confusion raised by the film's obliqueness and a felt prospect of the film expanding our sensitivity. The forest interlude is the most concerted expression of lyricism on offer in the film. Indeed, it bears the influence of two marvelous lyrical excursions in modern European cinema: the couples' flights from civilization in Ingmar Bergman's *Summer with Monika* (1953) and Jean-Luc Godard's *Pierrot le fou* (1965). Evoking Godard's Marianne (Anna Karina), Holly strolls along a riverbank at one point, lost in thought; and Kit's activities bring to mind Godard's Ferdinand (Jean-Paul Belmondo).[1] For each of these couples, however, the acute feeling of liberation proves short-lived.

Our transition into this scene (cued by "Gassenhauer") coincides with a lap dissolve from Kit and Holly's car to a shot in which the camera fluidly circles around driftwood in a river. The camera has hitherto occasionally moved in the film but never with such elegance. Further signaling a change in register, Holly's voiceover becomes less detached, less monotone. Responding to the new environment, the film offers focus pulls that scrutinize organic life up close, phenomena that give Holly pause, muting her narration for a moment: grass blades, roots and stems, an insect on a bristly plant. A lyrical force runs through intercut scenes of the couple constructing and booby-trapping a woodland fort, washing up at their makeshift sink, and dancing to Mickey & Silvia's "Love is Strange." Chromatically, the synthetic yellows that punctuated a number of the earlier scenes in town have given way to natural greens made radiant by sunlight. Commenting at once on the painterliness of these scenes and on the couple's romanticized view of their predicament, a camera move relates their sleeping figures to a print of Maxfield Parrish's gleaming if kitschy landscape painting, *Daybreak* (1922), which they have taken from Holly's house and exhibited in their "bedroom" (Morrison and Schur 71–2). Many critics have noted that she, more than he, awakens to the surroundings. "I grew to love the forest," she professes in voiceover as the same music

Figure 11.1   Holly (Sissy Spacek) walks and contemplates waterside: *Badlands* (1973). Digital frame enlargement. Courtesy of Warner Bros.

comes back, its initiatory bars blending with the tranquil sounds of the river, "the cooing of the doves and the hum of dragonflies in the air . . . When the leaves rustled overhead it was like the spirits were whisperin' about all the little things that bothered 'em." We see her excited, wide-eyed response to an alpaca she spies with binoculars. The pensive vitality she experiences in the forest suggests her standing as a spectator within the film, and this is made more explicit when she examines a series of photographic "vistas" through her late father's stereopticon. The music now underscores her reverie on mortality, fate, and contingency, this being one of the few times in *Badlands* where we find ourselves movingly dialed into her character's interiority, which itself has opened out onto the luminous world.

The idyll of this interlude and our contemplative alignment with Holly are interrupted by Kit's shooting of bounty hunters who descend on their fort. Following this brutal event, the film cuts to a landscape that contrasts mark-edly with the dense forest: a desolate grassy field below a cloudless sky. Their car soon appears on the horizon, headed toward us from the far background, but the planar compression produced by Malick's telephoto lens makes it look as if the vehicle is struggling to advance. This pictorial effect becomes a leitmotif in the latter half of the film as the couple drive westward across the Great Plains; it serves as a counterpart to the sense of fate that sets in as their relationship grows less and less sustainable and their arrest becomes increas-ingly imminent. The lyricism of the film doesn't fade in these moments but rather undergoes a shift. On the one hand, these landscapes, even as they flirt with intimations of freedom, suggest *containment*, this coming across through the telephoto flattening effect (Michaels 26) and a graphic emphasis on the horizon line, both of which circumscribe the couple's movement and render these scenes abstract. And yet, on the other hand, these same landscapes, which are among the most striking in the film, hold a wistful splendor for the viewer. "Gassenhauer," which will not recur until the end titles, has been replaced by more downbeat music (Erik Satie's *Three Pieces in the Shape of a Pear* and a stretch of James Taylor's "Migration") that combines with slow lap dissolves and a motif of billowing dust behind the couple's car to express a languor that overtakes them. But for us, these almost Rothko-like landscapes elicit feelings of awe that are only partially held in check by the fatalistic notes of the narrative.

All this is to say that Malick's lyrical sensibility manifests itself and gains force through a modulating dynamic of irony (by turns comic and somber) that contrasts our viewing experience with the deficiencies of the two protagonists, allowing for fleeting intervals in which they evince greater perceptual and reflective potentialities that fail to take *full and lasting* effect in the drama. Late in the film, Holly's narration recounts an epiphany brought on by her gaze through the car's windshield at night: she says that while staring at gas fires and city lights "at the very edge of the horizon" she made a vow to herself "to never again tag around with the hell-bent type, no matter how in love with him I was." We hear this passage over stark, nocturnal landscapes that illustrate her descriptions, but because they are static compositions, they do not replicate her point of view from a moving vehicle. The film then offers a shot from the front of the car, but, significantly, it is angled down at the ground from the viewpoint of the headlights, indicating a rupture from her vantage. I take it that her prosaic epiphany is a foil for the spectator's potentially more resonant connection with the atmospheric radiance of the world onscreen. Here, as elsewhere in the film's latter half, the horizon line occasions a lyrical heightening of our perception, over and against the felt limits of the characters' subjectivities.

The Grander Scheme of Things

In *Days of Heaven*, these basic elements of Malick's lyricism return on a more epic scale, and within a more boldly experimental enterprise. With a plot that concerns an itinerant, low-wage working couple who disguise their romantic relationship and scheme to inherit a fatally ill wheat baron's fortune in the grand and remote setting of the Texas Panhandle in 1916, the film contributes to a New Hollywood trend of reinventing the cinematic epic, doing so in a way that both luxuriates in and punctures national myths (Michaels 2009: 41). Here, too, the film's lyrical style, rather than being anchored in individual subjectivity, materializes through a disposition of atmosphere in and around the narrative episodes, putting the spectator in cryptic but powerfully hypnotic contact with a film consciousness – a thoughtful and poeticizing play of sensation and affect enabled by an elliptical style that more closely resembles that of Malick's later work. The construction of the film is more fragmentary and impressionistic; scenes with dialogue kept to a bare minimum are continually interrupted by seemingly unmotivated inserts and cutaways to the pastoral surroundings, which are captured in the orange-rose glow of "magic hour." The camera moves more often, with a hovering smoothness that owes to the Panaglide system, a precursor of the Steadicam. In collaboration with his two cinematographers, Nestor Almendros and Haskell Wexler, Malick pitches the feel of the imagery between meticulous control and a more chaotic extemporaneity. He also becomes more cavalier about pressing to its limits the light sensitivity of the film stock, which results in some of the decade's most resplendent compositions. Just as overwhelming, the use of Dolby multichannel sound lends *Days of Heaven* what Michel Chion calls an immersive sonic "lyricism" keyed to "the clamor of the world" – ambient rustlings and vibrations, both natural and mechanical, that vie with and at times melodically fuse with human speech, be it dialogue or the colloquial voiceover (132, 346).

More intensely than in *Badlands*, the lyricism of *Days of Heaven* comes into effect as a contemplative force that circulates between the spare psychological drama and a greater, more mysteriously encompassing environment. I am going to focus on just one of the crucial motifs through which this lyrical style declares itself, a motif that couples film form with a particular immanent earthly element: wind. If the film is an ode to natural light, it just as vitally explores the poetic power of wind as an atmospheric current that both visually and sonically textures the events shown while amplifying the viewer's sensitivity.

Throughout the film, a wind motif underscores the feelings of the wealthy Farmer (Sam Shepard) toward Abby (Brooke Adams). Our narrator, Linda (Linda Manz) – the adolescent sister of Abby's lover and co-conspirator, Bill (Richard Gere) – addresses the Farmer's instant attraction to Abby by supposing, "Maybe it was the way the wind blew through her hair," her utterance coinciding with a windy shot of Abby at work. One of the most strongly accentuated objects in the film is a wind generator that spins atop the Farmer's house, providing electricity. This object is all the more pronounced because of the noise it makes, a relentless pulsing whirr we often hear offscreen in the section of the film where the Farmer gradually discovers Bill and Abby's swindle. When the Farmer sees overt evidence of Bill and Abby's surreptitious intimacy, he is standing next to the generator, spying down at them in a point-of-view shot, the high angle of which evokes a distinction in class. The anguish and rage in his face in the ensuing close-up are accented by the loud whirr, which mounts tension and blends with the emergent sound of a beating heart,

Figure 11.2   As the wind generator reels offscreen, the Farmer (Sam Shepard) trembles with rage and jealousy, having misperceived Bill (Richard Gere) and Abby's (Brooke Adams) interaction from his roof: Days of Heaven (1978) Digital frame enlargement. Courtesy of Paramount.

presumably his. He looks directly into the lens and there occurs a lap dissolve to shots that depict wind blowing through the ranch as geese and horses sense danger. This fierce wind seems to result from his exhalation before the shot change. In a prior scene, when he first detects signs of Bill and Abby's feelings for each other, this evidence appears to him (and to us) in the form of their silhouetted figures sneaking a kiss behind a white gazebo curtain at night, a "movie screen" of sorts rippling in the breeze. The tragic irony is that the Farmer doesn't know what Bill and the film's spectator certainly know at this point, that Abby's kiss is for old times' sake and that she has, in fact, begun to love the Farmer instead. The Farmer's limited, mistaken perception triggers his destructive outburst, a fatal turn of events that coincides with a plague of locusts facilitated by the wind. The fire that erupts and spreads through the wheat crop when the Farmer and his workers try to avert the insects blatantly recalls the flames of hell of which Linda speaks earlier in voiceover.

This isn't to suggest that the film relegates wind to the subordinate task of shoring up the human drama as an objective correlative that rather conveniently exteriorizes character emotion, in this case the Farmer's inner turbulence. As reflects the film's borrowing of figurative uses of weather from ancient Greek dramatic and Judeo-Christian theological sources, wind connotes a metaphysical agency that swirls around the farm and bodes tragedy (a notion that Linda's vocal narration supports with its parable-like undertones of pending disaster). That is to say, the film's use of wind serves to express "the presence and materiality of the invisible," at least flirting with the premise that this capricious natural element represents "the supernatural force presiding over Eden," albeit an Eden that the film unmasks as a "seeming paradise," a fallen world in spite of its undeniable lushness and beauty (Cohen 50).

At the same time, in Malick's spiritual cinema – no less than in Robert Bresson's, Andrei Tarkovsky's, or Jean-Luc Godard's – such an intimation of the metaphysical allows for no simple distinction from the physical, material, and terrestrial. If, at one level, the ubiquitous wind in the film evokes the super-natural in relation to the narrative, at another level this element works just as fervently to digress and divert attention away from the intrigue of the love tri-angle onto short-lived glimpses of the outside world. Cutaways offer a poetic inventory of the vegetation, terrain, wildlife, and climate, putting the narrative on hold and delineating a larger environment wherein humanity has no default place of privilege (McCann 81–6). It becomes, in this way, the primary task of the film's lyricism to mediate between two linked but somewhat different films occurring before us at once in cadenced alternation: the human-centered drama and something more like an observational nature documentary.

Synchronized to the film's rhythm of flux and commotion, as well as to its sensuous feel for the momentary in all its unpredictable delight, the wind gusts through treetops, grassy fields, the wheat crops in various stages of growth, and plants that surround the house. The wind has a *voice* in *Days of Heaven*, one not unlike Linda's narration in that it directs thought and curiosity onto a rapturous world to which the main adult characters are largely blind, impeded as they are by their ingrained alienation. Visually and sonically exploring the thresholds of internal/external, onscreen/offscreen, human/nonhuman nature, and quotidian/cosmic, this motif figures wind as a conductor of flows and forces of life to which the spectator is more keenly alert than are the Farmer, Bill, and Abby.

In his reading of *Days of Heaven*, Rybin shows that the lyrical intensity of the film serves to situate the sensory and contemplative experience of the audi-ence in partial counterpoint to the constrained sensibilities of the characters in the love triangle. As viewers, we perhaps never fully penetrate some of the film's enigmas either, but our knowledge of the world onscreen transcends theirs. More to Rybin's point, the film sumptuously affords us an opportunity to prevail over the obstacle that thwarts the characters both socially and as individuals: their inability to shake off their isolate, alienated subjectivity. As Rybin words it,

> Malick is not only giving *us* a cinematic space in which we might over-come our subjective isolation but also a series of poetic reverberations that gesture toward the new worlds that the *characters* might will into existence if only they could overcome their own solitary subjectivity. (77)

Having observed how the film implicitly engages the viewer in this fashion, it's tempting to state that this lyrical style that draws us into its peripatetic study of the natural world is nothing other than Malick's personal vision, a vision for which it seems no conciliation in the service of narrative tightness or psychological depth will do if it means having to lose, in the final edit, the striking marginal details on which his eye and ear have lingered. This style is the calling card of Malick's direction, to be sure, but it is essential to grasp that the windswept lyricism of *Days of Heaven* pushes into *im*personality. That is, it unfolds not so much as the avatar of an individual's inscribed point of view but as a *flight from* individual personhood, from what Emerson called the "jail-yard of individual relations" (221).

Instructive along these lines is Gilberto Perez's assertion that the film presents at its crux a tragedy not simply of individuals but of American individualism. To revisit the moments of the Farmer spying on Abby and Bill, his perspective misleads him precisely because it is inescapably individualized. As Perez writes:

> It is a fitting irony that the Farmer's point of view from above . . . gives him in fact no godlike grasp of the situation: even up there, he's only an individual with only his pair of eyes to go on. It is significant that his misapprehension, which has disastrous consequences, is due to no flaw in his character, to nothing other than the fact that an individual's perspective is necessarily limited: anybody else in his position would have drawn the same conclusion. (104)

By offering the spectator a cinematic escape from this constraint that proves catastrophic in the plot, the wind motif has a double function. If, at some intervals, it riffs on character affect and evokes some wrathful spiritual entity, at others it deserts this role, in and through magnificent natural landscapes that show us nothing so much as an ecological milieu going about its daily, immanent cycles regardless of the human turmoil. I have in mind two such stray shots, both of which are absent of people and sustained for just over ten seconds: a high-angle shot of a pond with its surface rippling into vectors under the breeze; and a more level shot of the dry, golden, iridescent wheat field undulating in the wind.[2] Both of these cutaways are wordless and without music: silent except for the whooshing of air. The first shot marks a radical hiatus in the plot. To see it as an objective correlative would be to ignore its *sheer indifference* the concerns of the narrative and to the very practice of character-driven psychological drama. The second shot ties in more with the human tragedy by stressing the wheat, but it, too, suspends narrative action to enforce a meditative pause.

Rybin, drawing on an observation by Adrian Martin, notes how these poetic images in the film convey "the sensuousness of things, before they are named," that is, a radiant world *before* the imposition of language (69–70). The added impact of the images I have singled out owes to their ephemerality and the fact that we receive them at an opportune instant – *right as* the wind animates the natural world. One senses that these atmospheric stirrings have been waited for and caught in the shooting stage, but more to the point, the epiphanic charge of these images strikes a rapport between the contemplative viewer and the film's impersonal lyrical style, which seems to have a mind of its own.

Although the lyricism at work in *Badlands* and *Days of Heaven* is highly distinctive (and perhaps inimitable), it would be wrong to treat Malick as a continent unto himself in the broader context of 1970s American filmmaking. Lloyd Michaels, writing of *Days of Heaven* specifically, recognizes that Malick's work belongs to a cultural milieu of disillusionment in the aftermath of Watergate and Vietnam, but Michaels is careful to say that this is "not the same disillusionment as, for example, *Straw Dogs* (1971), *The Godfather, Part II* (1974), or *The Deer Hunter* (1978)" (55–6). No doubt, these comparatively much bleaker films offer nothing of the lyrical promise we have seen in Malick's first two films, but Thomas Elsaesser, in offering an account of the period that shifts the focus from the Film Generation directors onto more peripheral, independent directors such as Rafelson, Hellman, Bogdanovich, and Schatzberg, suggests that Malick belongs to this loose cohort of outliers who, despite their failures to find favor with a mass public, contributed some of the decade's most indelible achievements, through poetic orchestrations of atmosphere in rural environments ("*Auteur* Cinema," 237–8). If this group, with whom Malick's early career is indeed linked to some extent (Horwath 94–6), constitutes a certain cinema of poetry, then let us view Malick as the group's exemplar of an ironic and impersonal lyricism that both registers disaffection in a fallen world *and* holds out the possibility of prevailing over it, in and through the relationship the film builds with the spectator.

NOTES

1. Malick's later films, *The Thin Red Line* (1998) and *The New World* (2005), evoke the lyrical interlude in *Pierrot le fou* through shots of a character walking across a fallen tree trunk, which echoes an action performed by Jean-Paul Belmondo's Ferdinand.
2. These shots occur respectively at 51:31 and 1:02:45 in the film's running time, on the Criterion Collection's Blu-ray edition of *Days of Heaven*.

WORKS CITED

Chion, Michel. *Film: A Sound Art*. Translated by Claudia Gorbman, Columbia University Press, 2009.
Cohen, Hubert. "The Genesis of *Days of Heaven*." *Cinema Journal* vol. 42, no. 4, 2003, pp. 46-62.

Culler, Jonathan. *Theory of the Lyric*. Harvard University Press, 2015.

Elsaesser, Thomas. "The Pathos of Failure: American Films in the 1970s: Notes on the Unmotivated Hero" [1975]. *The Last Great American Picture Show: New Hollywood Cinema in the 1970s*, edited by Thomas Elsaesser, Alexander Horwath and Noel King, Amsterdam University Press, 2004, pp. 279–92.

Elsaesser, Thomas. "*Auteur* Cinema and the New Economy Hollywood." *The Persistence of Hollywood*, Routledge, 2012, pp. 237–55.

Emerson, Ralph Waldo. "The Poet" [1844]. *Ralph Waldo Emerson: Selected Essays, Lectures, and Poems*, Bantam, 1990, pp. 207–28.

Henderson, Brian. "Exploring Badlands," *Wide Angle*, vol. 5, no. 4, 1983, pp. 38–51.

Horwath, Alexander. "A Walking Contradiction (Partly Truth and Partly Fiction." *The Last Great American Picture Show: New Hollywood Cinema in the 1970s*, edited by Thomas Elsaesser, Alexander Horwath and Noel King, Amsterdam University Press, 2004, pp. 83–106.

McCann, Ben. "'Exploring the Scenery': Landscape and the Fetishization of Nature in *Badlands* and *Days of Heaven*." *The Cinema of Terrence Malick: Poetic Visions of America*, edited by Hannah Patterson, Wallflower, 2007, pp. 77–87.

Michaels, Lloyd. *Terrence Malick*. University of Illinois Press, 2009.

Morrison, James and Thomas Schur. *The Films of Terrence Malick*. Praeger, 2003.

Petric, Vlada. "*Days of Heaven*." *Film Quarterly*, vol. 32, no. 2, 1978–79, pp. 37–45.

Perez, Gilberto. "Film Chronicle: *Days of Heaven*," *Hudson Review*, vol. 32, no. 1, 1979, pp. 97–104.

Rybin, Steven. *Terrence Malick and the Thought of Film*. Lexington Books, 2012.

Sitney, P. Adams. *Visionary Film: The American Avant-Garde, 1943-2000*. Third ed. New York: Oxford University Press, 2002.

12. ELAINE MAY: SUBVERTING MACHISMO "STEP BY TINY STEP"

Kyle Stevens

Elaine May is not only one of the brightest American comic minds of the twentieth century, she is one of Hollywood's historically unsung *auteurs*. This neglect is all the more tragic given that she is one of the few female *auteurs* in studio history. May began her career as half of comic duo Nichols and May in the late 1950s, and went on to become a playwright, actress, screenwriter, and director. Yet she only directed four films: *A New Leaf* (1971), *The Heartbreak Kid* (1972), *Mikey and Nicky* (1976), and the legendary commercial flop *Ishtar* (1987). Each is a gem, but given the scope of this collection I will discuss only the first three. I leave it to others to detail the stories of these films' production, the histories of May's troubled relations with studio executives, her baroque editing sequences, relationships with collaborators, and so forth. My aim in the following pages is rather to demonstrate a specific May sensibility – the stylistic and thematic consisten-cies across her films – and to argue that such an auteurist lens helps surface meanings in, and aspects of, each film that may otherwise go unnoticed. In particular, and by moving most carefully through her directorial debut, *A New Leaf*, I will show that May's films critique Hollywood tropes concern-ing the expression of the concepts of men and women, and their relations. May's films were seen in line with extant mainstream American cinematic genres and styles, but what critics have missed is that her films are *about* those genres and styles. This attention is not accomplished through the sort of reflexivity one might associate with other modernist-Brechtian films of the 1960s and 1970s, but rather, May's reappraisals operate at the meta-level, elucidating how the character types around which certain genres revolve reinforce objectionable gender norms.

In the early 1970s, the initial flush of excitement and experimentalism that accompanied the New Hollywood of the latter 1960s began to fade, and, not coincidentally, the Film School Generation emerged to institute a new industrial order. But not only were these lauded directors all men, their narratives tended toward the macho. Women were situated as obstacles or muses, always existing in relation to the male characters. This was a departure from the 1940s and 1950s, when studios made concerted efforts to appeal to female audience members through stories in which female characters had multiple forms of agency (though we might well object to their assumptions about female tastes). Yet this period of film history also coincides with second-wave feminism, and the "consciousness-raising" work of activists regarding cultural conceptions of women and femininity – including expressions of these ideas onscreen. Within the disciplinary memory of Film Studies, the years of 1974 and 1975 loom large. In particular, Molly Haskell's *From Reverence to Rape* (1974) and Laura Mulvey's "Visual Pleasure and Narrative Cinema" (1975) called out Hollywood's sexist thematic and formal conventions.

Alongside calls for equitable onscreen treatment were calls for more female authorial voices. (Ironically, these criticisms overlapped with the "death of the author," not coincidentally at the very moment that women and members of minority communities garnered more access to the means of making films).[1] Outside of Hollywood, filmmakers such as Barbara Kopple, Lina Wertmüller, and Barbara Loden were seeing their work circulated. But within Hollywood, there was only May. Yet, May was not particularly celebrated by feminist film critics, as the films she directed concentrate on men and their fragile masculinity. In this respect, it is important to appreciate that May is first and foremost a comic. The joke must be on the powerful (men, in this case) lest it be cruel. Comedy is usually subversive. It is, as May says, "closer to life" than drama, which is free to pose problems in ways both vague and personal, provided that they're moving. The earnest is easily agreed or disagreed with, and dramas can *tell* the audience that they are grand – and, indeed, can often heighten the sense of grandness. By contrast comedies cannot *tell* the audience that they are funny or important; doing so would undermine their humor.

Before delving into her films of the 1970s and providing a brief bit of biographical background, I want to quote May on her theory of comedy. It is a long quotation but instructive for understanding her approach to comedy, and to what she seeks to achieve through it. It is also itself funny:

> You can do something dramatically or you can do it funny. You can kill somebody dramatically or you can kill them funny. Funny is closer to life. If you kill somebody in a drama you get a gun and shoot them and

they die, and then you're left to face the consequences of your act. If you kill somebody in a comedy you have to start out by finding a place where you can buy a gun that can't be traced. Or you have to buy a gun and then spend your evenings and weekends filing off the serial number. Then you have to buy cartridges. Then you have to learn how to load the gun and fire it. Then you have to put the gun and cartridges somewhere where they won't be found by the maid or your wife. Then when the right time comes you have to get the guy you're going to kill either to come up to your apartment or make a date to meet him some place where you can fire a gun and no one will notice. Like Central Park. If you can get him to meet you in Central Park without making him nervous, you will have to put the gun in your pocket and try to decide whether to leave the safety off and risk shooting your foot off, or leave the safety on and find some way to take the gun out of your pocket gracefully and release the safety in front of your victim without rousing his suspicion. If you manage to actually kill someone under these circumstances, you then have to get rid of the body and get out of Central Park alive. Getting rid of the body has got to be a hair-raising experience. Especially if you've decided to kill somebody bigger than you are, which you probably have, because in a comedy almost everybody is bigger than you are. Comedy is almost entirely the doing of something in detail, step by tiny step. Drama sort of sweeps everything away. (Probst 134–5)

Before Hollywood

May was born Elaine Berlin in Philadelphia, Pennsylvania on April 21, 1932. She grew up performing in her father's traveling Yiddish vaudeville company and studied acting under Maria Ouspenskaya, but it was at the University of Chicago (where she was sitting in on classes un-enrolled) that her career took off. There she met Mike Nichols. The two became involved with the on-campus improvisational troupe, Tonight and 8:30, and then were instrumental in the founding of America's first improvisational theater, The Compass Theater (which evolved into The Second City). It was Nichols and May's sketches that drew attention, and the pair went on to appear on television and radio, record extremely successful LPs (*Improvisations to Music* [1958], *An Evening with Mike Nichols and Elaine May* [1960], *Nichols and May Examine Doctors* [1963]), and star in their own Broadway revue, *An Evening with Mike Nichols and Elaine May* in 1959 (directed by Arthur Penn). Throughout their work, Nichols and May lampooned 1950s American middle-class attitudes toward sex, gender, class, fame, psychoanalysis, and more.[2]

After Nichols and May went their separate ways, Nichols immediately began to direct, first on Broadway, presenting Neil Simon's work, and then, more famously, in Hollywood, beginning with *Who's Afraid of Virginia Woolf?* (1966) and *The Graduate* (1967). May instead turned to writing, even winning the 1969 Drama Desk Award for most promising playwright for *Adaptation*. She went on to write a screenplay under the nom de plume Esther Dale, which would become *Such Good Friends*, directed by Otto Preminger and released in 1971. The premise is straight out of a Nichols and May sketch: a man, Richard, goes into the hospital to have a benign mole removed and dies from a sequence of complications. Forces that promise to improve your life inevitably make it worse. The story, though, is about Richard's wife Julie, as she first deals with her frustration at dealing with her duties as wife, mother, and daughter, and then her anxiety as Richard prepares for surgery, then her sadness and rage as she discovers that for years he has been having affairs with all the women she knows. As is typical of May's films, it is difficult to describe the narrative in terms of a traditional arc. It does not build to a traditional climax, nor does it offer a conventional resolution. *Such Good Friends* is about Julie's journey to let go of her attachments to people who inhibit her ability to *lead* her life. Although none of the films May directed in the 1970s focuses on a female character, here every scene centers on Julie. She has an imaginative inner life and an active sex drive, and, as in *A New Leaf*, May plays on the cultural anxiety around, and fascination with, women's breasts. There are also classical May jokes, as when the doctors try to reassure her by telling her, "Now that your husband is so damaged, the care will be the finest," or when, her appetite having been lost while she anxiously awaits news of her husband's condition, a friend tells her, "Try the turkey [sandwich]. I promise you won't enjoy it."

A New Leaf

1971 also saw the release of *A New Leaf*, which May directed, wrote, and starred in (and for which she was nominated for a Golden Globe Award for Best Actress in a Musical or Comedy). May plays Henrietta, an absent-minded heiress and botanist targeted for marriage by Walter Matthau's newly bankrupt playboy Henry Graham. The film is a farce, a genre difficult for cinema to love, for farces lean further toward theatricality than movies typically like to (with their attachment to recording pro-filmic reality). Yet May was made for them. Her comedy had always been documentary-like anyway, sussing out how, despite their best efforts to hide neuroses, prejudices, and feelings, people's words eventually give them away.

When *A New Leaf* begins, its screen and an electrocardiogram, beeping ominously, are coextensive. We wonder who might be dying, and our anxiety is soon displaced onto a nervous Henry, who refuses to leave the doctor's side until hearing that "she'll be alright." Only then does the camera pull back to

Figure 12.1   Elaine May and Walter Matthau as, respectively, Henrietta Lowell and Henry Graham in *A New Leaf* (1971). Digital frame enlargement. Courtesy of Paramount Pictures.

reveal the feminine patient to be Henry's beloved Ferrari. This fop brings his car in two or three times a week, or every time he drives it, so when he receives the diagnosis – "There was carbon on the valves." – his response is a stony "Yes, there always is." He speeds away only to get immediately stuck in traffic. We are thus introduced to a world in which prized machines are not expected to work and where automobiles designed to achieve fantastic speeds cannot get anywhere. May establishes an unsettling mood of constricted amusement, right on the edge of laughter.

Cut to Henry being towed home to his chic Manhattan high-rise, still behind the wheel, helmet on head. The film jumps to him on horseback, lecturing his riding partner on the tribulations of having "carbon on the valves." The repetition of the phrase (six times in a matter of seconds), though funny, also imbues a sense of ennui. It reminds us of Henri Bergson's theory of comedy by suggesting something machine-like about Henry, and invites us to laugh at him.[3] His language is predetermined, and we begin to wonder what keeps *him* from running smoothly. Next, we see Henry sitting in a two-seater plane, listening to the pilot complain about the aircraft's incessant need of repair. What is the trouble? Carbon on the valves. May has now so thoroughly emptied the phrase of meaning that we realize just how many mechanical explanations sound *like* this, but amount to just such nonsense. (This is particularly so as carbon is simply everywhere; it needn't be said to begin with!) This is quintessential May.

Each of these moments has ended with Henry receiving an urgent message that someone named Beckett (William Redfield) wants to see him. Henry has been riding this series of vehicles, it turns out, not because he has anywhere to go but because he has someone from whom he wants to get away. So, while Beckett may be waiting for Henry, we are now waiting for Beckett. He arrives as Henry's attorney and accountant, in a wood-paneled room that confers the weight of authority upon him. A dearth of money, it turns out, is the carbon on Henry's valves. He is unable to grasp the thought, and Beckett struggles to find new ways to explain to him that he has depleted his trust fund. Henry, childlike, demands, "Don't treat me like a child." Matthau plays Henry like a patrician W. C. Fields, or as though he resents not being allowed to wear a Fauntleroy suit as (saving a check) he indignantly throws a tantrum: "Do you realize this check bounced? Like I'm some indigent?"

Thoroughly shaken (and filmed with a shaky, handheld camera), Henry staggers into the glinting sunlight on New York's Fifth Avenue, muttering, "I'm poor" with increasing realization. He whispers good-bye to the first-class buildings, to the best haberdasheries, to polo. He visits his favorite restaurant to "look at the room once more," and is unsure he can even enter his gentlemen's club, as though he bears some visible mark of penury. Swooping in to counterpoint this sequence of Henry's despair is a Disneyesque orchestral score, made even more excessive by its cheery birdsong descant.

Back home, Henry caresses his possessions, including his "gentleman's gentleman," Harold (George Rose), before a horrific vision of his future – buying his clothes off-the-rack, going to the YMCA, driving a Chevrolet – sends him to the brink of suicide. The ever-reliable Harold, an obsequious six inches shorter than his master, is not ready to give up. As he dresses Henry in evening cravat and smoking jacket, he encourages his mettle by earnestly declaring, "You have managed, sir, in your own lifetime to keep alive traditions that were dead before you were born!"

Harold advises marriage, "the only way to acquire property without labor." Henry is repulsed by the thought, but Harold insists, informing him that,

> If you do not commit suicide, sir, you will be poor. Poor in the only real sense of the word, sir, in that you will not be rich. You will have a little after you've sold everything, but in a country where every man is what he has, he who has little is not very much. There's no such thing as genteel poverty here, sir.

Despite Harold's paean to American capitalism, this will be no yarn of rugged individualism. Henry has all the greed with none of the ambition. Without appetite for work, he admits, "I have no skills, no resources, no ambitions. All I am, or was, is rich, and that's all I've ever wanted to be." Only after

Harold states that if Henry does not marry "the worst will have happened: your credit rating will be impugned," does Henry fully accept the gravity of his situation. Sinking into his chair, he mutters, "I can't. I can't. Better death or murder." He summarily agrees with himself that the latter is preferable.

So, convinced he "can engage in any romantic activity with an urbanity born of disinterest," Henry is off to wive wealthily, and to kill. If this premise sounds straight out of Alfred Hitchcock, there is good reason. May decided to adapt the story after reading it (titled "The Green Heart") in *Alfred Hitchcock's Mystery Magazine*. The writer, Jack Ritchie, was a regular contributor not just to Hitchcock periodicals but to *Alfred Hitchcock Presents* (which featured both Matthau and Redfield) and *The Alfred Hitchcock Hour*. We might see *A New Leaf* as May's intervention into familiar tales that threaten uxoricide, such as *Rebecca* (1940), *Suspicion* (1941), *Dial M for Murder* (1954), and George Cukor's *Gaslight* (1944) (which might remind us just how witty and near farce Hitchcock often is). *Suspicion*, in particular, hinges on the anxiety that a gold-digging husband may be trying to kill his wife. Several of Ritchie's events appear in the movie, but *A New Leaf*'s humor and concern with class and gender is all May. Given that throughout her career May both participated in and mocked the interlocked histories of comedy and Jewish ethnic identity in America, we might also see the fact that she and Matthau are of Jewish extraction as disrupting Hollywood orthodoxies. Suppose Hitchcock had cast Matthau in a blue-blooded Cary Grant or Laurence Olivier role? Or the fidgety, alert May instead of wan, anodyne Joan Fontaine?

Beckett, who sets the absurd narrative in motion, is also May's invention. And here we cannot miss the invocation of absurdist playwright Samuel Beckett, for whom words (like money for his namesake) are a dubious medium of exchange, without inherent value and likely to cause trouble between parties (which is not to say that the *act* of speaking is worthless). Henry – who never wanted to *do* anything – is suspended in the tension between the injunction to act and the pointlessness of acting, between the futility of action we find in Beckett's dramas and the terribly determined space of Hitchcock, where actions, both virtuous and villainous, take on consequences beyond their intentions.

Over the course of the film, May unveils what it might *really* look like for a man to be willing to target, marry, and kill a woman for money. While in so many stories about men killing women, money (or its concomitant prestige) is routinely mixed up with the killer's motivation – picturing murder as both erotic and economic – Henry, being so univocally goal-oriented, is not interested in sex, as we witness during his first hunt for female prey. He attends an outdoor soirée, and the unstable handheld camera suggests his anxiety and awareness of his body, as a friend opines, "You know, Henry, I've never thought of you as terribly interested in women." Henry reassures him: "Well, it comes as rather a shock to me, too." He meets Sharon (Renée Taylor), who enthusiastically insists, by way of seduction, "I am a woman!" (a bit of news that causes Henry to stumble off his water-skis) and attempts to seduce Henry by removing her bikini top, which only causes him to flee, screaming, "No, don't let them out!"

Soon enough, Henry finds the right girl. At a tea party, as the hostess makes the introductions ("No, they are not the Boston Hitlers, they're from Glen Cove"), Henry spies Henrietta, a mousy wallflower performed by May. He inquires after her in classic May repartee: "Who's Henrietta Lowell?" "Old Guy Lowell's daughter." "Well, who's old Guy Lowell?" "Well, he's dead now." "Well, who was he when he was alive?" "He was an industrialist . . . or a composer." May elicits laughter at the possibility of confusing an industrialist with a composer, which, in turn, enjoins us to ponder why we might consider those professions more dissimilar than others. Henry is gripped with pleasure as he learns that Lowell's wealth was left intact, that there is an enormous house with servants, that Henrietta barely talks, and that she is a botanist who specializes in ferns. She is a "most isolated woman," a windfall.

May's entrance into the film is as meek as her character. She sits in the background, to the far right of the screen, bringing to mind Henrietta's object of study, that non-flowering plant generally confined to the corners of rooms. May's Henrietta – like the film – is lovely beneath a veneer of absentmindedness. Throughout the film, May shows a surprising aptitude for physical comedy (particularly a shtick with a Grecian nightgown). In addition, audiences at the time would have been familiar with May's voice, mostly from hit Nichols and May albums. She keeps Henrietta's voice at a relatively high pitch, breathy, possibly indicating the sort of dizzy heiress endemic to Hollywood comedies. But Henrietta is intelligent. She tends to accentuate words early in her sentences, speaking with great deliberation before rushing through the latter portions apologetically, as though constantly afraid she might be talking too much. This creates the impression of bashfulness born of a reticence to speak, not a lack of something to say.

Henry seizes his chance to ingratiate himself as Henrietta drops her teacup. After Henrietta proceeds to drop her glasses, her gloves, and a second cup of tea, it seems that she simply cannot keep anything upright – perhaps hinting at her effect on men (which, of course, only makes her more perfect for Henry). As the hostess scolds her, Henry comes to her defense, contriving to make it appear that she upends his beverage, too. His most chivalric gesture is to proclaim to the hostess: "Madame, I have seen many examples of perversion in my time, but your erotic obsession with your carpet is probably the most grotesque . . . I have ever encountered." Given that Henry himself will soon get upset when Henrietta spills wine on his own rug, we might apply his declaration to his own sexuality, too.

Henry tells Henrietta that he will escort her home, but they do not get far ("there is carbon on the valves"). We learn that Henrietta dreams not of wealth but of mattering. She has ambition without greed. She wants to "achieve immortality" by discovering a new species of fern, a frond of her own. Henry studies up on botany, orders her favorite drink (Mogen-David extra-heavy Malaga wine with soda water and lime juice), and proposes within the week: "I am a man and you are a woman and we don't have to let that interfere if we are reasonably careful . . . Will you marry me?" Henrietta's corrupt lawyer McPherson (Jack Weston) is none too pleased with the arrangement, and – in a perfectly Girardian bit of blocking on a sofa[4] – Henrietta is marginalized as the men fight over her, that is to say, over her fortune. Henry is saved when, to McPherson's horror, Henrietta decides to share custody of her fortune *before* the wedding so that no one can say he married her for her money.

After they wed, Henry gets immediately down to brass tacks. He spends the honeymoon trip researching poisons while she searches for ferns. In fact, it is on this trip that Henrietta discovers a new species. She names it after Henry: "*Alsophila Grahami.*" Perhaps not quite as moved as he ought to be to receive her gift of immortality, Henry is nevertheless pleased to learn that he will be "in all the textbooks as a footnote and in the atlases under G."

Given May's doctrine that comedy unfolds "step by tiny step," no cut to a well-lit glass of milk will do here. First, marriage must be a last resort. Henry must beg a rich relative for cash in the meantime. Then he must find a girl, woo her, plan the wedding, put up with her friends and relatives, marry her, and get her to agree to give him the money. Then he must read *Beginners Guide to Toxicology*, learn what poisons may be in the gardener's storehouse, and carefully plan the deed only to find out that the groundskeeper subscribes to "the organic method" and will not abide poisons. He must put Henrietta's house in order (it is, as Harold puts it, "incredibly democratic," which will never do). He has to organize the finances, figure out who has access to various accounts, fire the staff who are embezzling, hire new staff, study income tax law, and so forth, all before he can get around to knocking her off.

The opportunity to be rid of Henrietta finally presents itself when she asks Henry to accompany her on a research trip to the Adirondacks – just the pair of them. Canoeing down a river, they come upon whitewater rapids, echoed formally by suddenly rapid cuts. Henry can swim; Henrietta cannot. The boat capsizes, and Henry abandons Henrietta. Safely ashore, Henry starts to walk away when, implausibly, he chances upon an *Alsophila Grahami*. This sparks an epiphany that he might just miss her. Cursing the heavens that "nothing ever works out the way you plan," he rescues Henrietta. As they totter toward the setting sun, she confesses that she *knows* things have not turned out as he wanted. It seems Henry lives up to the movie's title, yet his recant is tepid. He *slightly* prefers her alive. He has gotten used to her. The darkness of this moment is stressed by the return of the overwrought orchestral theme and birdsong that precipitated events.

As satisfying as this ending is, it was not May's intention. She wanted to make a movie "in which someone gets away with murder" ("Elaine May in Conversation with Mike Nichols"). May even sued to have her name removed. According to reports, her version was an hour longer and included two murders before the studio wrenched it away. I speculate that the two victims are a blackmailer and his accomplice, Henrietta's lawyer (whom the hero of Ritchie's story bumps off). The idea that Henry successfully kills two people, though neither are the desired victim, is fitting, and it's a shame that the (male) studio executives could not allow May her vision.

THE HEARTBREAK KID

May's other two films of the 1970s are at least as intricate and ambiguous in tone. Space prohibits going into each in the same depth here, but I would like to devote a few paragraphs to showing how they comport with *A New Leaf*'s feminist agenda. In 1972, May followed with *The Heartbreak Kid*, the only of her movies whose screenplay she did not write (Neil Simon did). The story follows a "nice Jewish boy," Lenny (Charles Grodin), who is really a boring, lascivious man, and the vulgar, voluptuous, irritating, spoiled Jewish girl he marries, Lila (played by May's daughter, Jeannie Berlin). On their honeymoon, Lenny falls for his blonde fantasy shiksa, Kelly (Cybill Shepherd). Again, the story is about a man trying to dispose of his wife, but this time for the promise of sexual and romantic happiness. This premise, of following an

Figure 12.2   The Heartbreak Kid: Lenny Cantrow (Charles Grodin) and Lila (Jeannie Berlin) in *The Heartbreak Kid* (1972). Digital frame enlargement. Courtesy of Palomar Pictures/20th Century Fox

already coupled person pursue "the right one," is well known in Hollywood history. Again, May takes a classical narrative formula and flips it around by asking us to think more deeply about what was *really* going on with those poor shrill or schlubby "wrong partners," who were rarely seen as people worth caring about.

There is also, again, a Cary Grant connection. In Grant vehicles such as *The Awful Truth* (1937), *Holiday* (1938), *Bringing Up Baby* (1938), *In Name Only* (1939), and *My Favorite Wife* (1940), his characters abandon women who are deemed controlling, and so, unappealing, for far more exciting, erotic options. May points out that the "wrong partners" (to borrow Brian Henderson's description of this character type) are objectified not in Mulvey's visual terms, but because they are simply *there*. They are not objects of desire, but instruments in a process of self-discovery and personal evolution for the men, who treat them contemptibly for it. May also, in her generously sympathetic treatment of Lenny, confronts uncomfortable aspects of desire – that we might not be fully conscious of the contradictions and stories we tell ourselves about what, or who, we want. Is it merely unfortunate that he meets his dream girl on his honeymoon? It cannot, after all, be coincidental that Kelly is Lila's opposite, or at least appears to be, which allows Lenny to project that she actually is.

Kelly is in fact deliberately coy. She practices that kind of femininity familiar to the romantic comedy, one that pretends to have the upper hand by submitting, or playing as if she is not beholden to reason. We meet her as she inanely charges Lenny, a stranger, with taking her spot on the beach, her bar stool, and so forth. This is reminiscent of Susan (Katharine Hepburn) in *Bringing Up Baby*, who enters the film by purloining her paramour's golf ball, car, and appointments. The happy ending endemic to the Hollywood romantic comedies that May targets is achieved, but of course it is not so happy. For how can anyone know who they want when everyone dissembles?

Mikey and Nicky

May's third feature, *Mikey and Nicky*, follows a night – the last night – in the friendship of the titular characters, played by John Cassavetes and Peter Falk, respectively. The pair have been close since childhood, yet on this night we discover that Nick, a nervous two-bit crook, is being pursued by a hitman (Ned Beatty) – and that that hitman is being abetted by Mike. When we meet the characters in the first scene, it is, as in *Such Good Friends*, a minor ailment – a stomach ulcer – that propels the action. This little health blip – we do not know if Nick is a bit of a hypochondriac or if he has a real condition – introduces what we need to know about the characters: that Nick is childlike and impulsive and that Mike has historically acted as caretaker (he shows

Figure 12.3   Mikey and Nicky: Peter Falk (left) and John Cassavetes (right) as the eponymous *Mikey and Nicky* (1976). Digital frame enlargement. Courtesy of Castle Hill Productions/Paramount Pictures.

up with antacids at the ready). But things are changing. Nick refuses to take the antacids. Is he paranoid? There is something untrustworthy about Mike, so we, as an audience, are thrown into the paradoxical condition of justified paranoia. This uncomfortable affect is sustained throughout the film, and in various ways. Can Mike *really* be in on the killing of his dear friend? Can Nick *really* be a rapist? We are made to feel paranoid for wondering, and then think "surely not" as we come to know the characters, only to find the answer is an unequivocal yes.

So, we know what is happening, but we do not want to admit it. In this way, the film's thematic content echoes May's auteurist strategy. We always knew the darker sides of the character types Hollywood encouraged us to love; we just did not like to admit it. However, before considering what generic tropes this film mocks, I want to address the fact that *Mikey and Nicky* is formally a step away from May's more conventionally (if subtly) crafted prior movies. In fact, it is perhaps *because* the jagged visual edges and demanding soundscape of *Mikey and Nicky* superficially resemble the style of John Cassavetes's films that the film has received more critical attention than May's others. And to some extent, in this story that is manifestly about the guise and psychology of American masculinity (legendary acting teachers Sanford Meisner and William Hickey appear in cameos as mob bosses), May is commenting on the arguable machismo of Cassavetes's film style, a machismo which is also evident in the general effects that global New Wave cinema had on American film style. In his insightful essay "Male Narrative/Female Narration," Brad Stevens, thinking about just this question of style and explicitness, argues of May's earlier films that "If, then, desire for acknowledgment is a typically 'masculine' trait, it seems reasonable to claim that May's style is typically 'feminine'" (76). While difficult to pinpoint, there is an exaggerated quality to *Mikey and Nicky*'s visual grammar that I for one find not only humorous but also a highlight on the controlling, aggressive quality of formal choices that showcase the author's hand, almost a paranoia on a director's part that he may be neglected, even for a moment. To boot, the movie sides with neither character, such that the author's judgment is not felt as easily as it typically is in the films of other auteurs. Even the title gives this away. It construes them as the childlike derivatives of their names, names that are not used regularly throughout the film, but only at the precise moment each is at his most immature.

To return to the way that May's narratives mock genre and character types, Stevens situates *Mikey and Nicky* in relation to the spate of male buddy movies that filled theaters in the late 1960s and early 1970s – films like *Butch Cassidy and the Sundance Kid* (1969), *Easy Rider* (1969), *Midnight Cowboy* (1969), and *The Sting* (1973), which run on an anxiety about male intimacy. He writes that "it is of the essence of May's film that one feels that not only can it be read as a critique of the 'buddy' cycle, but that May has fully grasped the relevance of this cycle" (2015: 76). More specifically, Stevens points out that *Mikey and Nicky* exposes the fact that this generic cycle runs on the repression of homosexual desires between men. The first scene, for example, is easily read as two romantically entangled men having a spat – particularly in the way that Nick cradles Mike's face and holds him. I would add that *Mikey and Nicky* asks what it would *really* look like for two men – two men living amidst the infantilizing privileges and competitiveness of American capitalism – to be outlaws on a caper together. It would look like this: much of the relationship would be told via subtext, given the masculine injunction against overt emotional exchanges. And one man would eventually betray the other.

As well-known as *Mikey and Nicky* is the lore of its release. According to Jonathan Rosenbaum, May shot 1.4 million feet of footage in 1973, and spent two years meticulously editing and re-editing until studio executives wanted to release it themselves. May and her therapist (other accounts say it was May and Falk) broke into the studio in the dead of night and stole the footage. A compromise was reached for a 1976 release, but May's preferred version was not seen until 1980.

MISS MAY DOES NOT EXIST

After this frustration, May did not direct another film until 1987's legendary commercial flop *Ishtar* (which now enjoys a cult following). She went on to co-write *Heaven Can Wait* with Warren Beatty (1978), which won her a Writer's Guild of America Award, to contribute to the screenplays of *Reds* (1981), *Tootsie* (1982), and *Labyrinth* (1986), and to write *The Birdcage* (1996) and *Primary Colors* (1998) for Mike Nichols. Throughout her work, May never *tells* her audience that her movies are great, or what to think of her characters – though if we don't recognize spoiled, stunted men when we see them there's not much she can do about it. On reflection, audiences see that all the characters are trapped by gender expectations, capitalism, and marriage. Like any good comic, she can only play to an intelligent, discerning audience, one that is willing to think and not simply be swept up in sorrow, fear, and bonhomie. And unlike many Hollywood directors with aspirations to *auteur* status, May has given little guidance to audiences. She has, in fact, never sought the spotlight and is famously reclusive. Indeed, her biographical statement on the sleeve notes to the Nichols and May comedy album *Improvisations to Music* simply reads, "Miss May does not exist." Thank goodness her films do.

NOTES

1. For more on this point, and the midcentury history of film authorship more broadly, see Virginia Wright Wexman's *Film and Authorship*.
2. For a full history of Nichols and May, and an analysis of their comedy and its improvisational style, see my book, *Mike Nichols: Sex, Language, and the Reinvention of Psychological Realism*.
3. In thinking about the objects that spark laughter, Bergson emphasized that which appeared paradoxically automatic, machinic, or inelastic in human behavior. For more, see Michael North's book, *Machine-Age Comedy*.
4. René Girard famously writes of the centrality of the triangulation of desire to the structure of storytelling in the history of Western literature. For Girard, desire is "mimetic" in that a character comes to desire an object *because* another does. Typically, this takes the form of a hero desiring a female character, yet the story then marginalizes the female in favor of the conflict between the hero and his rival.

WORKS CITED

"Elaine May in Conversation with Mike Nichols." *Film Comment*, vol. 42, no.4., July/August 2006, www.filmlinc.com/film-comment/article/elaine-may-in-conversation-with-mike-nichols. Accessed 13 May 2020.

Girard, René. *Deceit, Desire and the Novel: Self and Other in Literary Structure*. Translated by Yvonne Freccero, Johns Hopkins University Press, 1965.

Kolker, Robert. *A Cinema of Loneliness: Penn, Kubrick, Scorsese, Spielberg, Altman*. Oxford University Press, 1988.

North, Michael. *Machine-Age Comedy*. Oxford University Press, 2008.

Probst, Leonard. *Off Camera: Leveling About Themselves*. Stein and Day, 1975.

Rosenbaum, Jonathan. "Mikey and Nicky." 6 April, 2017, www.jonathanrosenbaum.net/2017/04/mikey-and-nicky-liner-notes/. Accessed 13 May 2020.

Stevens, Brad. "Male Narrative/Female Narration: Elaine May's *Mikey and Nicky*." *Cineaction*, vol. 31, Spring/Summer 1993, pp. 74–83.

Stevens, Kyle. *Mike Nichols: Sex, Language, and the Reinvention of Psychological Realism*. Oxford University Press, 2015.
Wright Wexman, Virginia. *Film and Authorship*. Rutgers University Press, 2003.

13. PAUL MAZURSKY: THE NEW HOLLYWOOD'S FORGOTTEN MAN

Lester D. Friedman

During the 1970s, a wild bunch of flamboyant filmmakers threw wrenches into the factory system that had dominated the American cinema for decades. The result "was a time when film culture permeated American life in a way it never had before and never has since. Film was no less than a secular religion" (Biskind 17). Although mountains of general and academic writing analyze the works of the New Hollywood's iconoclastic auteurs, one of its most popular directors garners little contemporary attention from either scholars or fans: Paul Mazursky. Like other "elder" statesmen – such as Arthur Penn (1922–2010), Sidney Lumet (1924–2011), John Frankenheimer (1930–2002), and Woody Allen (b. 1935) – who intersected with the film-school-trained Movie Brats, Mazursky (1930–2014) was born before World War II, a circumstance that endowed him with a historical perspective about life and moviemaking that often set him apart from his younger colleagues. More than a decade before *Easy Rider* (1969) rolled into theaters, he had already appeared in bit parts during the studio period – *Fear and Desire* (1953) and *The Blackboard Jungle* (1955). He also worked for four years as a comedy writer on *The Danny Kaye Show* (1963–67) and as a performer/organizer in the Los Angeles Second City troupe. With his partner Larry Tucker he co-wrote the pilot and theme song for the popular TV show *The Monkees* (1966–68) and the script for *I Love You, Alice B. Toklas*! (1968), starring Peter Sellers. Although he had directed a twelve-minute parody of *Last Year at Marienbad* (1961) titled *Last Year at Malibu* (1962), Mazursky was thirty-nine years old before he directed his first feature movie. And he was not without contemporary

Figure 13.1   Bob&Carol&Ted&Alice: Ted (Elliott Gould), Carol (Natalie Wood)
Bob (Robert Culp) and Alice (Dyan Cannon) test the boundaries of sexual liberation
in *Bob&Carol&Ted&Alice* (1969). Digital frame enlargement. Courtesy of
Columbia Pictures.

honors. He received five Academy Award nominations (four for his screenplays and one as producer) and directed six Oscar-nominated performances
over the course of his long career: Dyan Cannon, Elliott Gould, Art Carney
(who won the award), Jill Clayburgh, Lena Olin, and Anjelica Huston. In
2011, the Los Angeles Film Critics Association gave Mazursky their Career
Achievement Award, and in 2014 he received the Writers Guild of America
Lifetime Achievement Award. For HBO viewers, Mazursky embodied the
recurring role of Norm, Mel Brooks's disdainful assistant, in Larry David's
Curb Your Enthusiasm during Seasons 4, who later meets his untimely death
(resulting from Larry's tirade on the golf course) in "The Black Swan" episode
(Season 7, 2009).

During his heyday, Mazursky received critical praise from the likes of Pauline
Kael (who dubbed him a "comic poet" in the mold of Fellini who "hasn't been
given his due" (Wasson 1/4), Stephen Farber (who characterized *Bob & Carol
& Ted & Alice* [1969] as the "most important film since *Bonnie and Clyde*
[1967] [Ehrenstein 59]), Andrew Sarris (who proclaimed him a "testament to
the sheer depth of American mainstream movies way back when directors knew
how to be funny and adult at the same time" [Wasson 4]), and Molly Haskell
(who claimed that he "is possibly the funniest and sharpest writer director of

his generation" [Wasson 87]). Roger Ebert (who said that "Mazursky has a way of making comedies that are more intelligent and relevant than most of the serious films around") usually admired his work as well. Richard Corliss, *Time Magazine* film critic and *Film Comment* editor, put both Mazursky and Truffaut in "the select circle of filmmakers who deserve to be called great" (Wasson 12–13) and dubbed the American as "the Horace with a heart of gold." He also encapsulated the preponderance of positive perspectives during these halcyon days, predicting that:

> Paul Mazursky is likely to be remembered as *the* filmmaker of the seventies. No screenwriter has probed so deep under the pampered skin of this fascinating, maligned decade; no director has so successfully mined it for home-truth revelations . . . Mazursky has created a body of work unmatched in contemporary American cinema for its originality and cohesiveness. ("Poet" 58)

Sadly, for Mazursky, Corliss's optimistic prophecy about his exalted status in the New Hollywood era and his lofty perch in the overall pantheon of American directors proved to be a false prognostication. Relatively few current movie lovers remember Mazursky and only some diehards sporadically wave his banner aloft. Writing in the *New York Times* (2001), Elvis Mitchell calls him "one of the most talented and subtle directors of the seventies" (1). Nat Segaloff, five years later, concludes that "no filmmaker captures the sensibilities of American society of the 1970s and early 1980s with as much honesty, humor and compassion" (222). A year later, The Film Society of Lincoln Center (2007) mounted a retrospective, "The Magic of Paul Mazursky," that screened eleven of his films along with his seldom-seen documentary *Yippee* (2006) about celebrating Rosh Hashanah in Uman (Ukraine) with 25,000 Hasidic Jews at Rabbi Reb Nachman of Breslov's grave; they also staged question and answer sessions with the filmmaker. Leonard Maltin calls Mazursky "American's most undervalued filmmaker" (Wesson, back cover). Finally, social historian Sam Wesson's book of conversations, *Paul on Mazursky* (2011), provides an insightful series of exchanges three years before the director's death, a collection that inspired Quentin Tarantino to conclude that, "Paul Mazursky is one of the great writer-directors of cinema. . . . His complicated, conflicted and comedic characters are some of that decade's finest" (qtd. in Wesson rear cover).

Yet Mazursky does not lack detractors. Bert Cardullo represents those who accuse him of generating "easy laughter at characters who all too often lapse into stereotypes" (*Screen Writing*, 7). For critics like Cardullo, Mazursky's "stale images" are trite, a formulaic collection of clichés that demonstrate how he never takes advantage of his medium, that his movies possess no visual sensitivity, contain shallow visions, and offer viewers a "suffocating sentimentality" (*Screen Writing*, 8). In another piece, he criticizes *Enemies, A Love Story* (1989) for the "sheer banality of its central idea" ("Lovers," 645). However, even such negative assessments usually acknowledge that Mazursky's films astutely encapsulate some of the decade's frustrating contradictions, but disparage them for a consistent degeneration into self-absorbed exercises in predictable filmmaking. For these critics, the director fails to probe beyond the surface gloss of complicated issues, often plastering a simplistic ending over the gaping holes in our cultural walls. But the response that most commonly characterizes current attitudes toward Mazursky's films is neither fulsome praise nor harsh criticism; it is silence, a lack of interest and consequently of attention. As a prime example, one of the most widely read books about the New Hollywood era, Peter Biskind's *Easy Riders, Raging Bulls* (1999), devotes only two pages to Mazursky's films, five pages less than he writes about "The Monkees." Such a dismissive assessment of Mazursky's output demonstrates how little his films engage even those who are writing about the New Hollywood cinema, much less American film history in general.

Between 1969 and 1980, Paul Mazursky directed seven movies: *Bob & Carol & Ted & Alice, Alex in Wonderland* (1970), *Blume in Love* (1973), *Harry and Tonto* (1974), *Next Stop, Greenwich Village* (1976), *An Unmarried Woman* (1978), and *Willy & Phil* (1980). The first and penultimate of these films were massive popular and financial hits that reverberated throughout the social zeitgeist: *Bob & Carol & Ted & Alice*'s production budget was $2 million and it grossed nearly $32 million in the United States; *An Unmarried Woman*'s budget was $2.5 million and it netted $24 million. The others, made on relatively small budgets, rarely lost money but failed to generate much in the way of box-office profits or critical enthusiasm: *Alex in Wonderland* (unavailable), *Blume in Love* ($2.9 million), *Harry and Tonto* ($4.6 million), *Next Stop, Greenwich Village* ($1.6 million), *Willy & Phil* ($4.4 million).

In these films, as I will discuss later, Mazursky explores areas that American filmmakers of the 1970s rarely entered, including the losses of old age (*Harry and Tonto*), fifties nostalgia (*Next Stop, Greenwich Village*), marital rape (*Blume in Love*), artistic indecision (*Alex in Wonderland*), and three-way relationships (*Willy & Phil*). In *Bob & Carol & Ted & Alice*, and to a lesser degree in *Alex in Wonderland* and *Willy & Phil*, Mazursky navigates the treacherous minefields of infidelity, sexual freedom, and new forms of coupling, while in *An Unmarried Woman* he probes the joys and pitfalls of an unexpected single life from the perspective of a newly divorced woman, a relatively new point of view at that time. Before looking at some of the individual films more deeply, I will first remark on an overriding sensibility that permeates almost all of Mazursky's movies.

MENSCHES AND MISHEGAS: MAZURSKY'S JEWISHNESS

With the exceptions of Woody Allen and Mel Brooks, no director is more influenced by his Jewish heritage than Paul Mazursky. But while Allen (né Konigsberg) and Brooks (né Kaminsky) both circumcised their surnames into WASPy conformity, Mazursky kept his ethnically evocative last name but changed his nerdy first name from Irwin to Paul; by doing so, he refused to bury the Eastern European heritage implicitly disclosed in his family name, rejecting the common attempt of Hollywood Jews to "pass" as the "same" to further their careers rather than being stigmatized as the "other," the foreigner. Mazursky is no undercover Jew furtively hiding in the closet of gentile conformity. His memoir, *Show Me The Magic: My Adventures in Life and Hollywood* (1991), begins by labeling himself as a "Jewish boy from Brooklyn" (3), describes his writing as "like a nice piece of halvah" (4), talks about waiting tables in the Catskills (23), and places his bar mitzvah photo as the first image in a collection of family pictures. Reading over many interviews with Mazursky during his career, the word "Jew" inevitably becomes part of the conversation, typified in his 14 January 2013 interview with Stacie Passon in which he characterizes George Segal and Richard Dreyfuss as "my Jews" and acknowledges that "all the actors I worked with underneath it, were me, some form of Jew" (3).

Indeed, relatively few of Mazursky's films don't contain recognizable Jewish characters. Sometimes, he even plays them himself in minor roles, like Sidney Waxman in *Down and Out in Beverly Hills* (1986), Hal Stern in *Alex in Wonderland*, Terry Bloomfield in *Tempest* (1982), and Leon Tortshiner in *Enemies, A Love Story*. As a bit player – a vestige of his early days and training as an actor – Mazursky habitually fashions a rather negative depiction of Jewish manhood: brash, pushy, loud, ostentatious, almost always eating and speaking with his mouth stuffed with food. Mazursky continually gives himself obnoxious roles – culminating in his appearance in drag as the dictator/president Alphonse Simms's (Richard Dreyfuss) mother in *Moon Over Parador* (1988). Shrinks take note. Many of Mazursky's lead characters are also overtly Jewish, such as Lenny's (Lenny Baker) family and his girlfriend Sarah (Ellen Greene) in *Next Stop, Greenwich Village*, Harold Fine (Peter Sellers) in *I Love You, Alice B. Toklas*, Willy Kaufman (Michael Ontkean) in *Willy & Phil*, Dave (Richard Dreyfuss) and Barbara (Bette Midler) Whiteman in *Down and Out in Beverley Hills*, Nick (Woody Allen) and Deborah (Bette Midler) Fifer in *Scenes from a Mall* (1991), Saul Kaplan (Alan Bates) in *An Unmarried Woman*, and Herman Broder (Ron Silver) and most of the characters in *Enemies, a Love Story*. Others, while not noted as such, also seem to read as Jewish, such as Ted Henderson (Elliott Gould) in *Bob & Carol & Ted & Alice* and Stephen Blume (George Segal) in *Blume in Love*. Along with Woody Allen, therefore,

Mazursky populates his films with more Jewish characters than any other Hollywood director.

The most memorable, and in many ways most clichéd, Jewish character in Mazursky's collection of films is Faye Lapinsky (Shelley Winters), Larry's mother in the director's nostalgic remembrance of things past: his young manhood in the 1950s as recollected in *Next Stop, Greenwich Village*. The film presents a decidedly ambivalent portrait of a Jewish family, almost totally ignoring the religious elements of Judaism and instead focusing on cultural Jewishness, the familiar traits audiences associate with Jewish screen characters. As Larry leaves his suffocating home life in Brownsville (Brooklyn) to move into his own Greenwich Village apartment, he literally replaces his yarmulke with a beret, a dismissal of his past and an embrace of his anticipated liberation. His mother's hysterical antics, her sense that he is "deserting them," makes his parting emotionally painful and induces guilt, but after Larry finally storms out of the apartment the soundtrack switches from the opera music that his mother so dearly loves to the jazz of Dave Brubeck and Charlie Parker: improvisational music as a soundtrack for a new and far more bohemian life. Despite his move, however, Larry's heated conflicts with his mother remain. Indeed, the film becomes a virtual compendium of Jewish mother–son clashes with enough pop Freudian psychology thrown in to delight any armchair psychologist. His parents' weekly visits are excruciating: his volatile mother listens to opera, his good natured but ineffectual father (Mike Kellin) reads the *Daily News,* and Larry anxiously waits for the minutes to tick slowly by until it is time for them to leave – until next week's repeat performance. When his parents appear, unannounced, at a raucous rent party, Larry seethes with resentment. He fears his mother will make a fool of herself but something even worse happens: she becomes the life of the party, dancing with his friends and enjoying herself – much to her judgmental son's disapproval.

Larry's fantasies about his mother incorporate all sorts of suppressed sexuality and anger. In one, he recites Shylock's famous "Hath Not" speech before members of his acting class, only to have his mother displace him onstage and surpass his performance. In another far more disturbing reverie, he acts out a scene from Clifford Odets with one of his female colleagues, only to have her replaced by his mother, whom he kisses on the lips. Finally, Larry dreams about delivering Hamlet's "To be or not to be" soliloquy before a hostile audience that pelts him with pies. His mother gleefully joins them, shouting, "Be a doctor!" Yet, despite all this barely disguised vitriol and furtive Oedipal desire, Mazursky never fully twists Faye into a raging Sophie Portnoy. Her sensitivity reveals itself as she weeps while listening to her opera records and she tearfully reveals that she yearns to see her favorite singer (Jussi Björling) perform at the Met. When Larry leaves New York City to take an acting job in Los Angeles, his mother, now far calmer than when he left for Greenwich

Figure 13.2   Lenny Lipinski (Lenny Barker) and his girlfriend (Ellen Greene) receive an unwelcome and uncomfortable visit from his father (Mike Kellin) and mother (Shelley Winters) in *Next Stop, Greenwich Village* (1976). Digital frame enlargement. Courtesy of 20th Century Fox.

Village, tells him to remember the bravery of his Jewish ancestors (as did Mazursky's own mother) and presents him with some apple strudel for the plane trip. "You're a funny lady, ma," he observes, to which she responds with uncharacteristic candor, "My life has not been very funny." At the film's conclusion Larry has learned to accept his mother's foibles. "I'm not angry anymore," he tells his long-suffering father, "I'm crazy, not angry." "Larry," his mother tells him as he exits without her histrionics, "Be a good actor." By the end of the film, therefore, Mrs. Lapinsky acquiesces to her son's decision to follow his dream, and Larry recognizes that whatever damage his mother has done to his battered psyche springs from her intense, if overbearing, love for him, however misguided.

As noted above, many of Mazursky's movies present portraits drawn from his Jewish roots. His move from Brooklyn to Manhattan to Hollywood – chronicled in *Next Stop, Greenwich Village* – is a psychological and emotional journey that shapes his worldview. In a sense, then, all of Mazursky's characters are immigrants. Strangers in a strange land, their lives have shifted radically, and they find the unstable topography of contemporary American life difficult to navigate. As Frank Rich wrote about Mazursky:

> As the American Jew has chosen or been forced to play roles that will enable him to fit into society – to assimilate – so affluent Americans have more and more had to choose among the ever-proliferating roles that the culture creates for their consumption; like the Jews who have left behind the ghettos, the heroes of Mazursky's films leave behind their middle class identities and try to fit into the new revamped America that emerged out of the social traumas of the 1960s. (5)

All Mazursky's characters invent and reinvent their identities, remodeling their values and renovating their priorities as situations present themselves, frequently rearranging a collage of ethical positions, points of view, and emotional ranges. They are, in essence, Wandering Jews, not trekking physically from place to place but rather traveling from one psychological state to another and doing their best to adjust to the sometimes distressing, sometimes exhilarating transformations in their lives.

Mazursky's artistic credo, summed up in his memoir, provides a context for the spectrum of major and minor Jewish figures who populate his movies: "I have always believed that the power of art is that the more specific it is, the greater chance it has to be universal" (4). Such an aesthetic reminds me of the famous declaration of another Jewish artist, the writer Cynthia Ozick, who proclaims: "If we blow into the narrow end of the shofar, we will be heard far. But if we choose to be Mankind rather than Jewish and blow into the wider part, we will not be heard at all" (177). For Mazursky, blowing into the "narrow end of the shofar" means incorporating an array of directly autobiographical characters and situations, most of whom are intimately connected to his ethnic background: aspiring artists in *Next Stop, Greenwich Village*, uptight lawyers in *Bob & Carol & Ted & Alice* and *Blume in Love*, the Wandering Jew in *Willy & Phil*, the affluent suburbanites in *Down and Out in Beverley Hills*, the Holocaust survivors in *Enemies, A Love Story*, the bickering Fifers in *Scenes From a Mall* – could there be a more archetypically Jewish couple than Woody Allen and Bette Midler? Mazursky's movies chronicle the plight of middle-class, mostly white characters who must wade through a sea of new realities that challenge the rock-solid beliefs of their forefathers. It is no surprise, therefore, that the overarching tension in Mazursky's films results from the clash between new-found freedoms and socially conventional traditions, a hallmark of the 1970s life in America and of Jews in America.

SELF-DISCOVERY VIA COMMUNAL ORGASMS

The advertising slogan for *Bob & Carol & Ted & Alice*, "consider the possibilities," remains an apt epigram for almost all of Mazursky's subsequent movies. At one point in the narrative his characters experience a traumatic event, either by chance or by their own choosing, that compels a full-blown reassessment of their lives from a decidedly different point of view, one that challenges their financially comfortable, cocooned existence. For *Bob & Carol & Ted & Alice*, it's a weekend marriage encounter; for Alex, a hit picture; for Blume, a careless affair; for Harry, the demolition of his apartment building; for Larry, a move to Greenwich Village; and for Erica, a divorce. Their new, cantilevered angle of perception obliges these figures to make fateful decisions that, in turn, encourages them to abandon the predictable paths and unambiguous set of values they have rather unthinkingly followed as definitive and final – and most of all safe. As a result, Mazursky's characters are galvanized to reexamine their previous choices and reconsider the new possibilities available for traveling down roads that inevitably lead to alternate lives. Such moments strike these figures as simultaneously confusing & illuminating & frightening & liberating, an intellectually scary but emotionally titillating scenario that posits a what-might-be as distinguished from a what-currently-is.

For example, in *Bob & Caro l& Ted & Alice*, Mazursky invites a generation drunk on the intoxicating promises of sexual freedom to consider the price to be paid for capriciously transgressing the socially sanctioned, moral boundaries that defined their parents' generation. The movie begins with Bob (Robert Culp) and Carol (Natalie Wood) attending a marathon encounter session at an Esalen-type retreat that motivates them to become more emotionally truthful and sexually honest with each other. Ultimately, each of them indulges in a brief infidelity and then reveals this fact to the other, establishing at least the semblance of an open marriage that condones sex with other people – as long as it is freely admitted. When they share their New Age revelations, as well as their bedroom exploits, with their far more conservative and sexually repressed best friends, Ted (Elliott Gould) and Alice (Dyan Cannon), their disclosure ignites a series of life-altering events that culminate with an evocative, iconic image that encapsulated the 70s sexual revolution that had migrated from the counterculture to the middle class: two naked couples in bed together contemplating a leap into sexual indulgence.

Poised on the brink of self-discovery via communal orgasms, while simultaneously contemplating the likely end of their friendship in its current formulation – and perhaps their marriages as well – the four realize that switching partners would push them beyond the emotional and psychological boundaries that govern their upper-middle-class lives: although Mazursky never shows us what actually transpires in the sumptuous hotel suite, apparently (at least I believe) his out of tune quartet leave the room without having sex; they stride down the hallway of their Las Vegas hotel with smiles on their faces, knowing they have tested the water and decided to remain in the shallow end of the pool rather than risk drowning in the deeper section. Mazursky ends the film not with a bang, but rather with a Fellini-esque coda: people milling around the hotel's parking lot (including both Mazursky and his writing partner, Larry Tucker) staring deeply in each other's eyes and repeating the exercise first seen in the encounter marathon. "What the World Needs Now is Love, Sweet Love" swells on the soundtrack, adding an ironic footnote. Maybe, offers the film, more love is needed in this brave new world of fluid lifestyles, but it should be ladled out carefully and it always exerts has a cost.

In a 1984 interview with Freida Lee Mock and Terry Saunders for the

American Film Foundation's TV series, *Words into Images: Writers on Screenwriting*, Mazursky characterizes his films as examining:

> Freedom, and the price of freedom; change and the price of change. We were suddenly told after World War II that you could do things differently, if you wanted to. . . . Can the middle class handle all the freedom it's now being offered? Does anybody really change? My pictures are about a reaction in the United States against and to authority, a reassessment of moral values and social mores, of how people live. (Desser and Friedman 233)

In these movies from 1969–80, therefore, Mazursky charts how people suddenly set adrift in a sea of options without the sustaining life jackets of religion, historical precedents, or cultural traditions float, swim, or drown.

Mazursky's Middle-Class Melodramas

Mazursky is a bard of the middle class. Almost all of his characters live privileged lives in their upper-middle-class, usually urban, mostly white worlds of material security; most have enough money to live quite comfortably, despite the winds of change that buffet them. Consequently, the problems, anxieties, and frustrations they suffer are the stuff of first-world angst, not questions about sufficient food, adequate clothing, or access to health care. This level of comfort holds true for Stephen Blume, Bob and Carol and Ted and Alice, and even Harry, the natty retired schoolteacher who can journey west and resettle in California. By situating his narratives in this protective milieu Mazursky received – as did Woody Allen (to whom he is often compared) – a steady diet of critical condescension and even derision. A typical comment would be that Erica in *An Unmarried Woman*, although facing an emotional crisis due to her husband's affair and abandonment, has the resources to cope with this unpleasant situation, unlike a woman from a lower socio-economic class forced to become a single mother. She can drink white wine with her friends at a trendy restaurant, work in a fancy gallery, talk about old Hollywood heroines, afford psychological counseling, and keep her daughter in private school. Mazursky, quite familiar with this line of attack over the years, spoke directly about it throughout his career: "Very few movies are made thinking of the audience as that fairly intelligent middle class" he told Terry Curtis Fox, "The middle class, I feel, is a class which is never dealt with romantically, although the passion which is felt there is as grand a passion as in the movies we used to see with Grace Kelly" (29). In a similar vein, he told Nat Segaloff that "because middle class characters are neither very rich nor very poor, they are rarely used as the subject of tragedy either" (229).

213

The dislocation Mazursky's characters feel, then, results mostly from the anxieties that accompany the bewildering social changes that surround them, particularly fluctuating gender roles and various forms of sexual experimentation. His characters undergo a disquieting sense of middle-class discontent not revolutionary zeal, the nagging feeling that other people are experiencing a better, more exciting, and ultimately more satisfying existence while they remain hopelessly stuck in a rut of mediocrity and boredom. Most of the time, however, they only dabble in new adventures; then, like groundhogs who catch a glimpse of their shadows and retreat to their dens, they scurry back to the sheltered confines of their comfortable values and mores. Bob and Carol and Ted and Alice never switch partners; Alex gets to meet his culture heroes (Federico Fellini and Jeanne Moreau); Blume and his wife reunite in Venice; Harry finds a new life on the West Coast (even without Tonto); Lenny goes to Hollywood; and Erica finds a suitable partner. Mazursky's characters may possess sufficient charm to carry us along on their various journeys, but one wonders if, by the time they reach their final destination, they really have changed or, for that matter, even learned much along the route. Are Mazursky's movies merely pseudo-Bildungsromans, rather than tales of true education or spiritual growth or coming of age (since the characters are way past that stage in their lives)? As mentioned above, such concerns lead some disparaging critics to dismiss Mazursky as a platitudinous filmmaker whose lengthy Hollywood career merely testifies to the feeble softness of mainstream movie making.

Many of Mazursky's best movies can aptly be classified as melodramas, part of a long tradition of films that strive to elicit audience emotions (usually tears) by focusing on personal relationships in classics like *Camille* (1936), *Stella Dallas* (1937), and *Mildred Pierce* (1945), and modern versions such as *The Bridges of Madison County* (1995), *Titanic* (1997), and *The Fault in Our Stars* (2014). The promises and pitfalls of marriage, as demonstrated in *Bob & Carol & Ted & Alice*, *Blume in Love*, and *An Unmarried Woman* provide fertile ground for Mazursky's budding narratives of disruption, as do strained family relations, as in *Harry and Tonto* and *Next Stop, Greenwich Village*. While many melodramas contain stories of love thwarted by the almost insurmountable impediments of social and economic class, the women in Mazursky's movies, as I have previously noted, inhabit a comfortable world; they are usually well educated figures who – like Nina Blume, Erica Benton, Beth Morrison, Shirley Coombes and the heroines in his later movies – never face the same basic monetary problems as many previous female inhabitants of this genre. They can rely upon having enough resources to help them deal with financial difficulties if they arise. If they do hook up with men from very different social backgrounds, like Nina with Elmo and Erica with Saul, it is because those new lovers provide a stark, and quite liberating, contrast to the more conventional husbands who betrayed them.

Bob & Carol & Ted & Alice presents viewers with two women who weather the cultural rip tides of the sexual revolution in the late 1960s quite differently. Carol Sanders embraces the new permissiveness allowed women at the dawn of the Aquarian Age. Her participation in the weekend marriage encounter session washes away any traditional notions of marital monogamy and sexual fidelity, allowing her to accept Bob's affair as merely a physical act rather than an emotional commitment that threatens their relationship. When Bob initially reveals his affair, Carol asks for more details, encouraging him to be specific about how the event occurred and the age of the woman with whom he had sex. Her matter-of-fact reaction actually upsets Bob, who accuses her of hiding her hostile feeling in a passive-aggressive attempt to chastise him – which never happens. Later in the film, after she meets the girl he slept with, Carol congratulates her husband on his good taste; eventually, she indulges in her own dalliance with a young tennis pro, not to obtain revenge but to seek pleasure. Indeed, it is Bob, far more than Carol, who becomes increasingly more troubled by the fluctuating moral currents of their marriage: he is perfectly willing to indulge in sex with another woman but, at least at first, feels wounded when Carol follows his example into their bedroom with another man. While Carol maintains the placid façade of an upper-middle-class housewife, holding neighborhood barbecues and pool parties and dinning in expensive restaurants, she has imbibed the waters of sexual discovery and, more than any of the film's other three main characters, swims with newfound confidence in her ability to avoid the treacherous undertow of jealousy.

Juxtaposed against Carol's acceptance of sexual openness beyond the conventional boundaries of marriage, Alice Henderson remains caught between her more traditional sense of marital fidelity, the changing attitudes of her best friends, and her husband's desire to have sex with other women, which he eventually realizes while away on a business trip. An outstanding example of Mazursky's comic timing takes place in Ted and Alice's bedroom when they return home after first learning of Bob's sexual fling. Ted is turned on by hearing this salacious news and wants to have sex with Alice who, appalled by Ted's infidelity and Carol's casual acceptance of it, just wants to go to sleep and forget about how her best friend has reacted so calmly to her husband's adultery. The result is a collision of actions and reactions, feints and dodges, deceptions and distractions, that would have made Preston Sturges, George Cukor, or any aficionado of Restoration Comedies applaud with appreciation, as we watch the horny husband desperately trying to seduce his dismayed wife and the various strategies she employs to fend off his clumsy advances. (Elliott Gould claims on the DVD's commentary track that this scene got them nominated for the Academy Awards.) "Do you want me against my will?" she asks Ted, who seems perfectly willing to take her any way he can. Finally, in the Las Vegas hotel room, it is Alice, the most sexually reticent of the foursome, who finally admits the truth: they came there to switch partners or, as she memorably puts it, "First we'll have an orgy and then go see Tony Bennett."

Almost a decade after Mazursky plunged into the murky currents of marital flexibility and casual sexual encounters with *Bob & Carol & Ted & Alice*, he dove back into those precarious waters again, this time from the point of view of the newly divorced Erica Benton in *An Unmarried Woman*. During interviews and on various DVD commentaries the director talks about what today would seem, quite presumptuously, his ability to understand "women better than I do men." But while some lauded the film's depiction of a newly emancipated woman and its frank discussions of sexuality and depictions of realistic nudity, others decried what they perceived as the film's retrograde ideology trussed up in slick modern garb. Two different articles, both published in 1982 and both written by renowned women scholars, demonstrate this dichotomy. Charlotte Brunsdon, in her essay for *Screen*, situates *An Unmarried Woman* as part of a group of Hollywood movies that "address and construct, however obliquely, changing concepts of the appropriate modes of femininity in contemporary Western culture" (21) and as such, reach out to a new female audience created by social, political, and economic changes that she labels the "Cosmo Girl":

> Cosmo Girl aspires to the sexual satisfaction that was connotatively denied to the 'career girl' of the '60s. However, her new subject position is potentially contradictory, retaining femininity, while moving into traditionally masculine modes (alert, aggressive, ambitious). There is thus a constant tension in the way she must always already be desirable (feminine), as well as desiring. (21)

Although Erica's journey is forced by Martin's decision to leave her for another woman, Brunsdon sees her coupling with the impossibly perfect Saul as a conventional melodramatic element and an acknowledgement that Erica has achieved a certain degree of growth by the time he appears late in the narrative. Brunsdon hits upon the dual, perhaps even paradoxical, nature of the narrative's conclusion. Given Erica's emotional progress, it would be a step backwards for her simply to accompany Saul to Vermont and essentially replicate a marriage without the ring and ceremony, but the film also posits true love – with all the sticky connotations of that term – as an actual possibility. In a similar vein, Joan Mellen applauds *An Unmarried Woman* for exploring how "a woman of our time, without the emotional protection of marriage, creates a life of her own . . . recognizing how friendships with other women form an important aspect of the life of the heroine" (529).

Julia Lesage's contemporaneous essay offers a less charitable reading of *An Unmarried Woman*, characterizing it as a "hegemonic fantasy" that "sets out a few issues which are treated as the key issues and deals with those issues in a socially acceptable and often predictable way: the hegemonic female fantasy is an historical creation – a visible projection in our fictions at any given date of how women are socially, by consensus, defined" (84). Lesage, like many other critics, felt that Mazursky solves the very real dilemmas faced by single women by means of a "fantasy fulfillment resolution" which, by its very nature, "delimits the parameters within which we are allowed to consider the woman's situation" (85). Even Erica's declaration of independence – not acceding to Saul's wish that she accompany him to Vermont for the summer – is undercut by the final image of her struggling on the windy New York City streets with the painter's outsized canvas, an apt symbol of how he now controls or at least substantially affects her life. Such a "present" is as much a burden as a gift. This narrative resolution, for Lesage, is conventional in many ways, particularly because the solution to Erica's situation, both her emotional and sexual problems, is "to become reglued into the social fabric by being part of a heterosexual couple" (88). In addition to this fantasy of the perfect male savior, *An Unmarried Woman* offers the myth of prosperity that allows Erica to continue to join her friends at expensive restaurants, that allows her to rent a spacious townhouse, and that provides a sense of independence denied women of lesser means.

While Erica grows emotionally during the course of the narrative, even refusing to take Martin back when he pleads with her to reconstitute their family, one wonders if that is enough, even in 1978. Within the overall flow of the movie, we are clearly meant to applaud her decision to stay in New York rather than attach herself to Saul as he works on his paintings, but beyond that liberating decision what are her aspirations now that she is no longer tethered to Martin and, in a few years, will not have her daughter Patty to raise? She gathers herself together enough to rent a new apartment, but seems in no hurry to do much else but go to therapy and talk with her friends. Perhaps this is asking too much of a woman at this still early stage of a new life she never thought she would be living, but beyond working at a part-time position in a gallery Erica tells us nothing about her higher ambitions or plans for the future. Of course, she has no desperate need to earn enough money to support herself and her daughter, but even so, should this be sufficient? Not for David Ehrenstein, who sees the ending of *An Unmarried Woman* as emblematic of "the New Hollywood brand of feminism, where the heroine is made to seem to take a stand for her own 'independence,' though the circumstances in which she resides have made no significant change since the Hayward-Crawford era" (61). While Mazursky clearly captured a moment of cultural change, his socially palatable form of feminism ruffles a few feathers and offers little designed to unravel the fabric of the society in which Erica functions.

Mazursky and the French New Wave

In *Bob & Carol & Ted & Alice*, Mazursky establishes the stylistic traits that will dominate the rest of his filmmaking career. To the eyes of a modern viewer, Mazursky is an "invisible" director, never brandishing visual flourishes or self-conscious techniques he labels derogatorily as "film school razzle dazzle" (Wesson 79). As a result, his minimal camera movement and his lengthy scenes resemble theatrical plays rather than frenetically edited moving pictures, a technique that distinguishes him from his younger counterparts. As Wesson and others repeatedly emphasize, however, Mazursky is a master of the long take, using deep focus to connect everything within the frame, and thereby compelling viewers to recognize the complementary relationships between all the elements in the mise-en-scène. As a result, he establishes the feel, the concrete reality, of a place and time. In many ways, therefore, Mazursky's technique foregrounds the philosophy expressed by the influential French critic André Bazin, evident in the style of many of the filmmakers he most admires, including Ford, Wyler, Cukor, Sturges, Wilder, Truffaut, and De Sica. In particular, Mazursky venerated the French New Wave critics and filmmakers who emerged in *Cahiers du Cinéma,* which Bazin co-founded. In basic terms, Bazin preached that a director should give the spectator the freedom to explore and make sense of the materials in the frame; as a result, he favored a realistic, depth of field composition that allowed for the relationships between objects to be revealed if the viewer paid close attention to the elements depicted. This "aesthetic rendition of reality" was augmented by an editing style we now would label as cutting to continuity that continues the illusion of reality by not drawing a viewer out of the screen narrative by calling attention to the technique of the filmmaker. (Ironically, the director Mazursky most reveres is Fellini, whose flamboyant visual style is not an aesthetic model for his own work.) Thus, the director maintains an "invisible" presence throughout the movie, never dragging the audience's attention to his/her flashy manipulation of the image through hyper-montages, dramatic lighting, or the exaggerated visual elements so characteristic of the German Expressionist movement. For Mazursky, like Bazin, everything must contribute to the reality of the image on the screen, and Mazursky proves a fitting pupil of this visual technique.

Following Bazin's aesthetic dictates, Mazursky believes that the types of long take, deep focus scenes that punctuate his movies endow the situations he creates with a tension and an emotional complexity that often gets eradicated by the barrage of quick cuts that characterize more contemporary movies, a strategy that often leaves viewers barely able to focus on an action or an environment before it gets whisked away and replaced by something new. Indeed, Mazursky, who remained more interested in reaction than in action throughout his career, reluctantly cuts away from a scene at the last possible moment and only when it finally feels emotionally necessary to move on to the next sequence. When Wesson asked Mazursky about his technique of shooting mostly in masters and close-ups, he responded:

> There are shots that hold for six or seven minutes and it's not static. You see a whole performance. One character moves into the frame and another character moves into the same shot. It's got depth of field so you can see back in the other room . . . You're showing a *life*. Real life is in masters, you know what I mean . . . When you shoot the thing, you see it one way: you see it real. But when you cut it up, you see the director manipulating it. He's lying to you. It's not true. It's not real. (43–5)

Thus, these long takes, sometimes interspersed with uncomfortably intimate close-ups, define Mazursky's filmmaking style but place him at odds with the MTV aesthetic that dominates contemporary moviemaking, much to the detriment of his critical reputation.

A Filmmaker of the 1970s

"During the 1970s," says Mazursky as part of his DVD commentary for *An Unmarried Woman*, "we were free to make the pictures we dreamt of." But

Figure 13.3   Director/Writer/Actor Paul Mazursky (1930–2014).

are Mazursky's films period pieces trapped in amber that have little relevance to the contemporary lives and cultural issues prevalent in the twenty-first century? Or, as some have suggested, is he just Woody Allen light: a reasonably kind-hearted satirical observer who skillfully fashioned a series of comedies of manners? Granted, Mazursky was an adroit director of actors, perhaps because of his own background and dramatic training. Most impressively, Art Carney, known primarily at the time as a TV comedian for his role in *The Honeymooners*, won for Best Actor for *Harry and Tonto*. Perhaps Mazursky is just too optimistic for the cynical age in which we live. As he told Terry Curtis Fox, "I believe in the affirmation of life. If we lose the possibility of it, we've lost an awful lot" (32). In fact, one of the more unique things about Mazursky's films is that no real villains exist within them. Certainly, self-centered and flawed characters who oftentimes act as their own worst enemy populate his frames, but no truly evil men or woman purposely seek to cause the hurt or destruction of others.

Paul Mazursky is a director of his time – and what a time it was. That, of course, should not necessarily be considered a bad thing. He travelled among the giants of the New Hollywood era and was seen as their equal by respected critics. Many directors would be content to have a career like his, one that allowed him to make the kinds of movies he wanted and that garnered attention and fame during his lifetime. But, despite his constant protestations that his films seem as relevant in the twenty-first century as they were in the 1970s, a refrain he expresses in all of his DVD commentaries at one point or another, I don't believe this is the case. As a director, he wants to please us so much, wants us to like his characters as much as he obviously does, that he drives right up to the edge of an interesting topic or difficult dilemma but then puts on the breaks, slips into reverse gear, and turns away from anything that might disturb the viewer too seriously. Mazursky certainly had compassion, a positive trait that many directors lack, but it limits him to never subject his characters to anything more than mild censure – even when they deserve it. That said, however, Mazursky was able to freeze moments of cultural unease for us to observe, now from a growing distance, and having done that deserves a far better fate than to be the forgotten man of the New Hollywood.

WORKS CITED

Biskind, Peter. *Easy Riders, Raging Bulls: How the Sex-Drugs-and-Rock 'N' Roll Generation Saved Hollywood* (4th Edition), Simon and Schuster, 1999.

Cardullo, Bert. *Screen Writing: Genres, Classics, and Aesthetics*. Anthem Press, 2010.

Cardullo, Bert. "Lovers and Other Strangers." *The Hudson Review*, vol. 43, no. 4, Winter, 1991, pp. 645–53.

Brunsdon, Charlotte. "A Subject for the Seventies," *Screen*, nos. 3–4, 1982, pp. 20–29.

Corliss, Richard. "Paul Mazursky: A Poet for People Like Us" *New York Times*, 3 April 1978, pp. 52–8.

Corliss, Richard. "Paul Mazursky: The Horace with a Heart of Gold." *Film Comment*, vol. 11, no. 2, March/April 1975, pp. 40–42.

Desser, David, and Lester Friedman, *American Jewish Filmmakers*. University of Illinois Press, 1993.

Ebert, Roger. "Roger Ebert Review of *'Down and Out in Beverly Hills'"* (January 31, 1986) Rogerebert.com. Accessed 8 February 2017.

Ehrenstein, David. "Melodrama and the New Woman," *Film Comment*, September/October, 1978, pp. 59–62

Fox, Terry Curtis. "Paul Mazursky Interview," *Film Comment*, vol. 14, no. 2, March/April, 1978, pp. 29–32.

Lesage, Julia. "The Hegemonic Female Fantasy," *Film Reader*, vol. 5, 1982, pp. 83–94

Maltin, Leonard. "Book Review – Paul Mazursky," Leonard Maltin website, September 2, 2011, www.leonardmaltin.com/book-review-paul-on-mazursky/. Accessed February 6, 2017.

Mazursky, Paul. *Show Me the Magic: My Adventures in Life and Hollywood*. Simon and Schuster, 1999.

Mellen, Joan. "The Return of Women to Seventies Films," *Quarterly Review of Film Studies*, vol. 3, no. 4, 1978, pp. 525–43.

Mitchell, Elvis. "Critics Notebook: Doing Justice to Mazursky, Long Bypassed," *New York Times*, 30 August 2001, p. 1

Ozick, Cynthia. "Towards a New Yiddish" *Art and Ardor*. Alfred A. Knopf, 1983.

Passon, Stacie. "Paul Mazursky Loves Talking to Women." *Filmmaker*,14 January 2013, pp. 1–4.

Rich, Frank. "Still Crazy after All these Years." *New York Post*, 7 February, 1976, p. 5.

Segaloff, Nat. "Paul Mazursky: A Map of the Heart." *Backstory 4: Interviews with Screenwriters of the 1970s and 1980s*, edited by Patrick McGilligan, University of California Press, 2006, pp. 222–61.

Wasson, Sam. *Paul on Mazursky*. Wesleyan University Press, 2011.

14. NEW HOLLYWOOD CROSSOVER: JOAN MICKLIN SILVER AND THE INDIE-STUDIO DIVIDE

Maya Montañez Smukler

Joan Micklin Silver's filmography presents a unique map of 1970s Hollywood in the way she traversed between independent and studio filmmaking, producing small, character-driven narratives at a time when the studios began to dominate screens with high concept blockbusters. She was one of the few directors during the 1970s who succeeded in making independent films a decade before film festivals such as Sundance and distributors like Miramax fortified a robust marketplace for independent filmmakers in the 1980s. In collaboration with her husband, Raphael (Ray) Silver (1930–2013), her as writer-director and him as producer-distributor, the couple produced and self-distributed the feature films *Hester Street* (1975) and *Between the Lines* (1977). In 1979, Micklin Silver transitioned from independent production to studio filmmaking when she wrote and directed *Head Over Heels*, later retitled *Chilly Scenes of Winter*, for United Artists.[1]

Her body of work during the 1970s examines the shifting dynamics within heterosexual romance under the influence of the era's social movements. These three feature films demonstrate the director's ability to push the well-known conventions of the romantic dramady to reveal the intricacies of intimate relationships by paying close attention to her characters' struggles as individuals as much as to the genre's familiar patterns of breaking up and coming together. Micklin Silver's gift for identifying new talent contributed to the originality of her characterizations – whether they were ensconced in a period piece about Jewish immigrants or focused on a contemporary group of middle-class friends in their late twenties grappling with the pressures of adulthood – and helped launch the careers of actors including Jeff Goldblum, John Heard, Marilu Henner, Carol Kane, Joe Morton, and Gwen Welles. Micklin Silver's interest in these kinds of themes and her commitment to young performers is what distinguishes her work during these years. However, her experiences making such films, and the particular challenges she faced, exemplify what has been historicized as Hollywood's conflicting creative and economic tendencies during this decade: the introspective, character-driven film versus the blockbuster.

As a woman making films in 1970s Hollywood, Micklin Silver belongs to the figurative "generation" who, while a statistically small group despite their historical significance, marked the first increase of female directors since the silent era. She and her peers, bolstered by the achievements of second-wave feminism, challenged the exclusivity of 1970s New Hollywood's male auteur canon.

The mythology of the 1970s is that it was "a time in the history of . . . the [US film] industry [when] almost anyone with talent and the will to do so could become a film director" (Cook 98). Hollywood during the late 1960s and into the 1970s was experiencing great insecurity and change. An influx of foreign and independent films – from art-house to low-budget exploitation and pornography – flooded the marketplace; the studios scrambled to keep up by introducing the MPAA's rating system to regulate film content while altering their own products in an effort to appeal to the large youth audience. While the studio system had maintained its power through vertical integration during the previous era, now corporate conglomeration decentralized executive authority and fragmented the production and distribution of motion pictures. Under these circumstances, Joan Micklin Silver's entry into a directing career, improbable for the generation preceding her, followed an unorthodox path that fit the era when traditions of industry meritocracy were being challenged by an incoming wave of filmmakers to an industry that was desperately trying to find its footing. But it is exactly what qualified her as an "outsider" breaking in, her difference as an independent and as a woman, that put her at odds with the era and the way it has so frequently been historicized.

MIDWESTERN DREAMS VS. HOLLYWOOD REALITY

Born in Omaha, Nebraska in 1935, Micklin Silver attended Sarah Lawrence College in the early 1950s during which time she met Ray Silver, a graduate of Harvard Business School and five years her senior. The two were married in 1956 and relocated to Ray's hometown of Cleveland where he would begin a career in real estate, establishing the company Midwestern Land Development Corporation; and Joan would begin imagining how to make a career in filmmaking. For Micklin Silver, watching Satyajit Ray's *Panther Panchali* at the Heights Art Theater in Cleveland was a revelation. The film's style of storytelling resonated with her deeply, but she didn't feel she could cultivate her own cinematic vision in Cleveland (Joan Micklin Silver, DGA). In 1967, when her husband had an opportunity to expand his business to the east coast, the family, now with three small daughters, ages four, seven, and nine, relocated to New York City; and the opportunity for Joan to explore a profession in film seemed possible.

Joan had imagined that writing would be her path to making movies. "I had a game plan," she told the *Los Angeles Times* in 1977. "First, I would write screenplays that would be directed by all the great directors, and then, at the proper ladylike moment, when I had thoroughly learned my craft, *I* would emerge as a great director" (Kent). In fact, Joan's "plan" did materialize at first. Soon after arriving in New York the couple attended a fundraiser for future mayor of Cleveland Carl Stokes, where Joan met Joan Ganz Cooney, soon to be co-founder of *Sesame Street*. Cooney connected her to Linda Gottlieb, vice-president of the Learning Corporation of America, which produced educational films (Joan Micklin Silver, DGA). She and Gottlieb began collaborating on projects, Joan as screenwriter and Linda as producer, one of which, *Limbo*, was made by Universal in 1972. However, the experience was a disappointment. Micklin Silver saw her script, a story about the wives of prisoners of war in Vietnam with a female-centric, anti-war commentary, altered into something resembling a soap opera by director Mark Robson. She fought for her original concept but was replaced by another writer, James Bridges. Robson, a Hollywood veteran (director of *Home of the Brave* [1949] and *Valley of the Dolls* [1967]), although displeased with her refusal to follow his rewrite instructions, recognized the novice filmmaker's ambition and invited her to visit the set.

> Although [Robson] didn't make a movie of *Limbo* that I respected, [he] was a very generous director. He invited me down to Florida, where the movie was being made . . . He let me talk to any actor, he let me look through the camera more than he was looking through the camera. He couldn't have been nicer . . . it was tremendous. It was like film school. (Joan Micklin Silver, DGA)

This was a turning point for Micklin Silver. Dismayed by her experience as a powerless screenwriter, but emboldened by the set visit, she understood that to protect her creative vision, she must direct. Joan returned to the Learning Corporation, and with Gottlieb as producer convinced William F. Deneen, filmmaker and founder of the company, that he should hire her to write *and* direct. Three successful short films followed: *The Immigrant Experience* (1972), *The Fur Coat Club* (1973), and *The Case of the Elevator Duck* (1974). With a screenwriting credit and the shorts that had done well on the educational media circuit, Micklin Silver was confident that her portfolio was small but promising. However, in the early 1970s the opportunity to get hired as a writer-director, from the east coast, coming out of educational films and as a woman, was a difficult combination.

The 1970s were a paradoxical time for female directors making narrative feature films. In this decade the number of women directors in Hollywood, and the independent production communities adjacent to the dominant film industry, increased for the first time in forty years. During the classic studio system there were two women directors. Dorothy Arzner made films for the majors from the late 1920s until her last picture in 1943, *First Comes Courage* for Columbia; and Ida Lupino, through her independent production company, The Film Makers, made her directorial debut, *Not Wanted*, in 1949. In 1966 Lupino directed *The Trouble with Angels* for Columbia Pictures: she was the only woman to direct for a major studio until 1971 when Elaine May wrote, directed, and co-starred in *A New Leaf* for Paramount. In the 1960s, independent filmmakers Shirley Clarke and Juleen Compton, both based in New York City, challenged dominant modes of production in their feature work: Clarke by drawing on traditions of documentary filmmaking; and Compton by invoking the influence of the French New Wave. Both financed their pictures outside of industry business norms and relied on film festivals and art-house theater circuits for distribution. In 1967, Stephanie Rothman wrote and directed her first feature, *It's a Bikini World*, for prolific low-budget exploitation producer Roger Corman. As a result of the studio system's decline and the expanding marketplace for a range of independent and foreign films; in combination with the broad impact of the national women's movement on all areas of social and public policy; and the movement's influence on feminist activism within the entertainment industry, the number of women directing features in the United States crawled upward.

Between 1970 and 1980 there were an estimated sixteen women (all of whom were white – women of color would begin to break through in the 1980s) who had directed at least one feature film intended for a commercial audience (see Smukler). Some, like Penny Allen, Karen Arthur, and Barbara Loden made independent art-house films; others such as Joan Darling and Jane Wagner each made a film for a major studio; Barbara Peeters made exploitation films for the drive-in audience; and Anne Bancroft, Lee Grant, and Joan Tewkesbury parlayed their established careers as performers and writers into directing. And yet the gap was insurmountable. In 1979, the Women's Committee of the Directors Guild released this statistic: Women had directed 0.19 percent – or 14 – of the 7,332 feature films made between 1949 and 1979 ("Letter to Signatories"). In 1972, Micklin Silver found herself at the apex of all that could be possible with the work she had generated through writing and making short films, and yet she was faced with an institutionalized impasse. "I had such blatantly sexist things said to me by studio executives when I started," she recalled at the end of the decade, "the most outstanding of which was, 'feature films are very expensive to mount and to distribute, and woman directors are one more problem we don't need'" (Joan Micklin Silver, AFI 1979).

Discouraged by her inability to gain access, Micklin Silver thought that in spite of her efforts she might never get the chance to make a film. "My husband saw my frustration and said, 'I don't know if you're talented or not but you certainly have the right to find out'" (Joan Micklin Silver, AFI 1988). With no prior experience in the film business, Ray Silver used his financial skills and business contacts from a successful twenty-five-year career in real estate to start another career with his wife. "I didn't feel that I was doing her a favor," Silver said of stepping up to produce for Joan. "I think it's a lot different for a woman in the creative world than it is for a man. Men have got this whole support system – the old boys" (Rosenthal). Deciding that the best, and possibly only, option to sidestep the sexist obstacles facing Joan was to create for themselves a different way of filmmaking, the couple entered a new partnership as director and producer-distributor. In agreement that the film had to be made for a small sum, the wife and husband team contributed personal funds in combination with investors to whom Ray had access from outside of the film industry, to raise a budget of under $400,000 for their first collaboration, *Hester Street* (Kent).

COMING TO AMERICA AND THE PERILS OF SELF-DISTRIBUTION

Born to Russian Jewish parents who had immigrated to the United States as children, Micklin Silver had grown up hearing stories about the experience of assimilating between cultures. Having already piqued an interest in the subject matter in her short film *The Immigrant Story*, about Polish immigrants coming to the United States at the turn of the century, she chose to adapt the short story "Yekl" by Abraham Cahan for the screen as her first feature. *Hester Street*, a period piece about Jewish immigrants living in New York City's Lower East Side in the early 1900s, focuses on the disillusionment of the marriage between Yankle and Gitl. Yankle has come to America ahead of his wife and in the time apart has reinvented himself as Jake and begun a relationship with another woman. When Gitl arrives, dowdy and awkward with "old country" tradition, the two struggle and ultimately are unable to reconcile what it is to be a New American family. The film began production in fall 1973 with a cast of relatively unknown screen performers, Carol Kane, Steven Keats, and theater veteran Doris Roberts in a supporting role. In order to create a convincing New York immigrant community in the early twentieth century, the movie was filmed in black and white on location in Greenwich Village with much of their small budget spent on costumes, sets, and a dialect coach for the portions of Yiddish dialogue. After being strong-armed by the Teamsters that the picture needed to be a union film, cast and crew were paid union scale; shooting was completed within thirty-four days.

What emerges in *Hester Street*, and becomes a constant in so much of Micklin Silver's work, in particular those projects that she wrote or independently produced, is an egalitarian attention to the female and male experience in romantic relationships. Gitl's transformation is a feminist one, but it is not done entirely at Jake's expense. He is flawed but at his core not a bad man. Micklin Silver portrays the demise of their marriage not without heartbreak and disappointment, and emphasizes that with what is lost as a couple comes a newfound self-awareness as an individual.

By the following year, Joan and Ray had a finished version of the film and began sending it around to studios in hopes of finding a distributor. Although they had an agent, Howard Housman, at William Morris in Los Angeles, the process of getting access to the people with power proved to be difficult. For new filmmakers with no industry standing Hollywood's pecking order was a deterrent. "You always want the top person," explained Ray. "But this is excruciatingly difficult since, as he's the most important person, he's also the least available" (Haskell). A small period-piece film, about Jewish immigrants with no well-known stars, made by first-time filmmakers, proved to be a challenge to sell to companies large and small. According to Ray, distributors rejected the picture because they thought it was "a totally ethnic, Jewish film and only old Jews would see it because younger people could not relate to the story" (McBride). For Joan, the reaction from distributors who refused to see past the ethnic identifiers of the film was disheartening: "I went through one of the worst winters of my life. The only offer was to release it on 16mm to the synagogue market" (Joan Micklin Silver, DGA).

Ray pursued the festival circuit, which was key in generating attention around the film. When *Hester Street* received positive reviews after screening for a predominately non-Jewish audience at the USA Film Festival in Dallas, held on the campus of Southern Methodist University, Joan and Ray's belief that their movie was not limited to a niche demographic was validated. The film screened at Cannes, where it received more favorable reviews. George Moskowitz, covering the festival for *Variety*, predicted that the film would be a "sleeper" hit; and singled out Micklin Silver as a new talent who "should be a filmmaker to be reckoned with after this effective and touching film." Charles Champlin, of the *Los Angeles Times*, was effusive about the movie, promising that it "goes beyond the particulars [Jewish subject] to touch the whole American immigrant experience, which is to say that it touches all of us at some point in our lives."

Buoyed by the festival buzz, Ray began to pursue domestic distribution

Figure 14.1 Greenhorn (Zane Lasky) meets with earlier arrivals in *Hester Street*'s (1975) story of Jewish immigration in the early 1900s. Digital frame enlargement. Courtesy of Midwest Films

options. However, the major studios dominated distribution outlets and they continually passed on the film, deeming it too small and too Jewish; and the minor companies, such as Cinemation and Cinema V, which were interested in the picture once the press began covering it, offered meager financial returns (Haskell). Helpful to Ray was John Cassavetes, who had self-distributed his own film *Woman Under the Influence* in 1974. The veteran director encouraged him to do the same. Important for the Silvers' success was to generate critical attention in New York and with those favorable reviews build some box-office earnings. Once the film was established as reputable in New York City, there was a better chance that the rest of the domestic market would be receptive (Verrill). While at Cannes, Ray was able to sell distribution rights to some European markets, making a profit that he could invest back into a wider domestic release effort. He hired Cassavetes's booking agents Blaine Novak and Jeff Lipsky to assist with the marketing; their publicity campaign was so successful that Carol Kane was nominated for an Oscar. For Ray, the choice to self-distribute was as much an act of necessity and self-preservation as it was defiance against a system that seemed inflexible. "At every step, the pros say an amateur is going to botch it up, but, My God!," exclaimed Silver, "the number of pros who have botched things up . . . there are no fixed ground rules. What you really need is commitment, an emotional involvement, and this is best secured from the people who did the film" (Haskell).

HESTER STREET (1975): CORPORATE TAKEOVER OF THE INDEPENDENT STRUGGLE

Hester Street grossed an estimated $5 million. With those profits the couple invested in their second film, *Between the Lines* (1977), directed by Joan, and produced-distributed by Ray. The story of a young and ambitious staff of an independent newspaper in Boston in the midst of a corporate takeover, the film featured an ensemble cast including Lindsay Crouse, Jill Eikenberry, Jeff Goldblum, John Heard, Marilu Henner, Bruno Kirby, Joe Morton, and Gwen Welles in some of their first starring roles. Written by Fred Barron, a journalist who based the script on his experience working for the independent Boston's independent *Real Paper*, the movie captured the complex dynamics of a group of friends and co-workers wrestling with the fading social and political idealism of the 1960s as they entered the 1970s and grappled with losing themselves and their relationships in the "Me"-generation narcissism associated with the new decade.

In 1983, Lawrence Kasdan's *The Big Chill*, made by Columbia Pictures, charmed the box office with its ensemble cast; but in 1977 distributors were uninterested in a group narrative. (Ironically, Goldblum would reprise in Kasdan's picture a character similar to the one he played for Micklin Silver.) Unable to garner interest from a distributor, once again Joan and Ray released the movie themselves through their company Midwest Film Productions. This time they found the experience more complicated than that of just a few years prior. "By 1978, when we were distributing *Between the Lines*, we found it difficult to get either the theaters we wanted or the numbers we wanted," explained Ray. "We'd ask for twelve theaters in Atlanta, and we'd get six" (Peary). In the late 1970s, the studios had begun to reestablish their power in the blockbuster formulas introduced by movies such as *Jaws* (1975), *Saturday Night Fever* (1977), and *Star Wars* (1977), films that opened wide, saturating the market and limiting access for smaller pictures, in particular non-sensational human-interest stories with a cast of young unknowns.

BETWEEN THE LINES (1977)

Critics found *Between the Lines*'s overarching theme of journalistic integrity in the face of corporate media's greed to be the least interesting part of the film. What did stand out to reviewers was the way Micklin Silver captured what Vincent Canby of the *New York Times* described as the twenty-year-olds' anguish of "growing up after you've already grown up." "[*Between the Lines*] is at its best," Canby went on, "when it ambles in and out of [the characters'] lives, overhearing lovers' quarrels, professional conflicts, office politics," emphasizing "the performances, which are uniformly first-rate, the kind of

Figure 14.2 *Between the Lines* (1977) traces the experiences of those running an alternative newspaper in Boston. Digital frame enlargement. Courtesy of Midwest Films.

ensemble work in which no actor is more or less important than another" (Canby, "Good Reading"). *Variety* was impressed with the film's estimated budget of $800,000: "Every cent of the budget shows on the screen and it should be received, with open arms, [by] the class of customers for which it has apparently been made – the young." This reviewer had nothing but praise for the film – the script, the performances, and "Joan Micklin Silver's firm director's touch," but suggested that "the overall handsomeness of the cast is one of the [film's] unbelievable aspects" ("Film Reviews: Between the Lines" 73). For a small film working outside of the star-package deal that defined Hollywood, this seemed like a critique Joan and Ray could take as a compliment.

Studio Turmoil and the Triumph of Modern Romance

Having successfully directed two independent features, as well as writing-directing *Bernice Bobs Her Hair* (1976), a short film starring Shelley Duvall made for PBS, and producing Ray's directorial debut, the prison drama *On the Yard* (1978; also produced-distributed by the couple), in 1979 Micklin Silver made her first studio picture: *Head Over Heels*, eventually re-released as *Chilly Scenes of Winter*. Based on Ann Beattie's 1976 novel *Chilly Scenes of Winter*, the film takes place in Salt Lake City and follows Charles – played by John Heard in his second film with the director – a thirty-year-old civil servant uninspired by the mundane nine-to-five life, who falls in love with a married co-worker, Laura (Mary Beth Hurt). The film was filled with a quirky cast of

Figure 14.3   John Heard and Mary Beth Hurt are the star-crossed lovers in *Head Over Heels* (*Chilly Scenes of Winter*) (1979). Digital frame enlargement. Courtesy of Triple Play.

characters: Charles's neurotic mother played by Hollywood veteran Gloria Grahame; and his best friend Sam, in an early role for Peter Riegert, who would star in Micklin Silver's next film, *Crossing Delancey* (1988).

The material had originally started with Triple Play, actors Griffin Dunne, Mark Metcalf, and Amy Robinson's newly formed production company, which had optioned the rights to the story. Micklin Silver, who had long been interested in the book, contacted the trio and a partnership was established with Joan adapting Beattie's novel for the screen. At the time, Micklin Silver had a two-picture development deal with 20th Century-Fox and was working with Claire Townsend, a creative executive at the studio who was friends with Robinson. The studio signed Micklin Silver to write and direct with Triple Play producing. Eventually, Fox lost interest in the film and Townsend took the deal with her when she left the company to work for United Artists as the vice-president of production, where the picture, relying on the cast and crew (including Joan) to defer a part of their salaries, was ultimately made for $2.2 million ("Three Actors Unite As UA Producers" 39).

HEAD OVER HEELS (1979)

Head Over Heels was marred as soon as it got to United Artists. The film was made during a time when the studio was in the midst of company turmoil. Prompted by a major dispute with its parent corporation, Transamerica, the longstanding and successful UA leadership had quit the company in 1978. This management upset, in combination with the studio's economic crisis suffered during the production of Michael Cimino's *Heaven's Gate* (1980), a film that went tens of millions of dollars over budget and led to the downfall of the company, impacted the small film. The studio had changed the film's name to *Head Over Heels* because they felt Beattie's original title, *Chilly Scenes of Winter*, was too dark and that audiences would think it was an Ingmar Bergman film rather than a bittersweet romantic comedy (Joan Micklin Silver, AFI 1988). *Head Over Heels* also misrepresented the film's depth of feeling with regards to its themes of romantic relationships. Beattie, who was supportive of the producers' and director's vision of her book, joked that *Head Over Heels* "sounded as if Fred Astaire should be dancing across the credits" (Atlas). On the contrary, both the book and the film portrayed a distinct and un-Astairelike male protagonist that had begun to emerge in Hollywood, most notably with Dustin Hoffman in *The Graduate* (1967), Warren Beatty in *Shampoo* (1975), and UA's own Woody Allen in *Annie Hall* (1977): a male lead who was romantic but not always successful, usually because of his own faults. Charles, like his cinematic compadres, drove the narrative with his adoration of Laura that was endearing yet obsessive, passionate but neurotic. He was an unlikely hero for whom audiences could root while unsure of his chances of succeeding. As in her previous films, Micklin Silver was drawn to characters who were compelling individuals but ill-suited as couples; and the resulting conflict and heartbreak was at the root of her kind of romantic dramady.

UA's marketing and distribution department was not enamored by the film-maker's rendition of modern love and found the movie peculiar and therefore difficult to sell. As a result they rushed the release, skipping over preview screenings that the director felt could have been worthwhile in gauging audience response as a way to fine tune the movie's final version. For Micklin Silver, she believed the company had purposefully maligned her work due to the corporate discontent taking place: "They felt the need to push somebody around and there was my little movie!" (Joan Micklin Silver, AFI 1988). The film received mediocre reviews. Vincent Canby was unsure as to what was wrong with this "tantalizing movie, seeming to be on the verge of some revelation of profound feeling that, at long last, never comes" ("Head Over Heels"). In an unlikely, and lucky, turn of events in 1982, UA Classics decided to re-release the film under the condition that Micklin Silver edit the ending that left Charles and Laura happily together. "When they said that to me," explained Micklin Silver, "I said 'Look, I've been dying to do this, this is wonderful'" (Joan Micklin Silver, DGA). No reshoots were necessary. The director cut the final scene, and the film – re-titled *Chilly Scenes of Winter* – closes on Charles alone and eager to start over. The small re-release of an already small film generated positive reviews. Sheila Benson writing for the *Los Angeles Times* was triumphant in her reaction: "'Chilly Scenes of Winter' [is] an impeccably performed comedy frosted with sadness ... Silver has assembled a splendid cast and achieved performances which are vivid and haunting. Her writing is almost equally successful." As for the title that United Artists had originally balked at, Benson forgave its gloominess. "For all its bleak title," she wrote, "'Chilly Scenes' is a warm, lovable, enormously appealing film."

CROSSED OVER: SURVIVING THE 1970S

The production history of *Head Over Heels/Chilly Scenes of Winter* is a symbolic ending for the 1970s and the romanticized notion that during this era a small film could be made by a big studio. By the close of the decade the hubris – which resulted in much success and failure – of many filmmakers and studio executives, of whom almost all were male, had shifted toward the star-studded, high-concept blockbusters with franchise potential. For the next decade of filmmakers starting off as independents, the production and distribution apparatus would have to change, and so it did. Joan and Ray's body of work was influential in what emerged next. Independent filmmaking in the 1980s would flourish with distribution companies such as Cinecom, First Run Features, Miramax, Orion Classics; the major studios' "classics" divisions that focused on smaller films; and the Independent Film Market and the Sundance Film Festival, which were crucial not only in creating a forum in which these films could be showcased but also in fostering a community of filmmakers. Further impacting exhibition trends, the ascendancy of the home-video market provided a financial incentive for distributors and extended the life of smaller, niche films.

In spite of ending the 1970s with the pallor of UA's misgivings, Micklin Silver entered the 1980s in good standing, but her time as a Do-It-Yourself independent had passed. She had paid her dues. In 1988 she made *Crossing Delancey* for Warner Bros., written by Susan Sandler and executive-produced by Ray. The film starred Amy Irving as Isabelle Grossman, a single, thirty-year-old New Yorker who teeters between her roots in the lower east side, where her lovable and meddlesome Jewish grandmother hires a matchmaker, and her identity as a 1980s "independent" single woman living uptown. *Crossing Delancey* serves as a bookend to the body of work that Joan and Ray created during the 1970s in the way the film continued to explore the complexities of "growing up after you've already grown up" crossed with the legacy of cultural heritage flirting with the present. Throughout the 1980s and into the early 2000s, Micklin Silver maintained a busy career directing television movies for networks such as PBS, HBO, and Lifetime Television. Her feature work – *Loverboy* (1989), *Big Girls Don't Cry ... They Get Even* (1992), *A Fish in the Bathtub* (1999) – tended towards more broad commercial material compared to the personal content of her early films. In 2016 it was announced that *Hester Street* would be adapted for Broadway by producers Ira Deutchman and Michael Rabinowitz, and the filmmaker would serve as a consultant. According to the producers, now more than ever there is a necessity for stories about immigrants and what it means to be American and this classic is worthy of revisiting (Winfrey).

The trope of the outsider, the maverick, the rebel, the misfit is a favorite not only for how Hollywood often describes its own and its most difficult in nostalgic reverie, but also for the historian in search of a protagonist through whom to understand major shifts in culture and industry. As this volume investigates, Hollywood during the 1970s was a period of much change that provided an opening for renegade filmmakers, while also clinging steadfastly to traditions, from how to sell a movie to who gets to make one. Joan Micklin Silver lives up to *and* confounds this New Hollywood ideal. She was an outsider from the Midwest, angling to break into the film business through the incongruous path of children's media. She was a woman in her late thirties (inconceivable to Hollywood) with three small children, who devised with her husband new ways to make their films when the existing system proved impossible. Her ability to capture the awkward and unresolved moments in relationships made her vulnerable to company abuse and popular with critics and audiences. These characteristics do not make her an exception to the rule, but reflect exactly what could be expected during these unique years when anyone with talent and the will to make a movie, woman or man, could.

Note

1. A version of this chapter appears in Maya Montañez Smukler, *Liberating Hollywood: Women Directors and the Feminist Reform of 1970s American Cinema* (New Brunswick: Rutgers University Press, 2019).

Works Cited

"Film Reviews: Between the Lines." *Variety*, 20 April 1977, p. 73.

"Three Actors Unite as UA Producers." *Variety*, 30 May 1979, pp. 3, 39.

Atlas, James. "How 'Chilly Scenes' Was Rescued." *New York Times*, 10 Oct. 1982.

Benson, Sheila. "Obsessive Love in 'Chilly Scenes'." *Los Angeles Times*, 21 Oct. 1982: J4.

Canby, Vincent. "Film: Good Reading 'Between the Lines'." *New York Times* 28 April 1977: p. 76.

Canby, Vincent. "Screen: 'Head Over Heels,' Drama, Open." *New York Times*, 19 Oct. 1979: C12.

Champlin, Charles. "Fiddler on 'Hester Street'." *Los Angeles Times*, 16 May 1975: F1.

Cook, David. *Lost Illusion: American Cinema in the Shadow of Watergate and Vietnam 1970-1979*. University of California Press, 2000.

Haskell, Molly. "How an Independent Filmmaker Beat the System (With Her Husband's Help)." *The Village Voice*, 22 Sep. 1975, p. 83.

Kent, Leticia. "They Were Behind the Scenes of 'Between the Lines'." *New York Times*, 12 June 1977, p. 83.

Letter to signatories from Michael Franklin regarding employment statistics. 20 June 1980. "DGA" Clipping File. Margaret Herrick Library, Academy of Motion Picture Arts and Sciences. Los Angeles, CA.

McBride, Joseph. "Overcome Exhibs Fear of Yiddish, 1896." *Variety*, 25 Feb. 1976, p. 7.

Moskowitz, George. "Film Reviews: Critic Week-Cannes, Hester Street." *Variety*, 14 May 1975, p. 27.

Peary, Gerald. "Getting It On: Or How to Make Deals and Influence Exhibitors." *American Film*, 1 September 1981, pp. 60–64.

Rosenthal, Sharon. "Two on An Island." *Daily News*, 23 Mar. 1981: M8.

Silver, Joan Micklin. "Interview." American Film Institute. Los Angeles, 1979 and 1988. Louis B. Mayer Library. American Film Institute, Los Angeles, CA.

Silver, Joan Micklin. "Interview with Michael Pressman." Directors Guild Visual History Project. New York City, 19 Sep. 2005. Directors Guild of America, Los Angeles, CA.

Smukler, Maya Montañez. *Liberating Hollywood: Women Directors and the Feminist Reform of 1970s American Cinema*. Rutgers University Press, 2019.

Verrill, Addison. "So They Distributed Film Themselves." *Daily Variety*, 18 Feb. 1976, p. 5.

Winfrey, Graham. "Why Indie Producing Veteran Ira Deutchman Is Moving from Films to Broadway." *IndieWire*, 25 May 2016. http://www.indiewire.com/2016/05/why-indie-producing-veteran-iradeutchman-is-moving-from-films-to-broadway-288723/. Accessed 12 May 2020.

15. MIKE NICHOLS AND THE HOLLYWOOD RENAISSANCE: A CINEMA OF CULTURAL INVESTIGATION

Nancy McGuire Roche

Two of the most successful films of 1967, Arthur Penn's *Bonnie and Clyde* and Mike Nichols's *The Graduate*, fueled a change in the content of American cinema and marked the onset of the Hollywood Renaissance. *The Graduate* also became the second highest grossing movie of the year, signifying a radical change in the content of popular film. Furthermore, *The Graduate*, alongside Nichols's film from the previous year, *Who's Afraid of Virginia Woolf?*, pushed at the limits of the Production Code, shifted narrative boundaries, and signified a profound change in Hollywood filmmaking. By 1968, the Motion Picture Association of America announced a new ratings system as a younger viewing audience made the Hollywood mainstream aware of its preferences, heralding a change in American filmmaking. The directors of the Hollywood Renaissance were not only the auteurs of a new brand of filmmaking, they also engaged more radically with American culture.

Critic Robert Kolker's *The Cinema of Loneliness* is considered one of the definitive books on this period, yet his analysis does not include Mike Nichols. Since *The Graduate*, along with *Bonnie and Clyde*, worked to kick-start the movement, it seems a glaring omission that Kolker's book does not include Nichols as it does Arthur Penn. Obviously, both directors' films mark a generational shift in cinema, and it may be argued that Kolker overlooked one of the most important directors of the era. Indeed, Geoff King, in his book *New Hollywood Cinema: An Introduction*, lists Penn's *Bonnie and Clyde*, Nichols's *The Graduate,* and Dennis Hopper's *Easy Rider* (1969) as the three definitive films that mark the advent of the New Hollywood.

Kolker states that his book "is an attempt to reach an understanding of the work, the independence, the compromise, and the effect of these filmmakers on American film, and the effect of that film on the culture at large" (viii). He furthers claims that cinema has "a cumulative effect, giving the culture a way of looking at itself, articulating its ideology, reflecting and creating its physical appearance and gestures, teaching and confirming its shared myths" (vii). Therefore, to omit Mike Nichols defeats his purpose, since Nichols's films so closely address and reflect American society. In the preface to the fourth edition, Kolker reiterates that he views movies as "ideological constructs responding or giving voice to dominant or recessive traits in the culture" (xi). Yet, to watch Nichols's movies from this period, *The Graduate*, *Catch 22* (1970), and *Carnal Knowledge* (1971), is to view the zeitgeist of an era. Whether Nichols is addressing antiwar sentiment, moral ambiguity, or sexuality, his work not only echoes the disenfranchisement of the time but also gives a portrait of a culture in flux. In his first two films alone, the universe of Production Code era Hollywood is upended. And indeed, *Who's Afraid of Virginia Woolf?* (1966) proved lethal to the Code, as a confluence of events liberated Nichols and his cohorts from outdated standards and launched the beginning of a new era.

Four years earlier, in 1962, Edward Albee's play *Who's Afraid of Virginia Woolf?* previewed on Broadway, just four months prior to the publication of Betty Friedan's *The Feminine Mystique*. By the time the film version was released in 1966, Friedan was a known cultural critic. Although the film's central female figure, Martha (Elizabeth Taylor), is angry, aggressive, and confidently liberated, the younger female character, Honey (Sandy Dennis), is of the generation Friedan describes. She is a "happy housewife" who lives for her husband and has no goals other than to support her spouse's career and make a comfortable home for him. Martha is anything but a happy housewife. She and husband George (Richard Burton) taunt and torment each other whenever they are drunk, tattling and telling their unwitting guests the darkest moments of their history.

Furthermore, Martha exhibits more typically masculine traits than George. She curses, drinks her liquor straight, and becomes a sexual aggressor as the night wears on. In fact, Martha is the most aggressive character of the narrative, which involves two competitive men she manages to best. She defeats her husband George with wit and wrath, while she conquers the young professor, Nick (George Segal), with a seduction that renders him impotent, even though he is the epitome of a virile young man: athletic, handsome, and self-assured. In *Who's Afraid of Virginia Woolf?* Albee, and later Nichols, creates a female aggressor who defies both gender roles and stereotypes.

In an article in *Modern Drama*, Clare Eby states:

> Martha demonstrates many masculine qualities, and her masculinity feeds off of George's emasculation. As she will later explain, 'I wear the pants in the house because somebody's got to.' She humiliates George by telling Nick about the time she donned boxing gloves and knocked her husband out cold. (604)

Martha prefigures second-wave feminism and she sees herself as an equal to her husband, or perhaps his superior. Arguably Martha is the character in Hollywood films most responsible for the destruction of the Production Code.

Geoffrey Shurlock, the Director of the Production Code Administration, was at the time lobbying for a classification system that would allow restricted ratings for controversial films instead of a blanket "unacceptable." And at this point (October 1965) Nichols, who had finished *Virginia Woolf?*, announced to Warner Bros. that he had not shot any back-up footage to substitute for the film's most controversial scenes, if it did not "pass." In tandem, the play won a Tony Award and a New York Drama Critics Circle award, and Edward Albee was nominated for the Pulitzer Prize. Additionally, the film's two stars, Taylor and Burton, were huge box-office favorites. Later that year, Warner Bros. voluntarily instituted a "no one under 18 policy" for the film's distribution, and Jack Warner engineered a meeting with the National Catholic Office for Motion Pictures, who begrudgingly approved the film uncut, as long as it would be restricted from viewers under eighteen years of age.

While helping to undermine the Production Code, Nichols also facilitated new modes of filmmaking. He did not shy away from controversial topics, and from the release of his first film he seemed compelled to document the sexuality of the unconventional 1960s. *Who's Afraid of Virginia Woolf?* is an American film text closely akin to the European New Wave films of its era, but it remains firmly entrenched in the complexities of American sexuality, gender, and class. From its black and white realist format, which echoes Italian Neorealism and French and British New Wave styles, to its exploration of contemporary society, *Who's Afraid of Virginia Woolf?* reflects an evolving American cinema. In his *New York Times* review, Stanley Kauffman states that Nichols had "gone to school to several film masters (Kurosawa among them, I would guess) in the skills of keeping the camera close, indecently prying". This aspect of Nichols's technique became even more efficient and disturbing over the course of his next three films. As a veteran Broadway director before he worked in film, Nichols framed scenes as he would have staged a play, favoring long takes and intense conversations with two actors firmly under the camera's gaze, in contrast to the standard shot-reverse-shot technique utilized in most Hollywood movies.

Mike Nichols had the eye of a Broadway director and the wit of a comedian, both professions he had mastered prior to moving into film. Along with his partner Elaine May, Nichols began as a comic. The duo eventually took their act to Broadway, where Nichols would move on to directing theater. Nichols's background and comedic sense of timing greatly informs his next movie, *The Graduate*, which focuses on alienation, privilege, and a widening generation gap. Since America had entered an era which heralded the loosening of both film censorship and public mores, Nichols would have no problem introducing his next controversial film text to the public. The new ratings system signaled to Nichols and screenwriter Buck Henry that the narrative they conceived of could now be made. In *Pictures at a Revolution*, Mark Harris states the two realized that "for the first time, it might be possible to make the adult sex comedy that Nichols had seen in the material all along" (236).

Leonard Leff and Jerald Simmons affirm that "along with *Blow Up*, *Bonnie and Clyde* and *The Graduate* contributed to the first box office boom since 1946" (270). In the case of the latter, Mike Nichols wanted to make a comedy, but he also intended to target the establishment, which for him meant California. Harris quotes Nichols as saying, "California is America in italics . . . a parody of everything that's most dangerous to us" (313). Nichols wanted to expose the perils of capitalism, materialism, and postmodern ennui. And he used as his weapons a spoiled young man (Dustin Hoffman) and a bored, predatory middle-aged woman (Anne Bancroft) who grimly breaks the moral bonds of society, a wholly sardonic character.

Nichols envisioned the world of *The Graduate* as a modern, wealthy playground. Writer Buck Henry wanted to convey "the disaffection of young people for an environment that they don't seem in synch with" (qtd. in Harris 313). The universe of *The Graduate* abounds with reflective surfaces, water and glass and mirrors, media that distort reality. The director had the idea that Benjamin (Hoffman) should constantly be isolated by glass or water. "Nichols and his art director Richard Sylbert wanted Benjamin to be shot through or against clear but impenetrable surfaces as often as possible, as if he were trapped in a fishbowl" (Henry qtd. in Harris 314). Thus, the audience sees Benjamin through an aquarium, a swimming pool, and a plate glass window that shelters his cries as if he were in a vacuum.

Mrs. Robinson (Bancroft) dominates the first half of the movie, as she drags Benjamin into her web of drink, sex, and boredom. It is she who defines what Benjamin seems destined to become should he follow in her generation's footsteps. She steals Benjamin from the nest of his home and family, robs him of interaction with his peers, and with sex somehow infects him with a lassitude available only to the bored upper class. The film features an innovative soundtrack to appeal to a younger audience. At one point, deep into his affair, Nichols creates a montage of Ben's summer, set to the music of Simon and Garfunkel, who wrote the entire soundtrack. The action occurs over the course of two songs, "The Sound of Silence" and "April Come She Will."

Figure 15.1   In *The Graduate* (1967), Benjamin is constantly surrounded by reflective surfaces to convey his isolation. Digital frame enlargement. Courtesy of Paramount Pictures.

The camera tracks Ben from the sunlight of his parent's home to the site of his surreptitious affair and back again, tracing the path of his post-graduate life: television, sex, beer, leisure, the narcotics of a wealthy boy with time to kill. The *mise-en-scène* emphasizes black and white, from clothing to furniture to interiors, blending the locations seamlessly as Benjamin follows the course of his emotional demise, a sordid maturity, which both robs him of optimism and paralyzes him in a liminal state between youth and adulthood. This is Nichols's take on the sexual revolution and youth: the temptations are the same no matter what one does. Wealth leads to decadence, and leisure to boredom.

It is significant to note that the character of Martha created by Albee for *Who's Afraid of Virginia Woolf?* is never portrayed through the lens of conventional morality that Nichols and Buck Henry use to dissect Mrs. Robinson. In many ways Mrs. Robinson is the protagonist of *The Graduate*, as she rescues the viewer from a sappy vision of puppy love between a blank, pretty co-ed and a confused young man who are both from the privileged class. In the iconic final scene of *The Graduate*, Ben and Elaine escape her wedding to leap onto a bus, but their smiles fade as they realize they have no real place to go. They are set adrift in a generation on the verge of something they do not yet comprehend. King states,

> The end of *The Graduate* is largely the stuff of romantic fantasy, although a certain sense of unease lingers over the final images of Benjamin and Elaine on the bus, overlaid by Simon and Garfunkel's 'The Sound of

Silence' . . . the song used to underpin the sense of alienation created in the film's opening sequence. (18)

Nichols captures a delicate ambivalence as Elaine and Ben escape into an unsure future, and he delegates Mrs. Robinson, finally, as a member of the establishment, a monstrosity who seduces a young man and later rejects him as "ruined." It is this very morality which will be reflected in the male seducers of his later film *Carnal Knowledge* (1971). They further represent the generation of Ben and Elaine's parents, the Braddocks and the Robinsons. Nichols's feature following *The Graduate*, *Catch 22*, takes on the anti-war sentiment of his generation, but in *Carnal Knowledge* he turns again to the topic of sexuality.

After the success of *The Graduate*, Nichols was given a big budget with which to adapt *Catch 22*, Joseph Heller's dark and complex book regarding the theater of war. The film was released at the height of the Vietnam War, and Nichols's retelling of Heller's novel reflects the generational divide of the 1960s even though its setting is World War II. *Catch 22* is resoundingly anti-establishment, as it attacks the very foundations of the Production Code era's portrayal of American life, savaging religion, war, and capitalism. Additionally, the shape of the narrative reflects Heller's novel, which unmoors temporal location in an avant-garde style. The central figure, John Yossarian (Alan Arkin), is doomed to live over and over the gruesome death of fellow bombardier Snowden (Jon Korkes) – and his obsession with the young soldier's demise haunts him in flashbacks throughout the film. The movie is a satirical metacommentary on American ideology: those in power amass wealth and more power at the expensive of the less privileged, while the most endearing and likable characters become completely disillusioned or die. In the 1960s, Heller's novel became very popular with a young audience who were dissatisfied with American politics and moral conservatism. Naturally, Nichols's film tapped into and amplified this disaffection because its anti-war sentiment appealed to the same market.

In an essay regarding "Hollywood's Post-traumatic Cycle (1970-1976)," Christian Keathley begins by quoting Pauline Kael: "Vietnam we experience indirectly in just about every movie we go to" (293). Keathley agrees. It is his opinion that many American films of the early 1970s reflect both Vietnam and a culture in crisis. As he proposes:

> Although none is set in and only a few make explicit reference to that war, these films represent and replay, in a displaced fashion, the Vietnam war's defining experience: the onset of trauma resulting from a realization of powerlessness in the face of a world whose systems of organization – both moral and political – have broken down. (293)

Figure 15.2 Nichols's Yossarian symbolizes the anti-establishment, counterculture perspective of the Vietnam War era in his *Catch-22* (1970). Digital frame enlargement. Courtesy of Paramount Pictures.

Yossarian is powerless to change his position in a corrupt military structure, yet he is also a hero for his abandonment of an unfair hegemonic system.

As with Nichols's previous two films, his characters receive meticulous attention, even if their intentions are never completely revealed. Yossarian is the central figure in a complex web of players who signify the hierarchical elements of a war machine. Moreso than Nichols's first two films, *Catch 22* is a dark comedy, rather than a comedy couched in the guise of drama. Each character is positioned as an elemental figure in a binary of innocence versus evil, pushed to the extreme through absurd and macabre circumstances. And here, Nichols also refines his artistic propensity for quick and witty dialogue, often intercut with long silences and long takes. Despite the fact that *Catch 22* was given a large budget due to the popularity of Heller's book and Nichols's success with his first two films, it may be argued that the film's style and content employ multiple elements of art-house film.

Yossarian is a likable anti-hero who fights the system, and even when given the chance for an honorable discharge (if he will support his superior's actions), he refuses and decides instead to head out as a deserter, a loner. The film has no exact conclusion and leaves many of the characters stranded in an unchanging hell. In his essay "The Art Cinema as a Mode of Film Practice," David Bordwell outlines multiple features of the art film of the early 1970s, many of which apply to *Catch 22*. The art film "defines itself against the classical narrative mode, and especially against the cause-effect linkage of events" (57). The narrative of *Catch 22* is circular and there are frequent flashbacks. Furthermore, as in Nichols's first two films, "characters and their effects on one another remain central" (58). Art Cinema also features protagonists for whom "choices are vague or nonexistent. Hence a certain drifting episodic quality to the art film's narrative. Characters may wander out and never reappear; events may lead to nothing" (58).

While not all of the traits of *Catch 22* align with Bordwell's definition, directors of the American New Wave often incorporated techniques found in European art cinema, and Nichols is no exception. His work further reflects Bordwell's assertion that "art cinema is less concerned with action than reaction; it is a cinema of psychological effects in search of their causes" (58). Nichols's camera closely tracks Yossarian's reactions to war and its casualties. He intercuts repeated flashbacks of the death of the young gunner Snowden, in fragments, throughout the plot arc; however, the viewer is left uncomprehending until the complete episode is disclosed. Each scene reveals a longer take until finally Snowden dies in Yossarian's arms, his entrails exposed. Yossarian's horror is foregrounded in the frame. Immediately prior to this final disclosure of trauma, Nichols's camera follows his protagonist through the bombed-out streets of Rome after he has informed Captain Nately's (Art Garfunkel) prostitute "fiancé" of the young soldier's demise. As Yossarian wanders aimlessly, the audience observes the consequences of war in a sequence that communicates murder, mayhem, and rape. An array of grotesque and unsettling images presages the full and final meaning of Snowden's gruesome death: the value of life is nil to the army.

As with his earlier two films, Nichols devises long reaction shots of actors, which imprint their responses and emotions onto the audience. Whether it is Martha berating George, Mrs. Robinson chastising Benjamin, or Yossarian registering Snowden's death, Nichols's camera holds fast to the image. His films reflect the disintegration of American values by utilizing irony, dark humor, and satire. *Catch 22* begins symbolically, with the visual intersection of beauty and terror, as a long take of sunrise over Pianosa becomes a surprising backdrop for images of combat – a cadre of bombers buzzing toward their target. As the engines roar, elements of the natural world are destroyed and displaced by the mechanics of war: flowers are crushed by the airplane's wheels, birds flee, and peace turns to chaos. This scene becomes a metaphor for the disruption and pandemonium to follow.

Geoff King asserts,

> The Hollywood Renaissance is often understood as a response to, or part of, a range of social upheavals in the United States in the late 1960s and early 1970s. It is hard to imagine some of its key films existing without that specific social context. (8)

Nichols's films expressly reflect an American culture in flux, and morality and sexuality are often his topics. His next film after *Catch 22*, *Carnal Knowledge*, takes place in the aftermath of the 1960s sexual revolution that *The Graduate* documents. The film is told from a male perspective. It is the story of two Amherst roommates, featuring their sexual escapades in college and beyond. Neither is especially likable, and both fit the profile of Thomas Elsaesser's "unmotivated hero," outlined in his work "The Pathos of Failure: American Films in the 1970s."

While writing primarily about ways Hollywood Renaissance films continue to reflect elements of Classical Hollywood, Elsaesser also emphasizes their differences. "The significant feature of this new cinema is that it makes an issue of the motives – or lack of them – in its heroes" (280), he observes. And while Elsaesser does not focus on Nichols per se, his argument aptly applies to *Carnal Knowledge*. Both Jack Nicholson's Jonathan and Art Garfunkel's Sandy may be seen as typical American males of the 1940s, obsessed with sex and uncertain about their future – but by the film's conclusion, both are middle-aged men confused by the enigma of their own sexuality.

As the plot arcs over the course of several decades, the men's motives change in relationship to their mid-life desires and the legacy of a "sexual revolution." In one of the final scenes, Jonathan "treats" Sandy and his young lover Jennifer (Carol Kane) to a slide show of his conquests, dismissing his lovers as "great tits," "frigid," "king of the ballbusters," "a real cunt," and "slob," after stating that he has forgotten many of their names. Hence, if Sandy and Jonathan are the "heroes" of *Carnal Knowledge*, then Nichols certainly "makes an issue" of their motives. Their motivation drives the film. At a loss to relate to women, in light of his personal history and the rise of second-wave feminism, Sandy takes a teenage lover, while the impotent misogynist Jonathan can achieve orgasm only with a prostitute. *Carnal Knowledge* follows these two from college to middle age in an attempt to determine their impulses, which resonate with, or more likely disturb, the viewer.

Nichols as director captures what he would have us know about his characters through the use of his camera, more so than with dialogue or plot. His close-ups hold the clue to each character, and therefore to the film's ultimate purpose. The film's opening credits occur over a black screen as two men discuss love, sex, and relationships. We know the duo's proclivities before seeing them. The two brag about their prowess, even while admitting they are virgins. Then, from the darkened screen, Susan (Candice Bergen) emerges, her pale skin and blond hair the film's first image. The camera stays tightly focused on Bergen's face as she walks through the room, until she crosses in front of Sandy and Jonathan and the shot abandons her for the two men. Jonathan states, "You like that? I give her to ya," implying that Jonathon already feels he possesses the young woman whom he has never met. Since the camera reveals

Bergen's Susan as the film's first image, however, Nichols implicitly empowers her. In *Carnal Knowledge*, the visual is more potent than words. Sandy and Jonathan refer to each other as "bullshit artists" and their discourse seems as false as they are; it is only through the use of the close up that Nichols's true meaning is conveyed.

After Sandy attempts to talk to Susan and loses his nerve, the personality of each man is readily established; Sandy is gentle and insecure while Jonathan is self-assured and blasé. Susan begins to date Sandy, but Jonathan's pursuit of his friend's love interest leads to an almost immediate and duplicitous love triangle between the three students, with Sandy kept in the dark. Jonathan has a sexual relationship with Susan first, but Sandy will manage to seduce her with his persistence, and eventually marry her. What seems to interest Nichols most, however, is how the pursuit of sexual conquest eventually leads to boredom. Sandy and Jonathan are in turn extreme versions of male bravado and insecurity, while their female counterparts are the most interesting and complex characters of the film: the bright, self-assured, and well-educated Susan, and the voluptuous and insecure Bobbie (Ann-Margret), who will become Jonathan's lover and finally wife. Yet in the diegesis of *Carnal Knowledge*, to become wife is to disappear from the screen, suggesting that to Sandy and Jonathan, once a woman is "acquired," she becomes irrelevant.

In many ways, *Carnal Knowledge* reads as a documentary of modern sexuality, as it exposes its characters without damning them. Bobbie is victimized but starts out with sexual agency; Jonathan is a misogynist, but the film's point of view is not; Sandy is passive and at times pathetic, while Susan exhibits a feminist sensibility when she informs Sandy that she intends to be a lawyer.

Figure 15.3 In *Carnal Knowledge*, Nichols's camera lingers on Susan and Bobbie's faces to register a series of complex emotions. Digital frame enlargement. Courtesy of Embassy Films.

Furthermore, she has sexual agency and makes her own choice between the two men. Susan drives the film's beginning, but she disappears after the first act. Only their amount of screen time and longevity determines that Nicholson and Garfunkel are the film's protagonists. And even then, it is easy to disassociate from these characters – until the camera brings the focus back to them, provoking unease and claustrophobia in the viewer.

In *Carnal Knowledge*, Nichols returns to the techniques and overlapping dialogue used in *Who's Afraid of Virginia Woolf?*. The two men's seduction of Susan and Jonathan's relationship with the model Bobbie contain multiple long reaction shots, which position the viewer as voyeur. Filmed five years before Laura Mulvey wrote her iconic essay on the male gaze and coined the term "to-be-looked-at-ness," Nichols trains his camera on Bergen and Ann-Margret; but his camera's intent is not to fetishize or sexualize as much as to humanize. Nichols's genius is that he is able to engender sexual narratives without visually exploiting his actresses. Bergen's Susan is often dressed in black and framed against darkness to emphasize her facial expression and emotion. In the film's first sexual encounter, Bergen's face floats out of a shadowy background and is partially obscured by her partner's black coat. It is only afterward that her lover is revealed as Jonathan and not Sandy (as the audience expects). In the 90-second scene, not a word is spoken – Nichols uses the close up to convey Susan's emotions.

Next, we see the trio together in a roadhouse. While Susan dances with Jonathan, and then Sandy, the film records, in turn, feelings of pleasure, doubt, guilt, complicity, and sexual attraction. The giddy movements of swing dance and the camera's rotation around the actors is disorienting. Subsequently, both men (off camera) are trying to make Susan laugh, and for a minute and forty seconds the camera never leaves its static position, recording her face – while Susan's hysterical laughter becomes actual hysteria, reflecting her inner turmoil. The consecutive scene focuses on a heated conversation between Jonathan and Susan in the parking lot. His jealously is uncontrollable, and he threatens to usurp her power and tell Sandy of their affair. "You are really something," he states. Susan replies, "I feel like nothing." Jonathan's intense pressure on Susan presages his treatment of women for the rest of the film – not just his words but his actions reveal a bully.

Nichols gives the audience little recovery time from one intense scene to the next. Most of the important conversations in the film occur in near darkness or confined spaces with the camera tightly focused on actors in tense situations. A fight between Susan and Jonathan in a stairwell, between university classes, uses Nichols's technique of keeping both actors onscreen simultaneously in an angry dialogue – but their break-up occurs during a phone conversation which employs a Hollywood standard shot-reverse-shot. In the following scene, Nicholson's face fills the screen as Susan and Sandy pack for a trip and joke about Sandy's lack of experience with camping. The camera stays tightly focused on Jonathan as he registers misery. Both Susan and Sandy are oblivious to his emotions, but the viewer's gaze is overwhelmed by this image.

Written by playwright Jules Feiffer, *Carnal Knowledge* readily breaks down into three separate acts. For the second act of *Carnal Knowledge*, the screen fades to white and a figure skater dressed in white emerges from the background, much like Susan emerges from darkness at the beginning of the film. Sandy and Jonathan have entered middle age but have not changed, as they discuss the woman's attributes, objectifying her. Admiration, however, is much easier than possession. This second section focuses on Jonathan's relationship with Bobbie, as simultaneously Sandy leaves Susan to date other women.

In the first scene between Bobbie and Jonathan, at dinner, the camera rotates around the couple, examining them. Later, in Jonathan's apartment, they have sex while the camera tracks through darkened rooms, searching for them. The next morning both characters are seen briefly naked, but Bobbie's face soon becomes the primary focus. Her emotional collapse when Jonathan leaves the room reveals her true feelings. After their relationship is established, Jonathan suggests she quit work. The following scenes disclose Bobbie's depression and ennui, as well as Jonathan's resentment of her presence in his space. Nichols's camera stalks a disheveled Bobbie, clothed in a dowdy housecoat with her hair unkempt, as she brings TV dinners to the bedroom, passing photographs of herself as a glamorous model, taken before she left her career for the confined space of Jonathan's apartment.

Film theorist and director Vsevolod Pudovkin posits, "The close-up directs the attention of the spectator to that detail which is, at the moment, important to the course of the action" (7). And indeed, for Nichols, it is the register of his characters' emotions that conveys the meaning of this narrative: relationships are tricky and painful. The camera unmasks these characters to the viewer, if not to others in the diegesis. And as early film theorists also insist, the "the significance of the close-up for the plot accrues to it less from its own content than from the manner in which it is juxtaposed with the surroundings shots" (Kracauer 187). Therefore, the notion of the close-up as an element in montage, which both propels the plot and unveils the characters, could not be more accurate for *Carnal Knowledge*.

Carnal Knowledge was well received by critics, unlike *Catch 22*. However, both its casual sexuality and its nudity contributed to an R rating, and in 1972 police presented a search warrant to a theater manager in Albany, Georgia for "distributing obscene material." The Supreme Court of Georgia upheld the ruling, but the US Supreme Court in Jenkins v. Georgia overturned the conviction two years later. The Justices validated their decision by stating: "The camera does not focus on the bodies of actors during scenes of ultimate sexual acts, nor are the actors' genitals exhibited during those scenes. The film shows occasional nudity, but nudity alone does not render material obscene" (JUSTIA, Georgia v. Jenkins). In general, the film's sex scenes are obscured by darkness and it is the actors' faces, not their bodies, which dominate the screen.

Linda Williams writes,

> Sex is an act and more or less of 'it' may be revealed but . . . it is not a stable truth that cameras and microphones either 'catch' or don't catch. It is a constructed, mediated, performed act and every revelation is also a concealment that leaves something to the imagination. (Williams 2)

This statement is certainly true of *Carnal Knowledge*, for even the Supreme Court of Georgia interpreted obfuscation as obscenity. In the end, an obscured sex scene is not as powerful as the naked emotion revealed onscreen. The performative action of *Carnal Knowledge* is mediated by the revelation of anger, lust, impotency, and boredom. It is the response to sex and not the act itself which may be deemed morally obscene, especially Jonathan's view of women as the film draws to its conclusion.

By the midpoint of *Carnal Knowledge*, the act of sex for Jonathan is necessitated by verbal stimulation, as we see him sexually aroused by Bobbie in the cab on their first date and then, at the film's finale, by the prostitute. The words either infantilize Bobbie or falsely praise Jonathan's sexual prowess and power. In the world of *Carnal Knowledge*, sex seems to be an either/or proposition. Once these two men take possession of the object of their desire, they no longer desire her. Sandy states that he can't be sexually attracted to someone he loves, and, after Susan, Jonathan can't seem to respect or love anyone who has sex with him. Or as Sandy tells Jonathan, "Maybe it's just not meant to be enjoyable with women you love." If the film is meant to be a satire of American masculinity, then it is certainly a brutal one, more a portrait of a cultural moment than an overall assessment of manhood. And this is Mike Nichols's signature, to know and reveal the era he inhabits.

Nichols's comedy partner Elaine May has stated, "Mike Nichols was so dazzling, so successful, yet his work was oddly underrated. His work, his best work, is about who we were at the end of the Twentieth Century, and who we were about to become" (PBS). A comedian and director of plays, movies, and television, Mike Nichols helped to create a film movement at a perfect intersection: the end of the Production Code, which he helped to defeat, and the beginning of a cultural revolution. His work catalogs the effect of disaffection, political upheaval, changing norms, and new sexualities. His films indict a diminishing old guard and gleefully celebrate an American New Wave. They are peopled with never-before-heard-of or -seen characters, and they reflect unique and transient moments of cultural history, captured impeccably. Mike Nichols therefore must be seen as an archetypal director of the Hollywood Renaissance.

WORKS CITED

Bordwell, David. "The Art Cinema as a Mode of Film Practice." *Film Criticism*, vol. 4, no. 1 1979, pp. 56–64.

Catch-22. Directed by Mike Nichols, Paramount Pictures, 1970. DVD.

Carnal Knowledge. Directed by Mike Nichols, Embassy Pictures, 1971. DVD.

Eby, Claire. "Fun and Games with George and Nick: Competitive Masculinity in *Who's Afraid of Virginia Woolf?*" *Modern Drama*, vol. 50, no. 4, 2007, pp. 601–19.

Elsaesser, Thomas. "The Pathos of Failure: American Films in the 1970s: Notes on the Unmotivated Hero." *The Last Great American Picture Show: New Hollywood Cinema in the 1970s*, edited byThomas Elsaesser, Alexander Horwath, and Noel King, Amsterdam, Amsterdam University Press, 2004, pp. 279–92.

Harris, Mark. *Pictures at a Revolution: Five Movies and the Birth of the New Hollywood*, The Penguin Press, 2008.

"Jenkins v. Georgia" 418 U.S. 153 (1974)." JUSTIA. Page 418 U. S. 154. Decided 24 June, 1974. https://supreme.justia.com/cases/federal/us/418/153/case.html. Accessed 6 May 2017.

Kauffman, Stanley. "Who's Afraid of Virginia Woolf?" *The New York Times*, 24 June 1966, http://www.nytimes.com/movie/review?res=EE05E7DF1731E774BC485 0DFB06. Accessed 17 April 2017.

Keathley, Christian. "Trapped in the Affection Image: Hollywood's Post-traumatic Cycle (1970-1976)." *The Last Great American Picture Show: New Hollywood Cinema in the 1970s*, edited by Thomas Elsaesser, Alexander Horwath, and Noel Kin, Amsterdam: Amsterdam University Press, 2004. pp. 293–308.

King, Geoff. *New Hollywood Cinema: An Introduction*. I. B. Tauris, 2002.

Kolker, Robert Phillip. *Cinema of Loneliness: Penn, Stone, Kubrick, Scorsese, Spielberg, Altman*. Oxford University Press, 2011.

Kracauer, Siegfried. "The Establishment of Physical Existence." *Film Theory & Criticism*, edited by Leo Braudy and Marshall Cohen, Oxford University Press, 2016, pp. 187–97.

Leff, Leonard J., and Jerold L. Simmons. *The Dame in the Kimono: Hollywood, Censorship, and the Production Code from the 1920s to the 1960s*. Grove Weidenfeld, 1990.

"Mike Nichols." *American Masters*. Directed by. Elaine May. PBS, THIRTEEN PRODUCTIONS LLC for WNET, New York, 28 Jan. 2016. Television.

Mulvey, Laura. "Visual Pleasure and Narrative Cinema." *Visual and Other Pleasures. Language, Discourse, Society*. Palgrave Macmillan, 1989. pp. 14–26.

Pudovkin, Vsevolod. "[On Editing]." *Film Theory & Criticism*, edited by Leo Braudy and Marshall Cohen, Oxford University Press, 2016, pp. 6–40.

The Graduate. Directed by Mike Nichols, MGM, 1967. DVD.

Who's Afraid of Virginia Woolf? Directed by Mike Nichols, Warner Brothers, 1966. DVD.

Williams, Linda. *Screening Sex*. Duke University Press, 2008.

16. "THERE WILL BE NO QUESTIONS": 1970S AMERICAN CINEMA AS PARALLAX IN ALAN J. PAKULA'S "PARANOIA TRILOGY"

Terence McSweeney

Parallax

noun

the apparent displacement of an observed object due to a change in the position of the observer.

AMERICAN FILM OF THE 1970S AS CULTURAL ARTIFACT

Is it really possible for a film to reflect the culture and the times in which it was made in any meaningful sense? What might it mean that the three films explored in this chapter, *Klute*, *The Parallax View*, and *All the President's Men*, all directed by Alan J. Pakula and often referred to as his "paranoia trilogy" (see Pratt; Brown; Kirshner; Richard T. Jameson), were described by Paul Cobley as being "emblematic of 1970s America" (74)? Cobley is just one of many writers who have made similar pronouncements about the relationship between certain films and the turbulent political climate of 1970s America in which they were produced. Of the paranoia trilogy in particular, Ian Scott in his *American Politics in Hollywood Film* (2011) wrote that

> Pakula's films provided the thread for an examination of American politics and society from beyond authority and accountability in the 1970s and in the process created cinematic form and content that would define the agency of paranoia cinema in its entirety. (138)

As many contributors to this volume have argued, a range of cinematic texts which emerged from the American film industry in the 1970s function as much more than disposable entertainment and should be regarded as engaging with the discourses of their era in a range of dynamic and visceral ways. According to this understanding of cinema, the fractious politics of the period are not merely a backdrop to films like *Chinatown* (1974), *The Texas Chain Saw Massacre* (1974), *One Flew Over the Cuckoo's Nest* (1975), *Taxi Driver* (1976), *Invasion of the Body Snatchers* (1978), and *The Deer Hunter* (1978), but rather a formative element in their construction and their reception, whilst the texts themselves form part of a cultural battleground on which a war of representation was waged. Writers like Peter Lev, Michael Ryan, and Douglas Kellner argue that the era becomes materialized within the frames of films like those mentioned above and, more importantly, that these texts were able to do much more than simply reflect the prevailing cultural discourse; in fact, they contributed to it in a range of palpable ways both at the time of their release and in the years after.

This chapter interrogates Alan J. Pakula's *Klute* (released June 1971), *The Parallax View* (released June 1974), and *All the President's Men* (released April 1976) which are a part of a range of American films often referred to as "the conspiracy cycle," other notable examples of which include *Executive Action* (1973), *The Conversation* (1974), *Three Days of the Condor* (1975), *Cutter's Way* (1981), and *Blow Out* (1981). For his part though, Pakula rejected the term "paranoia" as it is commonly used. In perhaps the most significant interview he ever gave about his work, conducted by Richard Thompson for *Film Comment* in 1976, Pakula stated,

> I think that paranoia is a terribly misused word, the sort of word that's used constantly today, unclinically and incorrectly. I use it to represent an excessive fear of the unknown, the unseen . . . Not a realistic fear of the unknown, but one that comes out of internal fears for oneself – one's internal anxieties being directed onto something outside of oneself. (qtd. in Thompson 19)

Yet what Pakula describes might be regarded as almost exactly what the three films discussed in this chapter do: they project some of the quintessential fears and anxieties of the decade on an external object, with that object being film.

What Is a Parallax?

The title of this chapter refers, of course, to *The Parallax View*, the middle part of the trilogy, and the eponymous fictional company The Parallax Corporation within the film's diegesis, but also to the term and the process defined in the epigraph to this chapter. A parallax is, broadly speaking, a "displacement or difference in the apparent position of an object viewed along two different lines of sight," that is, how any given object can *appear* to be different when viewed from different perspectives. It is my contention here that the cinematic medium is able to perform a social and cultural function analogous to the parallax in numerous ways: offering variegated political perspectives and insights into the cultures which produced such films at the time, but also unique perspectives for contemporary audiences, in the case of the "paranoia trilogy" more than forty years after they were made.

This use of the parallax as a metaphor is not entirely original, as it is one which has been returned to quite often in academic discourse: Slavoj Žižek titled his 2006 book *The Parallax View* without a single reference to the film of the same name within its pages, using the term to articulate "the confrontation of two closely linked perspectives between which no neutral common ground is possible" (4).[1] Fredric Jameson discussed the "paranoia trilogy" at some length in his essential *The Geopolitical Aesthetic: Cinema and Space in the World System* (1992), where he suggested that the trilogy offers alternate perspectives on the era and manifestations of the ideological currents of the times in which the films were made, which are represented *both* explicitly and at the same time in allegorical form. According to him, this is the only way that such a complicated concept as late-capitalism can ever be represented given that it is "so vast that it cannot be encompassed by the natural and historically developed categories of perception with which human beings normally orient themselves" (2).

The three films of the "paranoia trilogy" are entirely unconnected narratively but are referred to as a trilogy because they share themes, motifs, and similar political perspectives on the 1970s. They also happen to feature five of the most iconic performers of the decade (Donald Sutherland, Jane Fonda, Warren Beatty, Robert Redford, and Dustin Hoffman) and embody characteristics of what would come to define 1970s American cinema before the arrival of the blockbuster age, heralded by the likes of *Jaws* (1975) and *Star Wars* (1977) which were released the year before and after *All the President's Men* respectively. The political and social background of the "paranoia trilogy," as with many of the films discussed in this volume, includes the cultural trauma of the Vietnam War (1955–75), the aftermath of several high-profile assassinations, from the brothers John F. Kennedy (22 November 1963) and Robert F. Kennedy (5 June 1968), to Malcolm X (21 February 1965) and Martin Luther King Jr. (4 April 1968), US troops moving into Cambodia (1970), the Kent State shootings (1970), and the leaking of the Pentagon Papers (1971). The socio-political turbulence that surrounded the films also include the Watergate scandal (1972–74), the Pike Committee hearings (1975–76), and the tumultuous years of the Nixon presidency's second term (1973–74), events Barna William Donovan called "the very real international and financial concerns of the day" (77), which become subsumed within the frames of these key films, sometimes explicitly, sometimes in allegory, and sometimes in provocative combinations of the two.

KLUTE (1971): DISCONTINUITY, DISHARMONY AND INSTABILITY IN AN AGE WHERE "NOTHING IS WRONG"

The dates and events detailed above are certainly not arbitrary: Pakula's "paranoia trilogy," made in a five-year burst of creative activity between 1971 and 1976, overlaps and engages with real-world events in intriguing ways. Thus, *Klute* (June 1971) was released almost exactly a year before the Watergate burglary (17 June 1972) but is one of several films which have been described as participating in the "cultural foreshadowing" of Watergate by Stephen Paul Miller, author of *The Seventies Now: Culture as Surveillance* (79). As with the other films of the trilogy and indeed many films from the New Hollywood, *Klute* is defined by its utilization of some of the key cinematic devices which went on to characterize the filmmaking of the era. These techniques, which depart considerably from those of the Classical Hollywood period, are more than just stylistic flourishes but are significant aspects of how such films generate meanings and can be identified -- as Barry Langford asserted in his

Figure 16.1 While it is not her name in the title, Bree (Jane Fonda) is the defining character in *Klute* (1974), a film which taps into many of the most resonant fears and anxieties of the era in which it was made. Digital frame enlargement. Courtesy of Warner Bros.

Post-Classical Hollywood -- by how they foreground "ambiguity and actual narrative irresolution" (172). As a whole these are techniques which embrace not the stylistic and narrative continuity of the previous era but instead discontinuity, disharmony, and instability. Pakula's first act of disorientation with *Klute* is the very fact of its title, as Donald Sutherland's John Klute is not the film's main character, nor is he played by the film's top-billed star. Neither is his Klute the film's most compelling figure, by quite some margin. Indeed, the film might as well have been called *Bree*, as it is the prostitute played by Jane Fonda (in a performance for which she won the Academy Award for Best Actress in 1972) who is at the center of the film, the character who resonates most with audiences, then as much as now.

Pakula endeavors to destabilize audiences from the film's opening moments, which establish a sense of tone and also some of its central thematic motifs even before the credits. Without an establishing shot, the first image is a close up of a small portable tape recorder with the sounds of a conversation being played, but it is not initially clear who, what, or when the recording was made and even who is listening aside from us, the audience. Like the other two films of the trilogy, *Klute* tends to eschew conventional establishing shots, and scenes are regularly terminated abruptly and often transitioned between without explicit cues and information being provided to the audience, Pakula preferring instead the sense of immediacy/disorientation such devices provide. Donald Sutherland himself suggested "there were a lot of things in *Klute* that didn't make any sense in terms of movies" (qtd. in Kachmar 27). The scene that is being recorded, that we also then begin to see playing out in front of us, appears innocuous enough on the surface, as it is a brightly lit Thanksgiving dinner with a group of friends cheerfully interacting with one another. The eponymous Klute is not given priority at all in the scene, which instead focuses on the prosperous middle-class businessman Tom Gruneman (Robert Milli) and his wife Holly (Betty Murray). A jarring cut back to the tape recorder situated at the same table, at a moment now revealed to be sometime later, shows the police discussing with Klute and Holly the facts concerning Tom's disappearance and the crimes he is accused of committing. Pakula's trilogy dwells on how surface appearances mask far more complicated and ambiguous relationships underneath, on both personal and cultural levels, and begins a juxtaposition between private and public which will continue throughout all three films. Also at the dinner table, sitting next to Tom's wife, in a striking act of *legerdemain*, is the man who the audience will later learn is responsible for Tom's disappearance and murder, his seemingly amiable boss Peter Cable (Charles Cioffi).

Klute offers many more such moments of disorientation and discontinuity, which are implemented both narratively and stylistically as John Klute follows his enquiry into Tom's disappearance. All three films of the trilogy were shot by Gordon Willis, perhaps best known for his work on *The Godfather* (1972) and *The Godfather: Part Two* (1974). Willis frequently uses low-key lighting, off-kilter framing, and off-center compositions, with scenes often filmed in the shadows even if they take place during the day. This technique contributes to the sense of mystery and foreboding. Klute's investigation leads him to New York and the prostitute Bree Daniels, with whom he embarks on a complex sexual relationship. Bree is recorded on a number of occasions throughout the film, not just by a stalker revealed fairly early on to be the outwardly respectable Peter Cable, who uses recordings of Bree's own voice to terrorize her, but also by John Klute himself. While it is not explicitly articulated, there is a lingering suspicion that Klute, for all his apparent virtuousness, is not too far removed from Cable. Cable records Bree without her permission, as does Klute; Cable stalks Bree without her knowledge, as does Klute; Cable manipulates Bree, as does Klute. It is no coincidence that recording equipment plays a central role in all three films in the trilogy in a motif underlining the surface unreliability of images and sounds, at the very same time as recording devices were becoming something the public talked about more and more as the Watergate conspiracy unraveled.

Klute's stylistic devices, its challenging themes, and the ambiguous portrayal of Bree and Klute's relationship undoubtedly contributed to the ambivalence of responses to the film on its release and in the years since. For some *Klute* is a "vehemently anti-feminist" text about "the threat posed to patriarchy by second wave feminism" (Dunst 29) and for Colin MacCabe it was, in a common critical response, not "a film which goes any way to portraying a woman liberated from male definition, . . . [in actual fact] *Klute* exactly guarantees that the real essence of a woman can only be discovered and defined by a man" (57). Others though have seen more to the film, such as Helen Hanson, who wrote that it "offers ways of thinking through some complex questions of female identity/subjectivity that were being debated in the 1970s" (222). Whether the film is a commentary on the way women are viewed and manipulated by men or a perpetuation of dominant hegemonic values is a matter for debate, and on numerous occasions, somewhat paradoxically, it appears to emphasize both. These contradictions were observed by Michael Ryan and Douglas Kellner who wrote,

> *Klute* critically dissects the cultural stereotypes of the happy suburban family and offers a somewhat positive picture of an autonomous and sexually independent woman . . . Even if it is presented through the refracting filter of her role as a prostitute, Bree's open sexuality marks a breakthrough for the depiction of women in modern Hollywood film. (140)

Perhaps what connects *Klute* to the era most of all, however, is its criticism of power structures which begin at the personal level, but can be persuasively read as standing for broader cultural and social relationships (see Pratt; Miller; McDonnell). It is not the shady pimp Frank Ligourin (Roy Scheider) who is responsible for Tom Gruneman's murder and the stalking of Bree, as we are led to suspect, but the prosperous and reputable businessman Cable, who had even insisted that Klute originally take on the case for a reason never revealed, and about which the audience is left to speculate. As Miller wrote, "Although the dead Gruneman is redeemed, the system as a whole is shaken because a higher-up in the system, his boss, who is indeed the initiator of the investigation, is responsible for the crime" (80).

The film's most ambiguous moment is reserved for its ending, which, like those of *The Graduate* (1967), *Easy Rider* (1969), *The French Connection* (1971), *Three Days of the Condor, Chinatown,* and many other films of the Hollywood New Wave, is an uncertain but resonant dénouement. In the aftermath of Cable's exposure and death, the film concludes in Bree's apartment after she has apparently decided to leave the city and go and live with John Klute, trading the independence of her modern life for the supposed domestic harmony of middle-class America. It was an idea which reinforced some people's interpretation that the film's politics were essentially reactionary, as Brian McDonnell observed:

> This ending has caused concern for some critics who see it as the logical culmination of the film's conservative values. They see it as supporting the 'redemption' of an independent, if transgressive, woman by a man who offers her a traditional life as a wife. (253)

Yet what might have been a traditional happy ending for a heterosexual couple, an example of what Robin Wood memorably called the "ideological straightjacket" of Hollywood cinema (37), is undercut both by the film's mise-en-scène, as the coldness of Bree's empty apartment does not seem to suggest a celebratory move, and the layering over of her dialogue with her psychiatrist, to whom she confides, "I have no idea what's going to happen. I just can't stay in the city, you know? Maybe I'll come back. You'll probably see me next week . . ." This line is the film's final moment of contrast between the apparent and the real, and one which confirms the truth of James Monaco's suggestion that "*Klute* remains one of the most important films of the seventies. A film whose significance multiplies every year we get further away from it" (290).

THE PARALLAX VIEW AND THE "DISCOURSE OF DISTRUST"

Very soon after the release of *Klute*, Pakula moved on to his next project, *The Parallax View*, based on the best-selling novel of the same name by Loren

Figure 16.2   Joe Frady (Warren Beatty) goes on a physical and psychological journey in *The Parallax View* (1974) read by many as very much an embodiment of the fractious 1970s. Digital frame enlargement. Courtesy of Paramount Pictures.

Singer (1970). It is a film which has made an indelible mark, described by John Cettl as "a seminal political thriller of the 1970s (200) and by Fredric Jameson as the "greatest of all assassination films" (55). Despite their close proximity, much had happened between the production of *Klute* and the release of *The Parallax View* in June 1974: the 1971 publication of the Pentagon Papers, the re-election of Richard M. Nixon in November 1972, the Watergate burglary (of 17 June 1972), the signing of the Paris Peace Accords (January 1973), and the televised proceedings of the Senate Watergate Committee (17 May 1973 onward). The Watergate hearings had been broadcast into the homes of millions of Americans on a daily basis. Less than four months after the release of the film Nixon resigned from office in disgrace (9 August 1974).

   If the investigation and conspiracy at the center of *Klute*, though relatively personal in the context of the film, can be understood as evoking very real social and political tensions in American society at the time, *The Parallax View* offers far more extensive and explicit connections to the era's defining traumatic events. Pakula commented that the film was to be regarded as "sort of an American myth based on some things that have happened, some fantasies we may have had of what might have happened, and a lot of fears a lot of us have had" (qtd. in Brown 126). This thematic journey from private to public, as Kevin Gai Dean suggests, certainly opens a "discourse of distrust" (Ryan and Kellner 98) that is at the center of the film from its opening frames to its last.

The Parallax View begins with an assassination deliberately framed and shot to remind viewers of the shootings of both Robert Kennedy and John F. Kennedy. The film's victim is the progressive United States senator and potential presidential candidate Charles Carroll (William Joyce), of whom a journalist says he is "so independent that some say they don't know what party he does belong to!", murdered on Independence Day at the top of Seattle's futuristic-looking Space Needle in front of dozens of witnesses. An abrupt cut is then made to several months later as the results of the investigation into the event are revealed, deliberately evoking the Warren Commission (1963–64) in both its mise-en-scène and the language employed in their findings. With a grandly symbolic eagle placed prominently above them, the five members of the panel are bathed in light, whilst everything else in the frame is in absolute darkness. The camera slowly moves towards the group with the non-diegetic soundtrack becoming increasingly discordant as the man in the center recounts the results of the enquiry into Senator Carroll's death. This hearing comes to exactly the same conclusion as did the Warren Commission's reports into Lee Harvey Oswald's assassination of John F. Kennedy. The speaker states,

> It is our further conclusion that he acted entirely alone, motivated by a misguided sense of patriotism and a psychotic desire for public recognition. The committee wishes to emphasize that there is no evidence of any wider conspiracy. No evidence whatsoever. It's our hope that this will put an end to the kind of irresponsible speculation conducted by the press in recent months.

The narrative that follows, as Ryan and Kellner argue, "successful transcodes the popular discourse of conspiracy around the Kennedy assassination that thrived in the early seventies" (98) in a range of compelling and viscerally realized imbrications with reality, in a vivid example of the "parallax" which we suggested at the start of the chapter.[2] In the aftermath of the film's assassination, those who witnessed it mysteriously begin to die one by one, and the journalist Joe Frady (Warren Beatty), after a long and difficult investigation of his own, discovers several connections between these murders, which all appear to be accidents, and the shadowy Parallax Corporation. Singer's source novel describes Frady's revelation that it is all part of a large conspiracy in the following terms: "It was as though the country had revealed to him a great fissure in itself that engendered a deep and strong revulsion" (13). Singer makes it very clear that the Parallax Corporation is a parastatal branch of the United States government, but the film is more ambiguous in its dramatization of the prevailing fears that powerful institutions, whether governmental, corporate, or an uneasy conflation of the two, are so influential they can manipulate not just individuals but also the whole of society to do whatever they want without people ever being aware. Mark Fisher in his *Capitalist Realism: Is There No Alternative?* asks a question which the film itself never quite answers: "Who knows what the Parallax Corporation really wants? It is itself situated in the parallax between politics and economy. Is it a commercial front for political interests, or is the whole machinery of government a front for it?" (67). The fears the film dramatizes are both very real and at the same time allegorical, offering, as John Cettl remarked, "a metaphorical indictment of the corrupt institutions of patriarchal American capitalism" (200).

The Parallax View acutely renders the discomfort, alienation, skepticism, and distrust which characterized the seventies through both its narrative and the utilization of cinematic devices in a way similar to the strategy of Pakula and Willis in *Klute*. Its dark shadowy spaces, its claustrophobic settings, its juxtaposition between architecture and technologies new and old all result in a film which, according to Peter Lev in his *American Films of the 70s: Conflicting Visions* (2000), creates "a visual impression of American paranoia and despair, circa 1974" (54). There is no greater example of this than the film's most famous scene, as Frady is interviewed for a position at Parallax in an attempt to infiltrate the corporation. He is taken to a screening room and forced to watch an extended montage of images and words which evokes *The Manchurian Candidate* (1962), *A Clockwork Orange* (1971), and George Orwell's *1984* (1948). The words "father," "mother," "me," "country," "God" and "happiness" are initially connected to comforting, nostalgic, and traditional images of Americana, but as the sequence continues these words and images are alternated and juxtaposed with photographs of violence and destruction in 1960s and 1970s America. There can be no doubt that Pakula equates the images and the sequence to the impact of the challenges that the 1970s offered to some of the fundamental aspects of American national identity and values.

The film climaxes with another senator, George Hammond (Jim Davis), about to be killed and Frady provided with an opportunity to prevent the assassination. Frady's determination and the fact that he is played by one of the era's most charismatic stars lead us to believe that he will indeed be successful ... but he fails to prevent Hammond's murder and is shockingly even killed himself in the process. The film's coda returns to the very same committee which opened the film, with the same lighting design and the same eagle prominently placed above the panel, however this time the camera moves away rather than towards them as the figures become smaller and smaller in the frame. In almost exactly the same language as at the beginning of the film they inform the public that it was Joe Frady who assassinated Hammond and that he acted alone. The first committee sequence had ended with a freeze frame, but this time the individuals on the panel abruptly disappear, leaving their seats empty. What we are to understand by this provocative conclusion is ambiguous and left entirely for the audience to decide.

Figure 16.3   There can be no doubt that *All the President's Men* (1976) has shaped the perception and memory of the Watergate scandal (1972–74) in the cultural imaginary. Digital frame enlargement. Courtesy of Wildwood Enterprises/Warner Bros.

ALL THE PRESIDENT'S MEN (1976): RESURRECTING THE "AMERICAN HERO MYTH"

If *Klute* foreshadowed Watergate (see Miller) and *The Parallax View* rendered the fears and anxieties of the decade with a potency that is even now palpable (see Jameson), *All the President's Men* portrays the era far more explicitly, given the fact that it is based on the epoch-defining real-life events depicted in the bestselling book (of the same name) by Bob Woodward and Carl Bernstein (1974). The final film in the "paranoia trilogy" is certainly the most well-known of the three and has itself played a considerable role in how the Watergate scandal has come to be remembered in the cultural imaginary. The understanding of the aftermath of the Watergate burglary and the events leading to Nixon's resignation is now firmly aligned with how it is portrayed in Pakula's *All the President's Men* in a way that some have regarded as troubling, due to how the film departs quite distinctly from actual historical events, particularly the centralization of its two plucky, indefatigable journalists who are shown on a mission to uncover the truth which brought down a corrupt presidency (see Feeney; Toplin). Although the roles of Woodward and Bernstein in these events are indeed considerable, the truth, as one might expect, is much more complicated than this, yet these intricacies are eschewed in favor of an almost mythical depiction of heroism, one which has become the way the events have been understood by the public at large. *All the President's Men* therefore provides us with a remarkable example of the affectual power of film to shape public opinion and memory in ways analogous to what Alison Landsberg calls "prosthetic memories." Film can give us memories of events and experiences that we did not obtain first-hand. She states that

> what this suggests is that the experience within the movie theatre and the memories that the cinema affords – despite the fact that the spectator did not live through them – might be as significant in constructing, or deconstructing, the spectator's identity as any experience that s/he has actually lived through. (180)

After the release of *All the President's Men*, Pakula was interviewed by Richard Thompson at *Film Comment*. He described how a film critic had suggested to him that *The Parallax View* had "destroyed the American hero myth," to which he responded, "If that's true, *All the President's Men* resurrects it" (qtd. in Thompson 13).

In the same interview Pakula expressed the idea that there was a transition between the final two films in the trilogy, stating that "[*The*] *Parallax View* represents my fear about what's happening in the world, and *All the President's Men* represents my hope" (qtd. in Thompson 13). The absolute defeat of the individual by the system portrayed in *The Parallax View* is transmogrified into victory in *All the President's Men*, dramatized not just through theme and narrative but, as we have seen with the two other parts of the trilogy, through an artful manipulation of mise-en-scène and sound. The film adopts the visual style of both *Klute* and *The Parallax View*, but dilutes it somewhat given how it is tied to real-life events and people with whom many would have been familiar by the time it reached theaters in 1976. Its opening shot is one such example of this vivid use of cinematography, another statement of intent by Pakula in the form of an eighteen-second-long shot of pure white Eaton's Corrasable Bond paper before a sharp typewriter key stroke shatters the silence with the sounds of both a whip cracking and gunfire layered into the sound mix (see Thompson 16). The film creates a delicate balance between its use of real-life buildings and characters and how they are rendered cinematically: from the murkiness of the Watergate Hotel, the exaggerated brightness of the meticulously recreated Washington Post offices with accentuated sounds of typewriters and pencils, to the expressively lit and shot scenes with the whistle-blower Deep Throat (the real identity of the man was revealed only in 2005), whose face remains largely hidden in shadow. The film's most famous and justly celebrated shot takes place in the Library of Congress where Woodward and Bernstein are pursuing a lead, and begins with a close up on a small library ticket stub before retreating further and further up towards the ceiling, demonstrating both the scope of their investigation and, at the same time, that of the conspiracy in which they have become embroiled. Of this shot Pakula said,

> Starting with those little library slips as clues, filling the screen at first, enormous in their size, and then pulling back to the top of the Library of Congress, where the reporters are so small, gave me a chance to dramatize the endless time it takes to do these things, without being boring about it. It also gave me a sense of how lost they are in this thing, how tiny these figures are in terms of the enormity of their task, and the heroic job they're trying to achieve. (qtd. in Thompson 19)

The cumulative effect of this visual and aural design is the creation of "a larger sense of isolation around Woodward and Bernstein as they pursue the story. It's as if they're moving in a vacuum and chasing phantoms" (Feeney 261). But unlike those which led to the murder of Joe Frady in *The Parallax View*, these phantoms are vanquished by the climax of *All the President's Men*. Its final image is set quite specifically on 20 January 1973, as the two men type up the story that will make them famous, with Nixon shown taking the oath of office for his second term only on a television in the background, still more than a year before his resignation, but with the audience knowing exactly how the story will end.[3]

CONCLUSION: THE LINGERING RESONANCES OF THE "PARANOIA TRILOGY"

This chapter has argued that the "paranoia trilogy" is intimately connected to the times in which it was made and should be regarded as an affectual cultural artifact in the same way as many of the other films discussed in this volume. The idea that these films perform a function analogous to the parallax, then, provides a critical perspective from which to approach them that is stimulating, provocative, and fertile. What is most remarkable about many of the films discussed in this book is their interrogative nature and the fact that they ask questions of their audiences rather than providing them with answers, quite far removed from what we might term the ideological didacticism of new millennial American film. What they reveal is often ambiguous, sometimes even paradoxical, but it is certainly potent and affecting, leading them to function as a compelling testimony of the era, as they will no doubt continue to do in the decades to come.

NOTES

1. For others who return to the idea of parallax as metaphor in very different fields: see Bjerg, and Cumings. The absence of Pakula's *The Parallax View* from Žižek's *The Parallax View* is rather striking given how it chimes with some of the central ideas he puts forward and that he does find time to mention films as diverse as *Rashomon* (1950), *The Graduate* (1967), *The Sacrifice* (1986), *The Fugitive* (1993), *The Passion of the Christ* (2004), and *Star Wars: Episode III Revenge of the Sith* (2005).
2. Ryan and Kellner are here writing before the release of Oliver Stone's *JFK* (1991) which revived interest in the assassination and shaped the way it was seen. Michael L. Kurtz suggested that "with the exception of *Uncle Tom's Cabin* . . . *JFK* probably had a greater impact on public opinion than any other work of art in American history" (174).
3. In a development which suggests that the events portrayed in *All the President's Men* still resonate more than forty years later, Steven Spielberg's *The Post* (2017) dramatizes the publication of the Pentagon Papers (June 1971) and concludes with the break-in at the Watergate Hotel which opens Pakula's film. At various moments in the film it is made fairly explicit that Spielberg regards *The Post* as particularly relevant in the Trump era, something he confirmed in interviews when he commented, "The urgency to make *The Post* was because of Trump's administration" (qtd. in Freedland 2018).

WORKS CITED

Bjerg, Ole. *Parallax of Growth: The Philosophy of Ecology and Economy*. Polity Press, 2016.

Brown, Jared. *Alan J. Pakula: His Films and His Life*. Back Stage Books, 2005.

Cettl, John. *Terrorism in American Cinema: An Analytical Filmography, 1960-2008*. McFarland & Company, 2009.

Cobley, Paul. "Justifiable Paranoia: The Politics of Conspiracy in 1970s American Film." *Shocking Cinema of the Seventies*, edited by Xavier Mendik, Noir Publishing, 2002, pp. 74–86.

Cumings, Bruce. *Parallax Visions: Making Sense of American–East Asian Relations at the End of the Century*. Duke University Press, 1999.

Dean, Kevin Gai. "Pakula, Alan J." *Conspiracy Theories in American History. An Encyclopedia. Volume 1. A-L*, edited by Peter Knight, ABC-Clio, 2003.

Donovan, Barna William. *Conspiracy Films: A Tour of Dark Places in the American Conscious*. McFarland, 2011.

Dunst, Alexander. *Madness in Cold War America*. Routledge, 2017.

Feeney, Mark. *Nixon at the Movies: A Book About Belief*. University of Chicago Press, 2004.

Fisher, Mark. *Capitalist Realism: Is There No Alternative*. Zer0 Books, 2009.

Freedland, Jonathan. "Steven Spielberg: 'The Urgency to Make *The Post* Was Because of Trump's Administration'." *The Guardian*, 19 Jan. 2018, www.theguardian.com/film/2018/jan/19/steven-spielberg-the-urgency-to-make-the-post-was-because-of-this-administration. Accessed 13 May 2020.

Hanson, Helen. "The Big Seduction: Feminist Film Criticism and the *Femme Fatale*." *The Femme Fatale: Images. Histories, Contexts*, edited by Helen Hanson and Catherine O'Rawe, Palgrave MacMillan, 2010, pp. 214–28.

Jameson, Richard. T. "The Pakula Parallax." *Film Comment*, vol. 12, no. 5, Sept./Oct. 1976, pp. 8–12.

Jameson, Fredric. *The Geopolitical Aesthetic: Cinema and Space in the World System*. Indiana University Press, 1995.

Kachmar, Dianne. *Roy Scheider: A Film Biography*. McFarland & Company, 2002.

Kirshner, Jonathan. *Hollywood's Last Golden Age: Politics, Society, and the Seventies Film in America*. Cornell University Press, 2013.

Kurtz, Michael L. "Oliver Stone, *JFK*, and History." *Oliver Stone's USA: Film, History and Controversy*, edited by Robert Brent Toplin, University of Kansas Press, 2000, pp. 166–77.

Landsberg, Alison. "Prosthetic Memory: *Total Recall* and *Blade Runner*.". *Cyberspace/Cyberbodies/Cyberpunk: Cultures of Technological Embodiment*, edited by Mike Featherstone and Roger Burrows, Sage, 1995, pp. 175–90.

Langford, Barry. *Post-Classical Hollywood*. Edinburgh University Press, 2010.

Lev, Peter. *American Films of the 1970s: Conflicting Visions*. University of Texas Press, 2000.

MacCabe, Colin. "Realism and the Cinema: Notes on Some Brechtian Theses." *Contemporary Film Theory*, edited by Antony Easthope, Routledge. Originally published in *Screen*, vol. 15, no. 2, Summer 1974, pp. 7–27.

McDonnell, Brian. "*Klute*." *Encyclopedia of Film Noir*, edited by Geoff Mayer and Brian McDonnell, Greenwood Press, 2007, pp. 251–3.

Miller, Stephen Paul. *The Seventies Now: Culture as Surveillance*. Duke University Press, 1999.

Monaco, James. *American Film Now. The People, The Power, The Money, The Movies*. Oxford University Press, 1979.

Pratt, Ray. *Projecting Paranoia: Conspiratorial Visions in American Film*. Kansas: University Press of Kansas, 2001.

Ryan, Michael and Douglas Kellner. *Camera Politica: The Politics and Ideology of Contemporary Hollywood Film*. Indiana University Press, 1990.

Scott, Ian. *American Politics in Hollywood Film* (Second Edition). Edinburgh University Press, 2011.

Singer, Loren. *The Parallax View*. Dell, 1970.

Thompson, Richard. "Mr Pakula Goes to Washington." *Film Comment*, vol. 12, no. 5, Sep./Oct, 1976; pp. 12–19.

Toplin, Brent. *History by Hollywood: The Use and Abuse of the American Past*. University of Illinois Press, 1996.

Wood, Robin. *Sexual Politics and Narrative Film, Hollywood and Beyond*. Columbia University Press, 1998.

Žižek, Slavoj. *The Parallax View*. MIT Press, 2006.

17. GENRES OF THE MODERN MYTHIC IN THE FILMS OF SAM PECKINPAH

Daniel Sacco

In the late 1960s, Hollywood directors were engaged in a dramatic reimagining of commercial "genre" filmmaking. Far from offering the escapist thrills of B-movie drive-in fare, filmmakers such as Arthur Penn, Stanley Kubrick, and Roman Polanski were infusing genre frameworks with palpable realism and considerable prestige. *Bonnie and Clyde* (1967) set its fairly typical gangster action against a landscape of socioeconomic reality and morally complex characterizations. *2001: A Space Odyssey* (1968) replaced the intergalactic warfare of 1950s drive-in sci-fi with delicate and sophisticated musings of the utmost philosophical profundity. *Rosemary's Baby* (1968) transcends the cheese-ball gimmickry of its producer William Castle's catalogue, infusing its occult themes with a social-realist treatment of urban life and paranoia. It is perhaps this sort of experimentation that paved the way for the 1970s films of Coppola, Scorsese, and Spielberg more than any other factor. Such works stand as fountainheads for the films of the "renaissance" period and are distinguished by, as Glenn Man notes, "a combination of technical innovation, reflexivity, genre transformation and radical themes" (5). The effect of this strategy was so profound that one could perhaps consider Sam Peckinpah's celebrated western *The Wild Bunch* (1969) as coming at the dramatic end of classical genre cinematic storytelling as an artistic touchstone. Peckinpah's brutal yet reflective entry into the western canon fated subsequent attempts to exploit genre conventions without critically engaging their relationship to the "real world," to appear uninspired, derivative, or naive. Peckinpah, who at that time had made a number of more traditional westerns including *Ride the High Country* (1962), ratchets up the genre's grittier and rough-edged elements so extensively in *The Wild Bunch* that it would be nearly thirty years before Clint Eastwood's *Unforgiven* (1992) would revive talks of "revisionist" westerns. In one fell swoop *The Wild Bunch* had perfected and obliterated the Hollywood western.

Peckinpah himself was clearly cognizant of this fact, as he subsequently began to explore a richer wealth of inspiration and technique. While he continued to make westerns, including *The Ballad of Cable Hogue* (1970) and *Pat Garrett and Billy the Kid* (1973), these comprise only a portion of his prolific output from 1970–74, which also included the gritty modern crime classics *Straw Dogs* (1971), *The Getaway* (1972), and *Bring Me The Head of Alfredo Garcia* (1974). Though gaining a substantial cult appreciation, Peckinpah's output during this period at times bewildered audiences and critics who sought and failed to place their action into immediately recognizable and previously established modes of storytelling. These films represent the work of a director who was endlessly fascinated by the mythic substructure of the western, but who simultaneously understood that he had taken the genre's visual iconography and dramatic signifiers as far as they could go. What Peckinpah's stunning crime films of the early 1970s do most inventively and unapologetically is foster a conceptual intersection of the mythic and the mundane; the antiquated and the avant-garde; the extinct and the extant. This chapter will examine sequences from four films, *The Wild Bunch*, *Straw Dogs*, *The Getaway,* and *Bring Me the Head of Alfredo Garcia* in hopes of pinpointing with some precision those moments in which Peckinpah, like a selection of his contemporaries, altered the course of genre filmmaking forever by casting aside its stultifying escapism.

Washers

Much of the scholarship devoted to Peckinpah's output focuses on his skills at rendering a massacre. The robbery of the Starbuck railroad offices that opens *The Wild Bunch* encapsulates what has now become known as his signature stylization of violence. The scene is brutal, chaotic, tragic, and exhilarating. It shows the sheer destructiveness of violence in combinations of real-time and slow-motion chaos, as bounty hunters, innocent bystanders, and half of the Bunch are gunned down, trampled by horses, and left bleeding in the dusty streets. Less frequently remarked upon, however, is the nearly seven-minute dialogue scene which immediately follows, in which the surviving members of the Bunch pause to divide the loot in pursuit of which so many have just met a violent demise. The aging leader of the group, Pike (William Holden), is shown rendezvousing with Willie (Edmund O'Brien), a disheveled former gunslinger who sat out the robbery to keep watch on the Bunch's horses. Seeing the Bunch approaching, now reduced in size, he begins to asks, "Those others . . .?" To which Pike interrupts, "They're not coming." Pike sits on a concrete slab catching his breath. Two members of the gang, Lyle Gorch (Warren Oates) and Tector Gorch (Ben Johnson) seize an opportunity to air their grievances. They claim, because of their seniority, to deserve a more ample share of the loot than Angel (Jaime Sánchez) who is "just starting out." Pike responds, "If you boys don't like equal shares, why in the hell don't you just take all of it?" After a pause, he springs to his feet, shouting, "Well, answer me, you yellow-livered trash!" The tension thickens as Pike's second in command, Dutch (Ernest Borgnine), lays his palm on the revolver holstered at his side, ready to draw. The Gorch brothers relent, with Lyle conceding: "Alright, we divide it up just like you say." The exchange establishes Pike as a man of principle but also one ready at any given moment to use violence in order to maintain his leadership over the rowdy and often fractured collective. As he threateningly remarks, "I either lead this group or end it right now."

As the gang gathers around their sacks of loot, ready to divide the spoils and rejoice in their newfound wealth, their expectations are shattered by the discovery that the bags contain only piles of worthless steel washers. Lyle Gorch stares in disbelief: "We shot our way out of that town for a bunch of steel holes?" In a clever twist of screenwriting, *The Wild Bunch*'s complex thematic concerns are concisely laid bare for the audience. The bloodshed that permeated, indeed engulfed, the preceding sequence was all for nothing. The Bunch have been outsmarted by state and business officials who are becoming better and better equipped to counter the renegade strategies that have provided outlaws like Pike with means to survive for decades. As many scholars have noted, the film's early-twentieth-century setting points toward a time of transformation, in which the lawless frontier of the "west" is rapidly disappearing into the capitalistic order of modern civilization and the systems that enforce it. Of course, this transformation is synergistically mirrored in Peckinpah's own transformation of the western as a genre. The pre-modern west is disappearing in the film, as the pre-modern western is disappearing from Hollywood. The reality of modernity is not lost on Pike: "We've got to start thinking beyond our guns . . . those days are closing fast." Watching from a distance, Angel sees an opportunity to return the disrespect shown to him by the Gorches moments before. "Gringo . . .," he addresses Lyle Gorch, "you can have my share." Angel and the Gorch brothers draw their pistols, ready for battle. The tension is palpable and accentuated by the low rising tones of Jerry Fielding's orchestral score. Dutch, his hand once again on his pistol, adds, "Walk softly, boys . . ." While Peckinpah is often celebrated (and equally derided) for his stylization of violence, his work (particularly following *The Wild Bunch*) more consistently and stunningly captures the constant *threat* of such violence that permeates the interactions and behavior of his male characters (taking center stage most notably in *Straw Dogs*, discussed further below).

As the Gorches reconsider and lower their pistols, Lyle's protestations at Pike's leadership continue: "All your fancy talkin' and plannin' nearly got us shot to pieces over a few lousy bags of washers." His voice rises: "We spent all our time and money getting ready for this!" Pike shoots back: "You spent your time and money running whores in Hondo while I spent mine setting it up . . ." and then concedes, "Hell, I should have been running whores instead of stealing Army horses." Chuckles emerge from the Bunch. Dutch joins in laughing heartily: "You boys were getting your ropes pulled while Pike was dreaming of washers." The banter continues as the gang bellow with laughter, their cohesion as a unit reaffirmed, while two children from a nearby village watch from a distance, smiling to one another. The scene is a tour-de-force of eloquent dialogue, impeccable acting, and delicate dramatic shifts that represents Peckinpah's moral and cultural universe at its most articulated. While the reference to "Hondo whores" reflects the careless misogyny of which Peckinpah's detractors have often charged him, it also serves to display with frankness "how men behave around each other" (Fulwood 57). The members of the Bunch are neither perfect heroes nor perfect villains. They are volatile and brash, and bounded by codes and principles of honor that are not only less and less adaptable to the modern world but undermined by a primitive violence that threatens constantly to emerge from between the cracks fracturing their group unity.

Peckinpah will reprise this sequence of laughter during what Michael Bliss refers to as the

> apotheosis at the film's end, by which time they are in their most perfect cohesion: that of mutual death . . . reminding us of the Bunch's better

Figure 17.1 (l. to r.) William Holden, Jaime Sánchez, Ernest Borgnine, Warren Oates, Ben Johnson, and Edmond O'Brien in *The Wild Bunch* (1969). Digital frame enlargement. Courtesy of Warner Bros/Seven Arts.

selves, their ability to laugh about their shortcomings and to be joined in joyous union. (92)

While *The Wild Bunch* is credited for reinventing the western through its technologically sophisticated presentation of onscreen violence (including montage, slow-motion, and explosive squibs), the transformative impact of its characterization and psychological richness cannot also be overstated. While the violence of today's genre thrillers at times bears a superficial aesthetic resemblance to Peckinpah's, his skillful staging of human interaction, distinctly modern in its design and treatment, wields a more profound continued influence on contemporary films.

Here Kitty Kitty

Many critics consider *The Wild Bunch* to be Peckinpah's defining statement on the subject of violence, his primary artistic obsession. However, this is likely due primarily to the director's association with the conventional western in the popular imagination, based on the assumption that since he so frequently explored this genre's themes, motifs, and iconography they must naturally have provided the ideal elements for making his views on the subject clear. One could instead argue, in fact, that the director's post-*Wild Bunch* crime films of the 1970s, wherein he explores violence in a context removed from history and classical genre, are indeed far *more* reflective of his beliefs about brutality and male aggression in the contemporary world. In *Straw Dogs, The Getaway,* and *Bring Me the Head of Alfredo Garcia* Peckinpah elaborates and significantly expands upon his previous thematic concerns, but by way of the same sophisticated technical and psychological treatments of characters and the harsh realities of human behavior. These three films transpose earlier themes onto contemporaneous settings and periods but also employ the modern realist tendencies of early seventies Hollywood filmmaking. These films are certainly not entirely divorced from genre frameworks, but rather explore certain thematic concerns of the western by way of the horror film, the heist film, and the revenge film respectively. Each of these genres (or sub-genres) was transformed to a degree by Peckinpah's authorial touches and penchant for morally complex scenarios and volatile anti-heroes. *Straw Dogs* is an especially effective stepping-stone between Peckinpah's work in the western genre and his subsequent exploration of evil and human-authored carnage, owing to is transposition of the dramatic "siege film" structure, made famous in films like Howard Hawks' *Rio Bravo* (1959), to a very particular contemporary socio-economic and cultural context. To this point, it is perhaps no coincidence that the rape-revenge sub-genre that *Straw Dogs* pioneered was subsequently subsumed by the horror genre. Stripped of western genre trappings, Peckinpah's simultaneous concerns about (and fascination with) violence indeed become horrific.

While *Straw Dogs* is rarely considered a conventional "horror film," it may be constructively thought of as *post-horror*, a film that seeks to frighten its audience while eschewing any treatment of supernatural forces or gothic narrative traditions. One scene in particular encapsulates this inventive mix of tones and traditions. A young couple, David (Dustin Hoffman) and Amy (Susan George), are retiring to bed in their Cornish farmhouse. The scene arrives approximately one third of the way through the film, which for the most part so far has explored the strained relationship between the couple and the menacing but unspoken hostility that David, an American mathematician, has experienced in the company of the Cornish locals since the couple's recent arrival in rural England. In the previous scene, David engaged in a passive-aggressive game of one-upmanship with the local reverend, in which he flaunted his intellect and knowledge of philosophy while subtly belittling the glamorous Amy, whom he does not consider his intellectual equal. That night, as David gets undressed, Amy playfully calls him out on his frequently obnoxious behavior from under the sheets of their shared bed: "You were awful to the Reverend tonight." David recourses to his particular brand of denial: "No, no, he's alright." "David," she continues referencing the earlier scene, "what's a binary number?" He condescends: "Zeroes or ones, plus or minus . . ." Asserting her own intellectual capability, she finishes his sentence, "in sequences of twos." David is surprised. "Hey that's right, you're a bright lady. Y'know you're not so dumb." Amy conceals the emotional hurt that David frequently causes her: "Sometimes I need help."

The scene is thus far a psychologically nuanced portrait of a marriage in crisis, one that once again brushes up against Peckinpah's oft-construed misogyny. Yet, the audience's sympathies are undoubtedly with Amy as she struggles emotionally against her husband's arrogance and condescension. The scene would find itself perfectly at home in the style of the other adult realist classics featuring Hoffman that were making waves in Hollywood at the time, including *The Graduate* (1967) and *Midnight Cowboy* (1969). Yet this sequence, indeed the entire film, is about to take a sinister and unexpected turn. David moves toward the bedroom closet, to retrieve his pajamas. As he yanks on the chain of the closet light, his movements become tense and spastic. We see, as David sees it, a quick flash of an undefined mass of black fur. David reflexively yanks the chain two more times – the light turning off and on again. The mass becomes plainly visible: it is the couple's pet cat, whose disappearance has hitherto been repeatedly mentioned. The animal has been strangled and hanged with the very chain on which David is pulling. Beholding the gruesome sight, David appears to shut down. He soberly closes the closet door and sheepishly crosses the room, collapsing on a chair. Sensing

Figure 17.2   Dustin Hoffman in *Straw Dogs* (1971). Digital frame enlargement.
Courtesy of ABC/Talent Associates

the disturbance, Amy too approaches the closet and, seeing the hanged cat, lets out a piercing scream.

By Peckinpah's own admission, *Straw Dogs* is a "western" of sorts. It deals explicitly with themes of territorial tension and frontier lawlessness. Scenes like the one described above, however, have a spectacularly transformative effect on the boundaries of genre and their implications of fantasy escapism. The hostility and violence that David will be forced to contend with by the film's climax are currently awaiting him out on the plains, but will eventually come "home," invading the most intimate spaces of his domestic existence. The revelation of the cat killing is a shock moment on par with any offered by horror filmmaking of the period, even with the bar irrevocably raised two years later by William Friedkin's *The Exorcist* (1973). Friedkin's film would become the first of its genre to receive Oscar-recognition (taking the prize for its screenplay and sound mixing), a symbolic affirmation of horror's increasing social relevance, earlier escalated by *Rosemary's Baby*. It could be argued, however, that the critical and commercial attention paid by audiences to *Straw Dogs* also contributed significantly to the mainstreaming of shock-horror film-making in the late sixties and early seventies. As Stephen Prince has claimed, Peckinpah's work "helped propel American film toward explorations of sub-terranean aspects of human behavior that had been too dark or twisted for the industry to countenance in earlier decades" (4). Like Friedkin and Polanski, Peckinpah's brand of horror does not provide escapism by showcasing mon-sters as simple symbolic stand-ins for sociocultural anxieties. It represents, by contrast, the inextricable interweaving of monstrosity and anxiety. Evil in Peckinpah's world does not threaten society from the outside; it is rather part and parcel of it, all too human and pervasive in the interactions of individual actors. From his treatment of surprise and shock-horror in *Straw Dogs*, it is clear that Peckinpah was cognizant of something his audience did not recognize: that the true face of violence, made to appear less destructive and horrific when bound up in western genre trappings, becomes more recognizable for what it is when set against the psychological veracity and moral ambiguity of realist drama.

Shotgun Wedding

The Getaway is often thought of as Peckinpah's most purely commercial genre outing, this reading seemingly confirmed by his lack of extensive public comment about the film's thematic preoccupations. As such, *Getaway* provides a somewhat unique opportunity to assess his distinctive style as a storyteller (as opposed to an author). It is indeed true that the narrative of *The Getaway* is more typical of the heist-film dramatic structures that both preceded and followed it. Even so, Peckinpah includes remarkable artistic flourishes that contain his signature blending of the mythic and mundane. Whilst, when taken as a whole, the film is perhaps the least challenging and radically unconventional of Peckinpah's films considered in this chapter, an examination of its most memorable and adeptly executed sequence provides no shortage of material for critical analysis. The film follows Doc (Steve McQueen) and Carol (Ali McGraw) who, after a successful bank robbery, cross the deserts of Texas struggling to evade a multitude of state officials, greedy gangsters, and treacherous former accomplices in hot pursuit. The sequence in question takes place approximately two-thirds of the way into the film, before the couple's criminal pursuers have caught up to them, but immediately after the state officials have learned of Doc's identity and have publicly released his mug shot.

On the populated main street of a small Texas town, Carol waits in the couple's car while Doc enters an electronics store. He asks the clerk for a radio, presumably to monitor the news for mention of the robbery's investigation. This effort is made redundant when, moments later, Doc's face appears on the screens of several televisions scattered throughout the store. As Doc abruptly exits the store without his radio, the clerk notices the screens and promptly telephones the police. Outside, Doc approaches the car and informs Carol: "We've got trouble." He then crosses the street and enters a gun shop, approaching the counter and curtly asking the clerk for a "Shotgun, twelve gauge, pump." He continues: "Lemme have a pack of those double-aught bucks." Doc's desired firepower surprises the clerk, who responds, "What are you gonna' do? Knock a wall down?" This evocation of property damage whets the audience's appetite for the inevitable outcome of this Chekhovian moment. Upon the clerk's insistence that Doc fill out a piece of paperwork, Doc points a pistol at the clerk's chest. "You know what this is, don't you Mr.?" Mildly annoyed, the clerk answers "Yeah." Neither seems particularly uncomfortable with the implicit threat of violence just issued. The clerk wraps up a shotgun, which Doc leaves the store carrying at his side. Now in the broad daylight of a busy public street, Doc sees two police officers leaving their car to approach Carol, who is standing a short distance away. A standoff is imminent and viewers, as well as the town's many citizen onlookers, wait with bated breath.

Despite his forays into particularly dark territory such as in *Straw Dogs*, Peckinpah is not fundamentally interested in evil. Endlessly fascinated by outlaws, he nonetheless "seems to have realized fairly early on that men who are merely bad don't make for very interesting characters, themes, or drama" (Seydor 50). Like the eponymous Wild Bunch, Doc's moral status is certainly skewed by his criminal activity. However, Peckinpah's antiheroes are often redeemed through their retribution against villains who are even less morally scrupulous, such as the corrupt pillager General Mapache (Emilio Fernandez) in *The Wild Bunch*, or Doc's treacherous former partner in crime, Rudy (Al Lettieri). While audiences will offer baseline sympathy for criminal characters doing what they must to "survive," this concession would not likely extend to any wish to see Doc gun down two innocent police officers. When the Wild Bunch "shoot their way" out of the film's opening robbery, for example, their pursuers are mostly greedy bounty hunters hired by corrupt economic interests from within the railroad industry. Transposed to a contemporary modern setting and sensibility, gleeful violence against random innocent police officers would read as purely nihilistic and artistically indefensible (as in Mr. Blonde's

Figure 17.3   Steve McQueen in *The Getaway* (1972). Digital frame enlargement. Courtesy of First Artists/Solo.

[Michael Madsen] horrifying showcase in Tarantino's *Reservoir Dogs* [1992]). And yet, standing in the sun-drenched streets of Texas with a twelve-gauge shotgun, Doc is very much the classic outlaw archetype. We expect him to toe a moral line yet still require of him some brazen, anti-authoritarian, anti-establishment gesture. Peckinpah delivers as Doc fires a round in the back-left tail light of the now empty police car and shouts: "Get those guns out on the street!" The two panicked officers comply, throwing down their guns and lying face down in the dirt, hands behind their heads.

Having seemingly neutralized the immediate threat, Doc next acts to facilitate one of the film's many eponymous *getaways*. He fires again at the empty police car. And again. And again. In total, he pumps five rounds of the high-velocity shots at the empty vehicle. The windows, side mirrors, rear bumper, and trunk explode in a series of slow-motion medium shots, in which glass and metal debris float gracefully through the air with a dazzling balletic quality. It is a remarkable explosion of cinematic violence, yet one notably devoid of the bloodshed and pain so frequently on display in Peckinpah's work. The entire sequence is perhaps also an ideal visual metaphor for the entrance of the director's old-west style of outlaw violence into a contemporary setting, in this case channeled via its modern technology – the radio, the TV, the automobile. However, it is the brief dramatic touch that follows and ends the scene that elevates it to the level of Peckinpah's highest storytelling genius. Satisfied with his obliteration of the police vehicle, Doc approaches Carol in the getaway car. Then, as he is entering the vehicle, Carol suddenly reverses it a few feet, knocking Doc to the ground, shotgun still in hand. He calmly picks himself up and shouts with visible frustration: "What the hell's the matter with you?" Carol does not respond. It is an exceedingly surprising and peculiar moment of black comedy, one informing the style of countless subsequent Peckinpah imitators. Every element of Doc's assault on the police car is designed to elevate his character to mythic outlaw status. Yet, this brief comic beat that follows grounds him once again in the banality of human foibles and the tragic comedy of everyday life.

THE HEAD OF THE GORGON

Peckinpah's most prolific and creatively fruitful period is bookended by *The Wild Bunch* in 1969 and *Bring Me the Head of Alfredo Garcia* in 1974. The latter is a gritty revenge thriller that combines more of the dark thematic subject matter of *Straw Dogs* with the black comedy touches of *The Getaway*. Having examined one of *The Wild Bunch*'s opening scenes, the beginning of *Straw Dogs*'s second act, and the veritable climax of *The Getaway*'s second act, I turn now to *Alfredo Garcia*'s concluding final moments. Alcoholic piano player Benny (Warren Oates) has, by this point in the film, undergone a soul-

Figure 17.4   Emilio Fernández and Warren Oates in *Bring Me the Head of Alfredo Garcia* (1974). Digital frame enlargement. Courtesy of Optimus/Estudios Churobusco Azteca S.A.

eroding journey through the criminal underworld of Mexico, accompanied by the severed head of a stranger for which "treasure" he hopes to collect a bounty. Throughout the film, sixteen people have died as a result of the reward issued for this head, including many innocents and, most distressingly to Benny, his lover Elita (Isela Vega). By this time, Benny seems less concerned with the prospect of financial reward than with seeing his mission through and confronting the criminal kingpin whose demand has caused so much carnage. Benny arrives at the hacienda of the powerful ruler El Jefe (Emilio Fernandez), carrying the decomposing severed head of Alfredo Garcia in a wicker basket, chilled by blocks of ice. He finds El Jefe at the baptism of his newborn grandson, whom his daughter conceived with Garcia, setting the bounty in motion. Benny follows El Jefe into a spacious, temple-like office. He speaks hesitantly: "Here's the uh . . . merchandise you wanted." One of El Jefe's armed guards produces a briefcase containing Benny's reward. "Take it and go," El Jefe tells Benny, "and don't forget to take that [the head], and throw it to the pigs."

Benny shows little interest in the reward, which had previously consumed his attention. His guilt over the death of Elita, whom he had involved in the violence of the ordeal, has overcome his greed. Further, he has developed an odd companionship with Garcia's head, which he affectionately refers to throughout the film's latter half as "Al." Benny places the basket on El Jefe's desk and opens the lid, remarking, "Sixteen people are dead because of him . . .," before removing a block of ice and throwing it on the desk, ". . . and you . . .," another block punctuates his speech, ". . . and me." Benny withdraws a pistol from the basket as he adds: "And one of them was a damn good friend of mine!" El Jefe's guards immediately raise their rifles at Benny who, as if by miracle, dodges their fire in a series of balletic slow-motion shots. He kills the guards and turns his pistol on El Jefe, uttering as if half to himself, "The first time I saw him . . . he was dead." El Jefe's teenage daughter, who has been in the background all along and whose loyalties also fall with the severed head, coldly demands: "Kill him!" Benny fires twice, killing El Jefe. Once again, Peckinpah significantly complicates a straightforward genre trajectory. In fact, Benny's "revenge" for the death of Elita has already been exacted upon those who actually murdered her, but this is not enough. In El Jefe, Benny rightly sees the corrupted authority at the root of the sordid affair – the source of the malicious whim that set the film's events in motion. The obvious irony, however, has to do with Benny's own culpability as the one who involved Elita. "Come on, Al," he mutters defeated, "let's go home." As Benny no doubt anticipates, a hail of bullets will end his life as he drives out of the hacienda. He knows as well as the audience that there is no longer any "home." Benny must join his enemies in death before moral restitution will truly be made.

Alfredo Garcia has been called Peckinpah's most "modern" film, a claim supported by the fact that it "ranges broadly through different physical environments and cultures, and does so with realistic attention to details, often significant details" (Simon and Merrill 177), and further evidenced by its oddly and violently black comedy (which would later become a staple of 1990s crime film). Yet scholars such as Simon and Merrill have also noted its simultaneous strong narrative similarities to Elizabethan and Jacobean revenge tragedies (177). The origins of the scene described above, however, are more ancient. Benny's brandishing of Garcia's head before bringing death upon the man who ordered it is unmistakably reminiscent of the Greek myth of Perseus. Sent by Polydectes to retrieve the head of the gorgon Medusa, Perseus returned only to find that the corrupt ruler had abused (perhaps even raped) his mother in his absence. Rather than offer the head as a reward to Polydectes, Perseus brandishes it as a weapon before him, turning Polydectes and his fellow nobles to stone. In both narratives, the protagonist avenges wrongdoing against a woman he loves by vanquishing the powerful figure who initially demanded the severed head. While Benny's subsequent death modernizes the tragic framework by highlighting his mortality and complicity in the corruption, his association with Perseus elevates Peckinpah's storytelling once again to the realm of the mythic. The signature self-destructiveness of Peckinpah's male protagonists (also on display in *The Wild Bunch* and *Straw Dogs*) intersects with Benny's archetypical role as the righter of unjust wrongs in a complex manner, and it is within such elaborate intersections that Peckinpah achieves the marriage of the ancient and the distinctly modern.

CONCLUSION

With the rise of independent filmmaking, an influx in the availability of foreign film catalogues, and new generations of cinema-literate and wholly self-aware storytellers, it is becoming harder than ever to delineate between genres. While genre films continue to generate substantial receipts at multiplexes, the post-modern age has seen their boundaries collapsing inwards, giving way to an infinite number of sub-genres, the standardized elements of which are in a process of constant reformulation. The transience and inter-permeability of genres in the age of contemporary cinema owes a substantial debt to the filmmakers of the Hollywood Renaissance more generally, but Peckinpah's influence on the evolution of genre filmmaking cannot be overstated. *The Wild Bunch* epitomizes the transformation of genre material into prestige drama that late 1960s films including *2001, Bonnie and Clyde,* and *Rosemary's Baby* helped to engineer, but Peckinpah's early 1970s work, in particular, set a significant standard for the incorporation of pre-established, invented modes of archetypical storytelling into gritty realist drama and the blurring of categorical boundaries. Peckinpah's oft-touted old-fashioned masculinity and regressive treatment of women frequently sees him labeled as a conservative storyteller who, like the rogues of *The Wild Bunch*, was clinging to a rapidly disappearing past. However, as his plainly visible influence on subsequent storytellers and his modern reimaging of mythic narrative archetypes suggest, the filmmaker also had a visionary voice and paved a rich future for his followers. Though his films have not always received the recognition they deserve, their immeasurable influence persists.

WORKS CITED

Bliss, Michael. *Justified Lives: Morality and Narrative in the Films of Sam Peckinpah.* Southern Illinois University Press, 1993.
Fulwood, Neil. *The Films of Sam Peckinpah.* Batsford, 2003.
Man, Glenn. *Radical Visions: American Film Renaissance, 1967-1976.* Greenwood Press, 1994.
Prince, Stephen. *Savage Cinema: Sam Peckinpah and the Rise of Ultraviolent Movies.* University of Texas Press, 1998.
Seydor, Paul. "The Wild Bunch: The Screenplay." *Sam Peckinpah's The Wild Bunch,* edited by Stephen Prince, Cambridge University Press, 1999.
Simon, John L. and Robert Merrill. *Peckinpah's Tragic Westerns: A Critical Study.* McFarland & Company Inc., 2001.

18. BOB RAFELSON'S AMBIVALENT AUTHORSHIP

Vincent Longo

Ironically, Bob Rafelson is often considered an exemplary New Hollywood auteur, as well as a one-hit wonder. The overview of Rafelson's work provided by Douglas Hildebrand in the *Critical Guide to Contemporary North American Directors* states, "Had Bob Rafelson never made a film again after *Five Easy Pieces* (1970), his name would still be remembered in American history" (435). Film history has largely concurred with this statement, as *Five Easy Pieces* continues to overshadow Rafelson's two other films of the decade, *The King of Marvin Gardens* (1972) and *Stay Hungry* (1976).1 Yet in 1976 contemporary critics hailed Rafelson as being among the ranks of the great living directors with an impressive oeuvre (despite the mixed reviews of his later films). Critics had occasionally praised the director as an "auteur" during the early 1970s – usually during laudatory individual film reviews (Brackman 38). But during the release of his third feature of the decade, *Stay Hungry*, reputable film journals, trade papers, and cinema organizations began to focus on Rafelson's body of work as an accomplished whole: *American Cinematographer* released detailed coverage of his direction of *Stay Hungry*; prestigious journals like *Positif* and *Film Comment* published full-length retrospectives of his work; and the American Film Institute hosted a full-day retrospective, concluding with a sequential screening of his films and a Q&A with the filmmaker (Mitchell; Tato; Farber; Rafelson). John Russell Taylor, Alfred Hitchcock's authorized biographer, also produced a five-page interview with Rafelson for *Sight and Sound*, pointing in his introduction to Rafelson's "individual style and approach of an artist," built on what first appear as groups of "isolated oddities" (200). *The Globe and Mail* even announced that, with the release of *Stay Hungry*, "it's clear Rafelson can no longer be denied his place with Coppola, Scorsese, and the gang on the top rung of the new hierarchy" (Johnson 13).

Rafelson's own understanding of cinematic authorship in the 1970s seems to support the auteur reputation attributed to him. He fetishized an imagined authorial spirit of himself in his films throughout the decade. He made a point of requiring his films to be "unique," which he defined in the romantic terms used by critics enamored of auteurism: "By unique, I mean emanating solely from myself" (Taylor 204). And yet, despite sounding like an archetypical auteur, he always denied the specific label. Even in the *Los Angeles Times* interview in which he touted his need to have a "special vision" that considered no one but himself, Rafelson stated, "*Auteur* is a misunderstood concept and it doesn't apply to me" (Warga 122).

Instead of simply dismissing Rafelson's claims, as scholarship has typically done, this chapter argues that we have not paid enough attention to how individual directors understood and utilized his approach to authorship. As Timothy Corrigan reminds us,

> When auteurs and auteuristic codes for understanding film spread from France to the United States and elsewhere in the 60s and 70s, these models were hardly the pure reincarnations ... of literary notions of the author as the sole creator or of Sartrean demands of 'authenticity' in personal expression. (40)

And the directors themselves, like critics and viewers, neither understood nor adhered to auteurism in a single way. To better understand Rafelson's work we must place the director's ever-changing conceptions of authorship at the center of our analysis. Throughout the 1970s, Rafelson never clearly defined exactly what qualified as a "unique" film in his view. But his articulations about authorship – expressed both in interviews and in the construction of his films – intertwine with some of the period's most pressing historical issues, including the rise and fall of auteur cinema (and the related boom of blockbuster films) as well as representations of class. Indeed, the style, themes, and messages of Rafelson's films of the period are best understood in the context of the director's ambivalent relationship to the conventions and critical expectations of auteur cinema and the way this frames his depictions of inter-class struggle.

A CLASS OF HIS OWN

Rafelson had at least two definable conceptions of authorship during the 1970s, the first occurring before he directed *Stay Hungry* and the second being a direct reaction against the first. Self-producing his earlier films, enabling him to work without the usual studio-leveraged pressures (Schroeder 2003), Rafelson put great emphasis on authorial centrality. He heavily crafted *Five Easy Pieces* and *The King of Marvin Gardens* around autobiographical events (Boyer 1–4). Like David (Jack Nicholson) in *The King of Marvin Gardens*, Rafelson was a DJ with a competitive relationship with his brother; he wrote the opening monologue for a college English class (1–4). Rafelson also imagined Bobby from *Pieces* (Jack Nicholson) as a stand-in for his isolated, "existential-hero" sixteen-year-old self, who likewise abandoned a music-focused upper-middle-class upbringing (Tonguette). During four different sequences – many of the film's most pivotal moments, including the final scene where Bobby abandons his girlfriend Rayette (Karen Black) at the gas station (Fig. 18.1) – Bobby wears a black sweater that Rafelson had owned since he was in high school.

Scholars have often presented *Five Easy Pieces* as a case study in 1970s inter-class conflict (Nystrom 30–6; Menne 52–6; Kirshner 66–70; Schroeder 123–6). Yet it is worth recognizing that Rafelson's autobiographical brand of auteurism significantly shapes the depiction. Key members of the production company Rafelson co-founded, BBS, met on the LA counterculture party

Figure 18.1   Bobby (Jack Nicholson) wears Rafelson's black sweater when he crucially decides to abandon Rayette at the gas station and defect to Canada, in *Five Easy Pieces* (1970). Digital frame enlargement. Courtesy of BBS Productions/ Columbia Picturres.

circuit and were committed to affording individual directors nearly complete artistic control. This principle allowed BBS films to be politically diverse (though they were mostly left-leaning). As it happens, *Pieces* reveals more of Rafelson's political leanings than he was willing to disclose to interviewers. When then AFI student Cathy Galloway asked if he purposefully made films in which "upper-middle-class guys sort of slum with lower class people" Rafelson seemed confused or perhaps deflective: "I don't think so . . . I really don't know. I don't know that" (1-2). The film's representations, however, demonstrate a fascination with class division and hierarchy. *Pieces* follows Bobby Dupea (Nicholson), who appears at first to be a laborer in the California oilfields, fully immersed in working-class life and pleasures. Over time, the film establishes Bobby's disdain for some of his blue-collar life's most iconic elements: television, trailer parks, and his waitress girlfriend, Rayette, who wants nothing more than to marry him and to sing like popular country-music artist Tammy Wynette. Discovering his father has suffered a series of strokes, Bobby returns to his family home on a private island in Puget Sound, joined there (despite his reluctance) by Rayette, the film thus revealing only halfway through that Bobby left his family of renowned musicians and a promising career as a pianist for traffic jams and hard labor. Largely, however, he resents both worlds, which continue to clash throughout the remainder of the film.

Bobby's liminal position between his adopted blue-collar life and his upper-middle-class roots allows a critique of social identity across cultural and generational groups. Derek Nystrom argues that Bobby's working-class face is "less a signifier of his own identity, than it is a perspective from which to analyze and critique middle class existence" (32). I would add, however, that the reverse is also true: his upper-middle-class identity also works as a perspective from which to critique working-class life. Although Bobby often adopts one or another social-class mask when it is most beneficial, he largely rejects them no matter which class, upper or lower, they represent.

Despite the joy Bobby draws from dominating the working class at their own games and pleasures, his working-class job and domesticity are depicted as trailer and traffic-jam prisons. His entrapment in a Los Angeles traffic jam best displays this simultaneous critique of both upper and working classes. Several scholars (Nystrom 30–6; Schroeder 125–6). have previously argued that this scene demonstrates Bobby's ability to transcend the irritants of working-class life using his embodied cultural capital. When Bobby and Elton (Billy 'Green' Bush), his co-worker at the oilfields, are caught in the traffic jam its obvious constriction is matched by their tightly framed two-shot. The only negative space of the frame comes from the empty, fast-moving traffic going the other direction. Bobby quickly directs his angry outbursts not at the traffic jam itself or the pleasure-seeking exploits – gambling, copious drinking, late-night womanizing – that caused the foreman to remove him from work and subjected him to this torture, but rather at the "crazy" working-class people around him, whom he "can't believe start their day like this . . . [spending] the most beautiful part of the day" surrounded by the claustrophobic highway and migraine-inducing car horns that also cast blame at the other drivers. Bobby subsequently leaves his car and tries to find an exit route, climbing on top of a covered piano in the back of a moving-truck ahead of his vehicle. After seeing the next freeway exit, Bobby decides to uncover the piano and perform.

When Bobby incongruously plays Chopin's "Fantasy in F Minor," exuding his elevated social status, *Pieces* does appear to support his transcendence from working-class inconvenience. It is only when he climbs on top of the piano that Bobby notices the freeway exit, and only after he begins to lose himself in the music that the truck carries Bobby out of the pit of cars. The film also visually suggests that Bobby's piano skills loosen the confines of this working-class prison. He is positioned in the open air above the surrounding cars, and is freer than Elton, to whom Rafelson continually cross-cuts, tightly framed in his car, mimicking Bobby's piano playing like an excited chimpanzee clapping and yelling with excitement. Bobby's own barking at the dog in a neighboring car parallels Elton's animalistic actions, insinuating here, as Rafelson does in other films, that the working-class have animalistic tendencies. However, Bobby's cultural upbringing makes it possible for him, as it seems, to escape the freeway.

In a diner, Bobby famously outsmarts a complex of restrictive rules and the stickler waitress who enforces them but still does not get the side order of toast that he wanted; similarly, his cultural capital does get him out of the traffic jam but his protest is ultimately a fruitless action that does not position Bobby in a superior or beneficial situation. As soon as the truck he was riding on exits the freeway, the rest of the traffic begins to move without any sign of stopping again: only Bobby is in prison. The truck also delivers Bobby far beyond his intended destination, eventually dropping him off in a grungy part of the city outside a porn theater. His cultural capital might allow him to outwit waitresses and win a hand of cards, or soothe himself briefly with Chopin, but as a negotiation of class issues it leads nowhere productive. The working class might be animalistic and constricting, but the upper-middle-class intellectuals and artists in the film are also nothing but hollow statues filled with meaning-less cultural capital. Bobby's paralyzed and mute father best embodies this stereotype, and, as is insinuated by a neck brace he must wear, his brother Carl is on a similar path toward immobility.

Though *Five Easy Pieces*'s rather reductive negation of class identity and affiliation generally views both sides in negative light, the film eventually abandons the critique altogether. In this way, Rafelson seeks to transcend collective identities, ultimately emphasizing the romantic individualism of the artist – indeed, the auteur. One way this evasion occurs is through the film's "self-consciously elliptical narrative strategy," including a radical ending and other filmmaking techniques now iconic of New Hollywood, associating the director with the "privileged" class status of auteurs and artists (Nystrom: 35–7). Yet the film's ending is also romantic in its existential individualism. As a part of his authorial interpretation, Rafelson imagined Bobby as a stand-in for himself: it is self-obsession and self-blaming, rather than class, that define the film's ending. After examining himself closely in a gas station mirror (something he did once as an oil worker at the beginning of the film and once again on returning to his family home), Bobby leaves his wallet with Rayette in the car and hitchhikes, presumably on his way to Canada. Bobby's literal abandonment of his identification papers and his country act as a metaphor for the abandonment of his accumulated social self. But this situation in *Five Easy Pieces* is better classified as a self-alienation, as he is welcome in and can freely socialize with social circles up and down, appearing alien neither in the dusty denim of the oilfields nor among the fitted suits of his Puget Sound brethren. Bobby's alienation from and rejection of social classes ends up being rooted in a personal existential crisis; as Catherine (Susan Anspach) – Carl's fiancé and protégé with whom Bobby has a short affair – tells him the problem is him, not the apparent class issues surrounding them – squandering any truly productive negotiation of culture or class in the film.

A quick comparison of *Five Easy Pieces* with *The King of Marvin Gardens* supports a view of Rafelson eluding class critique. *Gardens* follows David Staebler (Jack Nicholson) as he attempts to help his brother Jason (Bruce Dern) in an obviously impossible get-rich scheme to build a resort in Hawaii. Set in a financially decaying Atlantic City before its casino-based revitalization, the brothers spend most of the film pretending they are successful businessmen that live like kings. This is most strikingly suggested when they ride white horses on the beach against the backdrop of the hard-hit city despite having to squat in a once-extravagant suite of the Marlborough-Blenheim hotel which no longer has even hot water. As the title insinuates, the brothers never had a chance at social mobility: they are not even the rulers of a child's board game. If anything, they are the kings of only a cheap and relatively worthless Monopoly property.

Five Easy Pieces and *King of Marvin Gardens* are stylistically, narratively, and thematically consistent. Through their episodic, elliptical narratives both films create thematic isolation and show personal failure in relationships and identity formation. Unlike *Pieces*, however, critics found *Gardens* too didactic, bleak, and unstructured. Most pertinently, like *Five Easy Pieces*, the ending of *Gardens* undermines any negotiation of class hierarchies through another self-reproaching, primarily existential, ending. Like Bobby in *Pieces* confessing to his awake but completely debilitated father, *Garden* ends with David confessing his personal failures to an unresponsive radio audience. And, in place of

Bobby's introspection in a mirror David later reflects upon his past and current life when he watches a 16mm film of himself and his brother as children playing carelessly at the beach. This film within the film, which his grandfather plays mourning Jason's death, is briefly projected directly into David's eyes, underscoring its role in his self-examination. Rafelson's pre-occupation with placeless, self-failing individuals once again takes primacy over collective issues seemingly at the film's center. With this shot, Rafelson again underscores David's realization that the brothers' problems were the result not of social inequality but of their naive inability to differentiate "hand-guns from water pistols," the real from the imaginary, and their incessant childlike fantasies of imagining meaningless kingdoms, whether a hotel in Hawaii or their sand castle in the home movie.

New Directions

The director's reconceptualization of authorship articulated in 1976 involved two significant changes to the visual style of his films: the elimination of both solid-color openings and static exterior shots. While these changes might seem trivial at first glance, Rafelson's reliance on these tactics tells us much about his contemporary conceptions of authorship. While discussing the role of opening his BBS films with a full screen of solid color (the yellow-orange inside of a backhoe in *Five Easy Pieces*; complete darkness in *The King of Marvin Gardens*), Rafelson mocked a vision of authorship that aligned with the conventions of auteurism, joking that he nevertheless ironically adhered to it while making the films. He told the audience at the AFI,

> Somebody once started to talk to me about auteurism, which I really don't know very much about. I decided that I would open up every picture with a solid color. Years later they can say, 'Ah, now we recognize that all these pictures were made by the same person...' I discarded this useful guide to my work in this last picture. No solid color opening. No Auteur. (44)

Despite their seeming flippancy toward authorial continuity, Rafelson's comments on his opening shots illuminate both his deliberate and meaningful changing personal conceptions of authorship and his ambivalence toward auteurism, especially regarding the importance of aesthetic continuity across his work. He explained the relationship between his solid color opening image and auteurism in more detail in *Positif* in 1978. There he suggested that the specific opening ensured obvious continuity among his works and authorial image:

If, in my first three films, I used this procedure, it is because I never would have imagined a spectator capable of seeing that the exact same sensibility about color functioned identically in all three films – at the same time allowing true amateurs to comment that Rafelson begins his films with an empty colored image. (Tato 31).[2]

The latter half of Rafelson's quote critiques what he deems a naive utilization of auteur criticism: the act of merely identifying the continuous elements across a filmmaker's work. This function still has benefit, but the true merit of this approach, according to Rafelson, is that such continuities signal and remind viewers that a single artistic understanding – in this case about color – cuts across numerous films. In other words, Rafelson valued these continuities as artistically important because they reminded viewers that his "unique" authorial sensibility was present in one film after another. This signaling played to critics' expectations as appeasement. Simply identifying these stamps of authorship by pointing out the similar colored openings was the superficial yet seemingly necessary layer that appeased critics looking for continuity. More importantly, however, the approach was also a sincere plea for artistic recognition. Asserting his authorial ownership in this way invited viewers to try to understand certain aspects of his films (e.g. color) as he did himself. Indeed, despite joking that they were empty signaling devices to appease critics, Rafelson took these continuities very seriously, affirming his romantic sense of authorial singularity. With his BBS films Rafelson used almost only static exterior shots, rationalizing his reliance with the authorial mantra that any scene can be filmed properly from only one vantage point that the director, and only he, could discover and decide upon (Tato 30).[3] Rafelson trusted this singular-perspective strategy so intensely that he threatened to break (or, in some retellings, chop off) cinematographer László Kovács's fingers if he dared to move the camera (Rafelson 45).

With *Stay Hungry*, Rafelson distanced himself from the techniques and approaches he had previously protected with threats of violence, and true to his decentering claims he never again pushed so aggressively for autobiography in his films. Instead, the director claimed that with *Stay Hungry* he would center the needs of the narrative and its characters. For example, he now vowed to motivate his camera movement solely by the action of the characters (Taylor 1976: 204). When asked in 1976 to justify his previous reliance on static exterior shots he said he now considered them empty gestures:

I had consciously to break myself of the habit, which I had come to think of as a conceit, and be much more flexible with my camera movement outdoors, since there was going to be much more action in the film. (Taylor 204)

When asked several different times during the same year to recall why he had adhered so stringently to this particular schema, Rafelson claimed to have forgotten: "It was for a very specific reason, though such reasons tend to dissipate as you look backwards and it comes to seem just as a stylistic flourish" (Taylor 203). What Rafelson dismisses here as a fanciful expression, he described as "heavy-handed" to *Film Comment* in 1976 and would retrospectively criticize derogatorily during the late 2000s, calling his flashiness "stupid," "absurd," "vain," "grandiose . . . egotistical and superficial," "very self-congratulatory . . . theoretical," and "too studied and arrogant" (Farber 4; Rafelson; Tonguette). By eradicating these techniques, Rafelson eliminated the "useful guide to his work" that he previously believed signaled his authorial presence and artistic sensibility to viewers. These changes, which perhaps go unnoticed by all but auteur critics invested in pointing out stylistic patterns and autobiographical references, were actually to him a radical decentering of his authorship of the film, and a loss of self-assurance. He was no longer so concerned that viewers could recognize that his own artistic sensibility and viewpoint necessarily guided a film.

Rafelson's gradual devaluing of authorial centrality was also tied to changing trends in Hollywood. During the mid-1970s, Rafelson believed that the dawning blockbuster era brought a lose-lose situation for "personal" filmmaking, only inviting attackers and making directorial autonomy impossible (Rafelson 11, 53). Perhaps Rafelson sincerely agreed that his authorship had been problematically self-obsessed, but if he did not change as a director and make less "personal" films – or at least appear to do so – he would likely be out of work. His directorial changes were thus as much as anything an act of economic self-preservation intended to dispel his auteur association.

Despite Rafelson's intentions to direct his films with more basis in the motivations of the characters, a close examination of *Stay Hungry*, especially its off-kilter, spectacle-filled ending, proves that rather than abandoning them he reconceptualized his practices of authorial centrality. These changes involved Rafelson dropping his signaling continuities, both in terms of style and autobiography, thus appearing less "personal" – less like an auteur according to his previous ideas.

His new ideas about cinematic authorship did, however, have consequences for his representation of inter-class conflict. *Stay Hungry*, like Rafelson's other often-cited films of the decade, embodies a timely class critique. Based on a book by the same name by Charles Gaines and noted for featuring the first dramatic film roles by Arnold Schwarzenegger and Sally Field, *Stay Hungry* resembles *Five Easy Pieces* in its story. In *Stay Hungry*'s "dropping out" narrative another upper-class young man, Craig Blake (Jeff Bridges), rejects his affluent and cultured upbringing and moves away from his family. However, the film begins with the death of Craig's parents; he has returned to their estate. Seemingly continuing to defect from their lifestyle and the money he has inherited, Craig denies ownership of their home and refuses to use his former bedroom in the usual way. Instead, he literally camps out there, sleeping on a mattress on the floor surrounded by his fishing and hunting equipment. Craig then joins a real-estate cartel trying to inconspicuously buy enough land in downtown Birmingham, Alabama to develop a mega-skyscraper. As part of this scheme, Craig is sent to buy the Olympic gym owned by Thor (R. G. Armstrong), known as the training place of Joe Santo (Arnold Schwarzenegger), a bodybuilder whom Thor had brought into the country to win the Mr. Universe contest. Craig quickly befriends Santo and the quirky cast of Southern working-class characters in his posse, including Mary-Tate (Sally Field), a receptionist at the gym who becomes Craig's girlfriend throughout most of the film.

Despite establishing a narrative of conflict centered around buying the gym and Santo's winning the contest, *Stay Hungry* is largely made up of episodic inter-class conflict between Craig, his upper-class clique, and his new working-class friends. These scenes do include moments of genuine pleasure and uncritical appreciation of working-class leisure. Largely, however, the film uses Craig's adopted inter-class identity to critique and often mock both upper (-middle) and working classes. Like Bobby in *Pieces*, *Hungry*'s Craig never truly defects from the world of affluence. This is evident from his camping in his parents' mansion. Instead of the showing his indoor camping as an indication of genuine adoption of the Southern working-class culture and a truly defiant act against his upper-class roots, Rafelson gradually reveals a continuation of the cozy camping entrenched in the socio-cultural (and economic) capital of big-game hunting. Craig might be sleeping on the floor, but he surrounds himself with thousands of dollars of hunting and fishing equipment and décor, including nearly a dozen fishing rods and gold statuettes adorning the fireplace.

Like other visual and narrative depictions of inter-class conflict in the film, the realization of Craig's insincerity comes largely at the expense and objectification of working-class women, whose sexuality Rafelson positions visually as the ultimate big-game trophy. After Craig and Mary-Tate have sex for the first time, she awakens in his bedroom, surrounded by outdoor gear. Mary-Tate stares at the many trophies and pictures of Craig with enormous trout, tuna, and bear that hang over the fireplace, each celebrating "the new experiences" he gathered during the past two years. Instead of adopting her point of view here, Rafelson shows these trophies in close-up from Craig's perspective, that is, from behind Mary-Tate's head. There is then a cut to a much wider point-of-view shot of Mary-Tate's naked body set against the backdrop of arrows and taxidermy animals, a composition clearly suggesting early on in the film that more than a businessman, Craig is a "white hunter," as Mary-Tate playfully refers to him (Fig. 18.2). A cruder use of this metaphor comes later, after Thor has sex with Mae (Laura Hippe), the prostitute

Figure 18.2   Framed against awards and pictures hung across the fireplace, Rafelson depicts sex with Mary-Tate (Sally Field) as Craig's newest hunting conquest in *Stay Hungry* (1976). Digital frame enlargement. Courtesy of Outov/United Artists.

sent as a bribe by the real-estate cartel. Mae hangs from her feet from a machine meant for vertical crunches, her hands swaying lifelessly below her. Here, Rafelson takes the revolting visual metaphor further, as Mae appears much like a hanging slaughtered deer draining of blood (we must wait for subsequent scenes to learn that Mae is alive). Thor even uses a bench-press bar like a spear to push Mae's lifeless body. Though Craig and Thor play disparate villainous roles in the film, Rafelson depicts sexual engagement in *Stay Hungry* not as a unification of class members but as a conquest of working-class women, who are animalized and portrayed as defenseless and gullible.

Craig also mocks his own social roots and values, as he and Mary-Tate play dress-up in the Blake mansion (Fig. 18.3). About half-way through *Stay Hungry*, the two flirtatiously dress in mismatched luxurious clothing. Craig tries on a jumble of club-house and formal wear, combining a tuxedo hat and jacket with wrinkled grey-khakis and an untucked blue button-down. Similarly, Mary-Tate clutches a Southern sunhat and wears a satin and lace night-shirt, overtop a hoopskirt meant to go underneath a formal dress. Throughout the scene the two impersonate robots, a corset-wearing mannequin in the mansion and a Frankensteinian monster. Although the beginning low-angle pan-down replicates the visual clichés of a royal ball entrance, Craig and Mary-Tate's severely unfitted, disheveled, incomplete formal clothes and their impersonations undercut the visual glamour, characterizing this material-driven world of

Figure 18.3   Mimicking the mannequin in the background, in *Stay Hungry* (1976) Craig (Jeff Bridges) and Mary-Tate (Sally Field) parody aristocratic fashion and mannerisms while playing dress up in the Blake estate. Digital frame enlargement. Courtesy of Outov/United Artists

Figure 18.4 The concluding moments of *Stay Hungry* (1976) capture in the style of Victorian silhouettes the renewed relationship of Craig' (Jeff Bridges) and Mary-Tate (Sally Field). Digital frame enlargement. Courtesy of Outov/United Artists

the upper class as rigid, emotionless, and lifeless, one to which they do not (or are at least trying not to) belong. Whereas Mary-Tate's clothes further drive home that she truly does not belong in this milieu other than for sex, Craig's again reveal his façade. The severely unfitting clothes she wears are clearly not her own and are so loose that Craig's light tug sends them cascading off, revealing her simple underwear. Craig's, in comparison, fit nicely, lacking only the polish of being pressed and tucked in.

In the film's most ironic moment, the only apparent upholder of the Blake family's upper-class values is William (Scatman Crothers), the African American family butler of fifty-two years who comparatively fits nicely into his tuxedo. Seeing their dress-up, William immediately quits, on the grounds that the apparent lack of respectability brings dishonor to the family. William's reactions lend credence to Craig's attempted defection and interest in working-class people, as Craig's actions have evidently propelled him down the social latter even in the eyes of the family's African American butler. However, as another upholder of class values, like the Dupea family in *Pieces*, William is characterized as comically rigid. Before storming out he promises to take his medieval armor, a gift from Craig's late parents, which, placed by the front door, acts as a decoration for the estate's foyer. William's continued desire for the armor suggests that his values are as anachronistic, socially immobile, and impractical as the ancient protection that primarily serves as a show-boat of material accumulation. As in a later country-club scene, which ends with Craig and Mary-Tate's break-up, Rafelson clearly indicates that these social groups cannot productively cohabitate or transfer without some degree of self-benefiting manipulation, usually on the part of the upper class. This implication that there is no mutually beneficial relationship between classes is common to all of Rafelson's works of the 1970s, despite the inconsistent endings of *Pieces* and *Gardens*.

Working with Gaines, Rafelson added several new ancillary characters, most prominently the shady group of businessmen and their real-estate subplot. The most significant divergence from the book, however, was the ending. Unlike other changes, alterations to the conclusion came because of Rafelson's demands alone (though all accounts indicate that Gaines happily conceded). Rafelson was most determined to change the book's bleak, alienating, and actually rather New-Hollywood-like ending. In the novel, Thor throws Mary-Tate to her death from a window, after which, according to Rafelson, "Blake remains basically unaffected by his experiences. He is in fact what [Mary-Tate] accuses him of being: a user of people" (Rafelson "Bob Rafelson" 40). This ending – which Rafelson "saw as the closest resemblance to my previous films" – was the element he initially most rejected and, after agreeing to direct the picture, was most determined to change (Taylor 204).

Rafelson concludes *Hungry* with an utter and surprising reconciliation among social classes. Craig stops Thor's attempted rape of Mary-Tate, after which the couple sells the Blake family mansion, packs up the family portraits with William's help, and begins life together as the film concludes. During the final minutes of *Stay Hungry*, William inexplicably now approves their romantic union and Craig's adopted rural working-class lifestyle. William even intends to open a thrift shop using any tradable object left to him from the Blake estate. Suddenly no longer the ironic upholder of class values – also suggested by his Hawaiian shirt – William doesn't see his previous lifestyle as viable or beneficial to Craig or himself. Even the material possessions William held dear during the role-playing sequence now resemble unwanted hand-me-downs fit for a thrift shop rather than a museum.

Rafelson desired an optimistic ending not because he believed the story deserved or necessitated one or because he simply wanted to create a film different from his previous work. Instead, in another effort to foreground a new authorial image, Rafelson stated he wanted *Hungry* to project his "exhilarating" sense of personal happiness. This elated state paradoxically stemmed from abandoning his previous conception of authorship which had him "unnecessarily terrified" to make a non-"unique" film (Taylor 204). Rafelson always explained these changes to the ending as having solely emanated from his emotional state: "At any rate I did not relent in my feelings about wanting to make a more optimistic film and express that aspect of myself" (Taylor 204). In fact, he also told *Film Comment* that he saw *Hungry* as an opportunity to dramatize his own feelings of "joy and ecstasy" (Farber 2). During the promotion of *Stay Hungry*, Rafelson was embarrassed to admit that he did not realize the similarities in story and class depictions to those of his two previous films until critics and audiences pointed them out ("Bob Rafelson" 2). Rafelson was discomforted by these similarities because he had deliberately adapted *Stay Hungry* to radically diverge from its source material and, more importantly, his previous authorial image.

For many contemporary reviewers, Rafelson's authorial insistence ruined the film. *Stay Hungry*'s ending reminded *Los Angeles Times*'s Charles Champlin of other forcefully imposed Hollywood "happy-ever-afters," and *Christian Science Monitor*'s David Sterritt affirmed that Rafelson could have worked "on a more convincing ending [for] the last five minutes are the weakest and the silliest in the movie, undercutting its skeptical but persuasive view of people and pleasures" (G1; 23). In general, critics found it unmotivated and representing a socio-cultural message at odds with what was suggested by the remainder of the film. The ending also includes the most clichéd and formalistic cinematography in *Stay Hungry*. In the final frame before the credits begin, Rafelson depicts Craig and Mary-Tate in an extremely backlit close-up with heavy shadows covering their faces, a shot reminiscent of framed Victorian silhouettes: a historically common way to celebrate the image of the affluent family that the film and its characters ultimately disavow (Fig. 18.4). In addition, the credit announcing "a film by Bob Rafelson" features the most exuberantly expressionistic composition in the film: body-builders posing on the criss-crossing fire escape of the Lyric Theater, a former vaudeville theater

Figure 18.5   A group of body builders flex on top of the intricate fire escape of the Lyric Theater, a former vaudeville theater in Birmingham, Alabama, in *Stay Hungry* (1976). Digital frame enlargement. Courtesy of Outov/United Artists.

in Birmingham, which bends in all the right places as if to flex itself (Fig. 18.5) just the way they're doing.

Surprisingly, Rafelson agreed with his critics even when promoting the initial release of the film, showing signs that he too found the ending absurd. At times, he veiled his concern behind a half-hearted belief that the ending straddled the edge of psychological realism and farce:

> There is that kind of challenge to see what would happen if the Martians landed, so to speak. This is not unlike, I suspect, the way people's lives are lived all the time: we are despairing and ecstatic in various degrees from moment to moment and day to day. (Taylor 204)

Surely, social conventions of realism allow for a wide latitude of unexpected situations and variations of psychological motivation, but having "Martians land" with only five-minutes left in a film that Rafelson himself often described as "naturalistic" presents a narrative shock far too disjointed from the remainder of the film to be considered anything but extremely peculiar. Rafelson explicitly discussed the absurdity of the ending with the AFI in 1976, admitting that he seriously considered cutting most of the ending despite his authorial reasons for creating it (40).

The ending does certainly qualify as farce, just as Rafelson feared. Eliminating the ending, however, would have meant sacrificing the underlying authorial intentions Rafelson had for *Stay Hungry*. But it also meant that he ludicrously disrupted the tone of the film: "Did you see the end sequence?" he rhetorically asked the AFI audience. "There were many images like that, and I just felt that it was going too far. But I do change" (43). For Rafelson, authorial differentiation and emotional expression outweighed classical motivation, cohesive storytelling, and class critique. Changing his previously entrapping conception of authorship left Rafelson with an overzealous sense of happiness; but instead of truly decentering himself from *Stay Hungry*, Rafelson let his dramatized emotions overtake the film, despite his own subtle regrets about ruining its tone and narrative arc – again, a romantic individualism rises to the fore.

However, I would argue that *Hungry*'s ending inadvertently completes the class critique that critics believed Rafelson abandoned at the film's conclusion. In relation to what comes before it, the ending is narratively and stylistically contradictory and inauthentic. Although *Stay Hungry*'s conclusion superficially disavows upper-class values and unites characters from both ends of its class spectrum, this occurs after Rafelson abandons all of the film's narrative conflicts, turning instead to the cathartic consumption of male bodies posing in the street and expressionistic cinematography. This also leads to the incongruous positioning of Craig and Mary-Tate as both abandoning and typifying affluent culture through a vignette shot. Just as unbelievable as all this is, so too is the unification of class groups in the conclusion. This reconciliation is especially unbelievable because it happens without any further conflict, learning experiences, or negotiation. Rafelson worked so hard to show his personal happiness that the conclusion inadvertently turned to farce. As a result, the class unification seems just as farcical. Consequently, Rafelson's overdetermined exuberance unintentionally allows New Hollywood's iconic disillusionment to inhabit a happy ending.

Rafelson gave no indication throughout the remainder of the decade of how he planned to calibrate his overcorrected approach to authorship. What we can see from the 1970s work is that his constant search to grow as a "unique" artist involved battles between his competing understandings of authorship – affected by pressures from critics, his understanding of auteurism, and the industrial shift favoring blockbusters. It also involved his failing to discover his ideal authorial relationship to his films, with each iteration affecting their preoccupation with class conflict in sometimes widely unexpected ways. Rafelson's struggles also help scholars get beyond using the word "auteur" to blanket over more nuanced, idiosyncratic, ambivalent, and ever-changing conceptions of what a "personal" film is.

NOTES

1. Unlike *Stay Hungry*, *The King of Marvin Gardens* has recently received some scholarly attention. See, Kirshner 70–7; Webb 100–25.
2. *De toute façon si dans mes trois premiers films j'ai utilisé ce procédé, c'est parce que je n'aurais jamais imaginé un spectateur capable de voir que le même type de sensibilité de couleur fonctionnait de façon identique dans les trois films tout en donnant quand même le plaisir aux vrais amateurs de s'exclamer que Rafelson commence toujours par une image colorée et vide.*
3. *La mise en place des images mais je crois qu'une scène ne peut être bien filmée que d'un seul point de vue, et c'est moi qui dois le trouver.*

WORKS CITED

Boyer, Jay. *Bob Rafelson: Hollywood Maverick*. Twayne, 1996.
Brackman, Jacob. "Five Easy Pieces." *Film 70/71*, edited by David Denby, Simon & Schuster, 1972, pp. 33–9.
Champlin, Charles. "'Stay Hungry' Stays Loose." *Los Angeles Times*, 12 May 1976:G1.
Corrigan, Timothy. "Auteurs and the New Hollywood." *The New American Cinema*, edited by Jon Lewis, Duke University Press, 2004, pp. 38–63.
Farber, Stephen. "Yesterday's Heroes, Today's Has-Beens?" *New York Times*, 7 Jan. 1973, p. 135.
Hildebrand, Douglas. "Bob Rafelson." *Contemporary North American Film Directors: A Wallflower Critical Guide*, edited by Yoram Allon, Del Cullen, and Hannah Patterson, Wallflower, 2002, pp. 435–6.
Johnson, Bryan. "Rafelson Shows his Muscle." *The Globe and Mail*, 17 Aug. 1976, p. 13.
Kirshner, Jonathan. *Hollywood's Last Golden Age: Politics, Society, and the Seventies Film in America*. Cornell University Press, 2013.
Menne, Jeff. "The Cinema of Defection: Auteur Theory and Institutional Life." *Representations*, vol. 114, no. 1, 2011, pp. 36–64.
Mitchell, Bob. "On Location with Stay Hungry." *American Cinematographer*, vol. 57, no. 2, Feb. 1976, pp. 170–236.
Nystrom, Derek. "Hard Hats and Movie Brats: Auteurism and the Class Politics of the New Hollywood." *Cinema Journal*, vol. 43, no. 3, 2004, pp. 18–41.
Rafelson, Bob. "Bob Rafelson: An American Film Institute Seminar on His Work." *The American Film Institute Seminars*, pt. 1, no. 138. 19 May 1976.
Rafelson, Bob. "Rafelson x 15" and "Reflections on a Philosopher King." *The King of Marvin Garden*. Criterion Collection, 2010. DVD.
Schroeder, Andrew. "The Movement Inside: BBS Films and the Cultural Left in New Hollywood." *The World the Sixties Made*, edited by Van Gosse and Richard Moser, Temple University Press, 2003, pp. 114–37.
Sterritt, David. "'Stay Hungry': Quirky, Flawed." *The Christian Science Monitor*, 10 May 1976, p. 23.
Tato, Anna Maria, and Bob Rafelson. "Entretien Avec Bob Rafelson." *Positif*, May 1978, pp. 27–33.
Taylor, John Russell. "Staying Vulnerable: An Interview with Bob Rafelson." *Sight and Sound*, 1976, pp. 200–4.
Tonguette, Peter. "Bob Rafelson and His Odd American Places." *The Film Journal*, 25 Mar. 2005, web.archive.org/web/20050324061241/http://www.thefilmjournal.com:80/issue11/rafelson.html. Accessed 26 August 2019.

Warga, Wayne. "Tune in as Bob Rafelson Answers Some Questions." *Los Angeles Times*, 25 Oct. 1970, p. 122.

Webb, Lawrence. "New Hollywood in the Rust Belt: Urban Decline and Downtown Renaissance in *The King of Marvin Gardens* and *Rocky*." *Cinema Journal*, vol. 54, no. 4, 2015, pp. 100–25.

19. WE'VE NEVER DANCED: ALAN RUDOLPH'S *WELCOME TO L.A.* AND *REMEMBER MY NAME*

Steven Rybin

It is a clear day in Los Angeles. In a taxicab, passenger Karen Hood (Geraldine Chaplin) gazes toward the camera, addressing a viewer who might also listen. She speaks of love, and of amorous deception. Is Karen Hood herself a deception, an illusion? She intones her words nearly catatonically, as if channeling some ghost from the past; and she is dressed in fur and a neat red beret, a charming try at high society chic. Later in the film, she will go to see Greta Garbo again, in *Camille* (1936); her pleasure here in the taxi and elsewhere is in play, in taking on the image of her favorite screen diva. Karen Hood is just one of several characters in Alan Rudolph's *Welcome to L.A.* (1976) who present themselves through artifice, all while asking questions about the love an artistic gesture or pose might reach. Retrospectively, it is not difficult to imagine Rudolph's entire body of work sitting in the backseat here, next to Karen, looking right at us and musing wistfully likewise. Rudolph's films are always probing the question of how romantic relationships secure permanence in insecure and unhinged worlds, and they are even more fascinated by how love is sought through performance, as private gestures and expressions yearn to become, as the seconds tick into the fullness of a social role, a show that might touch another person. From *Welcome to L.A.* and *Trouble in Mind* (1985) to *Mrs. Parker and the Vicious Circle* (1994), from *Made in Heaven* (1987) and *The Moderns* (1988) to *Afterglow* (1997) and *The Secret Lives of Dentists* (2002), Rudolph's work is absorbed by questions of fantasy and the fashioning of self-image, and with how fantasy is made manifest for ourselves and for our audience. Rudolph is interested in the ways his characters articulate identity and fashion connection through different varieties of social encounter, the borders of which are not always firmly distinguished from private reverie.

Rudolph nearly always begins with moments of solitude. As the first frames of *Welcome to L.A.* project before us, Karen Hood is as nearly alone as it gets, driven by an unseen taxi driver and speaking to a viewer she can only *hope* to touch. She is a daydreamer, snuggly swathed in pretense but alert to the possibility that the physical and gestural reality her dreams take on might find resonance with one who views her. And she's willing to wait to discover that moment and that person, comfortable with the idea that her performance might not always reach its most suitable watcher right away. "It's how you wait that's important, I think," she continues. She's willing to bide her time in wait for a fellow dreamer. Like nearly all of the characters in the film, Karen, although indulging a lot in private musings, will want eventually to share these flights of fancy with someone else. But as will often happen in Rudolph's cinema she begins this search in a self-spun cocoon. She will be careful, from within this private space, about how her public expression of emotion is shaped, but she won't be quite able to determine how feeling is received: her look into the camera is both assured and vulnerable, sharply performative but also susceptible in its nakedness – for the watcher is perhaps a viewer who might not be sympathetic to her playing.

"Reality is a negotiable subject for me," Rudolph has commented ("Collaborating with the Master," A7), and it is negotiable for his characters, too, who are happy to play with what reality might mean or be, so long as they find a faithful friend or a worthwhile lover to serve as audience. A gentle sway to-and-fro between groundedness and swooning romance, between social connection and private self-involvement, between a precise point in space and the emotional haze that can come to surround it: this is the dance that the viewer joins in watching Alan Rudolph's films. It is the dance that the viewer, like the character, waits to join. (And it is a shame when it is missed, as Martha Davis sings in the elegiac "We've Never Danced," the Neil Young-penned track that soars over the end credits of Rudolph's *Made in Heaven*.) We are always at one instant *here*, shyly and somewhat detachedly, in the manner of an introverted wallflower surveying the edges of a space or a scene – the Parisian art world of *The Moderns*, or the working-class rock'n'roll world of *Roadie* (1980), the dystopian criminal underground of *Trouble in Mind*, the world of literati and cognoscenti in *Mrs. Parker and the Vicious Circle* – then, an instant later, *there*, suddenly swept up by dream: in a fantasy that we are actually inhabiting this space (that, actually, as it turns out, we are not quite so shy, and have made a connection) or *there* with the character who, although slightly detached from us, is nevertheless dreaming, too. That the characters share our dreaming is a further sign that the act of viewing Rudolph's films, as is also the case in the New Hollywood Cinema of Altman, Bogdanovich, and Scorsese, is always reflexively doubled in the films themselves, full of characters who may or may not get to dance with their fellow dreamers.

Much of what concerns Rudolph throughout his work is already present in his first two major feature films, *Welcome to L.A.* and *Remember My Name* (1978). These are the two films I focus on here, not only because their dates locate them in the decade of American filmmaking which is the primary focus of this collection but also because they provide the best evidence for an argument seeking to position Rudolph among the unacknowledged masters of the New Hollywood Renaissance. Rudolph has received some critical attention (most notably in the book-length study by Richard Ness, but also in scattered articles and essays; see also, for examples, Rybin and Sallitt), yet in most discussions of American cinema in the 1970s he remains something of an adjunct to his mentor, occasional collaborator, and friend Robert Altman. In fact, Altman's reputation has somewhat obscured Rudolph's contributions to the American cinema of this period. The connection critics make between Altman and Rudolph is justified, of course, given the frequent preference of both directors for eccentric ensemble casts, musical accompaniment implicitly commenting on the lives of characters, and a somewhat cynical outlook that frequently takes dead aim at illusory fantasies promised viewers by the film, music, and culture industries. And Rudolph's films, like Altman's, also often revise and critique traditional genre molds; *Welcome to L.A.* might be taken as a modern variation of the screwball comedy, while *Remember My Name* makes sly reference to melodramas and film noir of the 1940s (for a discussion of these genre antecedents, see Ness 9–10 and 23). Both *Welcome* and *Remember* might also be understood as Los Angeles-set reworkings of two film classics: the roundabout, circuitous paths toward love taken by the characters in *Welcome to L.A.* as a reimagining of Max Ophüls' *La ronde* (1950); and *Remember My Name* as an oblique rearrangement of Alfred Hitchcock's *Psycho* (1960), in which Anthony Perkins, rather than hunter, is prey.

And like Altman's, Rudolph's is a deceptive mastery, cloaked in modesty: in interviews he will often deflect attention towards his actors. But Rudolph – who was employed by Altman as an assistant director on *The Long Goodbye* (1973), *California Split* (1974), and *Nashville* (1975), and as co-screenwriter on *Buffalo Bill and the Indians* (1976) – has a sense of what distinguishes his work from that of his mentor. "I'm more shamelessly romantic than Bob," Rudolph has said in comparing his work with Altman's;

> I look within, Bob looks without. He has a much broader view of things, he understands the workings of a subject. I get involved in the moment-by-moment emotional range. That's why I'm not really good at plots. My little individuals add up to a whole, and Bob's whole gets down to individuals. (Rudolph 13)

And Rudolph's is a deeply romantic whole, a vision of the world emerging from intimate portraits of wayward individuals who nevertheless possess sharp personalities. He may indeed be the Hollywood Renaissance filmmaker most given to swoon (he is less cranky than Altman, less tormented than Scorsese, and lacks the acerbic bite of Woody Allen). Thus his tendency to interrogate genre forms through a lightly modernist stylization does not come at the expense of an earnest curiosity about the onscreen figures who mesmerize him. This fascination is a generous and accommodating one, too, for Rudolph can find sincere emotion in what initially appears affected or arcane. Whatever arch quality may exist in Geraldine Chaplin's imitations of Greta Garbo in *Welcome to L.A.*, for example, is diffused by the sincere emotions her character means to express through that imitation, the connection with the world Karen Hood yearns for beneath and through her performative engagement with reality. In this sense Rudolph is as much a part of the Hollywood Renaissance as he is an influence on later independent filmmakers, such as Wes Anderson and Hal Hartley, whose filmic stylizations and studied aesthetic sensibilities finally generate an emotional engagement with reality that, no matter their posturing, is sincere and grounded.

WELCOME TO L.A.

Chaplin's Karen Hood is part of an ensemble characters in *Welcome to L.A.*, a loosely plotted story about amorous possibilities in the city of angels. As is often the case in Rudolph's films, the director's interest goes beyond the preoccupations of one character as it collects emotional impressions from a variety of players. In *Welcome to L.A.* we also meet Keith Carradine (playing the bachelor songwriter Carroll Barber); Sally Kellerman (as a romantically desperate real estate agent, Ann Goode); Viveca Lindfors (Barber's manager and ex-lover, Susan Moore); Denver Pyle (Carradine's estranged father, successful businessman Carl Barber); Harvey Keitel (Ken Hood, employee of Pyle, and emotionally detached husband of Chaplin's character); and Sissy Spacek (Linda Murray, a young woman who cleans and cooks for some of the central characters), among others.

An impressive collection of eccentric, sharp actors: Keitel, young and handsome here although again mentally afflicted (not spiritually so as in Scorsese's 1973 *Mean Streets*, and far less violently so than he will be again two years later in James Toback's *Fingers* [1978]); Kellerman, a figure from Altman's *M*A*S*H* (1971), achingly vulnerable for Rudolph's camera; Spacek, three years off Terrence Malick's *Badlands* (1973) and contemporaneous with *Carrie* (1976) yet, with *Three Women* (1977) and *Coal Miner's Daughter* (1980) still to come, slipping out of adolescent parts with a casual, if still slightly innocent, sexiness; and Carradine, the swinging bachelor, confidently good-looking and with an observational detachment, as in Altman's *Nashville*, that complements his songwriter occupation. These are characters who exist in their own fantasies as much as they do in reality, and their dreamy way of being is shared by the film's sensibility, which exudes romantic yearning and a curious, loving patience for people who just like to sit and watch (sometimes in taxicabs, or in front of a movie screen).

This longing is already signified through an opening credits sequence presenting each character, above the name of the actor, in a series of photographic portraits. Over this opening sequence floats the voice of Carradine, singing the title song whose lyrics lament the shaky boundary between a precise grounding in space and a desire for an elsewhere. The singer describes the green boundaries and icy mists of Canada, viewed from 30,000 feet above in an airplane, which slowly recede from view as the figure in the song descends towards Los Angeles. But the music is also diffuse with a misty pining for something lost or somewhere else, "that wet December night" during which the lover left behind his paramour for another, imagined one (she might be in Los Angeles, the song muses). In the film, Carradine's songwriter has arrived in L.A. to sit in on a recording of his compositions. The music we hear is already something of a remaking of reality, though; Carroll Barber's music, in the story world of the film, doesn't quite exist this way, because, in the recordings of his work as distributed in record shops in the film's story world, he doesn't sing. He writes songs that a popular musician named Eric Wood (Richard Baskin) will perform, a musician who ambles silently (except when he is singing Carroll's songs) throughout the film, a sort of gangly Art Garfunkel figure whose fans (including Linda Murray, Spacek's character) are oblivious to Barber's authorship of the songs. Carradine's singing is quite like what Chaplin is doing in the taxicab as the film opens, giving a little performance in which words are wrapped around emotions, fleetingly communicating some nuance to one who might also be vulnerable enough to catch their meaning.

Rudolph's character-driven films don't have much in the way of plot, and so the question of how time might be filled – typically answered in a conventional way by most mainstream Hollywood films, that is, through cause-and-effect and goal-oriented action – is perpetually posed. Christian Keathley, in an essay on the breakdown of cause-and-effect in New Hollywood films of the seventies, suggests that many of the films of the period "explore a cinema predicated not on action, but on the possibilities inherent in the interval *between* perception and action" (294), an idea informed by Gilles Deleuze's concept of the "affection image." David Deamer has probed this idea of the affection image a bit further, finding in it a kind of "internal intensity" that takes flight from the face or body of a figure in a film but that eventually disperses into the surrounding world in which the figures perform, wherein "affects are simultaneously de-individualising in that they are creations of autonomous powers and qualities" (83). *Welcome to L.A.* is a film brimming over with affection – with characters who feel intensely. But they find themselves unable to directly target partners or friends with these emotions, unable, through a precise action, to take a feeling as if it were an arrow on a Cupid's bow that might reach a certain lover. Wary and hurt, they have been deceived before. So Rudolph's lovers let the affects slip away, unsure of where they might land. Instead of finalizing their feelings through a climactic kiss, these characters tend to express feeling in dispersive, contingent ways, radiating affection that only *might* be caught by another in response. Rudolph's viewer, of course, is an integral part of this emotional roundabout, as the direct look into the camera (a recurring motif performed by nearly all the characters in *Welcome to L.A.*) suggests.

Part of the pleasure of Rudolph's cinema is in tracing all the various ways the director finds to stage and restage his characters' tendency toward this "affective diffusion," and in ways that position his camera as a sensitive receptor of feelings uncertain of their final site of reception. The ways in which Karen Hood – the film's emblematic character – seeks to find emotional connection have already been suggested in my description of her opening monologue. If the opening sequence finds her looking to the audience for a partner, in the diegetic world of the film it is Keith Carradine's Carroll Barber who becomes both her potential lover and a viewer of her eccentric, performative mannerisms. Carradine first encounters Chaplin on the side of the street. As he drives up, she's jotting something down in her notepad, wearing the same red beret and fur coat she always wears in her taxi. He's curious, so he pulls up beside

Figure 19.1   Keith Carradine and Geraldine Chaplin in Alan Rudolph's *Welcome to L.A.* (1976). Digital frame enlargement. Courtesy of Lion's Gate.

her. Rudolph frames much of their conversation from the passenger side of the car, as Carradine looks out the window at Chaplin. Carradine asks if she wants a ride – a simple enough question, met with artifice. (Chaplin first pretends not to hear, and then claims she can't go with him because she can't drive.) Rather than communicate directly Karen prefers to perform, sliding into her Garbo cough (again an homage to the film she adores, *Camille*) as she looks back down at her notepad.

"I've just been to a movie and I was the only person there," she tells him. "It's nice when you're by yourself," Carradine suggests. Karen is not quite sure if it is nice. "Well – men always have a better time," she answers, cryptically; "Maybe it's because they understand the situation." Rudolph cuts to a shot of Carradine, inside the car; Barber is now carefully contemplating her words – she is saying more than that she had a good time at the movies. *Camille* is a part of her, and she would have liked to have someone with her there to share those affects radiating from the screen on which it was projected. Here, as Carradine lingers on Chaplin's words, it becomes apparent that Karen Hood is performing Garbo mannerisms so as to hold onto the passions of *Camille* that she caught while watching it. Perhaps, in lingering on and with her now, Carroll is trying to catch a few of Karen's feelings, too. She continues coughing; he offers her a drink from his whisky bottle, extending this moment of encounter but also perhaps trying to help her out with her cough – maybe he wants to soothe it, so he can find out who Karen Hood really is. But she insists on Garbo; the drink has merely improved her coughing, which she performs again. "It was so sad when she died at the end – Camille," Karen tells him; "she said – *Nanine* .... *Nanine* ..." As Karen cries for Marguerite's maid, Carradine watches, bemused. The emotions Karen generates for him here are a different bundle of affects than those Carroll has encountered elsewhere in the film. He'll romance Karen like the other women he will meet in *Welcome to L.A.*, but without the sex he finds with Sally Kellerman's Ann Goode (and has already enjoyed from Viveca Lindfors's Susan Moore): there is a kind of gentlemanly *politesse* with which Barber treats Karen, swooning but keeping her at a gentle distance.

Perhaps more than any other character in the film Barber knows how to adjust his self-presentation to different qualities of encounter. He is, after all, the one character who receives, or is the target of, the various affections secreted into the world by the film's characters. That *Welcome to L.A.* should end with Carradine's Barber gazing into the camera lens, after regaling the non-diegetic audience with one final performance of the title song in a lonely recording studio, suggests that all the emotional textures in *Welcome to L.A.* only finally find their home in Barber's songs, the characters having failed to find final connection or secure commitment in the world itself. Is there a sense, though, that what we are falling for here as we listen to this song is a kind of affectation, a solipsism, a further entrapment in "the affection-image"? Royal S. Brown, in a commentary on the use of music in Rudolph's work, suggests that the romantic quest of the Carradine character in *Welcome to L.A.* for a "'meaningful' relationship" ultimately "gives way to a narcissistic attainment of imagehood" (246), a transition emblematized for Brown by the end of the film, in which we see Barber walk into an empty studio to perform his song, ending the film with a gaze to the camera that collapses the distinction between Carradine the actor and Barber the character. But to suggest, as I have above, that the song is a final testament to the emotions expressed by the characters in *Welcome to L.A.* is a more optimistic way to regard the ending of the film, one that would contrast with the suggestion that Barber's musical performance amounts to nothing more than narcissistic self-involvement. Rudolph's characters offer their inner lives to the world. That those emotional lives have been received, at least, in the performance of a song (itself another offering), suggests that there may be a hope for Rudolph's romantics, even if love finally remains elusive for some of them.

Remember My Name

Welcome to L.A. lingers in moments of waiting, its characters performatively soliciting social response from within private little bubbles. Rudolph's next film, *Remember My Name*, carries on this theme with new, and darker, variations. Emily (Geraldine Chaplin, in her second of three collaborations with Rudolph) has made a life of waiting. As the film goes on, it is revealed that the twelve-year prison sentence she has just finished (at the beginning of the movie) was given to her as a result of the murder of her ex-husband's lover. Emily has done her time: waiting to leave prison; waiting to journey westward to Los Angeles (she has been in prison in New York City, where the murder occurred); waiting patiently (but with her own arcane methodology) to enact revenge on Neil Curry (Anthony Perkins), the husband whose jilting motivated her act of murderous passion. When the film begins Emily is in her car, driving westward, smoking a cigarette. (It is the first of several cigarettes she enjoys in this jaggedly languorous film.) Even before we see her face, which is initially kept out of frame, we know her through her hands, which manipulate the steering wheel and hold a cigarette, two expressive actions that signify a tension between forward movement (Emily driving, walking, stalking toward Neil) and languid waiting (the cigarette indicating her willingness to wait and breathe it in, to time her revenge for just the right moment).

Her smoking is a sign that Emily is ultimately quite different from the character played by Chaplin in *Welcome to L.A.* Where Karen Hood's arch conveyance of emotion dispersed itself in the general direction of the audience (or to Carroll), Emily prefers to linger in her own interiority, her smoking a sign that she is inclined to wait in ways that are private rather than socially performative. In stark contrast to that dispersion of emotions performed by characters in *Welcome to L.A.*, Emily is guarded and wary: far from scattering affects out into her world, she keeps them interiorized, her intentions only slowly becoming manifest in her often unpredictable gestures, movements, and expressions, which jut into the world with angularity and anger when this wronged woman is pushed to the brink. She thus remains entangled in "the affection-image," but she uses this entrapment to her advantage, finding in it a source of vengeful power. And even once her reasons for trailing Neil are known, they are not our primary reason for watching and being fascinated with Emily. More intriguing is her continued effort to play close to the vest, to keep her inner life from slipping out carelessly into the world.

And there's something strange about this retribution Emily appears to seek, a peculiarity that will register especially to contemporary audiences weaned on cathartic visions of vengeance typically unleashed in Hollywood cinema. Unlike most vengeful characters, whose motivations are often worn on sleeves, Emily keeps her reasons for stalking Neil close to her chest. Likewise Rudolph, his camera hovering alongside the scenes, hides its reason, not revealing until almost an hour into the movie that Emily is fresh out of prison after serving a dozen years for murdering the lover with whom Neil was cheating on her.

In Rudolph's other films this sort of self-containment is often contrasted to emotional nakedness and open vulnerability (of the kind exhibited by many of *Welcome to L.A.*'s fragile characters). In *Trouble in Mind*, for example, the impulsive and indulgent Coop (Keith Carradine) immerses himself in the criminal underworld of Rain City almost as soon as he arrives, styling himself as a glam-rock gangster and looking for action wherever he can find it. This eccentric and exteriorized behavior is thrown into relief against the gruff but stoic mannerisms of Hawk (Kris Kristofferson), an ex-con whose tough visage betrays a deeper desire to avoid more trouble. Rudolph's later film *Afterglow*, too, presents different kinds of emotional bearings expressed through varieties of performance. Both Lara Flynn Boyle's Marianne Byron and Julie Christie's Phyllis Mann suspect their respective husbands of infidelity but their physical responses to these qualms are distinct (Marianne takes to the neurotic rearrangement of furniture while Phyllis, a former actress, retires to her home to watch herself in old movies). *Remember My Name*, a sparse and measured work, intriguingly lacks these kinds of stark emotional contrasts so typical in Rudolph's other films: all of the characters keep their performance restrained and economical, staying on one side of public declaration and waiting carefully for the right moment, the right gesture, the right viewer.

Emily, indeed, has lithe ways of *not* being seen, of keeping private and guarded. Rudolph's camera joins her in this private dance. She ducks stealthily beneath window and shrub as she follows Neil's wife, Barbara (Berry

Figure 19.2   Neil Curry (Anthony Perkins) warily confronts Emily (Geraldine Chaplin) in *Remember My Name* (1978). Digital frame enlargement. Courtesy of Columbia Pictures.

Berenson), who puts groceries away while Emily watches, unseen. More pointedly in terms of the film's theme of romantic revenge, Emily will hover near the edges of the frame as she circles around Neil in the first half of the film, making her presence known to him only later in the movie when she dons a *femme fatale* get-up and begins patrolling his construction site. In this way, Emily plays with nearly everyone in the film, finding ways to appropriate space and manipulate perspective in relation to the camera in order to preserve her private and solitary place.

Halfway through the film, Emily is taking a cigarette break in an alley outside the department store where she works. She is framed in long shot, sitting down on a box next to a pile of pallets, the upper half of her back leaning against the exterior wall as her knees jut sharply out into the space in front of her. She is interrupted by one of the store's managers, who drives up on a moped, all false swagger. "How's it goin' sweetheart?" he says, like a dolt; as he backs the bike up to meet her eyeline, the camera begins to dolly in towards a slightly tighter long shot. Emily begins to engage him in mock flirtation, cradling her left arm around his torso, offering him a cigarette, telling him he smells nice; these little gestural *bons mots* are delivered by Chaplin as stock lines, spoken quickly and directly, stripped of all affection. Her words are short (although not so sweet) and sharp; she inflects dopey pick-up lines with an acutely critical sense of ironic detachment. Chaplin does all this to mask her character's intentions – Emily's real and earnest affects – just as Rudolph's camera, proceeding in towards a closer two-shot of Emily and the manager, begins to mask the lower half of Chaplin's body. This re-framing of the *mise-en-scène*, which draws our attention squarely to Chaplin's face and the cigarette she holds in her right hand, also serves to draw our attention away from her feet. Rudolph cuts back to a long medium shot, taken from the same angle, but still keeping Chaplin's lower half out of view. "Hang on tight," the manager says, revving up the bike; but when he drives off, he does so without her, for now Chaplin has placed her feet firmly back onto the ground. The moment registers as a slight surprise not because we think there is any chance of Emily riding off into the sunset with this fellow. Rather, what takes Rudolph's viewer delightfully and repeatedly aback, in many of his films but in this film especially, is the perpetually surprising manner in which he arranges his movie people physically, with Emily, throughout the film, repeatedly and unpredictably intervening into the world around her with sharp new positionings of body and inflections of gesture that the men (and indeed some of the other women) in *Remember My Name* never seem quite ready for.

Rudolph's characters, even in his later films made after the end of the New

Figure 19.3   Geraldine Chaplin as Emily in Alan Rudolph's *Remember My Name* (1978). Courtesy of Joyce Rudolph and Columbia/Lion's Gate.

Hollywood cinema as a historical moment, do not finally find their way out of the "affection image." Nevertheless, they retain and invent ongoingly intriguing ways of inhabiting it, occasionally slipping out of it, and slyly working within it. Ten years after *Remember My Name*, in *The Moderns,* he tells a story of Parisian socialites and artists who use paintings as a way either to cheat or connect with the world. A similar dynamic informs *Mrs. Parker and the Vicious Circle*, with the literary dandies of the infamous Algonquin Hotel Round Table using words to carve out a social distinction that is nevertheless not entirely bereft of earnest emotion. And in *The Secret Lives of Dentists* to focus on a suburban husband who suspects his wife of an extramarital affair Rudolph uses dream images that convey the husband's entrapment in despairing visions of cuckoldry. In these later films Rudolph carries on the emotional tenor and spirit of his earlier work, cementing his status as a unique and sensitive spirit in Hollywood Renaissance cinema long after its moment of emergence has passed.

Works Cited

Brown, Royal S. *Overtones and Undertones: Reading Film Music.* University of California Press, 2009.

Deamer, David. *Deleuze's Cinema Books: Three Introductions to the Taxonomy of Images.* Edinburgh University Press, 2016.

Keathley, Christian. "Trapped in the Affection Image: Hollywood's Post-traumatic Cycle (1970-1976)." *The Last Great American Picture Show*, edited by Thomas Elsaesser, Alexander Horwath, and Noel King, Amsterdam University Press, 2004, pp. 293–308.

Ness, Richard. *Alan Rudolph.* Twayne, 1996.

Rudolph, Alan. "Disneyland by Night." *Film Comment*, vol 13, no. 1, January/February 1977, pp. 10–13.

Rybin, Steven. "Great Directors: Alan Rudolph." *Senses of Cinema*, vol. 80, August 2016, www.sensesofcinema.com/2016/great-directors/alan rudolph/#fn-27745-6. Accessed 13 May 2020.

Sallitt, Dan. "Alan Rudolph, 1985." *Thanks for the Use of the Hall*, 19 August 2016, sallitt.blogspot.com.au/2016/08/alan-rudolph-1985.html. Accessed 13 May 2020.

20. JERRY SCHATZBERG'S DOWNFALL PORTRAITS: HIS CINEMA OF LONELINESS

R. Barton Palmer

Hollywood in the early 70s was eager for new directorial blood, and New York City's Jerry Schatzberg, a fashion and art photographer, fit the industry's bill perfectly. Some might even consider him the poster child for the Hollywood Renaissance as in part a movement of cultural realignment. Schatzberg's surprising, meteoric rise exemplifies Hollywood's openness to talented outsiders in its time of continuing troubles, especially to those with deal-making *chutzpah*, which Schatzberg possessed in abundance. Though entirely inexperienced in the film business, the fortyish New Yorker was a nationally prominent artist, whose reputation and connections were useful as he sought the director's chair, which he attained after only a bit of adroit maneuvering.

Schatzberg made the most that he could from the chance he was given. In the course of three years he undertook, developed, and completed three low-budget A projects, working quickly and efficiently with such well-known producers as John Foreman, Dominic Dunne, and Paul Newman, while obtaining domestic and overseas distribution through Universal: *Puzzle of a Downfall Child* (1970), *Panic in Needle Park* (1971), and *Scarecrow* (1973). Most remarkably, however, this newcomer made use of the services of emerging A-list performers: Faye Dunaway, Gene Hackman, Roy Scheider, and Al Pacino. His striking portraits (a sine qua non promotional item for celebrities at the time) gave him an important standing with the illuminati. He found himself much in demand. Even the occasional visitor took advantage of his services, as had been happening for years. He also shot Fidel Castro during the leader's notorious and frenetic two-week NYC sojourn in 1959.

By the end of the 60s, Schatzberg had become acquainted with many of the era's big names, including a fair number of stage and film actors. Among these was Dunaway, then living in New York and working sporadically on Broadway. The two moved in together and soon planned to marry. As will become evident, their relationship and its eventual dissolution figure as crucial elements of Schatzberg's best film, *Puzzle of a Downfall Child*, where the actress delivers what is arguably her finest screen performance. The Schatzberg films showcased her considerable talents, and those of Hackman, Scheider, and Pacino as well. He had a knack for eliciting the detailed, complex character portraits that his camera was always perfectly positioned to capture.

By the end of the sixties and beginning of the seventies, Hackman and Dunaway (once together) had appeared in several major Hollywood productions (*Bonnie and Clyde* [1967], *The Thomas Crown Affair* [1968], *Downhill Racer* [1969], and *I Never Sang for My Father* [1970]). Before 1975, along with Pacino, they would separately star in several of that brief era's most successful films (*The Deadly Trap* [1971 in France], *The Godfather* I and II [1972/1974], *The Conversation* [1974], *Night Moves* [1975], *Chinatown* [1974], and *Dog Day Afternoon* [1975]). Scheider's breakthrough role came shortly after *Puzzle* wrapped, with *The French Connection* (1971), followed that same year by a memorable character portrayal in *Klute* (1971). In one of the era's most memorable male ensembles he was featured in *Jaws* (1976), briefly the industry's all-time top earner, as well as in its sequel *Jaws II* (1978), another huge box-office success. Showing an amazing range of technique, he went on to deliver one of the most impressive Hollywood performances of the decade, the mercurial Bob Fosse type in the biopic *All that Jazz* (1979).

Dunaway, Hackman, and Pacino – it bears noting – are all on the record as praising Schatzberg's work with actors (see for example Ciment, Newland). It simply was not Scheider's style to praise directors. Instead, his film and television work was often marked by disputes and petulance; Steven Spielberg and William Friedkin found themselves at times in epic battles with the actor, so it is certainly noteworthy that Schatzberg collaborated smoothly with him. Perhaps the most striking element of Schatzberg's early career is that this newcomer to directing worked three times with actors who would go on to be among the most acclaimed and bankable performers of the era. Many established directors never had a single such opportunity, and that all four agreed to work with him offers indirect praise of his deal-making ability and personal magnetism. Even if they were not as aesthetically inventive and artistically successful as they are, Schatzberg's early films would be crucial to any account of this period (and indeed of the New Hollywood in general) simply because they feature carefully sculpted performances from four of the post-studio era's most significant performers.

In an important sense, Schatzberg was of course no neophyte. Directors need to have a good photographic eye and, if they work in studios with models, the ability to coach performance while at least helping to design the *mise-en-scène*. Directors also need to be competent managers, sensitive to many commercial realities, including the financial bottom line. Schatzberg had honed these skills during his decades in the highly competitive New York industry. He delivered his work on time and according to specification, and also achieved considerable success with gallery exhibition of his portraits of celebrities and nude studies. His street scenes demonstrate an inventive compositional sensibility, while his more abstract fashion set-ups are often enigmatic and mysterious, going beyond the haughty self-consciousness of glamour that had become a cliché of model demeanor by the late 60s. His mild iconoclasm, which played with notions of attractiveness, was coming into fashion. His most famous colleague, Richard Avedon, was celebrated for revolutionizing "the 20th-century art of fashion photography, imbuing it with touches of both gritty realism and outrageous fantasy and instilling it with a relentlessly experimental drive" (Avedon).

Schatzberg shared the same artistic instincts (see Schatzberg for a useful selection of his art photographs; a general appreciation of the period's aesthetics is to be found in Katur and Bowles). He was more mature and experienced than colleagues who had gone straight from film school to stand behind the camera. Martin Scorsese was only thirty-one when his breakout film, *Mean Streets*, was released in 1973, Francis Ford Coppola thirty-three when *The Godfather* had been named Best Picture the year before. Schatzberg was able on his own initiative to break in as a director and then solidify his position by demonstrating the work ethic and talent needed to complete three different features in three years. None of these was a box-office success. Yet that was because he was committed to avoiding industry formulae and producing films of great artistry that would engage with filmmaking as then defined by the international art cinema. These films were clearly meant to appeal mainly to a cine-literate, upscale viewership. Accordingly, they received only an indifferent handling from US distributors and exhibitors, while the national critical establishment showed itself uniformly incapable of understanding his aesthetics and themes, entirely missing the playful autobiography of *Puzzle*.

American audiences received little help from the nation's reviewers, then enjoying perhaps their greatest cultural influence, in appreciating what they found unfamiliar, even though *l'affaire Bonnie and Clyde* had just recently demonstrated that the domestic critical establishment was out of touch with international cinematic fashion (see the Introduction to this volume for details). Writing for *The New Yorker*, Pauline Kael had by 1970 become the nation's most noted if unpredictable judge. Though she recognized the value of many of the era's groundbreaking releases (*Bonnie and Clyde* and *M*A*S*H* chief among them), Kael missed her chance with *Puzzle* at a time when Bergman,

Godard, and Varda, among others, were offering similarly striking portraits of the discontents of female experience. Of *Puzzle* she lamely observed, "I have a constitutional aversion to movies about women whose souls have been lost, stolen or destroyed, especially when it isn't made clear – and it never is – whether the heroine had a soul in the first place" (Kael, "Puzzle" 250; See Godfrey 60 for an interesting discussion of this review). Clearly this is American Philistinism at its most obtuse.

During the era, however, Schatzberg was among the newly minted US cineastes most praised by the critical establishment in France, where knowledgeable filmgoers appreciated his adroit inflection of the art cinema approach. Likewise, Dunaway refused to accept the role of glamorous Hollywood film star, refusing a number of unchallenging commercial projects and instead taking roles that offered her complex characters to incarnate. Though she broke off their engagement in 1968, the two remained close friends, and both were especially attracted to the art cinema. In her early career, Dunaway would work with three prominent international personalities, Marcello Mastroianni, René Clement, and Roman Polanski, while assaying difficult stage roles in Harold Pinter and Tennessee Williams properties. Though both she and Schatzberg would subsequently work within post-Renaissance Hollywood on projects that, even when commercially successful, offered little in the way of artistic value, they retained connections with and an interest in the international art cinema. Consider, for example, Dunaway's startling performance in Roger Avary's *The Rules of Attraction* (2002) and Schatzberg's work with a German/French/British consortium in bringing Fred Uhlman's 1971 Holocaust novel *Reunion* to the screen (in 1989) with a script by Harold Pinter. Like many of Schatzberg's films, *Reunion* was nominated for the Palme-d'Or at Cannes, though unsurprisingly in the US it received only indifferent exhibition and was barely reviewed.

By the end of the seventies, what American producers saw in Schatzberg had nothing to do with his talent as such but rather reflected his ability to develop and then finish a commercial film on time and under budget. He continued to work in the industry, if not steadily. In the aftermath of the demise of auteur filmmaking during the mid-70s, Schatzberg produced acceptable results even when working *contre-coeur* with well-worn formulas (*The Seduction of Joe Tynan* [1979], a political melodrama; *No Small Affair* [1984], a comedy/drama). However he failed, and sometimes badly, with other genre pieces, notably *Sweet Revenge* (1976), a car chase actioner, and *No Small Affair* (1984), an insipid entry into the teen/young adult comedy genre whose potential for incisive and poignant social comedy John Hughes would soon exploit. In the later decades of his career Schatzberg proved able to turn out films of artistry and substance when provided with suitable material and the requisite artistic freedom. However, nothing equals his first three projects, whose excellence is due in large measure to the unusual cinematic moment that permitted a more personal approach to filmmaking. Schatzberg was a bright flash in what proved to be that false dawn of an American art cinema.

He has been more appreciated as a photographer. Always based in New York City, where he was born in 1927, he apprenticed in his early twenties with Bill Helburn at the ad agency Doyle Dane Bernbach, a leading shop in fashion journalism at the time. He soon made a name for himself in a competitive world where art and commerce were complexly interconnected in a fashion reminiscent of Hollywood. During the 60s, Schatzberg's striking, often idiosyncratic images appeared on the covers and in the pages of *Vogue, McCall's, Esquire, Glamour,* and *Life.* Along with Helburn, Richard Avedon and Irving Penn were then the leading lights in the field, and Schatzberg was fortunate to work with, and learn from, all three. Like them, he managed his own studio, not only doing contract work for the magazines (never accepting an editor's position) but simultaneously pursuing a career as an art photographer.

By the early 60s, Schatzberg was well known in the city's arts community. A *habitué* of its gatherings and events, he found that his outgoing personality and sharp business sense were useful to self-promotion. In managing his career, he benefitted from the tutelage of *Vogue*'s fashion editor Alex Liberman, a Russian émigré who prided himself on being a sophisticated and worldly intellectual. Liberman enjoyed extensive contacts with the European and New York City art worlds, to which the personable Schatzberg now had an entrée. Schatzberg is also grateful to have learned much from Alexey Brodovitch, a similar *éminence* in the fashion world, who was for a time the artistic director at *Harper's Bazaar* (see Ciment and Schatzberg 10).

The young photographer did not lack for clients, as he became something of what we would now call a global citizen. He developed a considerable reputation with his portraits of celebrities he met and charmed, an interesting and quite heterogeneous roster of politicians and artists including Robert Redford, Edie Sedgwick, Harold Pinter, Castro, Roman Polanski, and Francis Ford Coppola. These photos advertised their subjects, but they also attested to his fine eye for the character-revealing power of the camera if provided with *l'objet juste,* which the portrait photographer needed to help produce, not simply find. It was in what filmmakers call the *mise-en-scène* that Schatzberg discovered he possessed considerable talent. He soon found himself in the front rank of portraitists working in a finely grained black and white style.

Reflecting the ideas of both Avedon and Liberman, he never posed his subjects. Instead, the people he photographed were given the opportunity to reveal themselves to the camera, which they often did with humor and self-mockery, responding to the photographer's gentle cajoling. Schatzberg was in the process developing an aesthetic that recalls the Neorealist commitment to discovering, within the material that the camera is placed to photograph, something of its inherent meaning. This was an approach that had recently been explored by fellow New Yorker Siegfried Kracauer in his *Theory of Film* (1960), where in his analysis of the medium the esteemed member of the Frankfurt School argues for the pre-eminence of the photographic capturing of reality (see Kracauer).

In the mid-60s, Kracauer, then enjoying a post as a research coordinator at Columbia University, was a prominent member of the New York intellectual and artistic scene. It would be odd if Schatzberg had not become familiar with Kracauer's extensive writings on photography in addition to his theory of film – or, indeed, with the man himself, since they moved in similar circles. The social realism for whose value Kracauer argued bucked the formalist trends of much then-current art-cinema practice and theorizing. Interestingly, this aesthetic appealed not only to Schatzberg but also to others in the American auteur movement. As a style of filmmaking engaged with contemporary political and social issues, and committed to an authenticity of approach that rejected, or at least interrogated, industry formulas, 70s auteurism traces its history back to several previous production trends. These include foreign and domestic postwar realist films that likewise promised more substantial seriousness than what the average industry entertainment vehicle had on offer (for further discussion see the introduction to this volume).

Schatzberg attracted the notice of the younger generation with his widely reproduced studies of singer Bob Dylan, especially the image used on the cover for his 1966 album *Blonde on Blonde*. Eventually receiving an offer to direct TV commercials, then an increasingly complex form, Schatzberg developed considerable skill in handling actors and molding performances. Directing for TV a series that focused on the world's most beautiful women, including Claudia Cardinale (of whom he also shot a memorable portrait), he took the next step after coming to feel a certain disenchantment with a business and art that, so he assessed, had passed its prime. With an idea or two in mind, he decided to put together a film project, eventually released as *Puzzle*, that drew on the interest and assistance of such cultural luminaries as French screenwriter Jacques Sigurd, critic Michel Ciment (soon to become editor of the important journal *Positif*), actor and producer Paul Newman and his partner John Foreman, and the writer Carole Eastman. Perhaps the most influential "player" in French film culture, Pierre Rissient, catching a screening of the film by chance, rode to Schatzberg's rescue when critical indifference threatened to derail *Puzzle*'s US exhibition, which was being handled by Universal (on Rissient see Genzlinger). Box-office and critical success followed in Europe, and the film's overseas reception helped sustain Schatzberg's career in the US cinema.

No other Renaissance neophyte commanded similar interest and support from those prominent in the global industry. Schatzberg, let us admit, was very lucky indeed in his friends. *Puzzle* was the first – and by any account the most artistically successful – film he finished in a directorial career that would last (if only sporadically) for more than three decades, while continuing to ply his craft as a photographer. Photography is the art he emphasizes at present on his professional website (see Schatzberg). Even though he formed interesting relationships with many in the US and international film communities, Schatzberg never became a Hollywood figure or "personality," and this is perhaps one reason why the histories of Renaissance filmmaking rarely mention him.

Puzzle offers a sharp but not shrill account of the ego-busting and dehumanizing aspects of a business in which human beings are objects that are carefully manipulated to arouse consumer desire to purchase the clothes for a "look" that is in some sense "modeled." The film's agenda, however, was clearly broader than an engaged social criticism that was especially timely since middlebrow culture had become increasingly aware of the marketing manipulations that had fueled the postwar commercial boom. *Puzzle* is no flashy fictional exposé of the ad industry (then routinely referred to as "Madison Avenue") that had been thoroughly anatomized a few years previously. In his bestselling and widely acclaimed study of modern advertising, *The Hidden Persuaders* (1957), Vance Packard had shown how the carefully constructed images produced by ad agencies, and published in glossy monthlies, engage what he identifies as the eight "compelling needs" that influence consumer buying habits but of whose power most of us are hardly conscious (see Packard).

Most intriguingly, perhaps, in the personal vein of art-cinema filmmaking, Schatzberg's maiden effort explores the intersection of art and life (*his* life and art, in particular). Like Jean-Luc Godard, the director is "in" this film, even if only in ways that would be recognized most easily by those who knew him. The subject of *Puzzle* is the "child" whose "downfall" provides a through line of sorts. Lou Andreas Sand (Faye Dunaway) is a top model in her twenties who, her career ruined by the jealousy of others and her own fecklessness, has withdrawn to self-pitying isolation in a remote beach house. Aaron Reinhardt (Barry Primus), for years one of her photographers, has now decided to become a filmmaker and intends to a write a script based on her life, in which he has been much involved as a collaborator, friend, and (perhaps) lover. Tape recorder in hand, Aaron has sought her out so that she can provide him once again with something he needs.

The extended interview to which Lou Andreas submits constitutes the film's present frame, with her memories imaged, usually without specific comment, in a number of enigmatic flashbacks. Some of these correspond to the answers she gives to Aaron's questions, but others emerge as it were unwilled and un-cued, corresponding – sometimes -- to what Lou remembers and will not say. Most significant are the alternatives, perhaps corrections to what she does say. She seems at time to trade in deliberate lies, but then perhaps she is the victim of her mind playing tricks, protecting her from what is too threatening to remember, including a rape (if this did in fact happen). Aaron, listening, never learns the apparent truths made available only to the viewer, in oppositional gestures that recall the crucial revelations of the camera, freed from the narrative control of the characters, in the closing sequences of Orson Welles's *Citizen Kane* (1941).

Like Schatzberg, Aaron is a talented young maverick who exists on the margins of the commercial mainstream; he is more interested in the portraits he takes in furtherance of art (for example, striking compositions shot at dawn in an empty Central Park) than the commissions he completes for the industry. At least, this seems to be how he thinks of himself. In that cramped studio, he is a mostly silent assistant. An arrogant older photographer named Falco holds sway there, and, angry that she is late and obviously never disposed to be polite, he roughly and rudely handles Lou's initial session. Dressed in an elaborate costume, she is shockingly required to hold an unhooded and quite threatening hunting bird. This is an *à clef* moment, but quite private, since Falco is played by Emerick Bronson.

Bronson would not be recognized by most viewers since he is no professional actor, but any major player in the fashion industry and art photography world would recognize the man whose work was exhibited in both Paris and New York (see Bronson). Here he plays a version of himself, and we might assume that he was persuaded to take this acting turn by the director; both of whom worked at *Vogue* at the time. Interestingly, Schatzberg never unmasked his identity in any of the interviews he gave about the film. Bronson's incarnation of a character is true to professional stereotype and probably was close to his true working self. He is all concentration on craft, no time for manners or kindness, and his presence adds to the authenticity of the striking sequence, in which, appropriately, the outrageously incongruous bird of prey is clearly the master of ceremonies, in a bit of compositional legerdemain that should have made Richard Avedon smile. The image makes the cover of *Vogue*, so the film reveals, but in a revealing irony it has been cut to include all of the hawk and just the hand of the model on which he perches. No clothes, the purported objects advertized, are visible.

In a general sense, the film comments somewhat acidly on the use that artists make of the images or stories of others, which become material to advance their careers as they turn them into signed productions. *Puzzle*'s narrative lightly fabulizes Schatzberg's obtaining of material from a model he knew professionally and personally, even as his career turn to filmmaking is re-enacted. Throughout, the film is intriguingly pseudo-autobiographical, deploying a nexus of personal references, as in the case of Bronson, while proffering meanings that are available only to those in the know about the film and its creator. Schatzberg was not reticent to admit in interviews that he had obtained in the

Figure 20.1   In *Puzzle of a Downfall Child*, Lou Andreas Sand (Faye Dunaway) poses for her first cover image, in an outrageous set-up that satirizes the extremism then prevalent in high fashion photography. Digital frame enlargement. Courtesy of Universal Pictures.

same way as Aaron does what became the basis of the film's narrative from Anne Saint-Marie, with whom it seems Schatzberg had carried on a romance of sorts. Faye Dunaway was pleased to be cast as Lou Andreas. *Puzzle* thus casts one former lover in the role of yet another former lover, as the film stands in extra-textually for the unnamed project that Aaron is pursuing. Schatzberg, like his fictional avatar, is in pursuit of a truth that only a gentle relentlessness, sympathetic yet self-serving, can render up.

Indeed, the film provided Faye Dunaway the opportunity to assay a complex, often contradictory character, with the script offering her extended performance moments, often a monologue in effect, in which different emotions and moods succeed one another often at a dizzying pace. It was this kind of acting (requiring just the right close-up and lighting) at which she has shown herself skilled. Among a host of examples, compare her confessional scene with Jack Nicholson's detective in *Chinatown*, as the unbearable truth of her experience drips agonizingly from her, elicited by Polanski with a camera that is just intimate enough, similar enough to Schatzberg's approach to be a direct borrowing. Like the three international art-cinema figures who also worked with her, Schatzberg provided Dunaway with a role that allowed her to explore a character more complex than those which Hollywood had recently provided (as the sexy but very bright insurance investigator, the romantic foil of Steve McQueen's amateur bank robber in *The Thomas Crown Affair*). In its engagement with the pseudo-autobiographical, *Puzzle* invites comparison with the most ostentatious, if ultimately opaque, attempts at directorial self-revelation: Fellini's *8 ½* (1963) and Woody Allen's *Stardust Memories* (1980).

Like those two noted attempts at cinematic autobiography, *Puzzle* had deep personal roots, and it is confessional in an unusual way. Consider how Dunaway, the director's live-in fiancée, is used as a barely disguised version of the fashion model Anne Saint-Marie, with whom Schatzberg had worked at *Vogue* and who was the subject of several of his most memorable portraits and covers. In the fictional version of these relationships, the sympathetic photographer Aaron is very much like Schatzberg himself, eager to help a friend in need but, in so doing, providing himself with material for his next project as his career takes a turn in a different direction. Lou Andreas Sand, first an object for the photographer's camera, becomes another kind of thing for the would-be filmmaker. What she has to tell now has more value than her still glamorous looks, which the camera carefully suggests have deteriorated little with the passage of time and neglect for her appearance. His visit is simply another kind of "session," as he now "directs" her transformation into a different object of value. No longer is he interested in taking her to Central Park for a "shoot." His is now the more thorough and potentially intrusive possession of the storyteller, who appropriates, as he will, his friends, family, and world in order to construct a fictional reflex, to create what seems to have been but no longer can claim to be. This is one of the great self-reflexive themes of modern fiction, common to Proust and Joyce, and, with perhaps less claim on artistic seriousness, Philip Roth's pseudo-autobiographical *Portnoy's Complaint*(1969), which was achieving a significant *succès de scandale* as the film entered production.

Its personal references revealed, *Puzzle* reveals itself as a complex metafiction and an intriguing *mise-en-abîme* configuring the director's experiences in two senses: not only in regard to the gathering of the story it recycles aslant, but also, extratextually, with regard to the casting decisions that brought it to life. It is significant that Barry Primus is a Schatzberg lookalike in addition to playing a role that precisely mirrors the director's early career and his relationship with Saint-Marie. Faye Dunaway's casting provides yet another level of relevant autobiographical resonance since until recently she had been Schatzberg's fiancée. Dunaway, who had broken the engagement after falling for Marcello Mastroianni, perhaps found that her scenes with Schatzberg's fictional stand-in were interestingly energized by her recently broken attachment to the man directing them. Aaron's interrogation of Dunaway's character, including her emotional instability and promiscuity, surely gave the director something of a frisson as shooting proceeded. Lou Andreas's romantic life, it should be noted, includes her leaving her fiancé, played by Roy Scheider, without explanation at the altar, afterward offering the bewildered man little in the way of an "I'm sorry" as she packs a suitcase and hurtles out of the apartment they share.

Figures 20.2a and b Lookalike actor Barry Primus, as a wannabee director, emphasizes the autobiography in *Puzzle of a Downfall Child* (1970). Digital frame enlargement. Courtesy of Jerrold Schatzberg Productions, 1970.

In general terms, of course, the film engages with the slippery notion of character and the difficulty, perhaps impossibility, of coming to know someone else, themes elsewhere explored during the period in two art-cinema classics, Ingmar Bergman's *Persona* (1966), and Federico Fellini's *Juliet of the Spirits* (1965). Sometimes Aaron plays the therapist, giving the lie to his subject's self-deceptions, but in three crucial instances a debunking in the service of truth is accomplished by "objective" flashbacks, with no voiceover, that contradict her commentary and memories. These counter-memories, as it were, are of course only present to the viewer and not to Lou. Do these sequences depict truths that she will not or cannot admit? Alternately, are they repressed memories that surface unwilled as she responds to Aaron's questioning? In yet a further possibility, do these flashbacks represent wishes or bypassed possibilities? Lou's fervent proclamation that she is reticent about sex because of early abuse is "illustrated" by a flashback showing her being picked up and bedded by a stranger. Are dialogue and image meant to be understood as delivering complementary or contradictory truths? Is the past, and hence the "character" of the downfall child that it might be thought to constitute, recoverable? Undecidability and irresolution are key to modernist narratives that refuse the recuperative, restorative effects of Hollywood storytelling, which explicitly sets itself the task of leading somewhere.

Nothing makes this clearer than the film's finale, which at first glance seems to offer only the most banal of Hollywood romantic clichés: a gesture of momentary rapprochement and revelation that ratifies a once-satisfying connection now seen as belonging only to the past. Why is it, Lou whispers seductively, that they never slept together? Taken aback, Aaron reminds her that of course they did, if only once. This was a free and frank encounter, he reminisces, satisfying to them both. Lou has no answer, only smiles. So doing, she silently puts into question the value, so dependent on her memory, of their extended and at times quite painful dialogue. What else of importance has she forgotten? If she remembers their tryst, why does she lie? What other lies has she told?

In terms of artistic quality if not ticket sales, Schatzberg delivered spectacularly during the brief flourishing of the auteur cinema. Unfortunately, he was best suited for a kind of filmmaking that would never work for Hollywood. In the early seventies, he directed (and in effect produced) three of the era's most "intimate and remarkably intense character studies," films that share "a poignant focus on the discontented, abused, and socially marginal" (Harvard Film Archive). Schatzberg's first film differs substantially from the two that soon followed, however, even if all three can be described as character studies in which genre plays no role. *Puzzle* was a thinkpiece, presenting viewers with neither an easily understood story nor a straightforwardly likeable main character, even as it engaged with issues, including ethical ones, to which no easy answers were forthcoming. This likely explains why the film did not do well in domestic exhibition. As Roger Greenspun observed in the *New York Times*, what the photographer and director turned out "values its mysteries and does not pretend to solve them." This was not a formula designed to please US audiences, especially when developed with what the reviewer identifies as "the wildest self-indulgence" (Greenspun).

The film's unabashed artiness, quickly pronounced uncommercial by US critics, almost ended Schatzberg's directorial career before it had properly begun. It must have been disappointing when *Puzzle* did poorly in its domestic exhibition, and the film likely would have sunk out of sight had not Pierre Rissient, traveling in the US, caught a screening at a San Francisco festival by chance. Taken with Schatzberg's evident talent, he talked Universal into letting him buy the rights for French exhibition in an act of cultural appropriation that seems entirely justified. Rissient soon was not the director's only champion. Michel Ciment was also convinced of the neophyte's sensibility and talent. He did much to help the young American establish his reputation in French circles. So, thanks to the sponsorship of Rissient and Ciment, French cinephiles were introduced to Schatzberg. The American cinema did not include influential *patrons* who took a similar interest in promoting artistic excellence as the centerpiece of a cinematic *patrimoine*. In America there was little to counter the crass commercialism of box-office receipts used to measure the success of the nation's cineastes. Wild self-indulgence, or what some thought that was, would simply not do as a plan.

Wishing to remain in the game, Schatzberg made it clear that he had received the message. The projects he accepted for his next two films are nothing like *Puzzle*; they avoided what Greenspun saw as "mysteries," but in their avoidance of industry conventions (especially the happy ending that endorses conservative values) they clearly belong to the developing alternative tradition soon to be known as the Hollywood Renaissance. *Panic in Needle Park* (1971) started life as a photo essay in *Life* magazine, the movie rights for which were purchased by maverick New York producer and writer Dominick Dunne. Dunne arranged for his brother, John Gregory Dunne, and sister-in-law Joan Didion, to write the screenplay. The material was sensational because it dealt with drug addiction, with the community that addicts had informally created for distribution in Sherman Square, not far from the tony neighborhoods of the Upper West Side and just a few blocks from the Guggenheim Museum. John Gregory Dunne, frequent contributor to *Vanity Fair,* was likely one of the Manhattan glitterati that Schatzberg had come to know in the course of his photographic career. He was not a Hollywood figure. Filmed on the streets of New York City, *Panic* traces the precarious lives of two heroin junkies, thrown together by circumstance and now in love even though held tight in the grip of addiction and facing incarceration or worse.

Scarecrow (1973) was based on an excellent script by Gary Michael White that was intended, so it seems, as a performance piece, with two actors who had achieved success in renowned A-productions (Al Pacino and Gene Hackman) given a chance to create a film that is little more than a succession of sharply observed *scènes à deux*. In *Scarecrow*, two ill-assorted homeless adventurers, who meet up by accident on the road, navigate disappointment, a lack of money, and the occasional threat as they pursue different dreams of deliverance: for one, reconciliation with a wife he abandoned and for the other, somewhat inexplicably, ownership of a car-wash business. Romantic fulfillment and a respectable place in the social order – the banal goals of Hollywood storytelling–are here demonstrated as unattainable for those who seem by nature ill-disposed to conform to the rules of regular living.

Figure 20.3   In *Scarecrow*, Schatzberg was able to cast two of the most celebrated actors of the decade and after: Al Pacino and Gene Hackman. Digital frame enlargement. Courtesy of Warner Bros.

Schatzberg was not interested in making social problem films (a well-established studio genre) in which deviations from middlebrow normality are shown to threaten the values, if not the functioning, of society, and thus call for expert surveillance and analysis. Amelioration by appropriate institutions restores the individuals affected to their appropriate places in the social order. The more aestheticized and thus prestigious examples of this kind of filmmaking that appeared in the postwar period, argues Chris Cagle, were sociological in their political focus, but could be "both middlebrow culture and a self-critical commentary on middle class life" (Cagle 15). By contrast, if Schatzberg's second and third films focus on the intimate lives of those living on the margins they deploy no sociological gaze and withhold moral judgment. Their realist aesthetic is furthered by the inventive use of actual locations, improvised dialogue and a de-dramatized performance style. *Panic* and *Scarecrow* are thus akin to a number of "personal" early Renaissance efforts such as Coppola's *The Rain People* (1969), Scorsese's *Mean Streets* (1973), Alan Pakula's *The Sterile Cuckoo* (1969), Bob Rafelson's *Five Easy Pieces* (1970), and Hal Ashby's *The Landlord* (1970).

A key point is that a taste for the "non-Hollywood" as a style, especially if it were provocatively transgressive, now co-existed somewhat uneasily with an enduring preference for the less challenging, more emotionally satisfying kind of stories upon which US filmmaking had depended from the beginning. The history of the New Hollywood, which begins with the Renaissance filmmaking of the early seventies, is marked by the industry's continuing accommodation of the art cinema (see Lewis on New Hollywood history). For example, as Barbara Wilinsky notes, by the seventies "many of the theaters that continued to screen art films focused on New Hollywood films," broadening the audience reach of auteur cinema productions (133). During the first decade or so of the New Hollywood, complex interconnections developed between auteur filmmaking and the art cinema. These deserve a broader analysis than they have yet received, with an emphasis on all aspects of the film sector, including financing, exhibition, journalism, reception, censorship, awards culture, tastemaking, as well as various forms of cooperation on the level of production – and this is by no means an exhaustive list.

Very much a transnational figure from the outset, even at the end of his directing career, Schatzberg continues to enjoy a substantial reputation in France even though he has not completed a project for years. Speaking of Schatzberg, Ciment suggests, "Though very American in spirit and culture he is much attracted to international cinema and its often more daring stylistic approach" (Ciment). Meanwhile many, perhaps most, American film scholars and enthusiasts know little if anything, about him. The French have admired him precisely because his films are radically different from the ordinary Hollywood product, and from the many Renaissance releases that honor, if in a lower key, time-honored industry conventions. Schatzberg's filmmaking career is interesting for its own sake, deserving attention in a volume like this that is dedicated to that spirit of respectful nostalgia with which US film scholars are refocusing on the auteur cinema of the seventies. It is surely time to fill in blank pages and rectify critical wrongs (see Kirshner and Lewis particularly in this regard). Yet there is a larger point to be made in a review of Schatzberg's career. From the perspective of the history of the auteurist cinema, his is a limit case, marking out just how much like the international art cinema Hollywood art-house-light films could aspire to be. The failure of the Schatzberg films in the American market, but their success in Europe, reveals the aesthetic gap between an established national cinema that celebrated film art and a Hollywood built on the entertainment model that viewed highbrow aesthetics with suspicion. What Schatzberg authored, working on the less monitored margins of commercial filmmaking, the US cinema ignored, neglected, or minimized, whereas in France his films were hailed as masterpieces. This is a pattern of rejection in the US and acceptance in France experienced by other Renaissance auteurs, most tellingly Francis Ford Coppola with a number of his later films, such as *Twixt* (2011).

For Ciment, and others within the French critical establishment, Schatzberg was a modernist who invited comparison with those in the international art cinema who also pursued a cinema of probing intimacy – especially Bergman, Resnais, Antonioni, and Carné. His youthful portraits of the downfallen offer thinly plotted, largely directionless stories in which contentious relationships provide the dramatic centers (as in much Broadway drama of the period such as Edward Albee's *Who's Afraid of Virginia Woolf?* [1962]). As the director admitted, looking back a decade later on this period, he was obsessed, as a photographer and director, with "images of those beings who had been broken in a world that afforded no protection" (Ciment and Schatzberg 12 – trans. mine). Eschewing glamor, spectacle, and romance, his films are especially revealing of the provocative themes and low budget approach of Renaissance filmmaking more generally. This was a production trend characterized by apparently unmediated, everyday atmospherics. In particular, Schatzberg's version of the cinematic connects deeply with "the era's movement toward personal, prismatic stories that refract the tumultuous cultural climate while also offering a more introverted variation of the fierce iconoclasm bred within the films of Robert Altman, Hal Ashby, Arthur Penn, et al." (Harvard Film Archive). Nothing about the Schatzberg films is tumultuous even if, very obliquely, they "refract" tumult in American society.

What makes his films so small in terms of production values and yet so rich in the dramatic scope they obtain from the director's patient restraint? The answer is the performers who, with the minimum of explicit instructions, were encouraged to allow their characters to reveal themselves to the camera. Schatzberg had perfected this technique in both his fashion work and in his "posed" art photography. In both genres, under the influence of Avedon and Liberman, he came to prefer abstract spaces and a minimum of props, often deploying strobe lighting (see Ciment and Schatzberg 9). Knowing that, as a photographer, he would be expected to make films consisting only of carefully composed, even pretty images, he consciously resisted the impulse to do so. Schatzberg's practice well suits the auteurist model for idiosyncrasy. With their observational technique, his films promote an uneasy intimacy with the characters by evoking a Bergmanesque claustrophobia and sense of no-exit. Carefully deployed silence and stasis reveal what Ciment calls "the unbelievable depth of a secret wound" (Ciment and Schatzberg 85).

Robert Kolker appropriately labels Renaissance films like these "a cinema of loneliness": a fictional world not only in which alienation prevails but where the failure of community also deeply registers its private anguish in order, to quote Ciment again, "to bear witness to the horror and despair of this world" (86). Schatzberg's films fit this microcosmic model perfectly. *Puzzle*, *Panic*, and *Scarecrow* are all small-budget projects that present characters in crisis who have failed to make safe and secure places for themselves in a contemporary America whose prosperous, respectable center lies far beyond their reach. They make only fleeting, often damaging contact with others, who fumble less with malevolence than with obtuseness or myopia. Life for them is picaresque, not predictable, but Lady Fortuna never smiles for long on their adventures. Chance encounters, sometimes promising, run their course into the blankest of futures; fantasies of control and dreams of success presage psychotic withdrawal or pointless persistence. Weaknesses, both moral and epistemological, their origins unexamined, prove insurmountable for the two homeless derelicts in *Scarecrow*, as for *Needle Park*'s pair of desperate addicts and the self-destructive former fashion model in *Puzzle*, whose erstwhile lover fails to halt her downward spiral but manages to turn her decline to his own purposes.

If subtly configured to suit Schatzberg, the films's settings are all "found" in real spaces, as, to take another interesting example, are the equally resonant (but also not unmodified) settings for Michelangelo Antonioni's *Blow-Up* (1966) and *Zabriskie Point* (1970). Like Antonioni, Schatzberg eschews a locative realism that explores the pro-filmic meanings of the world beyond the sound stage. Neither one is a guerilla filmmaker, imposing fiction onto facticity. Instead, again like Antonioni, Schatzberg's camera locates a "real" America in which (often unidentified) places can be deployed expressionistically, that is, carefully framed as symbolically dense backgrounds (see Palmer, *Shot on Location* for the distinction between setting and background). Schatzberg also achieves this effect in soundstage sequences that are staged in minimally dressed, constricting interiors. In these two forms of abstraction, betrayal, ignorance, and anger vitiate every gesture at lasting connection. Staging these failures to communicate, Schatzberg avoids sentimentalism. Like Bergman, he dramatizes incapacity without bitterness or irony, yet grants only minimal sympathy to characters whose plights are carefully, often relentlessly, anatomized. The endings of his films are poignant in the etymological sense of that word: piercing, wounding, unredemptive. No viewer's heart is warmed by them.

It is telling that Schatzberg identifies the subject of his first film as a "puzzle." This is a label that suits all three of the films discussed here. None of them climaxes at the traditional "point" that Hollywood narrative is usually configured to provide. No gestures of conventional virtue prettify the shabbiness and moral emptiness of lives misspent on the margin. Nothing dispels the unknowability of characters who seem incapable of articulating their most crucial truths. Experience offers no through lines for change, even as the films provide no intellectual framework for their understanding. Is Schatzberg a naturalist, resigned to the brutish facts of life, who believes that unfitness determines destiny? Alternatively, since he evokes the notion of fallenness, do these films offer (in the manner of his contemporary Paul Schrader) a slant Christian recognition of utter depravity, of an unmerited exile from blessedness of those not predestined for salvation? If so, no sign of grace, irresistible or otherwise, emerges to draw teleological distinctions, as it does, for example, in Scorsese's *Taxi Driver* (1976), scripted by Schrader, or Schrader's own

Hardcore (1979). Schatzberg's camera never catches sight of the inevitable blessed who prosper in the midst of abuse and corruption. The divine has no purchase in his fictional worlds, but then neither does conventional morality. Absent too are any manipulative machinations of the "establishment," then the accustomed target of widespread dissatisfaction. If there is blame for failure, it falls by default on the characters themselves who, free to choose, prove unable to act to their own ultimate benefit.

To put this another way, the Schatzberg films are politically agnostic in an era when this reticence might have been seen as cowardice, as a surrender to the unpromising decadence of an America then as now losing its way. The director, however, is more accurately described as a refusenik who simply will not go along with the crowd, the crowd in this instance being the many Hollywood directors of the past, both recent and remote, who extract a poignant melancholy from the subject of national discontent that pervades the era. Unlike those of many of his Renaissance colleagues, his films make no nostalgic reference to the Hollywood past. This cadre of melodramatists would include fellow auteurs like Peter Bogdanovich (*The Last Picture Show*, 1971) and Hal Ashby (*Harold and Maude*, 1971) (see Cagle).

For Schatzberg, as for the directors of the cinema of loneliness more generally, the impossibility of family or community metafictionally figures the self-imposed creative isolation of the auteur. In a larger sense, loneliness exemplifies the contrariness of this liminal cinematic movement, with its modernist and realist embrace of the essentially tragic nature of human life, and yet its residual, half-hearted commitment to providing emotionally satisfying visual drama, Hollywood-style. The Renaissance films do not collectively offer, in Fredric Jameson's apt phrase, a convincing "optical illusion of social harmony" that is the faux utopian goal of Hollywood narrative, its cherished legacy from nineteenth-century melodrama, all family values and timeless, never-questioned common sense (Jameson 26). Instead, its auteurs for the most part agree that irresolution and cultural instability are all, even if hope for brighter days should not be completely abandoned. Schatzberg's grim contributions to the movement, framed by his gestures at unknowability and moral agnosticism, constitute no exception to this general rule. As a critical position on Hollywood Renaissance filmmaking, traditional auteurism, with its serial focus on the careers of notable directors with a compulsion to reframe experience,, is difficult to avoid. In the final analysis, for these directors lonely singularity is all, both in the films and in the making of them.

Schatzberg did not have to make films in order to make a living or fulfill his artistic urges, of course. Taking pictures for money – and to please himself – he had already made his peace with the limited freedom available to art that is pursued within different forms of commerce. He had no big dream to fulfill, and was actually willing to spend some of his own wealth – which by then was considerable – to support an endeavor or two. He reveled in the accolades of the French. *Puzzle*, remarkably enough, was through the influence of Rissient and Ciment nominated along with Schatzberg for the Palme d'Or at Cannes. *Panic* earned the same honors the following year. Important for film history, it also offered Al Pacino his first starring role; and his co-star, Kitty Winn, won in the best actress category. In addition to Faye Dunaway's portrayal in *Puzzle*, hers is one of several outstanding but today largely forgotten performances by women in the early Renaissance releases (cf. Carrie Snodgress in Frank Perry's 1970 *Diary of a Mad Housewife* and Shirley Knight in Coppola's 1969 *The Rain People*). *Scarecrow* tied for the same award and played on French screens for months, even though it bombed in the US.

After almost half a century, there are signs that Schatzberg is finally receiving his due appreciation in the US. A recent retrospective at the Houston Museum of Fine Arts in May 2019, hosted by the filmmaker, perhaps indicates that more attention in this country will now be paid to him and his accomplishments (Houston). The transfer to Region 1 Blu-Ray of restored versions of *Panic* and *Scarecrow* makes it possible for contemporary viewers to see these beautifully photographed films in their best visual form. It is to be regretted that *Puzzle*, Schatzberg's masterpiece, remains unavailable in Region 1 DVD, despite the film having been restored and re-issued, including a Blu-ray version, by French distributors. The French DVD's special features include appreciations from several of that country's most influential critics, including Ciment, now the doyen of the Paris critical establishment. The launch of this edition in 2016 was treated as a very special event by the French press. It seems more than just that Schatzberg was flown to Lyon in order to be specially honored at that year's Lumière festival, where the just restored version of *Panic* was screened and fêted (see Jurgensen).

WORKS CITED

Balio, Tino. *The Foreign Film Renaissance on American Screens, 1946-73*. University of Wisconsin Press, 2010.
Barattoni, Luca. *Italian Post-Neorealist Cinema*. Edinburgh University Press, 2012.
Berliner, Todd. *Hollywood Incoherent: Narration in Seventies Cinema*. University of Texas Press, 2010.
Borde, Raymond and Étienne Chaumeton, *A Panorama of the American Film Noir: 1941-53*. Translated by Paul Hammond, City Lights, 2002.
Bordwell, David. *Narration in the Fiction Film*. University of Wisconsin Press, 1985.
Bronson, Emerick R. Obituary. *The New York Times*, 19 Oct. 1997, www.nytimes.com/1997/10/19/classified/paid-notice-deaths-bronson-emerick-r.html. Accessed 23 November 2019.
Cagle, Chris. *Sociology on Film: Postwar Hollywood's Prestige Commodity*. Rutgers University Press, 2017.
Chew Bose, Durga. "Jerry Schatzberg's Enduring Puzzle." *Interview Magazine*, 3 Dec.

2010, www.interviewmagazine.com/film/jerry-schatzberg-puzzle-of-a-downfall-child. Accessed 29 November2019.

Ciment, Michel. "Biography." www.jerryschatzberg.com/biography. Accessed 14 July 2019.

Ciment, Michel and Jerry Schatzberg. *De la Photo au Cinéma*. Sté Nlle des Éditions du Chêne, 1982.

Cook, David A. "Auteurs and the Film Generation in 1970s Hollywood" in Lewis (1998), pp. 11–37.

Cook, David A. *Lost Illusions: American Cinema in the Shadow of Watergate and Vietnam 1970-1979*. University of California Press, 2000.

Couston, Jerémie and Jacques Morice. "Pierre Rissient, Le cinephile au regard d'or." www.telerama.fr/cinema/pierre-rissient-le-cinephile-au-regard-d-or,132843.php. Accessed 19 August 2019.

Crowther, Bosley. "Bonnie and Clyde Arrives." *New York Times*, 14 Aug. 1967, www.nytimes.com/1967/08/14/archives/screen-bonnie-and-clyde-arrives-careers-of-murderers-pictured-as.html. Accessed 28 August2019.

Debruge, Peter. "*Silence* Review: Martin Scorsese Belabors his Passion Project." *Variety*, variety.com/2016/film/reviews/silence-review-martin-scorsese-1201935391/. Accessed 6 August 2019.

Easy Rider. IMDB www.imdb.com/title/tt0064276/

Foundas, Scott. "Overlooked and Undervalued: The Films of Jerry Schatzberg." *Village Voice*, 4 Sep. 2008, www.villagevoice.com/2008/09/04/overlooked-and-underval ued-the-films-of-jerry-schatzberg/. Accessed 24 August 2019.

Frank, Nino. "The Crime Adventure Story: A New Kind of Detective Film" in Palmer 1996, pp. 21–4

Friedman, Lester D., ed. *American Cinema of the 1970s*. Rutgers University Press, 2000.

Gelmis, Joseph. *The Film Director as Superstar: Kubrick, Lester, Mailer, Nichols, Penn, Polanski, and Others*. Doubleday, 1970.

Genzlinger, Neil. "Pierre Rissient, Behind-the-Scenes Force of Cinema, Dies." *The New York Times*, 7 May 2018, www.nytimes.com/2018/05/07/obituaries/pierre-rissient-81-behind-the-scenes-force-of-cinema-dies.html. Accessed 14 July 2019.

Giovacchini, Saverio. *Hollywood Modernism: Film and Politics in the Age of the New Deal*. Philadelphia: Temple University Press, 2001.

Godfrey, Nicholas. *The Limits of Auteurism: Case Structures in the Critically Constructed New Hollywood*. Rutgers University Press, 2018.

Greenspun, Roger. "Puzzle of a Downfall Child." *The New York Times*, 8 Feb. 1971, www.nytimes.com/1971/02/08/archives/-puzzle-of-downfall-child-with-faye-duna way-here.html. Accessed 20 November 2019.

Harvard Film Archive. "The Cinematic Portraits of Jerry Schatzberg." library.harvard.edu/film/films/2010octdec/schatzberg.html. Accessed 18 August 2019.

Hillier, Jim. *The New Hollywood*. Continuum, 1992.

Houston Museum of Fine Arts. "A Weekend with Filmmaker and Photographer Jerry Schatzberg." www.mfah.org/calendar/series/a-weekend-with-photographer-and-filmmaker-jerry-schatzberg. Accessed 24 August 2019.

Jacobs, Diane. *Hollywood Renaissance: The New Generation of Filmmakers and their Works*. Dell, 1979.

Jameson, Fredric. "Reification and Utopia in Mass Culture" (1979). *Signatures of the Visible*, Routledge, 1992, pp. 9–34.

Jurgensen, Gauthier. "Lumière 2016: Entretien avec Jerry Schatzberg, le doyen du Nouvel Hollywood." *Allocine*, 14 Oct. 2016, www.allocine.fr/article/fichearticle_gen_carticle=18656828.html. Accesed 13 May 2020.

Kael, Pauline. "The Frightening Power of 'Bonnie and Clyde.'" *The New Yorker*, 21 Oct. 1967, www.newyorker.com/magazine/1967/10/21/bonnie-and-clyde. Accessed 28 August 2019.

Kael, Pauline. "Puzzle of a Downfall Child." *Deeper into Movies*, Little Brown, 1973, pp. 250–1.

Katur, Alexandra and Hamish Bowles. *The World in Vogue*. Condé Nast, 2009.

Kirshner, Jonathan. *Hollywood's Last Golden Age: Politics, Society, and the Seventies Film in America*. Cornell University Press, 2012.

Klein, Amanda Ann. *American Film Cycles: Reframing Genres, Screening Social Problems, and Defining Subcultures*. University of Texas Press, 2011.

Kracauer, Siegfried. *Theory of Film: The Redemption of Physical Reality*. Oxford University Press, 1960.

Langford, Barry. *Post-Classical Hollywood: Film Industry, Style and Ideology since 1945*. Edinburgh University Press, 2010.

Lev, Peter. *The Euro-American Cinema*. University of Texas Press, 1993.

Lewis, Jon, ed. *The New American Cinema*. Duke University Press, 1998.

Madsen, Axel. *The New Hollywood: American Movies in the '70s*. Thomas Y. Crowell, 1975.

Menne, Jeff. *Francis Ford Coppola*. Illinois University Press, 2014.

Monaco, James. *American Film Now: The People, the Power, the Money, the Movies*. New American Library, 1979.

Naremore, James. "Hitchcock at the Margins of *Noir*." *Alfred Hitchcock: Centenary Essays*, edited by Richard Allen, and S. Ishi Gonzalès, BFI, 1999, pp. 263–77.

Newland, Christina. "Interview: Jerry Schatzberg." *Film Comment*, 21 March 2019, www.filmcomment.com/blog/interview-jerry-schatzberg/. Accessed 14 September 2019.

Palmer, R. Barton, ed. and trans. *Perspectives on Film Noir*. G.K. Hall, 1996.

Palmer, R. Barton. *Shot on Location: Postwar American Cinema and the Exploration of Real Place*. Rutgers University Press, 2016.

Palmer, R. Barton. "The Small Adult Film: A Prestige Form of Cold War Cinema." *Cold War Film Genres*, edited by Homer Pettey, Edinburgh University Press, 2017, pp. 62–78.

Pye, Michael and Lynda Myles, *The Movie Brats: How the Film Generation Took Over Hollywood*. Holt, Rinehart and Winston, 1979.

Richard Avedon obituary. *The New York Times*, 1 Oct. 2004, www.nytimes.com/2004/10/01/arts/richard-avedon-the-eye-of-fashion-dies-at-81.html. Accessed 13 May 2020.

Schatzberg, Jerry. www.jerryschatzberg.com/. Accessed 15 August 2019.

Sarris, Andrew. *The American Cinema: Directors and Directions 1929-1968*. E.P. Dutton, 1968.

Schaller, Nicholas. "Jerry Schatzberg: L'Interview Fleuve." *L'Obs*, 11 March 2012, www.nouvelobs.com/cinema/20120311.CIN9761/jerry-schatzberg-l-interview-fleuve.html. Accessed 2 September 2019.

Schatz, Thomas. *The Genius of the System: Hollywood Filmmaking in the Studio Era*. Pantheon, 1989.

Sherman, Eric and Martin Rubin. *The Director's Event*. Athenaeum, 1972.

Variety. "The Day the Ponies Come Back." 5 Sep. 2000, www.variety.com/2000/film/reviews/the-day-the-ponies-come-back-1200464418/. Accessed 15 August 2019.

Wilinsky, Barbara. *Sure Seaters: The Emergence of Art House Cinema*. University of Minnesota Press, 2001.

21. INSIDE JOHN SCHLESINGER OUTSIDE

Murray Pomerance

My belly's hollow breath sighs up through my heart
Allen Ginsberg, 4 October 1970

PRELUDE

Franz Kafka offers a powerful tale of the outside, that may backlight John Schlesinger's remarkable films leading into, and carrying through, the 1970s: *Midnight Cowboy* (1969), *Sunday Bloody Sunday* (1971), *The Day of the Locust* (1975) and *Marathon Man* (1976). To paraphrase:

Searching for The Law, a man comes to a gigantic gate, manned by a vicious-looking guard. "Let me in," he begs. The guard, standing firm, shakes his head. The man waits, and as time passes this conversation is repeated again and again. As the years wend on, a longer and longer chain of ever more imposing gates is visible, manned by ever more threatening guards. When, finally, the man is in his final hours and destitute, he begs his friend the guard to approach. "I am dying. Allow me one last question." "What is it?!" "I have noticed through all these years, while I have been waiting, that not one single other person has come here. Why?" The guard rises to his full height and gives a resonant bellow: "Because this gate . . . is *only for you*. And now I'm going to lock it" (Kafka 215-217).

Having caught the fancy of legion readers and scholars, "Before the Law" (1915) could motivate discussion of man's struggle with his own independence (the gate was always the visitor's to pass through, although he did not

Figure 21.1   Ratso Rizzo is walkin' here! Dustin Hoffman with Jon Voight (l.) in *Midnight Cowboy* (1969). Digital frame enlargement. Courtesy of Jerome Hellman Productions.

recognize it); or the associated problem of authority and its impositions. But most relevant as preface to a discussion of Schlesinger is the subject's utter loneliness, his disposition toward a search *that is now and always was his only*, shaped out of his own desiring consciousness with him set adrift on the vast social surface absent support, enduring love, or hope. Cut off, or held back, from his – albeit intensively decorated – surroundings and from social grounding, the hero follows his path regardless of difficulties; or else, doesn't follow it at all. The choice remains, but the solitary nature of that path: *that* is the shining feature of the Schlesingerian tale.

MIDNIGHT COWBOY

New York in the late 1960s, the Nixon era: signal center of Western culture outside Paris, urbanity epitomized, a hub of sophisticated attitudes, radical class distinctions, and urgent social and spatial mobility. Everybody is ravenous to *make it*; some few actually succeed (as must happen if the mass struggle is to be validated). The city is a maelstrom. Some drivers are accumulating thirty or more thousand dollars in unpaid parking tickets, so diffuse and pernicious are the challenges of street space, law, and order, and nobody does anything about it. The elderly clochards have their habits, occupying park benches day and night, often within the boulevard that capaciously divides upper Broadway, while at their elbows, as they rattle the *Times* in retreat, craven New Gentrians whiz past in limousines and cabs. This is an age of cosmopolitanism without terror. Manhattan is a borough of tiny and sharply defined neighborhoods, some defined by a predominant commercial activity (the Floral District, the Garment District, the Diamond District, the Gallery District) and some known by inhabitants as residential topoi (the sedate Upper West Side, the chic Upper East Side, the boho West Village, the hyper-boho East Village, throbbing not-yet-defined SoHo, and so on). At the time it was not an exceptionally challenging matter to find one's place in New York – some sort of place: a prospect of memorable edifices, a charmed corner, a collection of denizens who would give the recognizing eye. New York in 1969 was fundamentally sustaining and welcoming – if not always nourishing – notwithstanding its speed, pressures, and nervous flamboyance; or that crime existed, that the super-rich were incessantly hungry to find more and still more treasure, or that the lonely knew they inhabited a private, in many ways inaccessible, world.

The protagonists of *Midnight Cowboy* are outsiders: irremediably low, lumpen, of the *boue*. In the strictest classical sense they have only a *vulgar* commitment to New York life. Ratso Rizzo (Dustin Hoffman[1]) is a syphilitic pimp, his teeth rotting, his glance nervous as a rodent's. He walks with a clubfoot's stumble, flaunts a beggar's filth. At one precious moment early in the film a taxi pulls up a little too close while he crosses an intersection. "*I'm* walkin' here!,", he slams the hood with his palm, "*I'm* walkin' here!" (Hoffman is reputed to have improvised this action on the spot.) Rizzo is one of the uncountable untouchables, Schlesinger's forefronting of him a blunt indication that for all its glamour and style New York is the greatest caste society in America. The bourgeoisie who pay to see movies like this, Schlesinger knows, wordlessly bypass the Ratsos of this world, while here, for just under two hours, they gaze upon him with pleasured fascination. Without possessions, Ratso cannot boast the luxury of a keen moral sense. His etiquette, struck and modified upon the moment, depends on the exigencies of circumstance. He blows with the wind, as do all those who lack the capital foundation upon which to erect a sparkling edifice of achievement and pride.

Off the bus from the Texas boondocks (and rolling into Manhattan accompanied by Toots Thielemans blowing Harry Nilsson's "Everybody's Talkin'" on his harmonica: an award-winning performance) comes Joe Buck (Jon Voight), a late-twentieth-century version of the American yeoman, perhaps, fallen from grace because in the sweep of urbanization and modernity the force of agriculture (out of which he grew) is stymied, farms are foreclosed, the future is relocated to the city. Clothed in cowboy duds (deerskin jacket, broad-brimmed Stetson), culturally naive, socially maladroit (as are all persons outside of their native realm) and hungry to make good, Joe falls under Ratso's protection and tutelage. Of this tall, good-looking, muscular Adonis the creep from the gutters will fashion a utilitarian object of estimable proportions, a "midnight cowboy" who can entertain and engage capitalism's feverishly hungry movers by using the only tool he has brought to Manhattan, his body. The film is a Pygmalion tale turned on its head. In one hilarious sequence, Voight's Joe is caught in a society matron's apartment (Sylvia Miles), his pants dropped as she toggles between her husband on the phone, her poodle on the floor, and his genitalia. The two of them flop onto the bed, and as they writhe, her on top, his naked buttocks flip channels on the TV remote so that their moans are accompanied by Jack LaLanne, Bette Davis, Sandy Duncan, Godzilla, and a host of other circus entertainers. The humor is diluted by the fact that both these lovers are starving.

The funders of Joe's dark picaresque are numerous and incomparable, a sketchy catalogue of archetypal "big city" social types. Sailing the unpredictably tempestuous currents of New York this "innocent abroad" comes of age, but if he is searching for The Law, Ratso's is the only one he will find. He learns – with pain – to see himself in urban terms, to lose touch with the country boy he "really" is. Ratso is hosting him in his "pad," an arbitrarily carved-out space inside a derelict tenement – not luxury living, but luxurious enough for two strangers who would otherwise be without a roof. Lovers, or just companions of the soul? Or is there a difference? Joe recognizes the utter helplessness of a man who knows his end is near. And at the film's conclusion we find the two offbeats aboard a bus heading to Florida, the suppurating Ratso cradled in Joe's frightened, unforeseeing arms.[2]

Schlesinger's narration is *ad hominem*, more or less claustrophobic. The choice is frequently made for a long lens, to draw the character's face closer to the camera and cause the background to recede. The story is thus a purely psychological view of a friendly bonding, a pair of portraits juxtaposed: Ratso sordid, Joe untouched; Ratso rotting, Joe virile and strong; Ratso with the endurance of the aged survivor, the one who has taken every conceivable hit and persevered doggedly in his path, while the other feels an urgent need for quick success and is prone to depression and resignation when the world doesn't go as he dreamed. Joe, indeed, is Edward Albee's "American Dream," save that in his case, signally for the story, no castration has taken place: It is his organic potential that Ratso sets himself to marketing, and that sets up his appeal to a wide-ranging clientele of hungry makers. Ratso is a contemporary, chewed-up Willy Loman, a man whose family life – such as it might conceivably have been – is all in the uncharted past, whose penchant for pitching, hawking, canoodling, manipulating, insinuating, and rationalizing has been honed and condensed in a closed waiting room, with desperation his fuel, trade his morality, rejection his lot. We angle back and forth between these differentially abject figurations, mundane encounters with the Moloch that is New York.

Even Schlesinger's minor characters deserve portraits. For a salient example, the stellar character actor John McGiver sweats around his one-room cell in a scarlet bathrobe, the light positioned to beam off his bald skull and his widely popping eyes making him a death's head of desire. There is a filthy, drooly gleam on his face, and his pounding imprecations that Joe get down on his knees so that they can "pray together" weave together incontinent homosexual energy and fearful subjection to the authoritative dictate of religious fervor. The man is a bible-thumper, in exactly the sense Joe would know from his agrarian roots, yet at the same time an utter alien, his warped spirit tempered in the furnace of metropolitan cravings and aspirations. He marches in a vast uncountable army of climbers and racers searching for tomorrow's reward.

Midnight Cowboy is an essay on this alienation and its accompanying, horrific integration: the inside quality of Ratso's rotting state of being and his kenning education of the outsider Joe. Because the two men are so clearly deviant in their commerce, however, so much beyond the pale of the world in which they make their lives, their alienation becomes its own kind of integration. In this way is the suggestion offered, with some modesty, that, when seen to its depths, all of New York is made up of types like these: outsiders to some fictive, presumptive, but entirely non-existent inside world, hangers-on for dear life who may think themselves marginal but in fact clearly represent the American type of the time.

Sunday Bloody Sunday

The figures in *Midnight Cowboy* are typifications, even animations. No viewer would reasonably suppose Ratso the only downtrodden soul of his sort in Manhattan, or Joe the only innocent to arrive from the farm belt with dreams of urban glory. In *Sunday Bloody Sunday*,[3] a poem on the fate of love in urban modernity under capitalism, the loneliness is of another, less superficial and more existential sort. The three central figures float in a bucolic and bourgeois English frame, skipping around their environment, like so many citizens of the early 1970s – here in the United Kingdom – with attachments that are subtle and traditional but not openly gregarious. In the age of "employment" and "employment counselling," life does not bring feelingful people together; it keeps them isolated in bubbles of privacy where knowledge and intimacy are converted to etiquettes and mannerisms, passion is scheduled, art commodified, truth rendered provisional and fleeting.

This is a film in which nothing happens and everything happens, at once. Daniel Hirsh (Peter Finch) is a middle-aged, gay, Jewish general practitioner,

Figure 21.2   Murray Head's uncertain head in Peter Finch's loving hands. *Sunday Bloody Sunday* (Vectia/Vic, 1971). Digital frame enlargement. Courtesy of Vectia/Vic/ United Artists.

with a healthy practice run out of a surgery in his comfortable London flat. Alex Greville (Glenda Jackson) finds unemployed executives jobs, helps her chums the Hodsons (Vivian Pickles and Frank Windsor) in Greenwich by sitting their house and children while they jaunt off for the weekend, and generally disports herself as helpful while being lost in her workaday world. Bob Elgin (Murray Head) is a narcissist in his late twenties, a creator of fascinating and beautiful sculptures, and bisexual. He is sleeping with both Daniel and Alex, in rhythmic alternation, fleeing one bedroom for the other in search of . . . what? – a self, a further round of pleasure, a muse . . .. Daniel knows about Alex, Alex knows about Daniel; and they are both friends to the elusive, boho Hodsons. More, they share a telephone answering service (by 1971, the later-ubiquitous personal home answering machine had not yet been marketed), through the agency of which we learn that each of them is constantly awaiting a call from Mr. Elgin that hasn't come in. If in seeing Daniel's tolerance of Bob's mobility we come to understand him as a man who has curtailed his romantic dreams so that they fit within the bounds of interpersonal civility and real opportunity, still there is an unmistakable sense in Finch's elegant performance of disappointment, better *chagrin*, so complexly personal as to be inexplicable. In an extended scene of his young nephew's Bar Mitzvah, for one example, we see his warm but too-nervous family, their genteel politenesses masking curiosity about how and why Daniel isn't married; but also the sense in which, smiling graciously, befriending folk young and old, this doctor is trapped in the disorderly personality that comes with modern life. His flat is meticulously clean and rational; but inside he has longings. In the rear garden is Bob's enormous glass-tube sculpture, bubbling in the night with green and blue fluids as the ethereal trio from Mozart's *Così fan tutte* fills the air. Daniel loves Bob. More, he adores him: Bob's youth, Bob's beauty, Bob's talent, Bob's irrepressible flair. But to *hold* Bob is an impossibility, since Bob is a sort of ghost. Daniel is therefore alone, horribly alone; although there isn't a moment in which he appears lonely.

Alex is on the point of quitting her middling job. A brief fling with a last-minute client (Tony Britton), a moment to pick up the cigarette stubs from her carpet, a weekend from hell with the four Hodson kids – most shockingly in a local park where the family dog, Kenyatta (of all names), is killed by a speeding lorry on the street nearby. How to let the children handle this death? Bob arrives, plays creative games with them on the kitchen table. But later, when the parents return, there seems to be no reaction at all: "We try not to pretend ... We're getting another one." The Hodson home is the microcosm of the bourgeois social scene in general, with productivity flourishing madly (read, reproductivity: four giggling, racing, untamed progeny); antiques fervently used and now falling apart; comfy decoration in place of classical form. There is a moment when Bob and Alex notice the four-year-old smoking marijuana, which mommy and daddy apparently hide behind the stereo. One senses in Alex the reek of desperation, her body and spirit taxed to the hilt by the children's ongoing energies, her loyalty challenged by Bob's coming and going, and her sexual need challenged by his frequent truancies with another lover she has already accepted and approved: or of whom she feels herself utterly unable to complain, in the name of overall peace and goodwill, the hallmarks of her bearing and class commitment.

For Alex comes from genuine money. We see a few brief moments of her at home, where her father (Maurice Denham) skips away from the dining table to take a trunk call about big money transfers, and her mother (Peggy Ashcroft) stolidly keeps up a mask of satisfied wifehood. The setting shrieks old money and privilege. Alex has run away from all this, for her young Bob; and with her beautiful pearl necklace the mother remains just a little – which is to say, just appropriately – envious, and also dismayed, because young men are, she need hardly say, flirtatious and incapable of real bonding. One of Schlesinger's deepest strengths is his understanding of the male condition – here and in other films – and his so piercingly accurate representation of Bob's attractiveness as being wedded to his insecurity.

The setting of *Sunday Bloody Sunday* is a cultural moment, and its composition is an array of pungently startling dramatic tableaux in rough sequence. Some of these are memorable in a way that is musical, haunting, and troubling at once. The dead Kenyatta, flaccid, with tongue dropped out, in Bob's arms, as he is lifted off the road. The astonishing sculpture in Daniel's garden, the bubbles rising hopefully, hopefully, hopefully, blue and green, green and blue, with the enchanted aria wafting through the air in the sedate London darkness. Daniel's composed face as he speaks to his patients in their moments of desperation, color in his cheeks, utter frankness in his crisp blue eyes. A drunken Scot hopping into Daniel's car at a crosswalk (Peter's son Jon Finch), a former lover evidently now in need of some painkillers so that Daniel has reason to stop at a druggist and leave this thief, as he turns out to be, alone in the car with his medical bag. The druggist's shop: a brave and starkly fluorescent vision with a gang of addicts and walking wounded waiting to collect their prescriptions. A scene in which Alex stands at the door of her bathroom watching Bob in the shower: the opaque vision of his warm orange body in the steamy cyan light. A culminating moment of embrace with the two men in bed, once the realization has dawned on Daniel that Bob is going to take up an invitation to visit New York (and thus put on hold, for the nth time, their dreamed-of idyll in Italy): he grasps Bob's face in both hands and holds it in silence, rather in the way a lover of art might clasp and stare at a Grecian head, dug up from the ruins.

An enormous number of shots in the film are extreme facial close-ups, it being deeply understood by Schlesinger what modernity has brought to the table: that there is no better keeper of secrets than the face, no more forbidding gate. And, to emphasize clearly and dramatically the connection between lost connections and the modern urban scene, the relation between technology and alienation, Schlesinger contrives to shoot Penelope Gilliatt's script, its bedtime conversations so repeatedly unaffected and mundane regardless of the gender of the lovers, in weave with a number of visions – abstracted in part from Hitchcock's *Dial M for Murder* (1953) and in part from Truffaut's *Baisers volés* (1968) – of the mechanical workings of the telephone switching system seen from inside and up close. When we hear conversational voices filtered through the answering service, or see telephones being dialed, we cut to wires, junction boxes, ratchets, pivots, transformers, what have you – it is a mystery quite by intention: the machine is actually doing the talking, the machine that is part of a system required because so many different people want to be talking to so many other people all at the same time. Talk talk talk talk talk talk. And in the end, a long shot of Bob's TWA jet taking off from Heathrow, up up up into the sky. "I'll be back," he promises both Daniel and Alex, but out of their sights he softly deposits their apartment keys on the entrance tables as he walks out.

Although it is shown only fragmentarily in the narrative, the Hodsons' Greenwich household centralizes a deep concern of Schlesinger's: the predominance of movement and doing, over talk. In this realm of anarchic liberality, where something is always – but perhaps incompletely – on the go, where there seems a matter-of-fact egalitarianism between educated adults and rambunctious children, where intelligence is embedded in every nook (even the dog reflecting through his name the esteemed leader of an African country, Jomo Kenyatta), where the bourgeois proprieties of neatness, order, deference, and age-division are systematically disavowed, we see a vivid representation of Cockaigne itself, an idealized, paradisiacal Britain conceived as utopian zone. Here all is effortless for those who have become citizens. This cannot be said yet of Alex, however, who labors rigorously to entertain the children and keep the house from falling apart. The open evidence of her labor, performed as a kind of show in front of Bob, makes dramatically plain that her having invited him to join her for the weekend was a subtle prelude to a more serious involvement. "How would Bob be as a marital partner, she may well be wondering," we may well conclude, as they lie abed together, with Bob cluelessly snacking upon a jar of Alva Hodson's breast milk from the jampacked refrigerator.

Daniel wants an enduring partnership with Bob, hence the planned Italian trip. But Bob is torn between the projects of his two lovers, each, in a private way, hoping to label, adorn, worship (and thus stultify) him in present form, his Narcissus self. Bob's own need, of course, is to grow, and to find his own terms for doing that. While his love bond with Daniel is less confining, even less irritating, it is no more likely to yield him genuine freedom. And as to Alex and Daniel themselves, they form their designs more or less unconsciously, naturally: not as a way of violating the young man or possessing him but merely to say, in the only language people of their generation know, "I love you."

THE DAY OF THE LOCUST

Based on Nathanael West's 1939 novel, this period reconstruction boldly asserts Schlesinger's outsider status as a professional at work in Hollywood. In this respect, suggests the film, he is like almost everyone there: eccentric if not suspected as such; a bad fit in a world of bad fits. *Locust* was the filmmaker's first foray into California. Lacking even the casual armature of interpersonal relationships that supports and constrains typical Hollywood filmmaking, he was able to see the place, and the industry which is its central economic feature, with a devastating clarity fully matching the New Yorker West's (who had gone to Hollywood after an inauspicious east-coast college career, in 1933, and with Boris Ingster written a later-discarded screenplay for what was to become Hitchcock's *Suspicion* [1941]). If the public face of Hollywood is a bacchanal without temporal limit, in which forces beautiful and talented revel in sybaritic enjoyment and the ongoing search for recognition; in the nostalgic recounting of shared legends; and in the admiration of an amenable climate and topography, in reality society is considerably isolating

Figure 21.3   William Atherton as Tod, the beleaguered designer, in *The Day of the Locust* (1975). Digital frame enlargement. Courtesy of United Artists/ Paramount Pictures.

there, competition the prevailing form, and the topography smaller than it appears onscreen: Edenic yet imperiled. The friendships, the chummery, the remembered histories of encounters are, if not wholly then at least frequently, business-oriented more than emotive. The main preoccupation is deal-making toward immense profit. Labor is intensive and exhausting, and human relations have labor in focus no matter their erotic charge and ebullience. The movie business has a class system, and in the early days of cinema that system was notably pronounced.

Schlesinger presents Hollywood extra Faye Greener (Karen Black) and Yale-graduated art designer Tod Hackett (William Atherton) as central figures, the earnest Tod besmitten by Faye and the flirtatious Faye perpetually teasing with his simmering desire. Numerous others populate what feels like a tropical circus: Faye's faded vaudevillian father Harry (Burgess Meredith, in a stunning performance); her eventual husband (or at least live-in partner – it's never made clear) Homer (Donald Sutherland), a pariah bird perched on the wire between repressed honor and scathing violence; the studio head of the art department Claude Estee (Richard Dysart, in a chilling take on the Cedric Gibbons type: he resides in an Art Deco house owned by his wife, whom he married in order to live there); Faye's girlfriend Mary Dove, eager to sell herself for a chance at fame (Lelia Goldoni); Earle Shoop (Bo Hopkins), another extra, also eager for Faye's attentions but a hanger-on to a cock fighter (Pepe Serna); Adore (Jackie Haley), a golden-haired youth living at the same Hollywood Blvd. hotel as

Tod and Faye and finally a victim of the buried jealousy, wrath, and violence underpinning the structure of Hollywood society. Faye's employment status leaves her stranded at the bottom of the vast studio underclass, paid by the day with no guarantee of a future in movies. Tod, talented and eager, is slotted in the vertical studio hierarchy, a bright young comer who must never stop toeing the line if he is to ascend.

Desperation and loneliness are ubiquitous here, set with canny precision in telling Hollywood locales such as Beachwood Canyon, Whitley Heights, and Hollywood Blvd. A pair of Inuit bit players, imported for Flaherty's *Nanook of the North* (1922), gloat about Greenblatt's Deli (on the Strip). Tod's attempts to warm Faye's heart are continually frustrated in any locale; and the pervading atmospheric toxicity of the studio compromises his sense of moral value. Faye seems perpetually lost (Black's wide-eyed stare emphasizing this condition), her father hopelessly unsalvageable and out of touch in his bubble from the past (in his door-to-door sales gig he approaches customers with old-time comedic schtick), her "love" relation with Homer at best equivocal, at worst brutally utilitarian, and frustrating to both of them. Estee is revealed as a hollow man, notwithstanding his consummate artistic flair. The studio bosses are craven – even criminal – opportunists puppeted by private greed.

Schlesinger's visual genius and sense of pace, his canny choices of focus and surprising compositions, his respect for the power of visual drama, and his keen sociological understanding of the Hollywood power structure are nowhere better evidenced than in a complex sequence set in a vast studio soundstage. At Estee's enthusiastic request, Tod has designed the set for the Battle of Waterloo, now being filmed with several hundred extras on a marvelous piece of construction involving rolling grassy hills mounting upwards on a fifty-foot-high platform of wooden scaffolding. Faye and Earle are both working the set, and Tod is lurking off-camera to watch the cinematic accomplishment of his first major Hollywood design. The director is on a crane with a megaphone (the scene's sound will be post-dubbed), ordering "soldiers" into the correct stance for bayonetting one another, and take after take proceeds. But suddenly Tod notices that the KEEP OFF warning signs intended for the understructure have been scrapped in a bin, and looking up he sees carpenters perched silently on the scaffolds while the take proceeds. He runs out and tries to shout the scene down, but in the melee no one can hear him, and suddenly the hills . . . collapse. "Oh! My God!" the director cries, but too late. Schlesinger archly cuts to a close shot of a couple of young kids dressed as drummer and piper, catching sight of the catastrophe and gawking at it with entertained smiles: the perfect childish response (from perfect children). Then, as some stagehands carelessly raise a ladder to save some of the extras trapped high in the air, more of the set collapses, until nothing is left of the hills but a swirling cloud of dust. Tod is calling out for "Faye? Faye Greener?!" And he thinks he sees her! But no, it's another extra – with the costumes and makeup, and not being stars, the extras all look alike.

Outside, trolleys bear the wounded away from the stage while extras from other shoots – some in tuxedoes, some dressed as Indians – rush up in concern (Schlesinger is cueing us to the multiple productions proceeding simultaneously, thus pointing to the economic logic of the studio as production facility.) Tod hops a ride, hearing people chat coldly about the levels of studio recompense depending on their injuries. He jumps off and finds Faye on an outside stairway. It is a moment *like* the tryst that would bring emotional closure for us after the pain of the disaster, yet not at all a tryst, since, as we recall in shocked dismay, these two never did get together. She begs a few dollars for streetcar fare and he asks a little too politely how she is, and Homer, and Mary Dove, trying for an instant to rekindle the ashes of hope. But now he is summoned to a meeting in the barber shop, whither he must race (as a star dressed à la Marie Antoinette is escorted in the background of the shot to the Rolls-Royce limo that will usher her a few feet down the road to the stage she is shooting on: the show must go on, and such a luminary must not be seen walking). This stark portrait of class difference at the studio – the star's privileged treatment; the lack of attention to the safety of extras – now gains full emphasis as the studio manager (Paul Stewart), in his barber's chair, shrugs off the accident, assured that the warning signs were up. "But – " tries Tod, to no avail.

Every human relationship in the film is shown somehow to spring from or pivot on the sort of production activity we see interrupted in this accident. The striving for Hollywood success is a frantic race to become the star in her Rolls. The working underclass are shown unprotected, uncared for, and routinely jeopardizing their lives (one of the assistant directors, we learn, is on the critical list and not expected to survive, like the cock torn to pieces in a nocturnal fight beneath the HOLLYWOODLAND sign). The old father represents a world out of which Hollywood film sprang, Mary Dove indexes the manipulation in gaining access to fame. Faye and Earle appear to have settled for lives out of the limelight: self-acknowledged rejects, willing to live on the margins of fame; but Tod intends to be a significant force in Hollywood film, until his utter disorientation (literally: his losing sense of the East, from which he came).

If the quest for fame and riches rushes through the story like a river, every character continually on the lookout for self-placement and for a way upward and forward, and if the setting is paradisiacal – too paradisiacal – the quest is feverish. Fever burns everywhere: Tod's inflamed hunger for Faye, coupled to his increasingly shocked perception of the film-world rat race in which he jogs; Faye's inflamed hunger for screen fame, because she comes from a "long line of show-business folk"; Harry's inflamed hunger for the old days, long lost, in which (at least as he imagines it now) he was loved and adored; Claude Estee's inflamed hunger for wealth, pleasure, control; Homer's inflamed hunger for the security of Faye's approval, which always seems over the horizon (when he serves up a bowl of strawberry ice-cream, she vitriolically washes it down the sink). Skipping, hopping, and taunting his or her way through the fever – unfeeling, uncaring, incendiary – is Adore, the (gender indeterminate) child star in the making, with curls too blonde and too long and a natty little two-step, spying, teasing, finally dying in the gutter as the Hollywood Blvd. of Grauman's Chinese explodes into movie-mob frenzy. These are the denizens of Hollywood's "Dream Dump," as Mike Davis names it, "a hallucinatory landscape tottering on apocalypse" (38); yet, as Schlesinger's images clearly tell and Carey McWilliams warned, "The state of mind, the utopian mentality, so vividly described by West, is a national, not a local phenomenon" (310).

Marathon Man

Having finished an undergraduate career almost ten years previously in *The Graduate* (1967), and having picked up a mouthful of rotten teeth in *Midnight Cowboy*, Dustin Hoffman returned as a graduate student who would suffer dental agonies in *Marathon Man*. If, like the central figures in Schlesinger's other 1970s films, his Babe Levy is an outsider, that status does not originate in any personal defect: this is an athletically healthy, vigorous, witty, and utterly charming young fellow. But Babe is caught up in a chilling international intrigue, finally discovering himself alone on earth as the only person who can

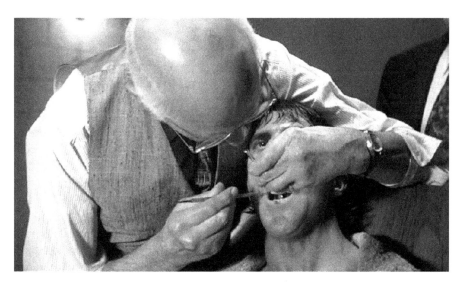

Figure 21.4 "Is it safe?" Laurence Olivier with Dustin Hoffman in *Marathon Man* (Robert Evans Company, 1976). Digital frame enlargement. Courtesy of Robert Evans Company/Paramount.

bring some semblance of justice to a sadistic and megalomaniac Nazi murderer. We are amid the bustle of mid- and uptown Manhattan, not John Lindsay's liberal-progressivist new city (of *Midnight Cowboy*) but Abe Beame's fragile urban bridge to the zany topos of Ed Koch that would follow. The villain here is Christian Szell (Laurence Olivier), a.k.a. Der Weisse Engel (The White Angel), who ran a concentration camp's medical and scientific "studies" in which countless unfortunates were tortured and slain. With Hitler's demise Szell had stowed away a treasure in diamonds, and has now left his South American jungle lair for New York in order to retrieve and market them. An old man not so hale, with a storehouse of interpersonal charm, his icily calculating method forbids sympathy of any kind. He is the epitome of evil, sporting a wristband-stiletto for slashing throats or carving the innards of any fool who comes too close. Olivier plays him as a man petrified by the panic of being discovered, interminably anxious that the contents of his magical safe-deposit box, purloined spoils of war, be kept secure.

The structure of *Marathon Man* has come to be familiar to fans of the thrillers that imitated it. Babe is surrounded early on by a pack of charming and intelligent "friends." He lives in relative ignorance of Szell and the Nazi undertakings rooted beneath the surface of the story. Carrying enduring (and indelible) memories of his suicided father, a brilliant historian felled by McCarthyism, Babe is accompanied in his present-day invigorations (through both jogging and thesis-writing: "The Use of Torture in American Political History") by Else (Marthe Keller), a lovely (and gorgeous) Swiss grad student he meets in the Columbia library; by his older brother Doc (Roy Scheider), a sell-out oil tycoon, and eventually by Janeway (William Devane), Doc's longstanding chum and business associate. Of course all this sweetness turns sour. Doc, it turns out, is working for Szell, and couldn't be less interested in oil. He is knifed in front of Lincoln Center, and, struggling to make his way to Babe's arms before dying, whispers something into the younger brother's ears. Confiding that he and Doc actually ran a secret operational group called The Division ("We supply." – "What?" – "Anything."), Janeway presses Babe to share the secret message, but to no avail, and soon enough our young historian is kidnapped and brought to Szell for torturing. Janeway arrives to rescue him, but soon Babe learns that this agent is also on Szell's payroll. Running half naked through the slick nocturnal streets to escape Janeway and his thugs, Babe finds a way, even in his weakened state, to trigger his jogger response, and finds freedom. He telephones Elsa to pick him up, and she drives him into the country, where it suddenly dawns upon him that she, too, is with the Nazis. After Janeway and friends arrive to recapture him, there is a shootout in which the whole gang are killed. Babe survives to come back into the city, locate Szell at his bank, and lead him at gunpoint to a reservoir control station in Central Park where the diamonds are tossed into the waterflow and the cupidinous

Szell, tumbling down the wrought-iron staircase, accidentally knifes himself to death.

Beyond his seemingly natural skill with actors and in choreographing action for camera, Schlesinger shines in the creation of revealing and pungent set pieces. The film opens, for one example, with a startling upper-east-side road rage sequence involving a German Nazi sympathizer and a New York Jew who begin screaming at one another from their moving cars as they careen down a narrow street. The interpersonal hatred, the mounting heat of the passions, the reanimation of World War II here in microcosm – "Nazi bastard!" – "Jude!" – coupled with the stunned gawking of onlookers as the cars speed by, all combine to transform a more or less standard action passage into a metaphor for racial division, irresolvable loathing, and historical guilt. Another: in a brief classroom scene with his supervisor (Fritz Weaver), who was a loyal pupil of Babe's father, it becomes apparent that the professor's practice of historical criticism is a paternal force both guiding and monitoring his student's scholarly life. Babe is a free man when he is jogging around the park, but here at Columbia, and in academic life, he is subject to the desire, memory, and hope of a senior who sharply embodies a past. The scene prefigures the dark variation that will be enacted between Babe and Szell. And there is a beautifully shot (hand-held) sequence in the diamond market, 47th Street between 5th and 6th Avenues, when Szell wishes to have one of his stones appraised. An old woman across the street recognizes him and shouts as he tries to escape through the crowded sidewalk, "Der Weisse Engel! Der Weisse Engel is here!!" The Nazi's only chances depend upon him *not* being seen to run, of course, so he must maintain his sangfroid as her voice grows louder and she implores people to "Stop him!!"

For most viewers who saw this film when it was released, however, there remains, drilled permanently into memory (in its way, like the atrocity of the camps), a group of related scenes in which Szell employs dental equipment to bring Babe to the limiting point of pain. "Is it safe?" the old man repeats, over and over, a diabolical mantra sung in every possible inflection of the voice (and nor any voice, but Olivier's resonant one). "Is it *safe?*" . . . "*Is it* safe?" Babe of course knows nothing, because what Doc whispered with his dying breath was only his younger brother's name. "Yes, it's perfectly safe . . . No, it isn't safe at all, it's very dangerous": coming from a face beleaguered by pain, confusion, darkness. It is hard to imagine a more agonizing picture of isolation, entrapment within the self, and despair.

NOTES

1. Hoffman neglected the emphatic advice of Mike Nichols, who had made him a star in *The Graduate* (1967), in agreeing to play Ratso for Schlesinger.

2. A polite directorial nod to the ending of *The Graduate*.
3. "Sunday," wrote Gilliatt, "almost always being bloody in the minds of English children: the day of stasis, of grown-ups going to sleep after too heavy a lunch" (online at criterion.com and included in the original screenplay, New York: Dodd Mead, 1986).

WORKS CITED

Davis, Mike. *City of Quartz*. Vintage, 1992.
Kafka, Franz. *The Trial*. Translated by Breon Mitchell. Schocken, 1998.
McWilliams, Carey. *Southern California Country: An Island on the Land*. Duell, Sloan & Pearce, 1946.

22. FIRE AND ICE: PAUL SCHRADER

Constantine Verevis

In *A Cinema of Loneliness*, Robert Kolker attends to the work of writer-director Paul Schrader mostly in terms of his collaborations with Martin Scorsese – *Raging Bull* (1980), *The Last Temptation of Christ* (1988), *Bringing Out the Dead* (1999), and in particular Schrader's (Bresson-inspired) screenplay for *Taxi Driver* (1976), an essay on "spiritual isolation and redemption" transformed (by Scorsese) into a film about the "despair and disintegration" of its protagonist, Travis Bickle (231). While Scorsese/*Taxi Driver* are undeniably key figures/works of the New Hollywood, this kind of emphasis occludes Schrader's own contribution as a filmmaker: specifically, four early films – *Blue Collar* (1978), *Hardcore* (1979), *American Gigolo* (1980) and *Cat People* (1982) – directed from Schrader screenplays and revisions. This chapter attends to these films, examining not only the ways in which the outsider character of Bickle recurs across Schrader's early works, but also interrogating the films to understand how each one activates key themes and prototypes that structure Schrader's career in, and contribution to, the New Hollywood.

Born in 1946 in Grand Rapids, Michigan, Schrader was raised in a strict Dutch Calvinist environment with restricted access to filmed entertainment. In the 1960s Schrader's ambition was to be a minister, but a chance meeting with Pauline Kael provided him with an introduction to UCLA film school where he fervently watched films and became a critic for the *LA Free Press*. In the early 1970s Schrader worked as an editor for *Cinema* magazine and published his MA dissertation as *Transcendental Style in Film: Ozu, Bresson, Dreyer* (1972). Schrader's first success as a screenwriter came with *The Yakuza* (1974), co-written with his brother Leonard Schrader, and his script output included *Taxi Driver*, *Obsession* (1976), and *Rolling Thunder* (1977). Schrader says he aspired to direct feature films from as early as the writing of his first (unproduced) screenplay, *Pipeliner* (1971), and planned for *Rolling Thunder* (ultimately directed by John Flynn) to be his first film as director (*Schrader on Schrader* 121).[1] Although not displeased with the way his screenplays had been produced, Schrader said:

> if you want to be in control of what you are doing as a writer you either have to become a novelist . . . or you have to get into directing. Being a screenwriter is . . . rather unsatisfying for an artist . . . In the end you don't really feel you have anything that represents you. (*SoS* 141)

In 1977, Schrader made his debut as director with *Blue Collar*, a film co-scripted with his brother Leonard. Set in Detroit, the film came out of a working-class milieu that the Schraders were familiar with from their upbringing in Grand Rapids, a place of manufacturing and a satellite town of the motor city (*SoS* 1–2). *Blue Collar* tells the story of three auto-workers – Zeke (Richard Pryor), Smokey (Yaphet Kotto), and Jerry (Harvey Keitel) – who, frustrated by the financial pressures of low-paid work and angered by the ineffectiveness of their union, decide to steal funds from the association's factory safe. The burglary leads them to discoveries of union corruption, and subsequent violent attempts to prevent that information from coming to light ultimately fracture the solidarity of the three workers. Schrader initially set out to make a film that would operate principally in the area of entertainment – a caper film, carried by three strong leads – but, as the script developed, he realized he had come to a "very specific Marxist conclusion":

> I didn't set out to make a left-wing film. I had no visions of making this into a concrete political thing . . . I wanted to write a movie about some guys who rip off the union because it seemed to me such a wonderfully self-hating kind of act, that they would attack the organization that's supposed to help them. (Crowdus and Georgakas 34)

In preparation for *Blue Collar*, Schrader conducted interviews with factory hands and rented several documentary films about workplaces and employees – *The Blue Collar Trap* (1972), *Finally Got the News . . .* (1970) and *Work* (1970) – which he transferred to videotape and watched several times (36). Like the similarly titled *Blue Collar Trap*, which deals with workers at a Ford Pinto plant in California, Schrader's film focuses on the alienation of workers and the methods by which they deal with their dissatisfaction. Specifically, he attends to the ways large corporations maintain control of conditions in

Figure 22.1   Smokey (Yaphet Kotto), Zeke (Richard Pryor) and Jerry (Harvey Keitel) in *Blue Collar* (1978). Digital frame enlargement. Courtesy of TAT Communications/ Universal Pictures.

the workplace by introducing tensions that make it easier to justify poor working conditions, and to hire and fire workers, because each worker is preoccupied with trying to get ahead of the next. In *Blue Collar*, this tension is explicitly created through the issue of race because – as Schrader describes it – "everybody has this big button called racism": "[*Blue Collar*] is about the impossibility of integration in a work situation; there are too many tensions that will destroy any racial harmony" (34). In the film, the friendship among the three workers (two black, one white) is tested when their attempted black-mail of the union is resisted: Smokey, considered the militant one of the group, is suspiciously killed in a paint-shop accident; Zeke, realising that cooperation with the bosses is his best chance to get ahead, is bribed into accepting a pro-motion to shop steward; and Jerry, terrified after his family is threatened and fearing for his life, goes to the FBI, only to be condemned by Zeke and fellow co-workers who see him as a fink. In the final confrontation, the former friends hurl racial abuse – "dumb Pollock ... jive white boy ... fuckin' nigger" – at one another. The film ends – in freeze frame – with Zeke and Jerry about to come to blows, and with Smokey's earlier comments on management's divisive politics of fear replayed in voiceover: "They pit the lifers against the new boy, the young against the old, the black against the white. Everything they do is to keep us in our place."

In his first film as director, Schrader experienced a number of difficulties on set. In particular there was tension among his three principal actors, each of whom believed he was the lead. This inadvertently created a situation that in some ways replicated the film's themes of resentment and claustrophobia. Schrader said: "*Blue Collar* was one of those legendary bad experiences. When it was all over, I thought, if that was what directing was, I didn't want any part of it" (Emery 159). Looking back, Schrader saw the film mostly as on-the-job training:

> I really didn't feel comfortable directing until *American Gigolo* . . . I told my script supervisor that I was just going to try to concentrate on story. I told her to make sure that I had the coverage and make sure the camera is doing something and looks okay. I really didn't concern myself that much about the technical aspects of the film. . . . There are a lot of ghost directors out there. Anybody can direct. Anybody listening to me can direct. All you do is hire a certain photographer . . . and they'll do that film for you. It won't have much of a personal stamp on it visually, but it will have a personal stamp in terms of the story as you've written it. So in *Blue Collar*, all I was trying to do was simply capture the story. (159)

Despite such sentiments *Blue Collar* was critically well received, and "the gritty working-class milieu" of the film was carried over into the more personal work of *Hardcore*, a story of a conservative Calvinist businessman from Grand Rapids who goes underground in the Los Angeles sleaze world of porn and snuff films to bring his supposedly abducted daughter home (Bliss 3). Schrader described *Hardcore*, along with the later *Light of Day* (1987), as "more or less autobiographical films" – the former about his father, the latter about his mother – and attributed their commercial failure to the fact of their being "a little too personal" (*SoS* 149). *Hardcore* opens with establishing shots of Grand Rapids, including views of a snow-covered Main Street festooned in Christmas decorations, and the First Christian Reformed Church. As the credits end, the opening sequence documents the domestic life of an extended Dutch Calvinist family, led by patriarch Jake VanDorn (George C. Scott), where, amid the Christmas festivities, parents discuss theology and children watch holiday specials on television. One adult responds impatiently to the latter, telling the children (in a line that Schrader attributes to one of his uncles): "You know who makes [this television]? All of the kids who couldn't get along here. They go out to California and make television. I didn't like them when they were here, and I don't like them out there" (*SoS* 149).

Schrader said *Hardcore* had its origins in a story about a girl who disappeared from their local high school in Grand Rapids only to later turn up working as a prostitute in Chicago (Kahan 4), but the prototype for *Hardcore*'s "bringing back lost sheep" narrative is more evidently John Ford's *The Searchers* (1956). As a film critic, Schrader had counted *The Searchers*, along with Hitchcock's *Vertigo* (1958), among the greatest films ever made, and the influence of the former – specifically, Ethan Edwards's (John Wayne) quest to rescue his kidnapped niece Debbie (Natalie Wood) from the Comanche chief Scar (Henry Brandon) – can be found not only in *Hardcore* but in Schrader's scripts for *Taxi Driver, Rolling Thunder, Patty Hearst* (1988), and *Bringing Out the Dead*. For Schrader, the significance of *The Searchers* lay not just in its "enormous technical expertise" but also (and more significantly) in its exposure of "the frailty of the great American hero" (*SoS* 155). As Schrader explains, with the character of Ethan Edwards,

> Wayne is playing with his persona; he hardly ever plays the outsider, but [Ethan] is a man who is deprived of the pleasures of hearth and home because he has blood on his hands. At the end of the movie he walks away and the door closes on him; he has returned the lost child to the home but he [himself] can't enter. (*SoS* 155)

Hardcore is not only a variation of *The Searchers* but also an insightful questioning of Schrader's own background. Schrader says he devised *Hardcore* as a revenge fantasy:

> I sort of wanted to make a film where my father was the revenge figure – to take somebody from my background, and that *is* my background, in *Hardcore*. . . . I tried to take a character like my father and put him in [the underworld of] Los Angeles. (Emery 160)

The action in *Hardcore* begins in earnest when VanDorn travels to California in search of his teenage daughter Kristen (Ilah Davis), who has disappeared from a Youth Calvinist Convention. At the suggestion of local police, VanDorn hires a private investigator, Andy Mast (Peter Boyle), who immediately alienates him, asking if Kristen "fucks around." But after months of investigation Mast eventually uncovers a lead in the form of a pornographic film featuring Kristen. Aghast, and frustrated by Mast's inability to actually locate his daughter, VanDorn decides to take up the search for Kristen himself, cruising the sex clubs and skin-flick stores of the Los Angeles neon porn underworld. Initially bewildered by what he finds, Jake gradually adapts his professional acumen to the local situation, posing first as a businessman seeking to invest in softcore and subsequently as a producer of pornographic movies in order to locate anyone with knowledge of Kristen's situation.

Throughout the film, Schrader draws upon his Calvinist upbringing to render Jake's journey through the Los Angeles porn underworld as a literal decent into Hell. Commenting on Schrader's own peculiar moral position – a Calvinist ("a lost sheep") residing in Hollywood Babylon – producer John Milius said:

Figure 22.2   Jake VanDorn (George C. Scott) goes to "hell" in *Hardcore* (1979). Digital frame enlargement. Courtesy of A-Team Productions/Universal Pictures.

> While we were making *Hardcore*, [Schrader] took me down Hollywood Boulevard. 'This is hell!' he said. 'You can go to hell any day, right here. Lost souls, burning and tormented' . . . He'd always known you could burn in hell, but he'd never realized you could drive your car through it. (Gehr 35)

Jake enlists a guide through the underworld, the parlour girl Niki (Season Hubley) who leads him to San Diego and San Francisco in search of Kristen. Along the way, in the film's most deliberate recall of Schrader's upbringing, Jake explains his religious views. Calvinists, he tells Niki,

> believe in the 'TULIP' . . . It comes from the Canons of Dort. Every letter stands for a different belief . . . T stands for Total Depravity – all men through original sin are totally evil and incapable of good. 'All my works are as filthy rags in sight of the Lord.' . . . U stands for Unconditional Election. God has chosen a certain number of people to be saved, the Elect, and He has chosen them from the beginning of time. L is for Limited Atonement . . . I is for Irresistible Grace . . . And P is for the Perseverance of the Saints. Once you are in Grace, you cannot fall from the number of the Elect.

VanDorn finally locates Kristen with Ratan (Marc Alaimo), a lethal dealer of snuff films, who is chased down and shot dead by Mast after a struggle with VanDorn. At long last reunited with his daughter, Jake is devastated when she reveals that she was not abducted but – like her mother – had chosen to run away to escape her stifling home environment. Kristen tells him (in words that anticipate the final scenes of Schrader's later "bringing back lost sheep" film, *Patty Hearst*):

> Don't touch me, you cocksucker. You never gave a fuck about me before ... I didn't fit into your goddamned world. I wasn't pretty or good enough for you ... I'm with people who love me now.

The film ends with Jake reaching out to Kristen: in a paraphrase of Ethan's words to Debbie, he tells her, "Let me take you home," but his actions and (religious) beliefs are, to the end, irreconcilable – "hardcore." Asking Mast whether there is anything he can do for Niki (whom he has exploited and discarded on the way to finding Kristen) Jake is told (in the final words of the film): "Go home Pilgrim. There's nothing you can do. You don't belong here." To the end an isolated man, VanDorn intrinsically connects to the "man and his room" protagonist of the earlier *Taxi Driver* and of Schrader's next film, *American Gigolo*.

Schrader wrote five scripts in 1976 – *Blue Collar*, *Hardcore*, *American Gigolo*, *Old Boyfriends* (directed by Joan Tewkesbury in 1978), and an unproduced Hank Williams film – and then spent the following three years directing the first three of these: "I was shooting *Hardcore* at the time *Blue Collar* opened and I was shooting [*American*] *Gigolo* shortly after *Hardcore* opened" (*SoS* 157). Unlike *Blue Collar* and *Hardcore*, *American Gigolo* referred not directly to the world of Schrader's upbringing but rather to the domain of films and filmmaking in which he had more recently been immersed (Tuchman 50). Schrader said the theme for *American Gigolo* – "the inability to express love" – came to him while he was conducting a writing workshop at UCLA, and the metaphor through which to convey this was that of the gigolo:

> I hit on this theme and realized that the character of the gigolo was essentially a character of surfaces; therefore the movie had to be about surfaces, and you had to create a new kind of Los Angeles to reflect this new kind of protagonist. (*SoS* 158)

To develop a high-concept style for the film, Schrader assembled a team of technicians (all of whom would carry over to Schrader's next film, *Cat People*): John Bailey for cinematography, Giorgio Moroder for music, and Ferdinando Scarfiotti for production design. Of the group, Schrader singled out Scarfiotti's contribution, and the influence of Scarfiotti's earlier work on Bernardo Bertolucci's *The Conformist* (1970): "I pretty much sat at Nando Scarfiotti's knee ... *The Conformist* was a very important film for my generation, because it was a film that reintroduced the concept of high style" (*SoS* 158–60).

American Gigolo is often characterized as the middle film in a trilogy of Schrader "man and his room" stories that begins with *Taxi Driver* (1976) and concludes with *Light Sleeper* (1992) (Smith 51). All three films draw their sense of loneliness and alienation from the film work of Bresson, but also share a number of qualities with film noir, in particular the professional code and "existential ethos" of the noir protagonist (Nichols 9). In *American Gigolo* the title character, Julian Kay (Richard Gere), is a former street boy who, through training and discipline, has positioned himself as an escort for wealthy women of many backgrounds and nationalities visiting Los Angeles. Julian's professional services can be purchased and are administered with absolute dedication, but he resists any involvement, and his room – an austere apartment – is a sanctuary that clients are not permitted to enter. Julian's position of privilege and his carefully controlled world begin to unravel, however, when he is asked by a friend and procurer, Leon Jaimes (Bill Duke), to take an assignment in Palm Springs with a couple, the Rheimans, who involve Julian in sado-masochistic sex. The following day, when Julian complains that he was set up for a "rough trick," Leon warns him of the precariousness of his situation:

> You know, you walk an awfully thin line, [Julian]. I wouldn't want to be in your shoes. I mean, you're getting awful cocky . . . You got all your rich pussy lined up: once a month tricks, a dip in the pool, a little tennis, an orgasm. I'm just trying to warn you as a friend: those bitches ever turn on you, you're through.

A larger problem emerges when Julian reads that Judy Rheiman (Patti Carr) has been murdered and, as the police now aware of the couple's bizarre sex life, Julian comes under the suspicion of Detective Sunday (Hector Elizondo). At the same time, Julian finds himself reluctantly drawn deep into a relationship with Michelle (Lauren Hutton), the alienated wife of Californian senator Charles Stratton (Brian Davies) whom he has mistaken for a wealthy French tourist at an exclusive bar. Realising his error, Julian attempts to excuse himself, but Michelle bluntly asks: "How much would you have charged me . . . [for] just one fuck?" Michelle not only sees through Julian's façade but also actively pursues him, arriving at his Westwood Hotel apartment and forcing him to change his rules for entertaining clients. Despite Julian's protestations, that he is not the solution to her problem, Michelle visits again, leading into a cold and detached – for Julian, a thoroughly *professional* – sexual encounter. As the police investigation intensifies – the ("rich bitch") client with whom Julian was with at the time of the murder won't confirm his alibi for fear of exposure – Michelle and Julian move closer, her offering him "a spiritual dimension to life wholly apart from his gigolo environment" (Nichols 9). At the end, Julian finds himself in jail awaiting trial for a murder he did not commit, and Michelle defies her husband, sacrificing her reputation to provide Julian with an alibi.

American Gigolo can be understood as a development of the formula – explicated in *Transcendental Style in Film* – by means of which the transcendent may be expressed in film. Although some have argued that Schrader failed to employ the formula (see Nichols), Schrader maintained that

> the trick of the film [*American Gigolo*] – and I guess if I ever try to do anything resembling transcendental style this might be it – is to try to create an essentially cold film in which a burst of emotion transforms it at the end. (*SoS* 160)

In *American Gigolo*, Julian's endeavour to perfect himself is rendered as his own personal hell, captured early in the film by the prowling camera that follows him into the "pinkly glowing inferno" of the bar in which he meets Michelle (Combs, "*American Gigolo*" 88). The materialist life (-style) to which Julian has surrendered is encapsulated right from the outset in the vibrant beat of Blondie's "Call Me" which opens the film, and continues through the abundant tracking shots that "exude power, authority, a rapture between camera and subject" (Nichols 11). Julian's world is one of sensation, but it is superficial, something literalized by the fact that he is frequently displayed in mirrors with his reflected image often shown first. At the end of the film Julian's arrest and decisive awakening is rendered through an abrupt shift in the film's style, which becomes austere and desaturated, the "bright pastel colours" that dominate the first part of the film giving way to a series of "washed-out blues and prison greys" and slow fades to white (Kouvaros 43). Julian's fall is also the occasion of Michelle's liberation, her hitherto perfunctory life finding a purpose. As Schrader describes it, *American Gigolo* is "about two professional arm-pieces. Male and Female. They both do the same job. One of them is actively empty, the other is passively empty. And they both do the opposite. He becomes passive by accepting her love, and she becomes active by sacrificing her marriage to him" (Wells 284). At the end, in a scene closely modeled on Bresson's *Pickpocket* (and later reprised in *Light Sleeper*), the characters break through the surface: Julian leans his head against the prison glass separating him from Michelle and breathes: "My God, Michelle, it's taken me so long to come to you."

Schrader said that with *American Gigolo* he felt he had "arrived as a director": "I felt confident about moving and placing the camera. I *saw* the movie for the first time" (*SoS* 164). While working on his next script, *Born in the USA* (later completed as *Light of Day*) Schrader took up an offer to direct a remake of the 1942 Val Lewton-produced and Jacques Tourneur-directed *Cat People*:

Figure 22.3   Julian Kay (Richard Gere) finds grace in *American Gigolo* (1980).
Digital frame enlargement. Courtesy of Paramount Pictures.

> It so appealed to me to do a film I didn't write, a big Hollywood film, a
> special effects film, a film that was about a woman, and a film that was
> not very realistic – it seemed to be very liberating to try and do something
> I'd never done before. (Crawley 15)

Although the writing credit for *Cat People* goes to Alan Ormsby, who had
developed the property as a sexually oriented contemporary thriller, Schrader
maintains he did substantial work on the script, sharpening the material's
obsessive and sensual aspects (Rebello, "Making" 32):

> I re-outlined the movie [for Ormsby] . . . Of the forty-six main scenes I
> think that there were about fifteen I wanted to keep . . . [Ormsby] turned
> around, wrote it, and we sat down and rewrote it together. (Thomson
> 51)

Aside from some small quotations, the final script retains little from the
1942 film, Schrader instead transforming the genre piece into a personal film
that – along with *Obsession* (1976) and *Forever Mine* (1999) – belongs to
his "Beatrice figure" cycle, and which (like *American Gigolo*) was shaped
by Schrader's collaboration with the "new axis" of Bailey, Moroder, and
Scarfiotti.

Accompanied by the Moroder-David Bowie theme music, *Cat People* begins
with a rust-tinted prologue used to explain the origins and destiny of the Cat

People, an ancient race whose members turn into black panthers when they mate and then must kill to return to human form. At the centre of the film is Irena Gallier (Nastassia Kinski), a nineteen-year-old orphan who has come to New Orleans to stay with her brother Paul (Malcolm McDowell), a Pentecostal minister who lives in their family home with the housekeeper, Female (Ruby Dee). A virgin who has yet to transform, Irena is terrified when told by Paul that she must mate only with him. Frustrated, Paul has sex with a prostitute and is captured in his panther form by Oliver Yates (John Heard), curator of the local zoo, and his assistant Alice (Annette O'Toole). Oliver meets Irena when she comes to visit the panther, and finds himself strangely attracted to her. After killing a zoo attendant, Paul regains his human form, only to be shot dead (by Alice) when he comes after Irena, transforms again, and attacks Oliver. Alone and confused, Irena realizes she cannot escape her destiny, has sex with Oliver, and kills to return to human form. Seeking to escape the cycle, Irena begs Oliver to kill her, but he instead ropes her to the bed and makes love to her, thereby allowing her to stay by his side as an exhibit in the zoo. The ending of *Cat People*, in which Oliver reaches out to the caged panther (Irena), is thus a "perverse" reprise of Bresson's *Pickpocket* (and *American Gigolo*): the two lovers, separated by prison bars, achieving a sort of consummation (Combs, "*Cat People*" 157).

Schrader said that his revision of *Cat People* – its movement from a horror piece to a more personal story – was achieved through the development of the character of the zookeeper as a pursuer of a Beatrice figure. Schrader imagined Oliver as an introspective intellectual, someone who separated himself from

Figure 22.4   Irena Gallier (Nastassia Kinski) visits her kind in *Cat People* (1982). Digital frame enlargement. Courtesy of RKO/Universal Pictures.

humans and preferred the company of animals, until coming across an innocent, virtuous young woman (Irena) worthy of his pursuit and idealization: "He's a man who lives with animals because he doesn't like humans very much. And this Beatrice appears and his greatest fantasy comes true, because [in this case] Beatrice is an animal" (SoS 166). Schrader's script for Obsession ("essentially a sort of remake of [Vertigo]," SoS 115) also had a Beatrice theme, but Cat People was Schrader's most deliberate rendering of the figure, with a sculpture of Beatrice appearing in the completed film, and Oliver – a casual student of Dante – at one point listening to a tape translation of La Vita Nuova. Schrader says that as he began to re-write Cat People he realized that what he had in the character of Oliver was an intellectual version of Taxi Driver's Travis Bickle: "This is my Calvinistic notion of the postponement of pleasure and the kind of sanctity of sex where you can really only be in love with something better" (Thomson 51). Once Irena embraces her destiny – loses her virginity and literally becomes a beast – Oliver achieves his fantasy of finding a creature that is divine, a Beatrice who lives in a pre-human state (Rebello, "Cat People" 45). As Schrader describes it: "At the end of the film, Oliver has set up his own little chapel and he goes in every day and lights a candle. He has his Beatrice and he has his shrine" (Thomson 52).

At the time of making his film, Schrader described the original Cat People as "basically a very good B-movie with one or two brilliant sequences" (Rebello, "Cat People" 43). Along with Bailey and Scarfiotti, he was particularly impressed with the original film's black and white cinematography and he became intrigued with the prospect of expressing the metaphysical concerns of the new version by returning to the "pre-nouvelle vague spirit" of such works as Orson Welles's The Trial (1962), Georges Franju's Eyes Without a Face (1960), and Jean Cocteau's Orpheus (1950) (Thomson 52). In order to transfer the luminous, monochromatic images of these films to color, Scarfiotti devised carefully controlled color arrangements of "salmon reds and chartreuse greens" (SoS 172). The restricted palette was taken even further in the film's most stylized sequences, such as that in which Irena dreams she is in a desert covered with coral-colored sand, where, led by Paul to a gnarled tree in which several panthers are perched, she discovers the myth of her cat ancestry. The fantasy aspects of the film – the explicit rendering of the timeless, other world of the cat myth – along with the movie's "explicit sex and good red gore" led some to complain that Schrader's version over-displayed everything that Tourneur had underplayed, so that "a film of absences [was] replaced by one of complete presence where everything is [laid out] there on the surface" (Romney 149). Schrader would later rue the fact that he hadn't changed the title of the film (so as to discourage comparisons with Tourneur's version), and admitted that in aiming to make a commercial and an existential horror film he had missed both target audiences, and so failed at the box office (SoS 172).

Commenting on his four "studio films," Schrader drew a distinction between his "schematic" (intellectual) films – *Cat People* and *American Gigolo* – and his "non-style" (working class) films – *Hardcore* and *Blue Collar* (Gehr 36). There is, nonetheless, a thematic consistency and interest in stylization across all four works, which Schrader would carry forward to his magnum opus, *Mishima: A Life in Four Chapters* (1985), a film that brings together the documentary style of Costa-Gavras, the Golden Age of Japanese cinema (Ozu, Naruse, Mizoguchi), and a color-coded rendering of three novels by Yukio Mishima: gold and green for *The Temple of the Golden Pavilion*, pink and grey for *Kyoko's House,* and *shu*-orange and black for *Runaway Horses* (*SoS* 177). For the next twenty years Schrader would work on smaller, independent productions until signing to direct *Dominion* (2005). A (failed) prequel to *The Exorcist* (1973), *Dominion* was to mark not only Schrader's return to big-budget filmmaking but also to the founding moment of the New Hollywood and to some of the existential questions that had structured his entire lifework.

NOTE

1. Hereafter cited as *SoS*.

WORKS CITED

American Gigolo. Directed by Paul Schrader, screenplay by Paul Schrader, Paramount, 1980.
Bliss, Michael. "Affliction and Forgiveness: An Interview with Paul Schrader." *Film Quarterly*, vol. 54, no. 1, Fall 2000, pp. 2–9.
Blue Collar. Directed by Paul Schrader, screenplay by Paul Schrader and Leonard Schrader, Universal, 1978.
Cat People. Directed by Paul Schrader, screenplay by Alan Ormsby, story by DeWitt Bodeen, Universal, 1982.
Combs, Richard. "*American Gigolo*." *Monthly Film Bulletin*, vol. 47, no. 552, May 1980, pp. 87–8.
Combs, Richard. "*Cat People*." *Monthly Film Bulletin*, vol. 49, no. 583, Aug. 1982, pp. 156–7.
Crawley, Tony. "Paul Schrader on *Cat People*." *Starburst*, vol. 55, Jan. 1983, pp. 14–15.
Crowdus, Gary and Dan Georgakas. "*Blue Collar*: An Interview with Paul Schrader." *Cinéaste*, vol. 8, no. 3, 1978, pp. 34–7, 59.
Emery, Robert J. *The Directors: Take Three*. Allworth Press, 2003.
Gehr, Richard. "Citizen Paul." *American Film*, vol. 13, no. 10, Sep. 1988, pp. 32–7.
Hardcore. Directed by Paul Schrader, screenplay by Paul Schrader, Columbia, 1979.
Kahan, Saul. "Schrader's Inferno." *Focus on Film*, vol. 33, Aug. 1979, pp. 4–12.
Kolker, Philip. *A Cinema of Loneliness*. 4th Edition. Oxford: Oxford University Press, 2011.
Kouvaros, George. *Paul Schrader*. University of Illinois Press, 2008.
Nichols, Bill. "*American Gigolo*: Transcendental Style and Narrative Form." *Film Quarterly* vol. 34, no. 4, Summer 1981, pp. 8–13.

Rebello, Stephen. "*Cat People*: Paul Schrader Changes His Spots." *American Film*, vol. 7, no. 6, April 1982, pp. 38–45.

Rebello, Stephen. "The Making of *Cat People*." *Cinefantastique*, vol. 12, no. 4, 1982, pp. 28–38, 43–7.

Romney, Jonathan. "New Ways to Skin a Cat: Paul Schrader's *Cat People*." *Enclitic*, vol. 8, nos. 1–2, 1984, pp. 148–55.

Schrader, Paul. *Transcendental Style in Film: Ozu, Bresson, Dreyer*. University of California Press, 1972.

Schrader, Paul. *Schrader on Schrader and Other Writings*. Rev. Edition, ed. Kevin Jackson, Faber and Faber, 2004.

Smith, Gavin. "Awakenings: Paul Schrader Interviewed." *Film Comment*, vol. 28, no. 2, March/April 1992, pp. 50–59.

Thomson, David. "Cats." *Film Comment*, vol. 18, no. 2, March/April 1982, pp. 49–52.

Tuchman, Mitch. "Gigolos: Paul Schrader Interviewed." *Film Comment*, vol. 16, no. 2, March/April 1980, pp. 49–52.

Wells, Jeffrey. "Paul Schrader: *American Gigolo* and Other Matters." *Films in Review*, vol. 31, no. 5, May 1980, pp. 284–87.

23. PETER YATES: ON LOCATION IN THE NEW HOLLYWOOD

Jonathan Kirshner

Peter Yates is often overlooked in the pantheon of American New Wave directors. One reason for this is that he is not easily cataloged according to the most common conceptions by which New Hollywood directors were classified. More than a decade older than the "movie brats" of the film-school counter-culture generation, the British-born Yates was also not affiliated with that more senior cohort of seventies directors like Sidney Lumet or Arthur Penn, who honed their skills (and earned their first laurels) during the golden age of live television in the US in the 1950s. Also working against Yates's prospects for a devoted following amongst cinephiles was that although his visual style was ambitious – he had a notably New-Wave commitment to location shooting and an outstanding eye for choosing and cannily framing locations – it was not a style that called attention to itself. In addition, Yates almost always chose to work with big stars, with the result that audiences, even in the savvy seventies, were rarely showing up for "A Peter Yates film"; rather, they more typically imagined they were lining up for, say, the new Robert Redford film. (In this regard, Yates can be compared with Sydney Pollack – it is not surprising to learn that he was once lined up to direct *Three Days of the Condor* (1975) [American Film Institute].)

But even if it would be hyperbolic to place him in the first rank among the leading directors of the New Hollywood era, Yates was, nevertheless, an active and accomplished figure in the movement. A notable participant in an important era, he made nine features between 1967 and 1977, most of which retain interest today – and the best of which stand out as landmarks. His first American film, *Bullitt* (1968), a path-breaking effort, is steeped in what would become the recognizable visual motifs of the emerging New Hollywood: saturated darkness, hand-held cameras, all-location shooting, and documentary style (along with its seventies-ready relatively downbeat conclusion). And Yates's masterpiece, *The Friends of Eddie Coyle* (1973), is one of the essential films of the era – and one that sets the standard for that fundamental hallmark of the New Hollywood: moral ambiguity. It is hard to think of a great seventies film – even entries such as *Chinatown* (1974) or *The Parallax View* (1974), two movies deservedly known for their bottomless nihilism – being as without any moral grounding as *Eddie Coyle* (and yet Yates's film still manages to leave the audience invested in its characters).

A graduate of the Royal Academy of Dramatic Art (RADA) (and one-time race-car driver, which certainly informed his celebrated chase-scenes), Yates first earned his filmmaking stripes as an Assistant Director in seven films from 1959 to 1961, including Tony Richardson's "New British Cinema" classic, *A Taste of Honey* (1961), an exemplar of that movement's gritty, working-class, "kitchen sink" aspiration to realism. Yates quickly graduated to the director's chair to helm the musical *Summer Holiday* (1963), which did not make much of an impression, and the comedy *One Way Pendulum* (1965), which flopped (Baxter; Weber). He then turned to television, where he honed his craftsmanship directing installments of high-quality suspense serials, including seven episodes of *The Saint*, starring Roger Moore, and then seven more of Patrick McGoohan's *Danger Man* (*Secret Agent*), including the final episode of that series, which was later combined with the penultimate episode to cobble together a feature-length offering after the series ended.[1]

After his work on *Danger Man* Yates returned to features, and on the strength of his early successes never turned back. *Robbery*, released in September 1967, was a very effective caper film, closely based on the daring "great train robbery" that grabbed headlines Britain in 1963. Early in the film, an initial small caper undertaken to finance the big robbery includes an impressive car chase. The oft-told story follows that producer-star Steve McQueen hired Yates to direct his next film, *Bullitt*, on the strength of that sequence. *Bullitt*, famously, would feature a remarkable and celebrated chase sequence through the streets of San Francisco (McQueen did a good bit of his own driving), that would set something of a revered standard for those who would follow. (The chase in *The French Connection* [1971] is the most prominent example of such efforts – director William Friedkin was among those who were determined to push the envelope even further.) And *Bullitt* was a hit, assuring that Yates would be afforded additional opportunities.

But the "hired because of the chase" story fails to do justice to either film. *Robbery* has more in common with *Bullitt* than merely speeding cars, which McQueen surely noticed as well. It was also the project of an ambitious producer-star (Stanley Baker, who had just completed *Accident* [1967] for Joseph Losey); it was shot, impressively, entirely on location[2]; and it was tight, and full of knowing, small observations. The location work underscored *Robbery*'s commitment to realism, as did the naturalistic lighting (including some nicely under-lit interiors), thoughtful camera movement (such as during a meeting at police headquarters – look also for the dangling phone wires), and several long, very fine, night-for-night sequences – the entire twenty-five minute heist sequence is set at night as well. Credit here must be afforded to the well-regarded cinematographer Douglas Slocombe, who shot *Freud* (1962) for John Huston and *The Servant* (1963) for Losey. In retrospect, *Robbery* can be seen as a trademark Yates film, especially with its extensive location work and evocative naturalism.

The same could be said for *Bullitt*. In the long history of the movies car chases come and go, but if you trimmed those heart-pounding twelve minutes of screen time, this excellent film would be no worse for wear. Seen today, two different sequences are the ones that stand out as exceptional – and much harder to imitate. The first is a long, mostly unhurried twenty-plus minutes in a (real) hospital, in the aftermath of a sudden and disturbing burst of consequential violence. With a cop down and a key witness gravely wounded, Yates shifts the movie to procedural mode, first at the crime scene and then, especially, overnight at that hospital. The second exceptional sequence is also an extended sequence (if with more "action") that also takes place at night, at the airport (shooting occurred after the last plane had landed and the airport was closed during the overnight hours – the crew had crowds of extras and three jumbo jets at their disposal [Yates "Director's commentary: *Bullitt*"].) The hospital sequence is also notable for its deftly-handled race and gender politics, in which hierarchies of power are definitively and implicitly understood, as Bullitt (McQueen) is confronted with the impossible, interfering ambitions of a callow politician (Robert Vaughn, so believable you want to vote against him) while trying to make sense of the case that just blew up in his face.[3] The airport scenes offer a clinic in suspenseful storytelling, and the saturated blacks on the runway (that's McQueen diving under a 707) offering still more glorious night-for-night shooting in the hands of cinematographer William Fraker.

Ultimately, if ironically given its reputation, *Bullitt* is a subtle and thoughtful film. The nominal plot is tissue thin – it does hold together and has a very nice twist regarding the identity of a murdered man, but all of that really matters little. Yates's approach to the material is a splendid example of Claude Chabrol's notion that if you work in the thriller genre, you can hold the good will of the audience by engrossing them in the mystery, enabling the filmmaker to go about the much more important purpose of having something to say. And *Bullitt*, as its title implies, is a character study, if an understated and minimalist one. We come to learn a good bit about the character – the movie even spends

Figure 23.1   "Integrity is something you sell the public": Robert Vaughn with Steve McQueen in *Bullitt* (1968). Digital frame enlargement. Courtesy of Solar/Warner Bros/Seven Arts.

a couple of minutes with him in a narrative-interrupting visit to a bodega, where his shopping rituals, like the way he indifferently grabs a stack of TV dinners in anticipation of next week's meals, illustrates his larger life choices (this small piece of business was one of many suggested by McQueen during the shoot [Yates "Director's commentary: *Bullitt*"]). Yates often deploys long lenses, pulling back the camera and withholding dialogue in order to let the images tell the story; he also brings out the best in McQueen, especially in silent passages where glances are substituted for words and the story is advanced by following McQueen's expressive eyes. As Renata Adler observed in the *New York Times*, the movie takes full advantage of McQueen's "special kind of aware, existential cool" (Adler). *Bullitt* also showcases Yates's signature, naturalistic, location-driven style (motel rooms, streetscapes, restaurants, morgues) and is thematically well-situated in the New Hollywood with its portrayal of corrupt institutions, compromised police brass, and crooked politicians. This is not always subtle: Vaughn's character goes so far as to assert that "integrity is something that you sell the public," and although he loses this round he nevertheless remains part of the larger problem, driving off in a chauffeured limousine that sports a "support your local police" bumper sticker as he turns his attention to *The Wall Street Journal*. But in 1968, the steely integrity of Bullitt and the struggle to preserve his humanity (Jacqueline Bisset is the love interest who reminds the audience that it's often not good for the soul to be a cop), paint a nuanced picture of contemporary social realities.

With back-to-back hits under his belt (*Bullitt* was the third-largest grossing film of 1968), Yates chose not to repeat himself, opting instead for something completely different – a small scale social drama. *John and Mary* (1969) tapped two stars coming off big hits – Mia Farrow (*Rosemary's Baby* [1968]) and Dustin Hoffman (*The Graduate* [1967] and *Midnight Cowboy* [1969]) – in a modest film about young people navigating the concurrent sexual revolution and emerging women's movement. Among *John and Mary*'s strengths are Yates's eye for New York City locations (he avoids the usual favorites) and his documentary-style realism. The film's conceit is to consider the aftermath of an anonymous one-night stand between the titular John and Mary, and then work both backward (flashbacks to show the evening before) and forward (do these intimate strangers have any prospects for the future?). It starts off promisingly, hitting the right cultural referents (Norman Mailer, Jean-Luc Godard) and letting the camera quietly observe the initial action and set-up. Yates is also successful in fracturing time (and also slowing down for a political speech) and in providing space for good supporting performances from Tyne Daily and Peter Tolan; the movie also lets Mary score some real feminist points. That said, *John and Mary* does not much rise above the "interesting effort" category – after a strong start the pacing is uncertain, the behavior and motivations of the principal players are often puzzling at best, and, most consequentially, there is little screen chemistry between them. As Molly Haskell observed, although the location work is well done ultimately *John and Mary* is limited by its "seductive but basically passive stars" (Haskell).

After a false start (there was talk of filming *Don Quixote* with Richard Burton [Williams 374]), Yates, in recognizable "have camera, will travel" mode, decamped to Venezuela to shoot *Murphy's War* (1971), an *African Queen*-like World War II river-bound adventure yarn (minus any remaining scrap of plausibility). Star Peter O'Toole isn't given much to do beyond embarking on an Ahab-like mission to avenge the death of his crewmates, massacred at the hands of a German submarine discreetly (for whatever reason) cruising rivers in South America. Yates, reunited with cinematographer Slocombe, ensures that the well-chosen locations are stunningly shot: O'Toole's preparations for his airborne attack have a deftly-orchestrated caper-like quality; and his first, terrifying flight (Murphy is teaching himself how to operate a plane on the fly, as it were) provides the film with something of a suspenseful chase-without-a-chase (by this point Yates was expected to provide such things), as airborne disaster is narrowly and harrowingly avoided obstacle-by-obstacle. *Murphy's War* is also distinguished by the vividness and stark realism of its initial atrocities, episodes which effectively raise the narrative stakes, and the film has the courage to stick with its fitting, very downbeat, New-Hollywood ending, on which Yates laudably insisted over some opposition (and which surely dampened the movie's commercial prospects) (Sellers 190). But there are more misses than hits in *Murphy's War*. The marvelous Philippe Noiret is saddled with a one-note sidekick role, and Sian Phillips (then married to O'Toole) is similarly underdrawn in a two-dimensional role that can be described as virginal-Katharine-Hepburn-without-the-awakening. And despite its strengths, *Murphy's War* starts out implausibly, and becomes increasingly head-scratching in the middle and frankly ridiculous by the end.

Perhaps running for cover, Yates next took on something close to a sure thing: a comedy-caper film with Robert Redford and George Segal leading a fine, familiar cast.[4] *The Hot Rock* (1972) played effortlessly to the director's strengths. It featured not one but four mini-capers, and outstanding New York City location work – and again, not the obvious choices but rather spots that showed a keen eye for the city (Yates was filming at the High Bridge Water Tower at a time when most New Yorkers probably didn't know what it was). And a long, extended helicopter sequence afforded spectacular views of the Big Apple – including a few shots looking through the unfinished top floors of the still-under-construction World Trade Center. Even though *Hot Rock*'s New York City is a little gentler than suggested by grittier, contemporaneous films like *Midnight Cowboy* and *The Panic in Needle Park* (1971) (it is a comedy, after all), the flavor of the era is still imparted by the ease with which a person can be mugged while standing across the street from a police station, and by the endemic levels of cynicism and corruption to be found in reputable walks of life. An evening's entertainment (Quincy Jones did the music) with moments of real suspense and humor, ultimately *The Hot Rock* was an audience-friendly shaggy dog story, and there was little for Yates to do but let his stars look good as they exchanged the witty banter that flowed from William Goldman's pen. Not that there's anything wrong with that – it's just not the kind of movie that makes a reputation.

The Friends of Eddie Coyle, on the other hand, is the sort of film that marks one's ticket to the Hall of Fame. A major work, *Eddie Coyle*, with *Bullitt*, establishes Yates as a filmmaker who must be included in any serious conversation of the New Hollywood. It is an exemplar of everything the moment aspired to achieve: a commitment to a certain type of "realism" (that pushed back against the flawless reassuring fantasies of the studio era) implying a naturalistic style of acting, location shooting, and downbeat, anti-sentimental endings. In addition, and in marked and measured contrast to the strict prohibitions of the shuttered Production Code Administration – "No picture shall be produced which will lower the moral standards of those who see it. Hence the sympathy of the audience shall never be thrown to the side of crime, wrongdoing, evil, or sin" – the New Hollywood was eager to traffic in that most forbidden taboo of the studio era: moral ambiguity (see Kirshner).

Finally, the New Hollywood was haunted by its nemesis, President Nixon, and *The Friends of Eddie Coyle* also captured the essence of a moment that could be called "peak Nixon." There is not a word in the film that mentions the Watergate scandal, or politics of any kind – but it is a Watergate film.

Fittingly, it was released the day after John Dean began his testimony before the US Senate, telling under oath everything he knew about *his* friends, having assessed, correctly, that they were about to first stab him in the back and then "throw him to the wolves" (this being the White House strategy regarding Dean, as memorably recorded on Nixon's tapes). That was how your friends treated you – certainly that is how Eddie Coyle's "friends" would treat him – in Nixon's America, where trust was for the hopelessly naive, intuitions were inherently and irretrievably corrupt, and very little distinguished the good guys from the bad.

Adapted by Paul Monash (who also produced the film), the screenplay drew heavily on the razor-sharp dialogue of George Higgins's debut novel. But the choices made by Monash and Yates in crafting the screenplay from the book are not to be underestimated – in fact they offer a model for how adaptation can stand as an art form of its own. The filmmakers invariably shed the weakest material, tightened some elements, added an additional layer of duplicity to the plot, introduced subtle but meaningful revisions (the tag line "Have a nice day" was a vast improvement over "Merry Christmas"), and moved a few pieces around. In particular, the book ends on a different note than the film, which draws on a cryptic conversation that appeared relatively early, on page thirty-eight of the novel, and which, moved to the closing scene, concludes the story more powerfully and effectively. (Monash and Yates also knew when to leave Higgins's gems alone – lines like "One of the first things I learned was not to ask a man why he's in a hurry," and "Life is hard, but it's harder when you're stupid" don't grow on trees.)

Shot on location in Boston – Yates's choices and command of location shooting here surpass even his own high standards – *Eddie Coyle* tells the story of small-time, middle-aged, that-stuff-just-fell-off-a-truck middleman. Robert Mitchum, in the performance of a lifetime as Eddie, finds himself with his back to the wall: he is staring down a few years of jail time – a sentence that, given his age (just over fifty) and family responsibilities (he has a wife and kids to support), he thinks is too much for him to handle. So in between buying guns from Jackie Brown (Steven Keats) and passing them on to his bank-robbing friends (Yates, as always, throws a great heist, as seen here in several gripping sequences) Eddie is reaching out to the Feds, in the form of Agent Dave Foley (Richard Jordan), to see if there is a deal that can be cut. Unbeknownst to Eddie, his friend Dillon (Peter Boyle) – part-time bartender, part-time hitman – is also friends with Agent Foley, and neither of them are looking out for Eddie's best interests.

Yates's film is never rushed, but it is tight as a drum, with each scene following logically on the heels of what came before, just as Hitchcock insisted they should. And it is a masterpiece of small observations, which bring every character to life with all their imperfections and uncertainties, as in that marvelous moment of Foley's indecisiveness ("Let me think") and his subsequent barely-contained self-control in a rush of excitement during a stake-out-gone-wrong at the railway station in Sharon. As noted, the location work is exemplary (Dillon's Bar, Eddie's home, Government Center, the Boston Garden), and is captured on film in faded pastels by day and saturated darkness at night – cinematographer Victor J. Kemper, who would also help bring the realism in *Dog Day Afternoon* (1975) and *Mikey and Nicky* (1976), made good on Yates's ambition that the film have a documentary-style look, "like a newsreel" (Bobrow 20, 21, 23).[5] And the performances are also uniformly outstanding – here, too, the director must be credited: this is not a movie from which clips can be pulled to showcase examples of attention-grabbing bravura *acting*, it is a film in which the players simply disappear into their characters. When Mitchum tells Keats that he'd better deliver, or "I'm going to come looking for you, and I'll find you, too, because I'm not going to be the only one that's looking," he doesn't raise his voice in anger – he's just telling the kid how the world works. And when Peter Boyle lectures a mob moneyman that he wants respect, and he deserves respect, and when he kills somebody, he does it his way – he doesn't chew the scenery, he just makes a pretty good case.

In addition to its story, performances, and visual coherence, *The Friends of Eddie Coyle* stands out by setting the standard for seventies moral ambiguity. In introducing the gunrunner Brown and the plainclothes agent Foley, Yates initially withholds information about each character, and it is impossible for viewers to understand at first who is the cop and who is the criminal. The actors also look alike, which can be confusing on a first viewing but further underscores the basic point – the movie doesn't see an important difference between them. When Foley uses Coyle, and then drops him without looking back, Eddie protests that it's "not right" but quickly realizes he should have seen it coming: "I should have known better than to trust a cop, my own mother could have told me that." (Foley's response: "Everybody ought to listen to his mother.") And the last time Foley talks with Dillon there is little doubt that he knows he's consorting with a killer – and doesn't care. ("I never asked a friend to do anything he couldn't do": moved to the ending by Monash and Yates, it is the last great line in the film.) As one critic noted, it's very seventies out there, with "criminals-and-police who wage an armed truce but might any day form an alliance which would spell the obliteration of everyone else" (Young 250).[6]

Most seventies of all is the way *The Friends of Eddie Coyle* leaves the audience empty handed. There are certainly no heroes in this story, but the audience has surely become attached to Eddie, who, despite operating outside the law, seems like a nice enough fellow, as far as it goes. He has an (age-appropriate) wife who loves him, cares about his kids, and has a decent, world-weary sense of right and wrong, regardless of what the law might say. The movie suggests

Figure 23.2 "I should have known better than to trust a cop": Robert Mitchum with Richard Jordan in *The Friends of Eddie Coyle* (1973). Digital frame enlargement. Courtesy of Paramount Pictures.

that guys like him are past their time. At the Boston Garden, he marvels at the great Bobby Orr – "What a future he's got." But of course, Eddie has no future. After the game he will be murdered by one of his friends, who was hired by some of his other friends, seeking revenge for something he didn't do. It's not that he wouldn't have done it, mind you – desperate times call for desperate measures – but his friend beat him to the betrayal, and then killed him to cover his tracks. And gets away with it. Have a nice day.

Unfortunately, Yates's next three films do not show a director moving from strength to strength – as he did with *Robbery* and *Bullitt* (and from there the still thoughtfully chosen and ambitious efforts that followed). Instead, as one observed noted, "his next films lacked individuality, suggesting a director for hire" (Baxter) – all the more puzzling because he wasn't: Yates was in a position at that moment to make his own choices and indeed was a co-producer on the second (and least distinguished) of these efforts. It is important to look at such fallow stretches with clear eyes, and acknowledge that they happen to the best of filmmakers. Many of the seventies' titans experienced rough patches, especially toward the end of this cinematic era – Altman, Bogdanovich, Nichols, Pakula, Penn, Peckinpah, and Rafelson are among those who come to mind – likely hastening its demise (although the end of the New Hollywood era was largely a function of social-cultural trends and changes to the industry's model with the ascension of the blockbuster.[7])

Yates followed *The Friends of Eddie Coyle* with *For Pete's Sake* (1974), a Barbra Streisand vehicle. This is the least representative of Yates's films, with the location shooting (in Brooklyn and elsewhere in the City) tellingly supplemented by studio work. And despite the presence of considerable talent on hand, including cinematographer László Kovács, *For Pete's Sake* never rises above its sitcom-ready script, and was possibly not intended to. Yates's own position on the film is clear: this was "a film to promote Barbra," and "you can tell ... it's not supposed to be taken seriously" (Yates "Director's commentary: *For Pete's Sake*"). There are some modest if unfulfilled gestures at class politics, but one gets the sense that the director took greater pleasure in his requisite chase sequence. Here Yates extracts some good-natured revenge on *The French Connection* (which was so determined to out-chase *Bullitt*), with its recreation of *Connection's* cat-and-mouse derring-do on the subway between Gene Hackman and Fernando Rey, here with Streisand just as nimbly outwitting the police dog on her tail (or so it seemed).

Mother, Jugs & Speed (1976), co-produced by Yates and Tom Mankiewicz, opens with promise, as Allen Garfield, one of the most intense actors of the New Hollywood (*The Conversation* [1974], *Nashville* [1975]), opens the film with a direct-to-the-camera diatribe of seventies despair that could have been one of the monologues Howard Beale (Peter Finch) puts forth in *Network* (1976, released later in the same year as *Mother*). But it turns out Garfield's Harry Fishbine is simply giving a pep talk to his employees in the threadbare, ethically challenged private ambulance company that he is struggling to keep afloat. The film depicts the trials and tribulations of its eponymous trio (Bill Cosby, Raquel Welch, and Harvey Keitel as Mother, Jugs, and Speed respectively), and the company's rivalry with a competing outfit. Once again we are back on location, there is some meritorious night-for-night work, and towards the end Cosby delivers a fine short speech that brings a fleeting moment of substance to the proceedings. But *Mother, Jugs & Speed* is a structurally unsound movie, with moments of real and consequential violence randomly interspersed in slapstick comedy trafficking in adolescent humor, with an under-motivated and less-than-plausible romance shoehorned into the action. The obligatory Yates chase, which involves an ambulance and a police car, breaks no new ground.

Yates closed his New Hollywood years with a box-office hit, *The Deep* (1977), which reunited the director with Jacqueline Bisset in a film designed to cash in on novelist-screenwriter Peter Benchley's follow-up to his mega-hit novel *Jaws*. A considerable improvement over *Mother, Jugs & Speed*, *The Deep* is more confidently Yatesian – the locations are striking, the chase offers a new twist (trucks vs. mopeds), sure-handed suspense is effortlessly delivered, and again we are treated to plenty of naturalism and inky night-for-night. In addition, there are some appealing elements and estimable moments: Eli Wallach shows up in a drunken sidekick role that has effective echoes of Walter Brennan's Eddie in *To Have and Have Not* (1944), and the negotiations between gray-market treasure-seeker Romer (Robert Shaw) and local mob boss Henri (Louis Gossett Jr.) at a cricket match bring us full circle to the haggling over terms between conspirators that takes place on location during a soccer game in *Robbery*. But however attractive, *The Deep* is a paint-by-numbers picture, with few if any surprises, and its players, including a still-finding-his-footing Nick Nolte in his feature-film debut, are hampered by weak dialogue. And, in a sure sign that the New Hollywood era had ended, *The Deep* sends its audience home smiling with a textbook happy ending.

As noted, limping to the New Hollywood finish line was the fate of many seventies' directors, and it does not diminish Yates's important role in the movement to note that he was among them. Especially with the path-breaking *Bullitt* and the masterpiece *The Friends of Eddie Coyle* – both of which are recognizable products of their director's distinct style – Yates holds a claim to his share of the New Hollywood glory. Moreover, he would soon regain his footing, resurfacing with one of his finest films, *Breaking Away* (1979) and a few years later with *The Dresser* (1983), continuing with a career that would stretch to the end of the century.

Notes

1. Neither the episode ("Shinda Shima") nor the subsequent feature ("Koroshi") are much distinguished. In general, the series was better in black and white, and both the series and Yates's contributions are more easily appreciated in earlier offerings such as "Man on the Beach."
2. Carefully chosen and at times quite intimate locations – similar to the search for realism in François Truffaut's *The Soft Skin* and John Frankenheimer's *Seconds*, Baker's character's house in *Robbery* was Baker's house in real life.
3. Implicit race and gender hierarchies are very much in play as Chalmers (Vaughn), goes "over the head" of African American surgeon Dr. Willard (Georg Stanford Brown) and dictates orders to the head nurse on duty.
4. Redford, who often sought out ambitious projects, was at that particular moment looking to participate in a less than challenging, well paying, New York City based production (Callan 177–8).
5. See also Yates "Director's commentary: *The Friends of Eddie Coyle*". Yates also talks at length in the commentary about the film's locations and his appreciation for the source material.
6. See also p. 251 on the film's "neutral" position; Yates "Director's commentary: *The Friends of Eddie Coyle*".
7. See for example Kael.

Works Cited

Adler, Renata. "Bullitt." *New York Times*, 18 Oct. 1968.
American Film Institute. "Three Days of the Condor," *AFI Catalogue of Feature Films*.
Baxter, Brian. "Peter Yates Obituary," *The Guardian*, 10 Jan. 2011.
Bobrow, Andrew C. "The Making of Friends of Eddie Coyle." *Filmmakers Newsletter*, vol. 6, no. 12, October 1973.
Callan, Michael Feeney. *Robert Redford: The Biography*. Knopf, 2011.
Haskell, Molly. "Film: John and Mary." *The Village Voice*, 18 Dec. 1969.

Higgins, George V. *The Friends of Eddie Coyle*. Knopf, 1972.

Kael, Pauline. "Why are Movies So Bad? Or, The Numbers." *The New Yorker*, 23 June 1980.

Kirshner, Jonathan. *Hollywood's Last Golden Age: Politics, Society and the Seventies Film in America*. Cornell University Press, 2012.

Sellers, Robert. *Peter O'Toole: The Definitive Biography*. St. Martin's Press, 2016.

Weber, Bruce. "Peter Yates, Filmmaker, Is Dead at 81." *New York Times*, 11 Jan. 2011.

Williams, Chris, ed. *The Richard Burton Diaries*. New Haven: Yale University Press, 2012.

Yates, Peter. "Director's commentary." *Bullitt*, Warner Bros. DVD, 2005a.

Yates, Peter. "Director's commentary." *For Pete's Sake*, Warner Bros. DVD, 2005b.

Yates, Peter. "Director's commentary." *Bullitt, The Friends of Eddie Coyle*, Criterion Collection. DVD, 2009.

Young, Vernon. "The Friends of Graham Greene" *The Hudson Review*, vol. 27, no. 2, Summer 1974.

INDEX

.

CPSIA information can be obtained
at www.ICGtesting.com
Printed in the USA
LVHW082215080321
680890LV00005B/128

9 781474 442640